Trends in Fixed Point Theory and Fractional Calculus

Trends in Fixed Point Theory and Fractional Calculus

Guest Editors

Boško Damjanović
Pradip Debnath

MDPI

Basel • Beijing • Wuhan • Barcelona • Belgrade • Novi Sad • Cluj • Manchester

Guest Editors
Boško Damjanović
Department of Mathematics
University Union—Nikola
Tesla
Belgrade
Serbia

Pradip Debnath
Department of Mathematical
Sciences
Tezpur University
Assam
India

Editorial Office
MDPI AG
Grosspeteranlage 5
4052 Basel, Switzerland

This is a reprint of the Special Issue, published open access by the journal *Axioms* (ISSN 2075-1680), freely accessible at: https://www.mdpi.com/journal/axioms/special_issues/4K4JA339IE.

For citation purposes, cite each article independently as indicated on the article page online and as indicated below:

Lastname, A.A.; Lastname, B.B. Article Title. *Journal Name* **Year**, *Volume Number*, Page Range.

ISBN 978-3-7258-5245-1 (Hbk)
ISBN 978-3-7258-5246-8 (PDF)
https://doi.org/10.3390/books978-3-7258-5246-8

Contents

About the Editors

Boško Damjanović

Boško Damjanović is a faculty member (Professor) in the Department of Mathematics at the University Union—Nikola Tesla, Belgrade, Serbia. His research focuses on nonlinear analysis, fixed point theory, operator theory, and applications of functional analysis. He has published widely in peer-reviewed international journals and actively contributes as a reviewer and editorial board member for several mathematics journals. Dr. Damjanović collaborates with mathematicians worldwide, fostering interdisciplinary approaches to fixed p oint t heory a nd i ts a pplications in differential and integral equations.

Pradip Debnath

Pradip Debnath is an Associate Professor in the Department of Mathematical Sciences at Tezpur University, India. He has been recognized among the World's Top 2% Scientists by Stanford University, published by Elsevier, for two consecutive years (2023 and 2024).

He has served as an Associate Editor for the Mathematics section of Heliyon (Elsevier) and is currently on the editorial boards of several leading journals, including *Scientific Reports* (Nature), Research in Mathematics (Taylor & Francis), *PLoS ONE*, and the *TWMS Journal of Applied and Engineering Mathematics*, among others. He is also a Topical Advisory Panel Member for *Axioms* and *Fractal and Fractional*, and has acted as Guest Editor for special issues in journals such as *Symmetry*, *Axioms*, and *Contemporary Mathematics*.

Dr. Debnath earned his Ph.D. in Mathematics from the National Institute of Technology Silchar, India. His research interests span fixed p oint t heory, f unctional a nalysis, s oft c omputing, and mathematical statistics. He has authored over 70 papers in internationally reputed journals, reviewed more than 450 manuscripts for 65+ international journals, and serves as a reviewer for Mathematical Reviews (American Mathematical Society). As editor and author, he has published 10 books with renowned publishers including Springer, CRC Press, De Gruyter, and World Scientific.

His academic career includes faculty positions at Assam University, Silchar, and the North Eastern Regional Institute of Science and Technology (NERIST). He has supervised Ph.D. students in nonlinear analysis, soft computing, and fixed point theory, and completed a major Basic Science Research Project funded by the UGC, Government of India. An academic gold medallist during his postgraduate studies at Assam University, he has also qualified in several national-level mathematics examinations in India.

Preface

It is our pleasure to present this reprint on Trends in Fixed Point Theory and Fractional Calculus, which brings together a diverse collection of recent advances at the intersection of two vibrant areas of mathematical analysis. Fixed-point theory continues to play a fundamental role in nonlinear analysis, variational inequalities, operator theory, and the solvability of integral equations, while fractional calculus extends classical differentiation and integration to non-integer orders, providing powerful tools for modeling memory effects and hereditary dynamics in applied sciences. The motivation for assembling this reprint arises from the growing synergy between these fields, particularly in addressing challenges in stability analysis, iterative algorithms, and fractional differential systems. This work is addressed to researchers, graduate students, and practitioners who seek both theoretical insights and concrete applications. We gratefully acknowledge the efforts of the contributing authors for their valuable research, the reviewers for their critical evaluations, and the editorial team of Axioms for their professional support. We hope that this collection not only highlights the state-of-the-art in the subject but also inspires further exploration and collaboration across mathematics and applied disciplines.

Boško Damjanović and Pradip Debnath
Guest Editors

axioms

MDPI

Editorial

Trends in Fixed Point Theory and Fractional Calculus

Boško Damjanović [1] and Pradip Debnath [2,*]

[1] Department of Mathematics, University Union—Nikola Tesla, 11158 Belgrade, Serbia; dambo@agrif.bg.ac.rs
[2] Department of Mathematical Sciences, Tezpur University, Assam 784028, India
* Correspondence: pradip.debnath@aus.ac.in or pradip@tezu.ernet.in

1. Introduction

This Special Issue of Axioms, titled "Trends in Fixed Point Theory and Fractional Calculus", presents a collection of ten high-quality papers reflecting the latest developments in two intertwined areas of modern mathematical analysis. Fixed-point theory serves as a cornerstone of nonlinear analysis, with far-reaching applications to functional equations, variational inequalities, and operator theory. Fractional calculus, by extending the concept of differentiation and integration to non-integer orders, has proven to be a versatile tool for modeling memory effects and hereditary properties in complex physical and engineering systems.

The synergy between these areas has become increasingly evident in the study of differential and integral equations, stability problems, and iterative algorithms. The contributions in this Special Issue span both theoretical advances, such as new contractive conditions, generalized spaces, and stability criteria, and practical applications, including integral equations and fractional differential systems.

2. Overview of the Published Papers

1. **Fixed-Point Theorems in Branciari Distance Spaces** (Seong-Hoon Cho) introduces σ-Caristi and generalized σ-contraction maps, establishing fixed-point results that extend Caristi's theorem and Banach's contraction principle and clarifying the relationships among various contraction conditions.
2. **m-Isometric Operators with Null Symbol and Elementary Operator Entries** (Bhagwati Prashad Duggal) investigates strict (m, X)-isometric operator pairs on Banach spaces, offering structural insights relevant to functional analysis and operator theory.
3. **Relational Almost (φ, ψ)-Contractions and Applications to Nonlinear Fredholm Integral Equations** (Fahad M. Alamrani et al.) presents new fixed-point results under relational strict almost (φ, ψ)-contractions, with applications to the solvability of nonlinear Fredholm integral equations.
4. **Fixed-Point Results of F-Contractions in Bipolar p-Metric Spaces** (Nabanita Konwar and Pradip Debnath) develops Banach-type and Reich-type theorems for F-contractions in bipolar p-metric spaces, supported by illustrative examples.
5. **Fixed Point Results in Modular b-Metric-like Spaces with an Application** (Nizamettin Ufuk Bostan and Banu Pazar Varol) introduces modular b-metric-like spaces, defines notions of ξ-convergence and ξ-Cauchy sequences, and proves fixed-point theorems with practical applications.
6. **Enriched Z-Contractions and Fixed-Point Results with Applications to IFS** (Ibrahim Alraddadi et al.) initiates a broad class of enriched (d, Z)-contractions on Banach spaces, establishing uniqueness and existence theorems and applying them to iterative function systems.

7. **Nonlinear Contractions Employing Digraphs and Comparison Functions with an Application to Singular Fractional Differential Equations** (Doaa Filali et al.) extends Jachymski's contraction principle via digraphs to study fixed points in graph metric spaces, applying the results to singular fractional differential equations.
8. **Stability of Fixed Points of Partial Contractivities and Fractal Surfaces** (María A. Navascués) examines a wide class of contractions in b-metric spaces, including Banach and Matkowski maps, providing convergence and stability results for Picard iterations with implications for fractal geometry.
9. **Three Existence Results in the Fixed Point Theory** (Alexander J. Zaslavski) offers three new existence theorems for fixed points of nonexpansive and set-valued mappings, generalizing known results on F-contractions and set-valued contractions.
10. **Fixed-Point Results of Generalized (φ, Υ)-Contractive Mappings in Partially Ordered Controlled Metric Spaces with an Application to a System of Integral Equations** (Mohammad Akram et al.) proves multiple fixed-point and coincidence point results, applying them to solve a system of integral equations.

3. Concluding Remarks

The contributions gathered here demonstrate both the diversity and the depth of current research in fixed-point theory and fractional calculus. From abstract generalizations in metric and Banach space settings to concrete applications in integral and fractional differential equations, these works collectively advance the frontiers of the field.

We thank all the authors for their valuable contributions, the reviewers for their careful evaluations, and the Axioms editorial team for their support in producing this Special Issue. We hope that these papers will serve as a source of inspiration for future research, fostering new connections between theoretical exploration and applied problem-solving.

Conflicts of Interest: The authors declare no conflicts of interest.

List of Contributions:

1. Cho, S.-H. Fixed-Point Theorems in Branciari Distance Spaces. *Axioms* **2025**, *14*, 635. https://doi.org/10.3390/axioms14080635.
2. Duggal, B.P. m-Isometric Operators with Null Symbol and Elementary Operator Entries. *Axioms* **2025**, *14*, 503. https://doi.org/10.3390/axioms14070503.
3. Alamrani, F.M.; Algehyne, E.A.; Alshaban, E.; Alatawi, A.; Mohammed, H.I.A.; Khan, F.A. Relational Almost (φ, ψ)-Contractions and Applications to Nonlinear Fredholm Integral Equations. *Axioms* **2025**, *14*, 1. https://doi.org/10.3390/axioms14010001.
4. Konwar, N.; Debnath, P. Fixed-Point Results of F-Contractions in Bipolar p-Metric Spaces. *Axioms* **2024**, *13*, 773. https://doi.org/10.3390/axioms13110773.
5. Bostan, N.U.; Varol, B.P. Fixed Point Results in Modular b-Metric-like Spaces with an Application. *Axioms* **2024**, *13*, 726. https://doi.org/10.3390/axioms13100726.
6. Alraddadi, I.; Din, M.; Ishtiaq, U.; Akram, M.; Argyros, I.K. Enriched Z-Contractions and Fixed-Point Results with Applications to IFS. *Axioms* **2024**, *13*, 562. https://doi.org/10.3390/axioms13080562.
7. Filali, D.; Dilshad, M.; Akram, M. Nonlinear Contractions Employing Digraphs and Comparison Functions with an Application to Singular Fractional Differential Equations. *Axioms* **2024**, *13*, 477. https://doi.org/10.3390/axioms13070477.
8. Navascués, M.A. Stability of Fixed Points of Partial Contractivities and Fractal Surfaces. *Axioms* **2024**, *13*, 474. https://doi.org/10.3390/axioms13070474.

9. Zaslavski, A.J. Three Existence Results in the Fixed Point Theory. *Axioms* **2024**, *13*, 425. https://doi.org/10.3390/axioms13070425.
10. Akram, M.; Alshaikey, S.; Ishtiaq, U.; Farhan, M.; Argyros, I.K.; Regmi, S. Fixed-Point Results of Generalized (φ, Ψ)-Contractive Mappings in Partially Ordered Controlled Metric Spaces with an Application to a System of Integral Equations. *Axioms* **2024**, *13*, 415. https://doi.org/10.3390/axioms13060415.

axioms

MDPI

Article

Fixed-Point Theorems in Branciari Distance Spaces

Seong-Hoon Cho

Department of Mathematics, Hanseo University, Seosan-si 31962, Chungnam, Republic of Korea;
shcho@hanseo.ac.kr; Tel.: +82-41-660-1316

Abstract: In this study, the concepts of σ-Caristi maps and generalized σ-contraction maps are introduced, and fixed-point theorems for such maps are established. A generalization of Caristi's fixed-point theorem and Banach's contraction principle is proved. The relationships among the various contraction conditions introduced in this paper are examined. Examples are provided to elucidate the main theorem, and applications to integral and differential equations are also discussed.

Keywords: fixed point; contraction; generalized contraction; Caristi map; metric space; generalized metric space

MSC: 47H10; 54H25

1. Introduction

In 1922, Banach [1] proved a famous fixed-point theorem, which is called the Banach contraction principle. Since then, this contraction principle has played an important role in mathematical analysis and applied mathematical analysis, and many authors have proposed generalizations and extensions of the Banach contraction principle. Many authors, such as [2–6] and those that are referenced in their studies, investigated various forms of contractive conditions and proved related fixed-point results.

On the one hand, many authors studied fixed-point theory in various spaces. Several authors generalized metric spaces and extended Banach's contraction principle. For example, Huang and Zhang [7], Matthews [8], Amini-Harandi [9], and Branciari [10] introduced the concepts of cone metric spaces, partial distance spaces, metric-like spaces, and Branciari distance spaces, respectively.

Guo and Lakshmikantham [11] investigated some coupled fixed-point results by introducing the concept of coupled fixed points, and an application to coupled quasisolutions of the initial value problems for ordinary differential equations. Samet and Vetro [12] introduced the notion of n-tuple fixed points as a generalization of coupled fixed points and established related fixed-point results. Rad, Shukla, and Rahimi [13] proved that the results of n-tuple fixed points in cone metric spaces and metric-like spaces can be obtained from fixed-point theorems; the converse is also true.

Antón-Sancho [14] also studied fixed-point theory in the field of Higgs bundles, pursuing another direction of research. He proved the existence of fixed points for automorphisms of the moduli spaces of principal bundles over a compact algebraic curve, and he [15,16] obtained fixed-point results for automorphisms of the vector bundle moduli spaces and involutions of G-Higgs bundle moduli spaces.

Axioms **2025**, *14*, 635 https://doi.org/10.3390/axioms14080635

Caristi [17] proved the fixed-point theorem in the so-called Caristi fixed-point theorem, which states that a map $S : X \to X$, where (X, d) is a complete metric space, has a fixed point provided that it satisfies the following condition:

$$d(x, Sx) \leq \phi(x) - \phi(Sx),\ \forall x \in X$$

where $\phi : X \to [0, \infty)$ is a lower-semicontinuous function.

After that, it was shown that this theorem is equivalent to Ekeland's variational principle and the Bishop–Phelps theorem, which have a great number of applications in many branches of mathematics and applied mathematics and are crucial tools in many fields, including nonlinear analysis, dynamic systems, optimization theory, game theory, economics modeling, equilibrium theory, optimization problems, computational methods, variational inequalities, differential equations, integral equations and control theory, population dynamics, and epidemiological methods. It is also known as the most beautiful and useful extension of Banach's contraction principle, and due to its importance, many authors, such as [18–21] and those that they reference in their studies, obtained generalizations and extensions of Caristi's theorem; in addition, some authors [22–26] presented new proofs of Caristi's theorem.

Very recently, Isik et al. [27] presented a generalization of Caristi's fixed-point theorem in complete metric spaces by using the concept of the control function.

In this study, we give the concept of σ-Caristi maps and prove the existence of fixed points for such σ-Caristi maps in Branciari distance spaces. We generalize the notion of σ-contractions and obtain related fixed-point results in Branciari distance spaces. We examined the interrelations among the various contraction conditions presented in this paper. In addition, we present examples to analyze the main theorems, and we give applications to integral equations and differential equations.

2. Preliminaries

Jleli and Samet [28] gave the concept of σ-contractions and used this notion to generalize Banach's contraction principle. Whenever $\sigma : (0, \infty) \to (1, \infty)$ is non-decreasing and satisfies (σ_1) and (σ_2),

(σ_1) For any sequence $\{u_n\} \subset (0, \infty)$,

$$u_n \to 0 \text{ (as } n \to \infty) \Leftrightarrow \sigma(u_n) \to 1 \text{ (as } n \to \infty);$$

(σ_2) There are $\varkappa \in (0, 1)$ and $\aleph \in (0, \infty]$:

$$\frac{\sigma(u) - 1}{u^{\varkappa}} \to \aleph \text{ (as } u \to 0^+).$$

Ahmad et al. [29] obtained an extension of the result of [28] to metric spaces by replacing (σ_2) with the condition that

(σ_3) σ is continuous on $(0, \infty)$.

Very recently, Işik et al. [27] generalized Caristi's result in metric spaces with (σ_2), (σ_3), (σ_4) and (σ_5), where

(σ_4) For any $\mu, \nu > 0$,

$$\sigma(\mu + \nu) \leq \sigma(\mu)\sigma(\nu);$$

$(\sigma_4)'$ For any $\mu, \nu > 0$,

$$\sigma(\mu + \nu) = \sigma(\mu)\sigma(\nu);$$

(σ_5) σ is strictly increasing;

(σ_6) For any $\mu, \nu > 0$,

$$\sigma(\mu - \nu) \leq \frac{\sigma(\mu)}{\sigma(\nu)};$$

(σ_7) For any $\mu > 0$ and $r > 0$,

$$[\sigma(\mu)]^r \leq \sigma(r\mu).$$

In 2000, Branciari [10] introduced the notion of Branciari distance spaces and extended the Banach contraction principle to Branciari distance spaces with two conditions:

(c_1) The topology generated by the Branciari distance is a Hausdorff space;
(c_2) Any Branciari distance is continuous in each coordinate.

Since then, the authors of [30,31] investigated the characteristics of Branciari distance spaces. They obtained the following characteristics.

(b_1) A Branciari distance does not have to be continuous at each coordinate;
(b_2) A convergent sequence does not have to be a Cauchy sequence;
(b_3) The limit of a convergent sequence is not guaranteed to be unique;
(b_4) An open ball does not necessarily need to be an open set. Hence, the existence of a topology compatible with the Branchiari distance is not guaranteed.

However, many researchers have realized that, despite the aforementioned topological disadvantages, Brancian distance spaces are attractive spaces for studying and developing fixed-point theory without additional conditions. It is for this reason that a considerable number of researchers ([30–39] and the references therein) have expressed interest in the Branciari distance spaces; consequently, they have undertaken studies of fixed-point theory in these spaces.

Recall the definition of Branciari distance spaces in [10].

Let $B(\neq \emptyset)$ be a given set. A map $\rho : B \times B \to [0, \infty)$ is called a Branciari distance, provided that for all $\upsilon, \zeta \in E$ and for all $\varsigma, \iota \in B \setminus \{\upsilon, \zeta\}$ with $\varsigma \neq \iota$,

($\rho 1$) $\rho(\upsilon, \zeta) = 0 \Longleftrightarrow \upsilon = \zeta$;
($\rho 2$) $\rho(\upsilon, \zeta) = \rho(\zeta, \upsilon)$;
($\rho 3$) $\rho(\upsilon, \zeta) \leq \rho(\upsilon, \varsigma) + \rho(\varsigma, \iota) + \rho(\iota, \zeta)$ (trapezoidal inequality).

Here , (B, ρ) is called a Branciari distance space.

Remark 1 ([40]). *For a Branciari distance space (B, ρ), the following holds:*

(i) *(B, ρ) is not reducible to a metric space;*
(ii) *In general, the topology on B generated by ρ does not exist.*

Remark 2. *A trapezoidal inequality holds whenever a triangular inequality is satisfied. However, the converse is not true. Metric spaces are included in the family of Branciari distance spaces.*

The concept of convergence in Branciari distance spaces is defined similarly to that of metric spaces.

Let (B, ρ) be a Branciari distance space and let $\{\xi_n\} \subset B$ be a sequence. Then, we say that

(i) $\{\xi_n\}$ converges to ξ if it satisfies

$$\lim_{n\to\infty} \rho(\xi_n, \xi) = 0;$$

(ii) $\{\xi_n\}$ is Cauchy whenever the condition

$$\lim_{n,m\to\infty} \rho(\xi_n, \xi_m) = 0 \text{ holds;}$$

(iii) (B,ρ) is complete when every Cauchy sequence in B converges to a point in B.

Let (B,ρ) be a Branciari distance space, and let τ_ρ be a topology on B such that, for any $E \subset B$ and any sequence $\{c_m\} \subset E$,

$$B - E \in \tau_\rho \Longleftrightarrow [\lim_{m\to\infty} \rho(c_m, c) = 0 \Rightarrow c \in E]. \tag{1}$$

Here, (B,τ_ρ) is called a sequential topological space (see [34]).

A map $T : B \to B$ is continuous [34] whenever the following condition holds.

For any sequence $\{c_m\} \subset B$,

$$\lim_{m\to\infty} \rho(c_m, c) = 0 \Rightarrow \lim_{m\to\infty} \rho(Tc_m, Tc) = 0.$$

In Example 1.1 ([31]) and Example 3 ([34]), we can see the properties $(b_1) \sim (b_4)$ of Branciari distance spaces.

In the following example, we can see some characteristics of sequential topology on Branciari distance spaces.

Example 1. *Let $B = \{1,2\} \cup \{1 - \frac{1}{n} : n = 1,2,3,\cdots\}$. Suppose that $\rho : B \times B \to [0,\infty)$ is a map defined by*

$$\rho(\xi,\zeta) = \begin{cases} 0, (\xi = \zeta), \\ 1, (\xi,\zeta \in \{1,2\}), \\ 1, (\xi,\zeta \in \{1-\frac{1}{n} : n \in \mathbb{N}\}), \\ \frac{1}{n}, (\xi \in \{1,2\} \text{ and } \zeta \in \{1-\frac{1}{n} : n \in \mathbb{N}\}). \end{cases}$$

Then, (B,ρ) is a complete Branciari distance space

It follows from (1) that the sequential topology τ_ρ on B generated by the Branciari distance space given in Example 1 is

$$\tau_\rho = \{\emptyset, B, \{1-\frac{1}{n} : n \in \mathbb{N}\}, \{1\} \cup \{1-\frac{1}{n} : n \in \mathbb{N}\}, \{2\} \cup \{1-\frac{1}{n} : n \in \mathbb{N}\}\}. \tag{2}$$

Remark 3. *We have some properties of sequential topology and sequential continuity on Branciari distance spaces.*

(i) From (2), we have that the sequential topological space (B,τ_ρ) generated by the Branciari distance space given in Example 1 is not a Hausdorff space.

(ii) ρ is not continuous with respect to (B,τ_ρ) because

$$\lim_{k\to\infty} \rho(1-\frac{1}{k}, 2) = 0 \text{ implies } \lim_{n\to\infty} \rho(1-\frac{1}{k}, \frac{1}{2}) \neq \rho(2, \frac{1}{2}). \tag{3}$$

Throughout this paper, unless otherwise stated, we let B denote a Branciari distance space with Branciari distance ρ. In addition, we represent by $\mathcal{CM}(B,B)$ the class of all self maps defined on a complete Branciari distance space B.

Lemma 1 ([41]). *Let (B,ρ) be a complete Branciari distance space. Assume that $\{\xi_n\} \subset B$ is a Cauchy sequence and $\xi,\zeta \in B$. If there exists $k_0 \in \mathbb{N}$ such that*

(i) $\xi_n \neq \xi_m \ \forall n,m > k_0$;

(ii) $\xi_n \neq \xi \ \forall n > k_0$;

(iii) $\xi_n \neq \zeta \ \forall n > k_0$;

(iv) $\lim_{n\to\infty} \rho(\xi_n,\xi) = \lim_{n\to\infty} \rho(\xi_n,\zeta)$,

then $\xi = \zeta$.

Lemma 2 ([37]). *Let $\{\xi_m\} \subset B$ be a Cauchy sequence such that*

$$\lim_{m\to\infty} \rho(\xi_m, \xi) = 0.$$

Then,

$$\lim_{m\to\infty} \rho(\zeta, \xi_m) = \rho(\zeta, \xi),\ \forall \zeta \in B.$$

3. Fixed Points

We introduce the notion of the σ-Caristi map on Branciari distance space; it is the motivation from the paper by Isik et al.

Let $\sigma : (0,\infty) \to (1,\infty)$ be a function.

Then, we say that $C \in \mathcal{CM}(B,B)$ is a σ-Caristi map if there exists an lsc function $\phi : B \to [a,\infty)$, where $a > 0$, such that

$$\sigma(\rho(\xi, C\xi)) \leq \frac{\sigma(\phi(\xi))}{\sigma(\phi(C\xi))}, \forall \xi \in B(\xi \neq C\xi). \tag{4}$$

Proposition 1. *Let $C \in \mathcal{CM}(B,B)$ be a σ-Caristi map with an lsc function $\phi : B \to [a,\infty)$, where $a > 0$.*

For each $\xi \in B$, let

$$R(\xi) = \{\zeta \in B : \zeta \neq \xi, \sigma(\rho(\xi,\zeta)) \leq \frac{\sigma(\phi(\xi))}{\sigma(\phi(\zeta))}\}.$$

If σ is non-decreasing and satisfies the condition (σ4), then the following hold:

(i) $R(\xi) \neq \emptyset$, $\forall \xi \in B$;
(ii) $\phi(\zeta) < \phi(\xi)$, $\forall \zeta \in R(\xi)$;
(iii) $R(\zeta) \subset R(\xi)$, $\forall \zeta \in R(\iota), \forall \iota \in R(\xi)$.

Proof. Since C is a σ-Caristi map, it satisfies that for all $\xi \in B$ with $\xi \neq C\xi$,

$$\sigma(\rho(\xi, C\xi)) \leq \frac{\sigma(\phi(\xi))}{\sigma(\phi(C\xi))}.$$

Hence, $C\xi \in R(\xi)$, and so $R(\xi) \neq \emptyset$. Thus, (i) is proved.

Let $\zeta \in R(\xi)$. Then, we have

$$\zeta \neq \xi \text{ and } \sigma(\rho(\xi,\zeta)) \leq \frac{\sigma(\phi(\xi))}{\sigma(\phi(\zeta))},$$

which implies

$$\sigma(\phi(\zeta)) < \sigma(\phi(\xi)),$$

and so

$$\phi(\zeta) < \phi(\xi).$$

Hence, (ii) is satisfied.

Let $\iota \in R(\xi)$, and let $\zeta \in R(\iota)$.

Then, we have that

$$\iota \neq \xi \text{ and } \sigma(\rho(\xi,\iota)) \leq \frac{\sigma(\phi(\xi))}{\sigma(\phi(\iota))},$$

$$\zeta \neq \iota \text{ and } \sigma(\rho(\iota,\zeta)) \leq \frac{\sigma(\phi(\iota))}{\sigma(\phi(\zeta))}.$$

Assume that $\varsigma \in R(\zeta)$.

Then, we obtain that

$$\varsigma \neq \zeta \text{ and } \sigma(\rho(\zeta,\varsigma)) \leq \frac{\sigma(\phi(\zeta))}{\sigma(\phi(\varsigma))}.$$

Hence,

$$\sigma(\phi(\varsigma)) < \sigma(\phi(\zeta)) < \sigma(\phi(\iota)) < \sigma(\phi(\xi)). \tag{5}$$

If $\varsigma = \xi$, then from (5), we have

$$\sigma(\phi(\xi)) < \sigma(\phi(\xi)),$$

which is a contradiction. Thus,

$$\varsigma \neq \xi. \tag{6}$$

Applying (ρ_3) and (σ_4), we infer that

$$\begin{aligned}
&\sigma(\rho(\varsigma,\xi)) \\
=&\sigma(\rho(\xi,\varsigma)) \\
\leq&\sigma(\rho(\xi,\iota))\sigma(\rho(\iota,\zeta))\sigma(\rho(\zeta,\varsigma)) \\
\leq&\frac{\sigma(\phi(\xi))}{\sigma(\phi(\iota))}\frac{\sigma(\phi(\iota))}{\sigma(\phi(\zeta))}\frac{\sigma(\phi(\zeta))}{\sigma(\phi(\varsigma))} \\
=&\frac{\sigma(\phi(\xi))}{\sigma(\phi(\varsigma))}.
\end{aligned} \tag{7}$$

It follows from (6) and (7) that

$$\varsigma \in R(\xi).$$

Thus, (iii) is proved. □

Remark 4. *Proposition 1 holds whenever (σ_4) and (σ_5) are satisfied.*

Theorem 1. *Let $C \in \mathcal{CM}(B,B)$ be a σ-Caristi map with an lsc function $\phi : B \to [a,\infty)$, where $a > 0$. If σ satisfies (σ_1), (σ_3), (σ_4) and (σ_5), then C possesses a fixed point.*

Proof. Assume that

$$\xi \neq C\xi,\ \forall \xi \in B.$$

Let $\xi_1 \in B$ be given.
Since $R(\xi_1) \neq \emptyset$, we can choose a point $\xi_2 \in R(\xi_1)$ such that

$$\phi(\xi_2) \leq \inf_{\iota \in R(\xi_1)} \phi(\iota) + 1.$$

Inductively, we can construct a sequence $\{\xi_n\} \subset B$ such that

$$\xi_{n+1} \in R(\xi_n) \text{ and } \phi(\xi_{n+1}) \leq \inf_{\iota \in R(\xi_n)} \phi(\iota) + \frac{1}{n},\ \forall n \in \mathbb{N}. \tag{8}$$

Since $\xi_{n+1} \in R(\xi_n)$,

$$\xi_{n+1} \neq \xi_n \text{ and } \sigma(\rho(\xi_n,\xi_{n+1})) \leq \frac{\sigma(\phi(\xi_n))}{\sigma(\phi(\xi_{n+1}))} \tag{9}$$

which implies

$$\sigma(\phi(\xi_{n+1})) < \sigma(\phi(\xi_n))\ \forall n \in \mathbb{N}.$$

Thus, the sequence $\{\phi(\xi_n))\}$ is decreasing.

We now show that $\{\xi_n\}$ is Cauchy.

Using (9) and (σ_4), we find that

$$\begin{aligned}\sigma(\phi(\xi_1)) &> \frac{\sigma(\phi(\xi_1)}{\sigma(\phi(\xi_n)}\\ &=\frac{\sigma(\phi(\xi_1))}{\sigma(\phi(\xi_2))}\frac{\sigma(\phi(\xi_2))}{\sigma(\phi(\xi_3))}\cdots\frac{\sigma(\phi(\xi_{n-1}))}{\sigma(\phi(\xi_n))}\\ &\geq\sigma(\rho(\xi_1,\xi_2))\sigma(\rho(\xi_2,\xi_3))\cdots\sigma(\rho(\xi_{n-1},\xi_n))\\ &=\sigma(\sum_{k=1}^{n-1}\rho(\xi_k,\xi_{k+1})),\end{aligned}$$

which implies

$$\sum_{k=1}^{n-1}\rho(\xi_k,\xi_{k+1}) < \phi(\xi_1).$$

Hence,

$$\sum_{n=1}^{\infty}\rho(\xi_n,\xi_{n+1}) < \infty. \tag{10}$$

Let $\epsilon > 0$ be given.

From (10), there exists a positive integer N such that

$$\sum_{n=N}^{\infty}\rho(\xi_n,\xi_{n+1}) < \epsilon.$$

Thus, we have that for all $n, m > N$,

$$\rho(\xi_n,\xi_m) < \sum_{n=N}^{\infty}\rho(\xi_n,\xi_{n+1}) < \epsilon.$$

Hence, $\{\xi_n\}$ is a Cauchy sequence.

By the completeness of B, there is $\xi_* \in B$ with

$$\lim_{k\to\infty}\rho(\xi_*,\xi_k) = 0. \tag{11}$$

Since ϕ is an lsc function and $\{\phi(\xi_n)\}$ is a decreasing sequence,

$$\phi(\xi_*) \leq \lim_{n\to\infty}\inf\phi(\xi_n) \leq \inf_{n\in\mathbb{N}}\phi(\xi_n) \leq \phi(\xi_n),\ \forall n \in \mathbb{N}. \tag{12}$$

We show that

$$\xi_* \neq \xi_n,\ \forall n \in \mathbb{N}. \tag{13}$$

If $\xi_* = \xi_l$ for some $l \in \mathbb{N}$, then it follows from (9) and (12) that

$$1 < \sigma(\rho(\xi_l,\xi_{l+1})) \leq \frac{\sigma(\phi(\xi_l))}{\sigma(\phi(\xi_{l+1}))} \leq \frac{\sigma(\phi(\xi_l))}{\sigma(\phi(\xi_*))} \leq \frac{\sigma(\phi(\xi_*))}{\sigma(\phi(\xi_*))} = 1,$$

which is a contradiction.

Thus, (13) holds.

Next, we assert that

$$\bigcap_{m\in\mathbb{N}} R(\xi_m) = \{\xi_*\}.$$

By (σ_4) and (9), we find that

$$\begin{aligned}&\sigma(\rho(\xi_n,\xi_m))\\ \leq&\sigma(\rho(\xi_n,\xi_{n+1}))\sigma(\rho(\xi_{n+1},\xi_{n+2}))\cdots\sigma(\rho(\xi_{m-1},\xi_m))\\ \leq&\frac{\sigma(\phi(\xi_n))}{\sigma(\phi(\xi_m))},\forall m,n\in\mathbb{N},m>n.\end{aligned}$$

Thus, from (12), we infer that

$$\sigma(\rho(\xi_n,\xi_m))\leq\frac{\sigma(\phi(\xi_n))}{\sigma(\phi(\xi_m))}\leq\frac{\sigma(\phi(\xi_n))}{\sigma(\phi(\xi_*))}. \tag{14}$$

Since (σ_5) is satisfied, (14) yields the following inequality:

$$\rho(\xi_n,\xi_m)\leq\sigma^{-1}\Big(\frac{\sigma(\phi(\xi_n))}{\sigma(\phi(\xi_*))}\Big). \tag{15}$$

By applying Lemma 2 to (11) to (15), we find that

$$\rho(\xi_n,\xi_*)\leq\sigma^{-1}\Big(\frac{\sigma(\phi(\xi_n))}{\sigma(\phi(\xi_*))}\Big),$$

which yields

$$\sigma(\rho(\xi_n,\xi_*))\leq\frac{\sigma(\phi(\xi_n))}{\sigma(\phi(\xi_*))},\ \forall n\in\mathbb{N}.$$

Hence,

$$\xi_*\in R(\xi_n),\ \forall n\in\mathbb{N},$$

and thus,

$$\xi_*\in\bigcap_{n\in\in\mathbb{N}}R(\xi_n).$$

Applying Proposition 1(iii) to $\xi_n\in R(\xi_{n-1})$, we find that

$$R(\xi_*)\subset R(\xi_{n-1})\ \forall n=2,3,\cdots,$$

which implies that

$$R(\xi_*)\subset\bigcap_{n\in\mathbb{N}}R(\xi_n). \tag{16}$$

Let

$$\iota\in\bigcap_{n\in\mathbb{N}}R(\xi_n).$$

Then, we infer that

$$\iota\in R(\xi_{n+1})\text{ and }\xi_{n+1}\in R(\xi_n)\ \forall n\in\mathbb{N}.$$

By applying Proposition 1(iii),

$$R(\iota)\subset R(\xi_n),\ \forall n\in\mathbb{N}.$$

From (8), we infer that $\forall n\in\mathbb{N}$,

$$\sigma(\rho(\xi_n,\iota))\leq\frac{\sigma(\phi(\xi_n))}{\sigma(\phi(\iota))}\leq\frac{\sigma(\phi(\xi_n))}{\sigma(\inf_{\iota\in R(\xi_n)}\phi(\iota))}\leq\frac{\sigma(\phi(\xi_n))}{\sigma(\phi(\xi_{n+1})-\frac{1}{n})}. \tag{17}$$

Since $\{\phi(\xi_n\}$ is decreasing and ϕ is bounded below by a, there exists $L \geq a$ such that

$$\lim_{n\to\infty} \phi(\xi_n) = L. \tag{18}$$

By letting $n \to \infty$ in Equation (17) and using (σ_3),

$$\lim_{n\to\infty} \sigma(\rho(\xi_n, \iota)) = 1. \tag{19}$$

It follows from (σ_1) that

$$\lim_{n\to\infty} \rho(\xi_n, \iota) = 0. \tag{20}$$

Applying Lemma 1,

$$\xi_* = \iota,$$

and hence,

$$\bigcap_{n\in\mathbb{N}} R(\xi_n) = \{\xi_*\}.$$

From (16), we find that

$$R(\xi_*) \subset \{\xi_*\}.$$

Because $\xi_* \neq C\xi_*$, it follows from (4) that

$$C\xi_* \in R(\xi_*),$$

and so

$$\xi_* = C\xi_*,$$

which leads to a contradiction.

Hence, C possesses a fixed point. □

Remark 5. *(i) If σ is a non-decreasing function in Theorem 1, then C possesses a fixed point.*
(ii) Theorem 1 extends Theorem 2 of [27] to Branciari distance spaces.

We now present an example to analyze Theorem 1.

Example 2. *Let $B = \{1, 2, 3, 4\}$, and let $\rho : B \times B \to [0, \infty)$ be a map defined as follows:*

$$\begin{aligned}
&\rho(1,2) = \rho(2,1) = 3,\\
&\rho(2,3) = \rho(3,2) = \rho(1,3) = \rho(3,1) = 1,\\
&\rho(1,4) = \rho(4,1) = \rho(2,4) = \rho(4,2) = \rho(3,4) = \rho(4,3) = 4,\\
&\rho(z,z) = 0,\ \forall z \in B.
\end{aligned}$$

Then, (B, ρ) is a complete Branciari distance space (see [32]).
Let $C : B \to B$ be a map defined by

$$C\xi = \begin{cases} 1 & (\xi = 1, 2), \\ 3 & (\xi = 3, 4). \end{cases}$$

Suppose that $\phi : B \to [a, \infty)$, where $a > 0$, is a map defined by $\phi(x) = 5x$, and let $\sigma(\iota) = e^{\iota}, \forall \iota > 0$.

Then, (σ_4) and (σ_5) hold, and ϕ is an lsc function.
We now show that C is a σ-Caristi map with lsc $\phi(x) = 5x$.

We infer that

$$\rho(\xi, C\xi) = \begin{cases} \rho(1,1) = 0 & (\xi = 1), \\ \rho(2,1) = 3 & (\xi = 2), \\ \rho(3,3) = 0 & (\xi = 3), \\ \rho(4,3) = 4 & (\xi = 4). \end{cases}$$

Hence,

$$\rho(\xi, C\xi) > 0 \Longleftrightarrow \xi = 2, 4.$$

Consider the following two cases.
First case: Let $\xi = 2$*.*
Then, we have that

$$\frac{\sigma(\phi(\xi))}{\sigma(\phi(S\xi))} = \frac{\sigma(10)}{\sigma(5)} = e^5 > e^3 = \sigma(\rho(\xi, S\xi)).$$

Second case: Let $\xi = 4$*.*
Then, we find that

$$\frac{\sigma(\phi(\xi))}{\sigma(\phi(S\xi))} = \frac{\sigma(20)}{\sigma(15)} = e^5 > e^4 = \sigma(\rho(\xi, S\xi)).$$

Hence, C is a σ*-Caristi map with* $\phi(x) = 5x$*. The suppositions of Theorem 1 hold, and there are fixed points 1 and 3 on the map C.*

Corollary 1. *Let* $C \in \mathcal{CM}(B, B)$ *be such that*

$$\sigma(\rho(\xi, \zeta)) \leq \frac{\sigma(\varphi(\xi, \zeta))}{\sigma(\varphi(C\xi, C\zeta))}, \forall \xi, \zeta \in B(\xi \neq \zeta), \tag{21}$$

where $\varphi : B \times B \to [a, \infty)$*, where* $a > 0$*, is lsc with respect to the first variable. If* σ *satisfies* (σ_1)*,* (σ_3)*,* (σ_4)*, and* (σ_5)*, then C possesses only one fixed point.*

Proof. For each $\xi \in B$, let $\zeta = C\xi$ and $\phi(\xi) = \varphi(\xi, C\xi)$.

Then, $\phi : B \to [a, \infty)$ is an lsc function. It follows from (21) that for all $\xi \in B$ with $\xi \neq C\xi$,

$$\sigma(\rho(\xi, C\xi)) \leq \frac{\sigma(\phi(\xi))}{\sigma(\phi(C\xi))}.$$

By Theorem 1, C possesses a fixed point.
We now show that C possesses only one fixed point.
Let $u = Cu$ and $v = Cv$ be such that $u \neq v$.
From (21), we acquire that

$$1 < \sigma(\rho(u, v)) \leq \frac{\sigma(\varphi(u, v))}{\sigma(\varphi(Cu, Cv))} = \frac{\sigma(\varphi(u, v))}{\sigma(\varphi(u, v))} = 1,$$

which leads to a contradiction.

Hence, C possesses only one fixed point. □

Corollary 2. *Let* $C \in \mathcal{CM}(B, B)$ *be such that*

$$\sigma(\rho(C\xi, C\zeta)) < \sigma(\phi(\rho(\xi, \zeta))), \forall \xi, \zeta \in E(C\xi \neq C\zeta), \tag{22}$$

where $\phi : [0, \infty) \to [0, \infty)$ is an lsc function with $\phi(t) < t$, $\forall t > 0$, and $\frac{\phi(t)}{t}$ is a non-decreasing function. If σ satisfies (σ_1), (σ_3), (σ_4), (σ_5), (σ_6), and (σ_7), where

(σ_6) $\forall \mu, \nu > 0$ *with* $\mu - \nu > 0$,

$$\sigma(\mu - \nu) \leq \frac{\sigma(\mu)}{\sigma(\nu)};$$

(σ_7) $\forall \mu, r > 0$,

$$[\sigma(\mu)]^r = \sigma(\mu r),$$

then C possesses only one fixed point.

Proof. As (σ_5) holds, it follows from (22) that

$$\rho(C\xi, C\zeta) < \phi(\rho(\xi, \zeta)),$$

which implies

$$0 < \rho(\xi, \zeta) - \phi(\rho(\xi, \zeta)) \leq \rho(\xi, \zeta) - \rho(C\xi, C\zeta).$$

Hence, we find that

$$\begin{aligned}
&\sigma\Big(\Big(1 - \frac{\phi(\rho(\xi, \zeta))}{\rho(\xi, \zeta)}\Big)\rho(\xi, \zeta)\Big) \\
=&\sigma\Big(\rho(\xi, \zeta) - \phi(\rho(\xi, \zeta))\Big) \\
\leq&\sigma\Big(\rho(\xi, \zeta) - \rho(C\xi, C\zeta)\Big).
\end{aligned}$$

Let $\varphi(\xi, \zeta) = a + \frac{\rho(\xi,\zeta)}{1 - \frac{\phi(\rho(\xi,\zeta))}{\rho(\xi,\zeta)}}$ for all $\xi, \zeta \in B$ with $\xi \neq \zeta$, where $a > 0$.

Then, $\varphi : B \times B \to [a, \infty)$ is an lsc function with respect to the first variable. Since $\rho(C\xi, C\zeta) < \rho(\xi, \zeta)$ and $\frac{\phi(t)}{t}$ is non-decreasing, it follows from $(\sigma5)$ and $(\sigma6)$ that

$$\begin{aligned}
&\sigma(\rho(\xi, \zeta)) \\
=&[\sigma(\Big(1 - \frac{\phi(\rho(\xi, \zeta))}{\rho(\xi, \zeta)}\Big)\rho(\xi, \zeta))]^{\frac{1}{1 - \frac{\phi(\rho(\xi,\zeta))}{\rho(x,y)}}} \\
\leq&[\sigma(\rho(\xi, \zeta) - \rho(C\xi, C\zeta))]^{\frac{1}{1 - \frac{\phi(\rho(\xi,\zeta))}{\rho(\xi,\zeta)}}} \\
=&\sigma\left(\left(a + \frac{\rho(\xi, \zeta)}{1 - \frac{\phi(\rho(\xi,\zeta))}{\rho(\xi,\zeta)}}\right) - \left(a + \frac{\rho(C\xi, C\zeta)}{1 - \frac{\phi(\rho(\xi,\zeta))}{\rho(\xi,\zeta)}}\right)\right) \\
\leq&\frac{\sigma\left(a + \frac{\rho(\xi,\zeta)}{1 - \frac{\phi(\rho(\xi,\zeta))}{\rho(\xi,\zeta)}}\right)}{\sigma\left(a + \frac{\rho(C\xi,C\zeta)}{1 - \frac{\phi(\rho(\xi,\zeta))}{\rho(\xi,\zeta)}})\right)} \\
\leq&\frac{\sigma\left(a + \frac{\rho(\xi,\zeta)}{1 - \frac{\phi(\rho(\xi,\zeta)}{\rho(\xi,\zeta)}}\right)}{\sigma\left(a + \frac{\rho(C\xi,C\zeta)}{1 - \frac{\phi(\rho(C\xi,C\zeta))}{\rho(C\xi,C\zeta)}}\right)} \\
=&\frac{\sigma(\varphi(\xi, \zeta))}{\sigma(\varphi(C\xi, C\zeta))}.
\end{aligned}$$

By applying Corollary 1, C possesses only one fixed point. □

Remark 6. *Taking $\sigma(u) = e^u, \forall u > 0$ in Corollary 1 (or Corollary 2), we have Corollary 2.1 (or Corollary 2.3) of [20].*

A map $C \in \mathcal{CM}(B, B)$ is called a generalized σ-contraction if it satisfies the following condition.

There exists a function $\sigma : (0, \infty) \to (1, \infty)$ such that

$$\sigma(\rho(C\xi, C\zeta)) \leq \frac{\sigma(\phi(\rho(\xi, \zeta))}{\sigma(\phi(\rho(C\xi, C\zeta))}, \forall \xi, \zeta \in B(C\xi \neq C\zeta), \tag{23}$$

where $\phi : (0, \infty) \to (0, \infty)$ satisfies

$$\lim_{t \to 0^+} \phi(t) = 0. \tag{24}$$

Theorem 2. *Let $C \in \mathcal{CM}(B, B)$ be a generalized σ-contraction. If σ satisfies (σ_1), (σ_4), and (σ_5), then C possesses only one fixed point.*

Proof. Let $\xi_0 \in B$, and let $\xi_n = C\xi_{n-1}, \forall n \in \mathbb{N}$.

Then, we infer that $\xi_{n-1} \neq \xi_n, \forall n \in \mathbb{N}$. Otherwise, C possesses a fixed point. So, the proof is finished.

From (23), we find that $\forall n \in \mathbb{N}$,

$$1 < \sigma(\rho(\xi_n, \xi_{n+1})) \leq \frac{\sigma(\phi(\rho(\xi_{n-1}, \xi_n)))}{\sigma(\phi(\rho(\xi_n, \xi_{n+1})))}. \tag{25}$$

We now show that $\{\xi_n\}$ is Cauchy.

From (25) and (σ_4), we find that

$$\begin{aligned}
&\sigma(\sum_{k=1}^{n-1} \rho(\xi_k, \xi_{k+1})) \\
\leq&\sigma(\rho(\xi_1, \xi_2))\sigma(\rho(\xi_2, \xi_3)) \cdot \cdots \cdot \sigma(\rho(\xi_{n-1}, \xi_n)) \\
\leq&\frac{\sigma(\phi(\rho(\xi_0, \xi_1)))}{\sigma(\phi(\rho(\xi_1, \xi_2)))} \frac{\sigma(\phi(\rho(\xi_1, \xi_2)))}{\sigma(\phi(\rho(\xi_2, \xi_3)))} \cdots \cdots \frac{\sigma(\phi(\rho(\xi_{n-2}, \xi_{n-1})))}{\sigma(\phi(\rho(\xi_{n-1}, \xi_n)))} \\
=&\frac{\sigma(\phi(\rho(\xi_0, \xi_1)))}{\sigma(\phi(\rho(\xi_{n-1}, \xi_n)))} \\
<&\sigma(\phi(\rho(\xi_0, \xi_1))).
\end{aligned}$$

Hence, we acquire

$$\sum_{k=1}^{n-1} \rho(\xi_k, \xi_{k+1}) < \phi(\rho(\xi_0, \xi_1)),$$

which yields

$$\sum_{n=1}^{\infty} \rho(\xi_n, \xi_{n+1}) < \infty.$$

Thus, $\{\xi_n\}$ is Cauchy. Because B is complete, there is $\xi_* \in B$ such that

$$\lim_{n \to \infty} \rho(\xi_*, \xi_n) = 0.$$

By ($\rho 3$), (σ_4), and (23), we infer the following inequality,

$$\begin{aligned}&\sigma(\rho(\xi_n, C\xi_*)\\ \leq&\sigma(\rho(\xi_n,\xi_*))\sigma(\rho(\xi_*,\xi_{n+1}))\sigma(\rho(\xi_{n+1},C\xi_*))\\ \leq&\sigma(\rho(\xi_n,\xi_*))\sigma(\rho(\xi_*,\xi_{n+1}))\frac{\sigma(\phi(\rho(\xi_n,\xi_*)))}{\sigma(\phi(\rho(\xi_{n+1},C\xi_*)))}\\ <&\sigma(\rho(\xi_n,\xi_*))\sigma(\rho(\xi_*,\xi_{n+1}))\sigma(\phi(\rho(\xi_n,\xi_*))).\end{aligned} \tag{26}$$

Applying (24) to the term $\phi(\rho(\xi_n,\xi_*))$ in (26), we find that

$$\lim_{n\to\infty}\phi(\rho(\xi_n,\xi_*)) = 0,$$

because

$$\lim_{n\to\infty}\rho(\xi_n,\xi_*) = 0.$$

Hence, we infer that

$$\lim_{n\to\infty}\sigma(\phi(\rho(\xi_n,\xi_*))) = 1. \tag{27}$$

By letting $n\to\infty$ in (26) and applying (27),

$$\lim_{n\to\infty}\sigma(\rho(\xi_n, C\xi_*)) = 1,$$

which yields

$$\lim_{n\to\infty}\rho(\xi_n, C\xi_*) = 0.$$

Applying Lemma 1, we find that $\xi_* = C\xi_*$, and C possesses a fixed point.

We now show that C possesses only one fixed point.

Let $\mu = C\mu$ and $\nu = C\nu$ be such that $\mu \neq \nu$.

Then, it follows from (23) that

$$1 < \sigma(\rho(\mu,\nu)) = \sigma(\rho(C\mu, C\nu)) \leq \frac{\sigma(\phi(\rho(\mu,\nu))}{\sigma(\phi(\rho(C\mu,C\nu))} = 1,$$

which leads to a contradiction.

Hence, C possesses only one fixed point. □

Applying Theorem 2 to Newton's method, we can find the roots of equations.

We recall Newton's iterative scheme:

$$\xi_{n+1} = \xi_n - \frac{f(\xi_n)}{f'(\xi_n)}, n = 0,1,2,\cdots$$

where $f : X \to \mathbb{R}, X \subset \mathbb{R}$, is a differentiable function, and ξ_0 is an initial point for finding the root of the equation $f(\xi) = 0$.

Example 3. *Let $f(\xi) = \xi^2 - 4$, and let us apply Theorem 2 to determine the roots of the equation $f(\xi) = 0$.*

We define a map $C : [2,\infty) \to [2,\infty)$ using

$$C\xi = \xi - \frac{f(\xi)}{f'(\xi)} = \frac{1}{2}(\xi + \frac{4}{\xi}).$$

Then, we have that for $\xi \in [2,\infty), C\xi = \xi$ if and only if $f(\xi) = 0$.

Let $\sigma(u) = e^u\ \forall u > 0$ and $\phi(t) = 2t\ \forall t > 0$.

We find that for all $\xi, \zeta \in [2, \infty)$ with $\rho(C\xi, C\zeta) > 0$,

$$\sigma(\rho(C\xi, C\zeta)) = \sigma(\mid C\xi - C\zeta \mid) = \sigma(\frac{1}{2} \mid (\xi + \frac{4}{\xi}) - (\zeta + \frac{4}{\zeta}) \mid)$$
$$= \sigma(\frac{1}{2} \mid \xi - \zeta \mid\mid 1 - \frac{4}{\xi\zeta} \mid) \leq \sigma(\frac{1}{2} \mid \xi - \zeta \mid)$$
$$\leq \sigma(2 \mid \xi - \zeta \mid - \mid \xi - \zeta \mid) \leq \sigma(2 \mid \xi - \zeta \mid -2 \mid C\xi - C\zeta \mid)$$
$$= \sigma(\phi(\rho(\xi, \zeta)) - \phi(\rho(C\xi, C\zeta))) = \frac{\sigma(\phi(\rho(\xi, \zeta)))}{\sigma(\phi(\rho(C\xi, C\zeta)))}$$

By Theorem 2, C has a fixed point $\xi_* \in [2, \infty)$. In fact, $\xi_* = 2$. Thus, the equation $f(\xi) = 0$ has a solution $\xi_* = 2$.

Corollary 3 is obtained by taking $\sigma(\imath) = e^{\imath}\ \forall \imath > 0$ in Theorem 2.

Corollary 3. *Let $C \in \mathcal{CM}(B, B)$ be such that*

$$\rho(C\xi, C\zeta) \leq \phi(\rho(\xi, \zeta)) - \phi(\rho(C\xi, C\zeta)), \forall \xi, \zeta \in B(C\xi \neq C\zeta),$$

where $\phi : (0, \infty) \to (0, \infty)$ satisfies (24).
Then, C possesses only one fixed point.

Remark 7. *Corollary 3 generalizes and extends Theorem 4 [27] to Branciari distance spaces without the continuity of map C and $\phi(0) = 0$.*

Remark 8. *It follows from Remark 2 that our main theorems also hold in complete metric spaces.*

4. Corollaries

In this section, we give several fixed-point results and coupled fixed-point results that are obtained by applying the main theorem.

Corollary 4 (Caristi). *Let $C \in \mathcal{CM}(B, B)$ be such that*

$$\rho(\xi, C\xi) \leq f(\xi) - f(C\xi), \forall \xi \in B(\xi \neq C\xi), \tag{28}$$

where $f : B \to [0, \infty)$ is an lsc function.
Then, C possesses a fixed point.

Proof. Let $\sigma(\nu) = e^{\nu}, \forall \nu > 0$.
It follows from (28) that for all $\xi \in B$ with $\xi \neq C\xi$,

$$\sigma(\rho(\xi, C\xi)) = e^{\rho(\xi, C\xi)} \leq e^{f(\xi) - f(C\xi)} = \frac{e^{f(\xi)}}{e^{f(C\xi)}}. \tag{29}$$

We define $f : B \to [0, \infty)$ by

$$f(\xi) = -a + \ln(\sigma(\phi(\xi)))),$$

where $\phi : B \to [a, \infty)$, $a > 0$, is an lsc function.
Then, f is an lsc function. From (29), we acquire that for all $\xi \in B$ with $\xi \neq C\xi$,

$$\sigma(\rho(\xi, C\xi)) \leq \frac{e^{f(\xi)}}{e^{f(C\xi)}} = \frac{\sigma(\phi(\xi))}{\sigma(\phi(C\xi))}.$$

By Theorem 1, C possesses a fixed point. □

Recall that a map $C \in \mathcal{CM}(B,B)$ is called σ-contraction [28] if it satisfies

$$\sigma(\rho(C\xi, C\zeta)) \leq [\sigma(\rho(\xi,\zeta))]^k, \forall \xi,\zeta \in B(C\xi \neq C\zeta), \tag{30}$$

where $k \in (0,1)$, and $\sigma : (0,\infty) \to (1,\infty)$ is a function.

Jleli and Samet [28] proved that every σ-contraction $C \in \mathcal{CM}(B,B)$ possesses only one fixed point whenever σ is non-decreasing and satisfies (σ_1) and (σ_2).

By applying Corollary 2, we have Theorem 2.1 of [28].

Corollary 5 (Jleli and Samet). *Let $C \in \mathcal{CM}(B,B)$ be a σ-contraction. If σ satisfies (σ_1), (σ_3), (σ_4),(σ_5), (σ_6), and (σ_7), then C possesses only one fixed point.*

Proof. We define $\phi : [0,\infty) \to [0,\infty)$ by $\phi(s) = ks, \forall s > 0$, where $k \in (0,1)$.

Then, ϕ is an lsc function. By applying (30) and (σ_7), we have that for all $\xi,\zeta \in B$ with $C\xi \neq C\zeta$,

$$\sigma(\rho(C\xi, C\zeta)) \leq [\sigma(\rho(\xi,\zeta))]^k = \sigma(k\rho(\xi,\zeta)) = \sigma(\phi(\rho(\xi,\zeta))).$$

By Corollary 2, C possesses only one fixed point. □

Corollary 6. *Let $C \in \mathcal{CM}(B,B)$ be such that*

$$\sigma(\rho(C\xi, CC\xi)) \leq [\sigma(\rho(\xi,C\xi))]^k, \forall \xi \in B(C\xi \neq CC\xi),$$

where $k \in (0,1)$. If σ satisfies (σ_1), (σ_3), (σ_4), (σ_5), (σ_6), and (σ_7), then C possesses only one fixed point.

Remark 9. *Let (B,ρ) be a Branciari distance space such that ρ is an lsc function with respect to the first variable. If (σ_7) is satisfied, then the σ-Caristi map is a generalization of a σ-contraction. In fact, if $C : B \to B$ is a σ-contraction, then there is $k \in (0,1)$ such that*

$$\sigma(\rho(C\xi, C\zeta)) \leq [\sigma(\rho(\xi,\zeta))]^k, \forall \xi,\zeta \in B(C\xi \neq C\zeta).$$

Let $k = 1 - r, r \in (0,1)$.
We find that

$$\sigma(\rho(C\xi, C\zeta)) \leq [\sigma(\rho(\xi,\zeta))]^k = [\sigma(\rho(\xi,\zeta))]^{1-r} = \frac{\sigma(\rho(\xi,\zeta))}{[\sigma(\rho(\xi,\zeta))]^r},$$

which implies

$$\sigma(\rho(\xi,\zeta)) \leq \frac{[\sigma(\rho(\xi,\zeta))]^{\frac{1}{r}}}{[\sigma(\rho(C\xi,C\zeta))]^{\frac{1}{r}}} = \frac{\sigma(\frac{1}{r}\rho(\xi,\zeta))}{\sigma(\frac{1}{r}\rho(C\xi,C\zeta))}.$$

Let $\zeta = C\xi$ and $\phi(\xi) = \frac{1}{r}\rho(\xi, C\xi)$.
Then, we infer that

$$\sigma(\rho(\xi, C\xi)) \leq \frac{\sigma(\phi(\xi))}{\sigma(\phi(C\xi))}.$$

Hence, C is a σ-Caristi map.

Remark 10. *Inequality (23) of Theorem 2 is a generalization of a σ-contraction whenever (σ_7) is satisfied. In fact, if C is a σ-contraction, then*

$$\sigma(\rho(C\xi, C\zeta)) \leq [\sigma(\rho(\xi,\zeta))]^k, \forall \xi,\zeta \in B(C\xi \neq C\zeta) \text{ where } k \in (0,1).$$

Then, we have that

$$\sigma(\rho(C\xi, C\zeta)) \leq [\sigma(\rho(\xi,\zeta))]^{\frac{k}{1+k-\sqrt{k}}},$$

which implies that

$$[\sigma(\rho(C\xi, C\zeta))]^{1-\sqrt{k}} \leq \frac{[\sigma(\rho(\xi,\zeta))]^k}{[\sigma(\rho(C\xi, C\zeta))]^k}.$$

Hence, we infer that

$$\sigma(\rho(C\xi, C\zeta)) \leq \frac{[\sigma(\rho(\xi,\zeta))]^{\frac{k}{1-\sqrt{k}}}}{[\sigma(\rho(C\xi, C\zeta))]^{\frac{k}{1-\sqrt{k}}}} = \frac{\sigma(\frac{k}{1-\sqrt{k}}\rho(\xi,\zeta))}{\sigma(\frac{k}{1-\sqrt{k}}\rho(C\xi, C\zeta))}.$$

Let $\phi(s) = \frac{k}{1-\sqrt{k}}s, \forall s > 0.$
Then, we find that

$$\sigma(\rho(C\xi, C\zeta)) \leq \frac{\sigma(\phi(\rho(\xi,\zeta)))}{\sigma(\phi(\rho(C\xi, C\zeta)))}.$$

A map $C \in \mathcal{CM}(B, B)$ is called a σ-(ϕ, φ)-contraction if it satisfies the following condition. There exists a function $\sigma : (0,\infty) \to (0,\infty)$ such that

$$\sigma(\phi(\rho(C\xi, C\zeta))) \leq \frac{\sigma(\phi(\rho(\xi,\zeta)))}{\sigma(\varphi(\rho(\xi,\zeta)))} \forall \xi,\zeta \in B(\xi \neq \zeta) \tag{31}$$

where $\phi : [0,\infty) \to [0,\infty)$ is a continuous and strictly increasing function and $\varphi : [0,\infty) \to [0,\infty)$ is a continuous and non-decreasing function such that $\phi(t) = \varphi(t) = 0$ if and only if $t = 0$ and

$$0 < \phi(t) \leq t, \varphi(t) \geq t, \ \forall t > 0 \tag{32}$$

Note that $\phi : (0,\infty) \to (0,\infty)$ is a continuous and strictly increasing function and $\varphi : (0,\infty) \to (0,\infty)$ is a continuous and non-decreasing function such that (32) is satisfied.

Remark 11. *A generalized σ-contraction is a generalization of a σ-(ϕ, φ)-contraction, where σ is satisfied (σ_5). Actually, if $C \in \mathcal{CM}(B, B)$ is a σ-(ϕ, φ)-contraction, then from (31), we have that*

$$\phi(\rho(C\xi, C\zeta)) < \phi(\rho(\xi,\zeta)) \text{ because } (\sigma_5) \text{ holds.}$$

Hence, $\rho(C\xi, C\zeta) < \rho(\xi,\zeta)$ and, thus, $\varphi(C\xi, C\zeta) \leq \rho(\xi,\zeta)$. It follows from (31) that

$$\begin{aligned}\sigma(\phi(\rho(C\xi, C\zeta))) &\leq \frac{\sigma(\phi(\rho(\xi,\zeta)))}{\sigma(\varphi(\rho(\xi,\zeta)))} \leq \frac{\sigma(\phi(\rho(\xi,\zeta)))}{\sigma(\varphi(\rho(C\xi, C\zeta)))} \\ &\leq \frac{\sigma(\rho(\xi,\zeta))}{\sigma(\varphi(\rho(C\xi, C\zeta)))} \leq \frac{\sigma(\varphi(\rho(\xi,\zeta)))}{\sigma(\varphi(\rho(C\xi, C\zeta)))}, \forall \xi,\zeta \in B(C\xi \neq C\zeta).\end{aligned}$$

Hence, we infer that

$$\sigma(\rho(C\xi, C\zeta)) \leq \frac{\sigma(\varphi(\rho(\xi,\zeta)))}{\sigma(\varphi(\rho(C\xi, C\zeta)))}, \forall \xi,\zeta \in B(C\xi \neq C\zeta).$$

Remark 12. *A σ-contraction map is σ-(ϕ, φ)-contraction, where σ is satisfied (σ_5), (σ_6) and (σ_7).*
Let $C : B \to B$ be σ-contraction. Then there exists $0 < k < 1$ such that, for all $\xi, \zeta \in B$,

$$\sigma(\rho(C\xi, C\zeta)) \leq [\sigma(\rho(\xi,\zeta))]^k.$$

Let $\phi(t) = t, \varphi(t) = rt, r = 1 - k$ and let $\sigma(t) = e^t$, $\forall t > 0$.

Then, we have that

$$\sigma(\phi(\rho(C\xi, C\zeta))) \leq [\sigma(\rho(\xi,\zeta))]^{1-r} = \frac{\sigma(\rho(\xi,\zeta))}{[\sigma(\rho(\xi,\zeta))]^r}$$
$$= \frac{\sigma(\rho(\xi,\zeta))}{[\sigma(r\rho(\xi,\zeta))]} = \frac{\sigma(\phi(\rho(\xi,\zeta)))}{\sigma(\varphi(\rho(\xi,\zeta)))}, \ \forall \xi \neq \zeta.$$

Hence, C is a σ-(ϕ,φ)-contraction map.

The following example shows that σ-Caristi map is not a σ-contraction map, and it is not a generalized σ-contraction.

Example 4. *Let $B = [0,\infty)$ and $\rho(\xi,\zeta)) =\mid \xi - \zeta \mid, \ \forall \xi,\zeta \in B$.*

Let us define a map $C : B \to B$ by $C\xi = \sqrt{\xi}$, and let $\phi(t) = \varphi(t) = t, \sigma(t) = e^t, \ \forall t > 0$.

Then, we infer that, for all $\xi \in B$,

$$\frac{\sigma(\varphi(\xi))}{\sigma(\varphi(C\xi))} = \sigma(\varphi(\xi) - \varphi(C\xi)) = \sigma(\xi - \sqrt{\xi}) = \sigma(\rho(\xi, C\xi)).$$

Hence, C is a σ-Caristi map.

We now show that C is not a generalized σ-contraction map.

Suppose that C is a generalized σ-contraction map.

Then, for all $\xi,\zeta \in B$ with $\xi > \zeta$,

$$e^{\sqrt{\xi}-\sqrt{\zeta}} = \sigma(\rho(C\xi, C\zeta))$$
$$\leq \frac{\sigma(\varphi(\rho(\xi,\zeta)))}{\sigma(\varphi(\rho(C\xi, C\zeta)))} = \frac{\sigma(\rho(\xi,\zeta))}{\sigma(\rho(C\xi, C\zeta))}$$
$$= \frac{e^{\xi-\zeta}}{e^{\sqrt{\xi}-\sqrt{\zeta}}} = e^{(\sqrt{\xi}-\sqrt{\zeta})(\sqrt{\xi}+\sqrt{\zeta}-1)}.$$

Hence,

$$\sqrt{\xi} + \sqrt{\zeta} - 1 \geq 1$$

which leads to a contradiction, for $\xi = \frac{1}{4}, \zeta = \frac{1}{16}$.

Hence, C is not a generalized σ-contraction.

Example 5. *Let $B = [5,\infty)$ and $\rho(\xi, y) =\mid \xi - y \mid, \ \forall \xi, y \in B$.*

Define a map $C : B \to B$ by $C\xi = \frac{1}{5}\xi + 4$, and let $\phi(t) = t, \varphi(t) = \frac{1}{2}t, \sigma(t) = e^t \ \forall t > 0$.

$$\sigma(\rho(C\xi, C\zeta)) = \sigma(\frac{1}{5} \mid \xi - \zeta \mid)$$
$$\leq \sigma(\frac{4}{5} \mid \xi - \zeta \mid) = \sigma(\phi(\mid \xi - \zeta \mid) - \phi(\mid C\xi - C\zeta \mid))$$
$$= \sigma(\phi(\rho(\xi,\zeta)) - \phi(\rho(C\xi, C\zeta))) = \frac{\sigma(\phi(\rho(\xi,\zeta))}{\phi(\rho(C\xi, C\zeta))}.$$

Thus, C is a generalized σ-contraction map.

We now show that C is not a σ-Caristi map.

We infer that, for all $\xi,\zeta \in B$,

$$\frac{\sigma(\phi(\xi)}{\sigma(\phi(C\xi))} = \sigma(\phi(\xi) - \phi(C\xi)) = \sigma(\frac{2}{5}\xi - 2)$$
$$< \sigma(\frac{4}{5}\xi - 4) = \sigma(\rho(\xi, C\xi))$$

This implies that C is not a σ-Caristi map.

The following figure is derived from the previously mentioned remarks and the above examples. Here, the conditions of σ applied in each remark are also applied.

The following Figure 1 was created with reference to [42].

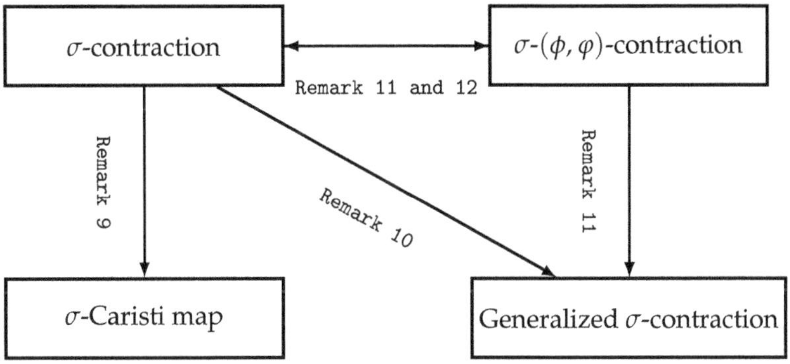

Figure 1. Relationships between different types of contractions.

From the above figure, it can be seen that a σ-contraction implies a σ-Caristi mapping, a generalized σ-contraction, and a σ-(ϕ,φ)-contraction. Moreover, a σ-(ϕ,φ)-contraction also implies a σ-contraction. On the other hand, there is no implication relationship between the generalized σ-contraction and the σ-Caristi mapping.

By taking $\sigma(u) = 1 + \ln(1+u), u > 0$ in Theorem 1, we acquire Corollary 7.

Corollary 7. *Let $C \in \mathcal{CM}(B, B)$ be such that*

$$1 + \ln(1 + \rho(\xi, C\xi)) \leq \frac{1 + \ln(1 + \phi(\xi))}{1 + \ln(1 + \phi(C\xi))}, \forall \xi \in B(\xi \neq C\xi),$$

where $\phi : B \to [a, \infty)$ is an lsc function, $a > 0$.

Then, C possesses a fixed point.

We apply Theorem 1 to prove the existence of coupled fixed points.

Let B be a nonempty set, and let $P : B \times B \to B$ be a map. A point $(\xi, \zeta) \in B \times B$ is said to be a coupled fixed point of P if it satisfies

$$P(\xi, \zeta) = \xi \text{ and } P(\zeta, \xi) = \zeta.$$

Lemma 3 ([43]). *Let B be a nonempty set, $(\xi, \zeta) \in B \times B$, and let $P : B \times B \to B$ be a map. We assume that $Q : B \times B \to B \times B$ is a map defined by*

$$Q(\xi, \zeta) = (P(\xi, \zeta), P(\zeta, \xi)). \tag{33}$$

Then, we find that

$$P(\xi, \zeta) = \xi \text{ and } P(\zeta, \xi) = \zeta \iff Q(\xi, \zeta) = (\xi, \zeta).$$

Lemma 4. *Let (B, ρ) be a complete Branciari distance space. We define $\hat{\rho} : B^2 \times B^2 \to [0, \infty)$ by*

$$\hat{\rho}((\xi, \zeta), (\varsigma, \iota)) = \rho(\xi, \varsigma) + \rho(\zeta, \iota). \tag{34}$$

Then, $(B \times B, \hat{\rho})$ is a complete Branciari distance space.

Proof. Let $(\xi,\zeta),(\varsigma,\iota) \in B \times B$. Then, we have that

$$\hat{\rho}((\xi,\zeta),(\varsigma,\iota)) = 0 \Leftrightarrow \rho(\xi,\varsigma) + \rho(\zeta,\iota) = 0 \Leftrightarrow (\xi,\zeta) = (\varsigma,\iota).$$

Thus, (ρ1) is satisfied. Obviously, (ρ2) holds.

We infer that for all $(\xi,\zeta),(\varsigma,\iota) \in B \times B$ and for all distinct points $(\mu,\nu),(\kappa,\omega) \in B \times B \setminus \{(\xi,\zeta),(\varsigma,\iota)\}$,

$$\begin{aligned}
&\hat{\rho}((\xi,\zeta),(\varsigma,\iota)) = \rho(\xi,\varsigma) + \rho(\zeta,\iota) \\
\leq &\rho(\xi,\mu) + \rho(\mu,\kappa) + \rho(\kappa,\varsigma) + \rho(\zeta,\nu) + \rho(\nu,\omega) + \rho(\omega,\iota)\} \\
\leq &\rho(\xi,\mu) + \rho(\zeta,\nu) + \rho(\mu,\kappa) + \rho(\nu,\omega) + \rho(\kappa,\varsigma), \rho(\omega,\iota) \\
= &\hat{\rho}((\xi,\zeta),(\mu,\nu)) + \hat{\rho}((\mu,\nu),(\kappa,\omega)) + \hat{\rho}((\kappa,\omega),(\varsigma,\iota)).
\end{aligned}$$

Thus, (ρ3) holds. Hence, $(B \times B, \hat{\rho})$ is a Branciari distance space.

We now show that $(B \times B, \hat{\rho})$ is complete.

Let $\{\varpi_n = (\xi_n,\zeta_n)\} \subset B \times B$ be a Cauchy sequence, and let $\epsilon > 0$ be given.

Then, there exists $n_0 \in \mathbb{N}$ such that for all $m > n > n_0$,

$$\hat{\rho}(\varpi_n, \varpi_m) < \epsilon,$$

which implies that

$$\rho(\xi_n,\xi_m) < \frac{1}{2}\epsilon \text{ and } \rho(\zeta_n,\zeta_m) < \frac{1}{2}\epsilon \text{ for all } m > n > n_0.$$

Hence, $\{\xi_n\}$ and $\{\zeta_n\}$ are Cauchy sequences in B. From the completeness of B, there exist $\xi,\zeta \in B$ such that

$$\lim_{n\to\infty} \rho(\xi,\xi_n) = 0 \text{ and } \lim_{n\to\infty} \rho(\zeta,\zeta_n) = 0.$$

Hence, there exists $n_1 \in \mathbb{N}$ such that for all $n > n_1$,

$$\rho(\xi_n,\xi) < \frac{1}{2}\epsilon \text{ and } \rho(\zeta_n,\zeta) < \frac{1}{2}\epsilon.$$

Thus, we have that for all $n > n_1$,

$$\hat{\rho}(\varpi_n,(\xi,\zeta)) = \hat{\rho}((\xi_n,\zeta_n),(\xi,\zeta)) = \rho(\xi_n,\xi) + \rho(\zeta_n,\zeta) < \epsilon.$$

Hence, we have the desired result. □

Corollary 8. *Let (B,ρ) be a complete Branciari distance space. We assume that $P : B \times B \to B$ is a map such that for all $(\xi,\zeta) \in B \times B$ with $(\xi,\zeta) \neq (P(\xi,\zeta), P(\zeta,\xi))$,*

$$\sigma(\max\{\rho(\xi, P(\xi,\zeta)), \rho(\zeta, P(\zeta,\xi))\}) \leq \frac{\sigma(\hat{\phi}(\xi,\zeta)))}{\sigma(\hat{\phi}(P(\xi,\zeta), P(\zeta,\xi)))} \tag{35}$$

where $\hat{\phi} : B \times B \to [a,\infty)$ is an lsc function, $a > 0$. If σ satisfies (σ_1), (σ_3), (σ_4), and (σ_5), then P possesses a coupled fixed point.

Proof. Let Q and $\hat{\rho}$ be defined as in (31) and (32), respectively.

Then, from (33), we find that for all $(\xi,\zeta) \in B \times B$ with $(\xi,\zeta) \neq Q(\xi,\zeta)$,

$$\sigma(\hat{\rho}((\xi,\zeta), Q(\xi,\zeta)) = \sigma(\max\{\rho(\xi, P(\xi,\zeta)), \rho(y, P(\zeta,\xi))\})$$

$$\leq \frac{\sigma(\hat{\phi}(\xi,\zeta))}{\sigma(\hat{\phi}(P(\xi,\zeta),P(\zeta,\xi)))} = \frac{\sigma(\hat{\phi}(\xi,\zeta))}{\sigma(\hat{\phi}(Q(\xi,\zeta)))}.$$

By Theorem 1, Q possesses a fixed point. Thus, P possesses a coupled fixed point. □

The following result is obtained using Remark 2.

Corollary 9. *Let (B,ρ) be a complete metric space. We assume that $P : B \times B \to B$ is a map such that for all $(\xi,\zeta) \in B \times B$ with $(\xi,\zeta) \neq (P(\xi,\zeta),P(\zeta,\xi))$,*

$$\sigma(\max\{\rho(\xi,P(\xi,\zeta)),\rho(\zeta,P(\zeta,\xi))\}) \leq \frac{\sigma(\hat{\phi}(\xi,\zeta)))}{\sigma(\hat{\phi}(P(\xi,\zeta),P(\zeta,\xi)))} \tag{36}$$

where $\hat{\phi} : B \times B \to [a,\infty)$ is an lsc function, $a > 0$. If σ satisfies (σ_1), (σ_3), (σ_4), and (σ_5), then P possesses a coupled fixed point.

Lemma 5. *Let (B,ρ) be a complete Branciari distance space. Suppose that σ satisfies (σ_1), (σ_3), (σ_4), and (σ_5).*

Then, the following assertions are equivalent.

(i) We assume that $P : B \times B \to B$ satisfies the condition

$$\sigma(\rho(P(\xi,\zeta),P(\xi_*,\zeta_*)) \leq [\sigma(\rho(\xi,\xi_*))]^{\alpha}[\sigma(\rho(\zeta,\zeta_*))]^{\beta} \tag{37}$$

for all $\xi,\zeta,\xi_*,\zeta_* \in B$, where $0 < \alpha+\beta < 1$.

Then, P possesses a unique coupled fixed point.

(ii) We assume that $C : B \to B$ satisfies the condition

$$\sigma(\rho(C\xi,C\zeta)) \leq [\sigma(\rho(\xi,\zeta))]^{k} \tag{38}$$

for all $\xi,\zeta \in B$, where $0 < k < 1$.

Then, C possesses a unique fixed point.

Proof. Firstly, we show that (i) implies (ii).

Let $k = \alpha+\beta$. Then, for all $\xi, y, \xi_*, y_* \in B$, it follows from (i) that

$$\begin{aligned}
&\sigma(\hat{\rho}(Q(\xi,\zeta),Q(\xi_*,\zeta_*)\\
=&\sigma(\hat{\rho}((P(\xi,\zeta),P(\zeta,\xi)),(P(\xi_*,\zeta_*),P(\zeta_*,\xi_*)))\\
=&\sigma(\rho(P(\xi,\zeta),P(\xi_*,\zeta_*))+\rho(P(\zeta,\xi),P(\zeta_*,\xi_*)))\\
\leq&\sigma(\rho(P(\xi,\zeta),P(\xi_*,\zeta_*)))\sigma(\rho(P(\zeta,\xi),P(\zeta_*,\xi_*)))\\
\leq&[\sigma(\rho(\xi,\xi_*))]^{\alpha}[\sigma(\rho(\zeta,\zeta_*))]^{\beta}[\sigma(\rho(\zeta,\zeta_*))]^{\alpha}[\sigma(\rho(\xi,\xi_*))]^{\beta}\\
=&[\sigma(\rho(\xi,\xi_*))]^{\alpha+\beta}[\sigma(\rho(\zeta,\zeta_*))]^{\alpha+\beta}\\
=&[\sigma(\rho(\xi,\xi_*))]^{k}[\sigma(\rho(\zeta,\zeta_*))]^{k}\\
=&[\sigma(\rho(\xi,\xi_*))\sigma(\rho(\zeta,\zeta_*))]^{k}\\
=&[\sigma(\rho(\xi,\xi_*)+\rho(\zeta,\zeta_*))]^{k}\\
=&[\sigma(\hat{\rho}((\xi,\zeta),(\xi_*,\zeta_*)))]^{k}.
\end{aligned}$$

Hence, the proof follows from (ii).

Let us define a map $P : B \times B \to B$ using

$$P(\xi,\zeta) = C\xi.$$

It follows from (34) that for all $\xi, \zeta, \xi_*, \zeta_* \in B$,

$$\sigma(\rho(P(\xi,\zeta), P(\xi_*,\zeta_*))) \leq [\sigma(\rho(\xi,\xi_*))]^k,$$

which corresponds to (35) with $\alpha = k$ and $\beta = 0$.

Thus, by (i), P has a unique coupled fixed point $(\xi,\zeta) \in B \times B$. Hence,

$$x = P(\xi,\zeta) = C\xi \text{ and } \zeta = P(\xi,\zeta) = C\zeta.$$

From (26), we have

$$\rho(\xi,\zeta) = \rho(P(\xi,\zeta), P(\zeta,\xi)) \leq k\rho(\xi,\zeta),$$

which implies that $\xi = \zeta$.

Thus, C has a unique fixed point. □

Corollary 10. *Let (B,ρ) be a complete Branciari distance space. Suppose that ρ satisfies (ρ_1), (ρ_3), (ρ_4), and (ρ_5). We assume that $P : B \times B \to B$ satisfies the condition*

$$\sigma(\rho(P(\xi,\zeta), P(\xi_*,\zeta_*)) \leq [\sigma(\rho(\xi,\xi_*))]^\alpha [\sigma(\rho(\zeta,\zeta_*))]^\beta \tag{39}$$

for all $\xi, \zeta, \xi_*, \zeta_* \in B$, where $0 < \alpha + \beta < 1$.

Then, P possesses a unique coupled fixed point.

Proof. By Remark 9 and Theorem 1, C has a fixed point whenever the contractive condition in (36) is satisfied. Obviously, the contractive condition in (36) guarantees the uniqueness of the fixed point. From Lemma 5, we have the desired result. □

Remark 13. *The above result is an extension of Theorem 2.2 from [13], and Lemma 5 and Corollary 10 hold for n-tuple fixed points (see [13]).*

5. Applications

The most interesting application of fixed-point theory is its application to function spaces. In this section, we show the existence and uniqueness of solutions to integral equations and differential equations in function spaces.

Let $C([0,T],\mathbb{R}) = \{f \mid f : [0,T] \to \mathbb{R} \text{ be continuous}\}$, and let $\rho(f,g) = \sup\{\mid f(t) - g(t) \mid : t \in [0,T]\}$, where $T > 0$. Obviously, $(C([0,T],\mathbb{R}),\rho)$ is a complete metric space, and hence, it is a complete Branciari distance space.

5.1. Integral Equations

We consider an integral equation of the form

$$f(t) = p(t) + \int_0^T H(t,s)K(s,f(s))ds, t \in [0,T] \tag{40}$$

where $p : [0,T] \to \mathbb{R}, K : [0,T] \times \mathbb{R} \to \mathbb{R}$ and $H : [0,T] \times [0,T] \to \mathbb{R}$ are continuous, and $H(t,\cdot) : [0,T] \to \mathbb{R}$ is measurable.

Theorem 3. *We assume that $H(t,s) \geq 0$ for all $t,s \in [0.T]$, and $\int_0^T H(t,s)ds \leq 1$ for all $t \in [0,T]$, and we suppose that for each $t \in [0,T]$ and for all $f,g \in C([0,T],\mathbb{R})$,*

$$\mid K(t,f(t)) - K(t,g(t)) \mid \leq -1 + \sqrt{1 + (f(t) - g(t))^2}.$$

Then, the integral Equation (31) has a solution in $C([0,T],\mathbb{R})$.

Proof. We define a map $Sf(t) = p(t) + \int_0^T H(t,s)K(s,f(s))ds, t \in [0,T]$, and suppose that σ satisfies (σ_1), (σ_3), (σ_4), (σ_5), and (σ_6).

We infer that for all $t \in [0,T]$,

$$
\begin{aligned}
\mid Sf(t) - Sg(t) \mid =& \mid \int_0^T H(t,s)(K(s,f(s) - K(s,g(s))ds \mid \\
\leq& \int_0^T H(t,s) \mid K(s,f(s) - K(s,g(s) \mid ds \\
\leq& \int_0^T H(t,s)(-1 + \sqrt{1 + (f(s) - g(s))^2})ds \\
\leq& \int_0^T H(t,s)(-1 + \sqrt{1 + (\rho(f,g))^2})ds \\
\leq& -1 + \sqrt{1 + (\rho(f,g))^2}.
\end{aligned}
$$

By taking the supremum and applying (σ_6), we find that

$$\sigma(\rho(Sf,Sg)) \leq \sigma(-1 + \sqrt{1 + (\rho(f,g))^2}),$$

which implies that

$$
\begin{aligned}
\sigma(\rho(Sf,Sg)) \leq& \sigma(\rho(f,g))^2 - (\rho(Sf,Sg))^2) \quad (41)\\
=& \sigma(\phi(\rho(f,g)) - \phi(\rho(Sf,Sg))) \quad (42)\\
\leq& \frac{(\phi(\rho(f,g))}{\phi(\rho(Sf,Sg))} \ \forall f,g \in [0,T]
\end{aligned}
$$

where $\phi(t) = t^2$.

By Theorem 2, S has a fixed point. Thus, Equation (31) has a solution. □

5.2. Differential Equations

Our objective is to apply Theorem 2 to show the existence of a solution for the following first-order periodic boundary value problem:

$$
\begin{cases}
f'(t) = \theta(t,f(t)),\ t \in [0,T], \\
f(0) = f(T)
\end{cases}
\quad (43)
$$

where $f \in C([0,T],\mathbb{R})$, and $\theta : [0,T] \times \mathbb{R} \to \mathbb{R}$ is a continuous function.

Let $G(t,s)$ be a Green function defined by

$$
G(t,s) = \begin{cases}
\frac{e^{\eta(T+s-t)}}{e^{\eta T}-1},\ 0 \leq s \leq t \leq T, \\
\frac{e^{\eta(s-t)}}{e^{\eta T}-1},\ 0 \leq t \leq s \leq T
\end{cases}
$$

for any positive real number η with $\eta > T$.

Note that

$$\sup_{t\in[0,T]} \int_0^T G(t,s)ds = 1.$$

The preceding problem (34) is equivalent to the integral equation

$$f(t) = \int_0^T G(t,s)[\theta(s,f(s)) + \eta f(s)]ds. \quad (44)$$

We define the map $S : C([0, T], \mathbb{R}) \to C([0, T], \mathbb{R})$ by

$$S(f(t)) = \int_0^T G(t,s)[\theta(s, f(s)) + \eta f(s)]ds, \ t \in [0, T].$$

Then, f is a solution of (34) if and only if it is a fixed point of S. q

Theorem 4. *We assume that for any $f(t), g(t) \in C([0, T], \mathbb{R})$,*

$$\mid \theta(t, f(t)) + \eta f(t) - [\theta(t, g(t)) + \eta g(t)] \mid \leq \frac{-1 + \sqrt{1 + 4[f(t) - g(t)]^2}}{2} \tag{45}$$

where $t \in [0, T], \eta > T > 0$.

Then, Equation (34) has a solution.

Proof. Suppose that σ satisfies (σ_1), (σ_3), (σ_4), (σ_5), and (σ_6).

Applying (36), we infer that for any $f(t), g(t) \in C([0, T], \mathbb{R})$,

$$\begin{aligned}
&\mid S(f(t)) - S(g(t)) \mid \\
=& \mid \int_0^T G(t,s)[\theta(s, f(s)) + \eta f(s)]ds - \int_0^T G(t,s)[\theta(s, g(s)) + \eta g(s)]ds \mid \\
\leq& \int_0^T G(t,s) \mid \theta(s, f(s)) + \eta f(s) - \theta(s, g(s)) - \eta g(s) \mid ds \\
\leq& \sup_{t \in [0,T]} \mid \theta(s, f(s)) + \eta f(s) - \theta(s, g(s)) - \eta g(s) \mid \int_0^T G(t,s)ds \\
\leq& \frac{-1 + \sqrt{1 + 4[f(s) - g(s)]^2}}{2} \\
\leq& \frac{-1 + \sqrt{1 + 4[\rho(f, g)]^2}}{2}.
\end{aligned}$$

We take the supremum to find that

$$\rho(S(f), S(g)) \leq \frac{-1 + \sqrt{1 + 4[\rho(f, g)]^2}}{2},$$

which implies that

$$\begin{aligned}
&\sigma(\rho(S(f), S(g))) \\
\leq& \sigma([\rho(f, g)]^2 - [\rho(S(f), S(g))]^2) \\
=& \sigma(\phi(\rho(f, g)) - \phi(S(f), S(g))) \\
\leq& \frac{\sigma(\phi(\rho(f, g))}{\phi(S(f), S(g))}, \text{ where } \phi(t) = t^2 \ \forall t > 0.
\end{aligned} \tag{46}$$

By Theorem 2, S has a fixed point. Hence, Equation (34) has a solution. □

6. Conclusions

In this study, we give the concepts of σ-Caristi maps and generalized σ-contraction maps and have related fixed-point results in the setting of complete Branciari distances. By applying the main theorem, we have several corollaries, including Caristi's fixed-point theorem, Jleli and Samet's fixed-point theorem, and coupled fixed-point theorem. We give examples to illustrate the sequential topology and the main theorem. In particular, we provide an example of applying the main theorem to Newton's method to find the roots of an equation. We investigated the relationships among various contraction conditions introduced in this paper. As applications, we solve an integral equation and an ordinary differential equation with the help of our main result.

In the future, based on our main theorem, we will investigate the σ-Ekland variational principle and the σ-Takahashi minimization principle, and we will discuss their equivalence with our main theorem.

Funding: This research received no external funding.

Data Availability Statement: Data is contained within the article.

Acknowledgments: The author expresses his gratitude to the reviewers for their careful reading and valuable comments. This research was supported by Hanseo University.

Conflicts of Interest: The author declares that he has no competing interests regarding the publication of this study.

References

1. Banch, S. Sur les operations dans les ensembles abstraits et leur applications aux equations integrables. *Fundam. Math.* **1992**, *3*, 133–181. [CrossRef]
2. Edelstein, M. An extension of Banach's contraction principle. *Proc. Am. Math. Soc.* **1961**, *12*, 7–10. [CrossRef]
3. Jungck, G. Commuting maps and fixed points. *Am. Math. Mon.* **1976**, *83*, 261–263. [CrossRef]
4. Jungck, G. Common fixed points for noncontinuous nonself maps on nonmetric spaces. *Far East J. Math. Sci.* **1996**, *4*, 199–215.
5. Rhoades, B.E. A comparison of various definitions of contractive mappings. *Trans. Am. Math. Soc.* **1977**, *266*, 257–290. [CrossRef]
6. Van An, T.; Van Dung, N.; Kadelburg, Z.; Radenović, S. Various generalizations of metric spaces and fixed point theorems. *RACSAM* **2015**, *109*, 175–198. [CrossRef]
7. Huang, L.G.; Zhang, X. Cone metric spaces and fixed point theorems of contractive mappings. *J. Math. Anal. Appl.* **2007**, *332*, 1467–1475. [CrossRef]
8. Matthews, S.G. Partial metric topology. In Proceedings of 8th Summer Conference on General Topology and Applications. *Ann. N. Y. Acad. Sci.* **1994**, *728*, 183–197. [CrossRef]
9. Amini-Harandi, A. Metric-like spaces, partial metric spaces and fixed points. *Fixed Point Theory Appl.* **2012**, *2012*, 204. [CrossRef]
10. Branciari, A. A fixed point theorem of Banach-Caccioppoli type on a class of generalized metric spaces. *Publ. Math.* **2000**, *5*, 31–37. [CrossRef]
11. Guo, D.; Lakshmikantham, V. Coupled fixed points of nonlinear operators with applications. *Nonlinear Anal. Theory Methods Appl.* **1987**,*11*, 623–632. [CrossRef]
12. Samet, B.; Vetro, C. Coupled fixed point, f-invariant set and fixed point of N-order. *Ann. Funct. Anal.* **2010**, *1*, 46–56. [CrossRef]
13. Rad, G.S.; Shukla, S.; Rahimi, H. Some relations between n-tuple fixed point and fixed point results. *RACSAM* **2015**, *109*, 471–481.
14. Antón-Sancho, Á. Fixed points of principal E6-bundles over a compact algebraic curve. *Quaest. Math.* **2023**, *47*, 501–513. [CrossRef]
15. Antón-Sancho, Á. Fixed points of automorphisms of the vector bundle moduli space over a compact Riemann surface. *Mediterr. J. Math.* **2024**, *21* [CrossRef]
16. Antón-Sancho, Á. Fixed points of involutions of G-Higgs bundle moduli spaces over a compact Riemann surface with classical complex structure group. *Front. Math.* **2024**, *19*, 1025–1039. [CrossRef]
17. Caristi, J. Fixed point theorems for mappings satisfying inwardness conditions. *Trans. Amer. Math. Soc.* **1976**, *215*, 241–251. [CrossRef]
18. Chaira, K.; Eladraoui, A.; Kabil, M.; Lazaiz, S. Caristi-type fixed point theorem over Száz principle in quasi-metric spaces with a graph. *J. Math.* **2019**, *2019*, 8956083. [CrossRef]
19. Du, W.S. On Caristi type maps and generalized distances with applications. *Abst. Appl. Anal.* **2013**, *2013*, 407219. [CrossRef]
20. Khojasteh, F.; Karapinar, E.; Khandani, H. Some applications of Caristi's fixed point theorem in metric spaces. *Fixed Point Theory Appl.* **2016**, *2016*, 16. [CrossRef]
21. Suzuki, T. Generalized Caristi's fixed point theorems by Bae and others. *J. Math. Anal. Appl.* **2005**, *302*, 502–508. [CrossRef]
22. Du, W.S. A direct proof of Caristi's fixed point theorem. *Appl. Math. Sci.* **2016**, *10*, 2289–2294. [CrossRef]
23. Du, W.S. On Caristi type mappings without lower semicontinuity assumptions. *J. Fixed Point Theory Appl.* **2015**, *17*, 733–752. [CrossRef]
24. Du, W.S. A simple proof of Caristi fixed point theorem without using Zorn's lemma and transfinite induction. *Thai J. Math.* **2016**, *14*, 259–264.
25. Kozlowski, W. A purely metric proof of the Caristi fixed point theorem. *Bull. Aust. Math. Soc.* **2017**, *95*, 333–337. [CrossRef]

26. Pasicki, L. A short proof of the Caristi theorem. *Ann. Soc. Math. Polon. Ser. I Common. Math.* **1978**, *22*, 427–428.
27. Işiki, H.; Mohammadi, B.; Haddadi, M.R.; Parvaneh, V. On a new generalization of Banach contraction principle with application. *Mathematics* **2019**, *7*, 862. [CrossRef]
28. Jleli, M.; Samet, B. A new generalization of the Banach contraction principle. *J. Inequalities Appl.* **2014**, *2014*, 38. [CrossRef]
29. Ahmad, J.; Al-Mazrooei, A.E.; Cho, Y.J.; Yang, Y.O. Fixed point results for generalized θ-contractions. *J. Nonlinear Sci. Appl.* **2017**, *10*, 2350–2358. [CrossRef]
30. Samet, B. Discussion on "A fixed point theorem of Banach-Caccioppoli type on a class of generalized metric spaces" by A. Branciari. *Publ. Math.* **2010**, *76*, 493–494. [CrossRef]
31. Sarma, I.R.; Rao, J.M.; Rao, S.S. Contractions over generalized metric spaces. *J. Nonlinear Sci. Appl.* **2009**, *2009*, 180–182. [CrossRef]
32. Azam, A.; Arshad, M. Kannan fixed point theorem on generalized metric spaces. *J. Nonlinear Sci. Appl.* **2008**, *1*, 45–48. [CrossRef]
33. Bari, C.D.; Vetro, P. Common fixed points in generalized metric spaces. *Appl. Math. Commput.* **2012**, *218*, 7322–7325. [CrossRef]
34. Cho, S.H. Fixed point theorems for $\mathcal{L}_\gamma$ contractions in Branciari distance spaces. *Axioms* **2022**, *11*, 479. [CrossRef]
35. Cho, S.H. Fixed point theorems for Suzuki type generalized $\mathcal{L}$-contractions in Branciari distance spaces. *Adv. Math. Sci. J.* **2022**, *11*, 1173–1190. [CrossRef]
36. Das, P. A fixed point theorem on a class of generalized metric spaces. *Korean J. Math. Sci.* **2022**, *9*, 29–33.
37. Kirk, W.A. Generalized metrics and Caristi's theorem. *Fixed Point Theory Appl.* **2013**, *2013*, 129. [CrossRef]
38. Saleh, H.N.; Imdad, M.; Abdeljawad, T.; Arif, M. New contractive mappings and their fixed points in Branciari metric spaces. *J. Funct. Spaces* **2020**, *2020*, 9491786. [CrossRef]
39. Shatanawi, W.; Al-Rawashdeh, A.; Aydi, H.; Nashine, H.K. On a fixed point for generalized contractions in generalized metric spaces. *Abstr. Appl. Anal.* **2012**, *2012*, 246085. [CrossRef]
40. Suzuki, T. Generalized metric spaces Do not have the compatible topology. *Abstr. Appl. Anal.* **2014**, *2014*, 458098. [CrossRef]
41. Jleli, V.; Samet, B. The Kannan's fixed point theorem in a cone rectangular metric space. *J. Nonlinear Sci. Appl.* **2009**, 2, 161–167. [CrossRef]
42. Kottwitz, S. *Latex Graphics with Tikz: A Practitioner's Guide to Drawing 2D and 3D Images, Diagrams, Charts, and Plots*; Packt Publishing: Birmingham, UK, 2023; pp. 51–150.
43. Berzing, M.; Karapinar, E. Fixed point results for $(\alpha\psi, \beta\phi)$-contractive mappings for a generalized altering distance. *Fixed Point Theory Appl.* **2013**, *2013*, 205. [CrossRef]

axioms

MDPI

Article

m-Isometric Operators with Null Symbol and Elementary Operator Entries

Bhagwati Prashad Duggal

Faculty of Sciences and Mathematics, University of Niš, P.O. Box 224, 18000 Niš, Serbia; bpduggal@yahoo.co.uk

Abstract: A pair (A, B) of Banach space operators is strict (m, X)-isometric for a Banach space operator $X \in B(\mathcal{X})$ and a positive integer m if $\triangle^m_{A,B}(X) = \left(\sum_{j=0}^{m} \binom{m}{j} L^j_A R^j_B\right)(X) = 0$ and $\triangle^{m-1}_{A,B}(X) \neq 0$, where L_A and $R_B \in B(B(\mathcal{X}))$ are, respectively, the operators of left multiplication by A and right multiplication by B. Define operators $E_{A,B}$ and $\mathcal{E}_{A,B}(X)$ by $E_{A,B} = L_A R_B$ and $(\mathcal{E}_{A,B}(X))^n = E^n_{A,B}(X)$ for all non-negative integers n. Using little more than an algebraic argument, the following generalised version of a result relating (m, X)-isometric properties of pairs (A_1, A_2) and (B_1, B_2) to pairs $(\mathcal{E}_{A_1,A_2}(S_1), \mathcal{E}_{B_1,B_2}(S_2))$ and $(E_{A_1,A_2}, E_{B_1,B_2})$ is proved: if A_i, B_i, S_i, X are operators in $B(\mathcal{X})$, $1 \leq i \leq 2$ and X a quasi-affinity, then the pair $(\mathcal{E}_{A_1,A_2}(S_1), \mathcal{E}_{B_1,B_2}(S_2))$ (resp., the pair $(E_{A_1,A_2}, E_{B_1,B_2})$) is strict (m, X)-isometric for all $X \in B(\mathcal{X})$ if and only if there exist positive integers $m_i \leq m$, $1 \leq i \leq 2$ and $m = m_1 + m_2 - 1$, and a non-zero scalar β such that $I - \mathcal{E}_{\beta A_1,A_2}(S_1)$ is (strict) m_1-nilpotent and $I - \mathcal{E}_{\frac{1}{\beta}B_1,B_2}(S_2)$ is (strict) m_2-nilpotent (resp., $(\beta A_1, B_1)$ is strict (m_1, I)-isometric and $(\frac{1}{\beta}B_2, A_2)$ is strict (m_2, I)-isometric).

Keywords: Banach space; m-isometric; left/right multiplication operator; null symbol; strict m-isometric operator

MSC: 47A55; 47A05; 47A65; 47B25

1. Introduction

Let $B(\mathcal{X})$ (resp., $B(\mathcal{H})$) denote the algebra of operators, i.e., bounded linear transformations, on a complex infinite dimensional Banach space $\mathcal{X}$ (resp., Hilbert space $\mathcal{H}$) into itself. An operator pair $(A, B) \in B(\mathcal{X}) \times B(\mathcal{X})$ is (m, X)-isometric for some positive integer m, $m \in \mathbb{N}_+$, and operator $X \in B(\mathcal{X})$, if

$$\begin{aligned} \triangle^m_{A,B}(X) &= (I - L_A R_B)^m(X) = \left(\sum_{j=0}^{m}(-1)^j \binom{m}{j} L^j_A R^j_B\right)(X) \\ &= \sum_{j=0}^{m}(-1)^j \binom{m}{j} A^j X B^j \\ &= 0, \end{aligned}$$

where I is the identity of $B(\mathcal{X})$, L_A and $R_B \in B(B(\mathcal{X}))$ are the operators

$$L_A(Z) = AZ \text{ and } R_B(Z) = ZB,\ Z \in B(\mathcal{X}),$$

of left multiplication by A and right multiplication by B, respectively. (m, X)-isometric operators arise naturally in classical Function Theory and a study of the structure of such operators has been carried out by a number of authors in the recent past (see [1–8] and some of the references cited there). A number of the properties of (m, X)-isometric operators lie on the surface and are readily obtained. Thus,

$$(A, B) \in (m, X) - isometric \Longrightarrow \triangle_{A,B}^{m+t}(X) = \triangle_{A,B}^{t}(\triangle_{A,B}^{m}(X)) = 0 \text{ for all } t \in \mathbb{N};$$

$$\triangle_{A^n,B^n}^{m}(X) = 0 \Longleftrightarrow (I - L_A^n R_B^n)^m(X) = \left(\sum_{j=0}^{n-1}(L_A R_B)^j\right)^m (\triangle_{A,B}^{m}(X)) = 0 \text{ for all } n \in \mathbb{N};$$

$$\triangle_{A,B}^{m}(X) = 0 \Longleftrightarrow \triangle_{A.B}^{m-1}(X) = L_A R_B(\triangle_{A,B}^{m-1}(X)) \Longleftrightarrow \triangle_{A.B}^{m-1}(X) = L_A^n R_B^n(\triangle_{A,B}^{m-1}(X)) \text{ for all } n \in \mathbb{N}.$$

Some other properties of (m, X)-isometric operators lie deeper and their proof requires some argument. For example, if $\triangle_{A,B}^{m}(X) = 0$, $N_1 \in B(\mathcal{X})$ is an n_1-nilpotent operator for some positive integer $n_1 \in \mathbb{N}$, $[A, N_1] = AN_1 - N_1 A = 0$ (i.e., A commutes with N_1), then

$$\begin{aligned}\triangle_{A+N_1,B}^{m+n_1-1}(X) &= \sum_{j=0}^{m+n_1-1}(-1)^j\binom{m+n_1-1}{j}(L_{N_1}R_B)^j \triangle_{A,B}^{m+n_1-1-j}(X) \\ &= 0,\end{aligned}$$

since $\triangle_{A,B}^{m+n_1-1-j}(X) = 0$ for all $m + n_1 - 1 - j \geq m$, equivalently, $j \leq n_1 - 1$, and $L_{N_1}^j = 0$ for all $j \geq n_1$. Furthermore, if $N_2 \in B(\mathcal{X})$ is also an n_2-nilpotent operator which commutes with B, then

$$\triangle_{A+N_1,B+N_2}^{m+n_1+n_2-2}(X) = \sum_{j=0}^{m+n_1+n_2-2}(-1)^j\binom{m+n_1+n_2-2}{j}(L_{A+N_1}R_{N_2})^j \triangle_{A+N_1,B}^{m+n_1+n_2-2-j}(X) = 0,$$

since $\triangle_{A+N_1,B}^{m+n_1+n_2-2-j}(X) = 0$ if $m + n_1 + n_2 - 2 - j \geq m + n_1 - 1$, equivalently, $j \leq n_2 - 1$, and $R_{N_2}^j = 0$ if $j \geq n_2$. Conclusion: if (A, B) is (m, X)-isometric, N_i are n_i-nilpotent operators, and $[A, N_1] = [B, N_2] = 0$, then $(A + N_1, B + N_2)$ is $(m + n_1 + n_2 - 2, X)$-isometric.

Let $A, B, S, A_i, B_i, S_i \in B(\mathcal{X})$, $1 \leq i \leq 2$, and let $E_{A,B} \in B(B(\mathcal{X}))$ and $\mathcal{E}_{A,B}(S) \in B(\mathcal{X})$ be the operators defined by

$$\begin{aligned}&E_{A,B} = L_A R_B \text{ so that } E_{A,B}^n(S) = (L_A R_B)^n(S) = A^n S B^n \text{ for all } n \in \mathbb{N},\\ &\mathcal{E}_{A,B}(S)^n = E_{A,B}^n(S) = A^n S B^n \text{ for all } n \in \mathbb{N}, \text{ in particular } \mathcal{E}_{A,B}(S)^0 = S.\end{aligned}$$

This paper considers (m, X)-isometric pairs $(\mathcal{E}_{A_1,A_2}(S_1), \mathcal{E}_{B_1,B_2}(S_2))$ such that $\triangle_{A_1,A_2}^{m_1}(S_1) = 0 = \triangle_{B_1,B_2}^{m_2}(S_2)$ for some integers $m_1, m_2 \in \mathbb{N}_+$, and pairs $(E_{A_1,A_2}, E_{B_1,B_2})$. ($(m, X)$-isometric operators with entries $(\mathcal{E}_{A_1,A_2}(S_1), \mathcal{E}_{B_1,B_2}(S_2))$ have been called *(m, X)-isometric operators with null symbol entries* [2,7]; m-isometric operators with entries of type $(E_{A_1,A_2}, E_{B_1,B_2})$ have been considered by Gu [1], and Duggal and Kim [9,10].) Let X be a quasi-affinity. (Thus, X is injective and has a dense range.) Using little more than linear algebra, we generalise [2] (Theorems 1 and 2(iii)) to prove that "any two of the conditions (i) $(\mathcal{E}_{A_1,A_2}(S_1), \mathcal{E}_{B_1,B_2}(S_2))$ is (m, X)-isometric; (ii) there exists a positive integer $m_1 \leq m$ such that $I - \mathcal{E}_{A_1,A_2}(S_1)$ is m_1-nilpotent; (iii) there exists a positive integer $m_2 \leq m$ such that $I - \mathcal{E}_{B_1,B_2}(S_2)$ is m_2-nilpotent implies the third." Recall that an (m, X)-isometric pair is *strict (m, X)-isometric* if $\triangle_{A,B}^{m}(X) = 0$ and $\triangle_{A,B}^{m-1}(X) \neq 0$. In a similar vein, *we say that an operator A is strict m-nilpotent if $A^m = 0$ and $A^{m-1} \neq 0$*. Answering an open problem raised in [2] (Section 4), we give an elementary proof that the pair $(\mathcal{E}_{A_1,A_2}(S_1), \mathcal{E}_{B_1,B_2}(S_2))$ (resp., the pair $(E_{A_1,A_2}, E_{B_1,B_2})$) is strict (m, X)-isometric for all $X \in B(\mathcal{X})$ if and only if there exist positive integers $m_i \leq m$, $1 \leq i \leq 2$ and $m = m_1 + m_2 - 1$, and a non-zero scalar β such that $I-\mathcal{E}_{\beta A_1,A_2}(S_1)$ is strict m_1-nilpotent and $I-\mathcal{E}_{\frac{1}{\beta}B_1,B_2}(S_2)$ is strict m_2-nilpotent (resp., $(\beta A_1,B_1)$ is strict (m_1,I)-isometric and $(\frac{1}{\beta}B_2,A_2)$ is strict (m_2,I)-isometric).

Most of our notation is standard (and any non-standard notation will be explained at the point of its introduction). We write $A-\lambda$ for $A-\lambda I$, and $\sigma_a(A)$ for the approximate point spectrum of the operator A. We say that the pair (A,B) of operators in $B(\mathcal{X})\times B(\mathcal{X})$ is m-isometric if it is (m,X)-isometric for all $X\in B(\mathcal{X})$.

The plan of the paper is as follows. We consider null symbol operator pairs $(\mathcal{E}_{A_1,A_2}(S_1),\mathcal{E}_{B_1,B_2}(S_2))$ in Section 2, Section 3 considers pairs $(E_{A_1,A_2},E_{B_1,B_2})$, Section 4 consists of a concluding remark.

2. Null Symbol Entries: Pairs $(\mathcal{E}_{A_1,A_2}(S_1),\mathcal{E}_{B_1,B_2}(S_2))$

If $(A,B)\in B(\mathcal{X})\times B(\mathcal{X})$ is (m,X)-isometric for some $X\in B(\mathcal{X})$, then

$$\begin{aligned} 0 &= \triangle^m_{A,B}(X)=\left(\sum_{j=0}^m(-1)^j\binom{m}{j}(L_AR_B)^j\right)(X)\\ &= \left(\sum_{j=0}^m(-1)^j\binom{m}{j}E^j_{A,B}\right)(X)\\ &= \sum_{j=0}^m(-1)^j\binom{m}{j}\mathcal{E}_{A,B}(X)^j\\ &= (I-\mathcal{E}_{A,B}(X))^m=\nabla^m_{A,B}(X)\end{aligned}$$

(by the definition of the operator $\mathcal{E}_{A,B}(X)^n$, $n\in\mathbb{N}_+$). Hence, *the pair (A,B) is (strictly) (m,X)-isometric if and only if the operator $\nabla_{A,B}(X)=(I-\mathcal{E}_{A,B}(X))$ is (strictly) m-nilpotent.*

Recalling that (A,B) is strictly (m,X)-isometric if and only if $\triangle^m_{A,B}(X)=0$ and $\triangle^{m-1}_{A,B}(X)\neq 0$, it follows that if $\nabla_{A,B}(X)$ is strictly m-nilpotent, then the sequence of operators $\{\nabla^j_{A,B}(X)\}_{j=0}^{m-1}$ is linearly independent. Again, if (A,B) is (m,X)-isometric, then

$$\begin{aligned} &\nabla^m_{A,B}(X)=(I-\mathcal{E}_{A,B}(X))\nabla^{m-1}_{A,B}(X)=0\\ \iff\ &\nabla^{m-1}_{A,B}(X)=\mathcal{E}_{A,B}(X)\nabla^{m-1}_{A,B}(X)\\ \iff\ &\nabla^{m-1}_{A,B}(X)=\mathcal{E}^n_{A,B}(X)\nabla^{m-1}_{A,B}(X)\end{aligned}$$

for all $n\in\mathbb{N}$. Let A_i, B_i and S_i, $1\le i\le 2$, be operators in $B(\mathcal{X})$ such that

$$\nabla^{m_1}_{A_1,A_2}(S_1)=0=\nabla^{m_2}_{B_1,B_2}(S_2),\ m_1 \text{ and } m_2\in\mathbb{N}_+.$$

The following proposition relates (m_1,S_1)-isometric pairs (A_1,A_2) and (m_2,S_2)-isometric pairs (B_1,B_2) to (m,X)-isometric pairs $(\mathcal{E}_{A_1,A_2}(S_1),\mathcal{E}_{B_1,B_2}(S_2))$.

Proposition 1. *If $X\in B(\mathcal{X})$ is a quasi-affinity, then any two of the following conditions implies the third:*

(i) there exists $m\in N_+$ such that $(\mathcal{E}_{A_1,A_2}(S_1),\mathcal{E}_{B_1,B_2}(S_2))$ is (m,X)-isometric;
(ii) there exists $m_1\in N_+$, $m_1\le m$, such that $\nabla_{A_1,A_2}(S_1)$ is m_1-nilpotent;
(iii) there exists $m_2\in N_+$, $m_2\le m$, such that $\nabla_{B_1,B_2}(S_2)$ is m_2-nilpotent.
(Here, if (ii) and (iii) hold, then $m=m_1+m_2-1$.)

Proof. Let, for convenience, $\mathcal{E}_{A_1,A_2}(S_1)=A$ and $\mathcal{E}_{B_1,B_2}(S_2)=B$.

$(ii)+(iii) \Longrightarrow (i)$. Let $m_1+m_2-1=m$. By definition

$$\begin{aligned}\triangle^m_{A,B}(X) &= (I-L_AR_B)^m(X) = ((I-L_A)R_B+(I-R_B))^m(X)\\ &= \left(\sum_{j=0}^{m}\binom{m}{j}((I-L_A)R_B)^{m-j}(I-R_B)^j\right)(X)\\ &= \sum_{j=0}^{m}\binom{m}{j}(I-A)^{m-j}XB^{m-j}(I-B)^j\\ &= \sum_{j=0}^{m}\binom{m}{j}\nabla^{m-j}_{A_1,A_2}(S_1)XB^{m-j}\nabla^j_{B_1,B_2}(S_2)\end{aligned}$$

(since $[I-L_A,R_B]=[R_B,I-R_B]=0$). Since $\nabla^{m-j}_{A_1,A_2}(S_1)=0$ for all $m-j\geq m_1$, equivalently, $j\leq m-m_1=m_2-1$, and since $\nabla^j_{B_1,B_2}(S_2)=0$ for all $j\geq m_2$, $\triangle^{m_0}_{A,B}(X)=0$ for all $m_0\geq m$.

$(i)+(iii) \Longrightarrow (ii)$. Considering next (i) and (iii), we may assume without loss of generality that (A,B) is strict (m,X)-isometric and $\nabla_{B_1,B_2}(S_2)$ is strict m_2-nilpotent. Since

$$\nabla^{m_2}_{B_1,B_2}(S_2)=0 \Longleftrightarrow \nabla^{m_2-1}_{B_1,B_2}(S_2)=B^n\nabla^{m_2-1}_{B_1,B_2}(S_2)$$

for all $n\in\mathtt{N}$, the strictness implies that the sequence

$$\{B^n\nabla^j_{B_1,B_2}(S_2)\},\ 0\leq j\leq m_2-1$$

is linearly independent for all $n\in\mathtt{N}$. If (i) holds, then (see above)

$$\begin{aligned}0 &= \triangle^m_{A,B}(X)=\left(\sum_{j=0}^{m}\binom{m}{j}L^{m-j}_{\nabla_{A_1,A_2}(S_1)}R_B^{m-j}R^j_{\nabla_{B_1,B_2}(S_2)}\right)(X)\\ &= \sum_{j=0}^{m_2-1}\binom{m}{j}\nabla^{m-j}_{A_1,A_2}(S_1)XB^{m-j}\nabla^j_{B_1,B_2}(S_2)\end{aligned}$$

(since $\nabla^t_{B_1,B_2}(S_2)=0$ for all $t\geq m_2$). The linear independence of the sequence $\{B^n\nabla^j_{B_1,B_2}(S_2)\}_{j=0}^{m_2-1}$, taken along with the fact that X has a dense range, implies that

$$\nabla^{m-j}_{A_1,A_2}(S_1)X=0 \Longleftrightarrow \nabla^{m-j}_{A_1,A_2}(S_1)=0,\ 0\leq j\leq m_2-1.$$

In particular, letting $j=m_2-1$,

$$\nabla^{m-m_2+1}_{A_1,A_2}(S_1)=\nabla^{m_1}_{A_1,A_2}(S_1)=0.$$

$(i)+(ii) \Longrightarrow (iii)$. The proof here is similar to that of the previous case except for the fact that we now consider the adjoint operators

$$(\triangle^m_{A,B}(X))^*=\triangle^m_{B^*,A^*}(X^*)=\triangle^m_{\mathcal{E}_{B_2^*,B_1^*}(S_2^*),\mathcal{E}_{A_2^*,A_1^*}(S_1^*)}(X^*)$$

and

$$(\nabla^{m_1}_{A_1,A_2}(S_1))^*=\nabla^{m_1}_{A_2^*,A_1^*}(S_1^*).$$

Assuming strictness, it is seen that the sequence $\{A^{*n}\nabla^{j}_{A_2^*,A_1^*}(S_1^*)\}$ is linearly independent for all $0 \leq j \leq m_1 - 1$ and $n \in \mathtt{N}$; hence, since X is a quasi-affinity,

$$\nabla^{m-j}_{B_2^*,B_1^*}(S_2^*)X^* = 0 \Longleftrightarrow \nabla^{m-j}_{B_2^*,B_1^*}(S_2^*) = 0 \Longleftrightarrow \nabla^{m-j}_{B_1,B_2}(S_2) = 0$$

for all $0 \leq j \leq m_1 - 1$. In particular, $\nabla^{m-m_1+1}_{B_1,B_2}(S_2) = \nabla^{m_2}_{B_1,B_2}(S_2) = 0$. $\square$

If $(\mathcal{E}_{A_1,A_2}(S_1), \mathcal{E}_{B_1,B_2}(S_2))$ is strict (m,X)-isometric and $\nabla_{B_1,B_2}(S_2)$ is strict m_2-nilpotent, then the argument of the proof of the proposition shows that $\nabla_{A_1,A_2}(S_1)$ is strict $m_1 = m - m_2 + 1$ nilpotent. (Reason: if $\nabla_{A_1,A_2}(S_1)$ is t-nilpotent for some $t < m_1$, then (ii) and (iii) taken together imply $(\mathcal{E}_{A_1,A_2}(S_1), \mathcal{E}_{B_1,B_2}(S_2))$ is $(t + m_1 - 1(< m), X)$-isometric—a contradiction.) Indeed, if $(\mathcal{E}_{A_1,A_2}(S_1), \mathcal{E}_{B_1,B_2}(S_2))$ is strict (m,X)-isometric, $\nabla_{A_1,A_2}(S_1)$ is m_1-nilpotent, and $\nabla_{B_1,B_2}(S_2)$ is m_2 nilpotent, then

$$\begin{aligned}
\triangle^{m-1}_{A,B}(X) &= \sum_{j=0}^{m-1} \begin{pmatrix} m-1 \\ j \end{pmatrix} \nabla^{m-j-1}_{A_1,A_2}(S_1) X B^{m-j-1} \nabla^{j}_{B_1,B_2}(S_2) \\
&= \sum_{j=0}^{m_2-1} \begin{pmatrix} m-1 \\ j \end{pmatrix} \nabla^{m-j-1}_{A_1,A_2}(S_1) X B^{m-j-1} \nabla^{j}_{B_1,B_2}(S_2) \\
&\quad (\nabla^{j}_{B_1,B_2}(S_2) = 0 \text{ for all } j \geq m_2) \\
&= \begin{pmatrix} m-1 \\ m_2-1 \end{pmatrix} \nabla^{m_1-1}_{A_1,A_2}(S_1) X B^{m-j-1} \nabla^{m_2-1}_{B_1,B_2}(S_2) \\
&\quad (\nabla^{m-j-1}_{A_1,A_2}(S_1) = 0 \text{ for all } m-j-1 \geq m_1) \\
&= \begin{pmatrix} m-1 \\ m_2-1 \end{pmatrix} \nabla^{m_1-1}_{A_1,A_2}(S_1) X \nabla^{m_2-1}_{B_1,B_2}(S_2) \\
&\quad (\nabla^{m_2}_{B_1,B_2}(S_2) = 0 \Longrightarrow B^{m-j-1} \nabla^{j}_{B_1,B_2}(S_2) = \nabla^{j}_{B_1,B_2}(S_2) \text{ for all } j \geq m_2) \\
&\neq 0.
\end{aligned}$$

Thus

$$(I - A)^{m_1-1} X (I - B)^{m_2-1} \neq 0,$$

and the conditions $(I - A)^{m_1-1} \neq 0$ and $(I - B)^{m_2-1} \neq 0$ are necessary for $(\mathcal{E}_{A_1,A_2}(S_1), \mathcal{E}_{B_1,B_2}(S_2))$ to be strict (m,X)-isometric. These conditions are, however, not sufficient. For example, if we choose X to be such that it maps the range of $(I - B)$ into the null space of $(I - A)$, then $(I - A)^{m_1-1} X (I - B)^{m_2-1} = 0$ even though neither of $(I - A)^{m_1-1}$ and $(I - B)^{m_2-1}$ is the 0 operator. If, however, $(\mathcal{E}_{A_1,A_2}(S_1), \mathcal{E}_{B_1,B_2}(S_2))$ is strict m-isometric (i.e., strict (m,X)-isometric for all X), then, necessarily, $(I - A)^{m_1-1} X (I - B)^{m_2-1} = 0$ if and only if one $(I - A)^{m_1-1}$ or $(I - B)^{m_2-1}$ is 0. The proof of the following proposition uses little more than linear algebra to prove a necessary and sufficient condition for the operator pair $(\mathcal{E}_{A_1,A_2}(S_1), \mathcal{E}_{B_1,B_2}(S_2))$ to be strict (m,X)-isometric for a given quasi-affinity X.

Proposition 2. *Given operators $A_i, B_i, S_i \in B(\mathcal{X})$, $1 \leq i \leq 2$, and a quasi-affinity $X \in B(\mathcal{X})$, the pair of operators $(\mathcal{E}_{A_1,A_2}(S_1), \mathcal{E}_{B_1,B_2}(S_2))$ is a strict (m,X)-isometry if and only if there exist integers $m_i \in \mathcal{N}_+$ $(1 \leq i \leq 2)$ and a non-trivial scalar β such that $m = m_1 + m_2 - 1$,*

(i) $\nabla_{\beta A_1,A_2}(S_1)$ is a strict m_1 nilpotent, $\nabla_{\frac{1}{\beta}B_1,B_2}(S_2)$ is a strict m_2-nilpotent;

(ii) $\nabla^{m_1-1}_{A_1,A_2}(S_1) X \nabla^{m_2-1}_{B_1,B_2}(S_2) \neq 0$.

Proof. As before, for convenience, we let

$$\mathcal{E}_{A_1,A_2}(S_1) = A, \mathcal{E}_{B_1,B_2}(S_2) = B, I - \beta A (= I - \mathcal{E}_{\beta A_1,A_2}(S_1)) = \nabla(\beta A), \text{and}$$
$$I - \frac{1}{\beta}B = I - \frac{1}{\beta}\mathcal{E}_{B_1,B_2}(S_2) = 1 - \mathcal{E}_{\frac{1}{\beta}B_1,B_2}(S_2) = \nabla(\beta B).$$

To prove the "if part" of the theorem, we start by observing that

$$\triangle^m_{\beta A,\frac{1}{\beta}B}(X) = \left(\sum_{j=0}^{m}\binom{m}{j} L^j_{\beta A} R^j_{\frac{1}{\beta}B}\right)(X) = \triangle^m_{A,B}(X).$$

If $\nabla(\beta A)$ is m_1-nilpotent and $\nabla(\beta B)$ is m_2-nilpotent, then

$$\triangle^{m_1+m_2-1}_{\beta A,\frac{1}{\beta}B}(X) = \triangle^{m_1+m_2-1}_{A,B}(X) = \triangle^m_{A,B}(X) = 0.$$

Also, if condition (ii) is satisfied, then $\triangle^{m-1}_{A,B}(X) \neq 0$, i.e., (A,B) is strict (m,X)-isometric.

For the "only if part" of the proof, we start by recalling that

$$\begin{aligned}\triangle^m_{A,B}(X) &= \left(\sum_{j=0}^{m}(-1)^j\binom{m}{j} L^j_A R^j_B\right)(X) \\ &= \sum_{j=0}^{m}(-1)^j\binom{m}{j}\mathcal{E}^j_{A_1,A_2}(S_1) X \mathcal{E}^j_{B_1,B_2}(S_2).\end{aligned}$$

We claim that there exists a non-trivial $\beta \in \sigma_a(B)$. For this it will suffice to prove that $0 \notin \sigma_a(B)$. If $0 \in \sigma_a(B)$, then there exist sequences $\{x_n\}$ and $\{x'_n\}$, in $\mathcal{X}$ and (the dual space) X^*, respectively, such that

$$x'_n(x_n) = \langle x_n, x'_n\rangle = 1 \text{ for all } n \in \mathbb{N}_+ \text{ and } \lim_{n\to\infty}\langle Bx_n, x'_n\rangle = 0.$$

We have

$$\begin{aligned}\triangle^m_{A,B}(X) &= \sum_{j=0}^{m}(-1)^j\binom{m}{j} A^j X \lim_{n\to\infty}\langle B^j x_n, x'_n\rangle \\ &= 0\end{aligned}$$

for all j except for $j = 0$ when we have $\triangle^m_{A,B}(X) = X = 0$. The operator X being a quasi-affinity, this is a contradiction and our claim is proved.

Let $(0 \neq)\beta \in \sigma_a(B)$. Then, by an argument similar to the one used above to prove $0 \notin \sigma_a(B)$,

$$\begin{aligned}0 &= \triangle^m_{A,B}(X) = \left(\sum_{j=0}^{m}(-1)^j\binom{m}{j}\beta^j A^j\right)(X) \\ &\Longleftrightarrow \sum_{j=0}^{m}(-1)^j\binom{m}{j}\beta^j A^j = (I-\beta A)^m = 0.\end{aligned}$$

Let m_1 be the least positive integer such that

$$(I-\beta A)^{m_1} = (I - \beta\mathcal{E}_{A_1,A_2}(S_1))^{m_1} = (I - \mathcal{E}_{\beta A_1,A_2}(S_1))^{m_1} = 0.$$

Then $I - \beta A$ is strictly m_1-nilpotent and the sequence $\{\nabla^j(\beta A)\}_{j=0}^{m_1-1}$ is linearly independent. Since

$$\begin{aligned}
0 &= \triangle^m_{A,B}(X) = \triangle^m_{\beta A, \frac{1}{\beta}B}(X) \\
&= \left((I - R_{\frac{1}{\beta}B}) + (I - L_{\beta A})R_{\frac{1}{\beta}B}\right)^m (X) \\
&= \left(\sum_{j=0}^{m} \binom{m}{j} (I - R_{\frac{1}{\beta}B})^{m-j} R^j_{\frac{1}{\beta}B}(I - L_{\beta A})^j\right)(X) \\
&= \sum_{j=0}^{m} \binom{m}{j} \nabla^j(\beta A) X (\frac{1}{\beta}B)^j \nabla^{m-j}(\beta B) \\
&= \sum_{j=0}^{m_1-1} \binom{m}{j} \nabla^j(\beta A) X (\frac{1}{\beta}B)^j \nabla^{m-j}(\beta B) \\
& \quad (\text{since } \nabla^t(\beta A) = 0 \text{ for all } t \geq m_1) \\
\Longrightarrow & \quad X(\frac{1}{\beta}B)^j \nabla^{m-j}(\beta B) = 0 \text{ for all } 0 \leq j \leq m_1 - 1.
\end{aligned}$$

Since both X and B are injective, recall that X is a quasi-affinity and B is left invertible, $\nabla^{m-j}(\beta B) = 0$ for all $0 \leq j \leq m_1 - 1$. In particular,

$$\nabla^{m-m_1+1}(\beta B) = \nabla^{m_2}(\beta B) = 0.$$

The strict (m, X)-isometric property of the pair (A, B), taken in conjunction with the fact that $m_2 = m - m_1 + 1$, implies that $\nabla(\beta B)$ is strict m_2-nilpotent. The necessity of condition (ii) having already been seen (above), the proof is complete. □

The Hilbert space case In the case in which $A_1^* = A_2 = A$ and $B_1^* = B_2 = B$ are Hilbert space operators,

$$\mathcal{E}_{A^*,A}(I)^n = E^n_{A^*,A}(I) = A^{*n}A^n, \ \mathcal{E}_{B^*,B}(I)^n = E^n_{B^*,B}(I) = B^{*n}B^n,$$
$$\triangle^n_{\mathcal{E}_{A^*,A}(I),\mathcal{E}_{B^*,B}(I)}(X) = \sum_{j=0}^{n} \binom{n}{j} A^{*j}A^j X B^{*j} B^j$$

for all $n \in \mathbb{N}_+$. Proposition 2 in such a case takes the following form.

Corollary 1. *Given operators $A, B, X \in B(\mathcal{H})$, X a quasi-affinity, the pair $(\mathcal{E}_{A^*,A}(I), \mathcal{E}_{B^*,B}(I))$ is strict (m, X)-isometric if and only if there exist positive integers $m_i \leq m$, $m = m_1 + m_2 - 1$, and a (non-trivial) positive scalar β such that $(\beta A^*, A)$ is strict (m_1, I)-isometric, $(\frac{1}{\beta}B^*, B)$ is strict (m_2, I)-isometric, and $\triangle^{m_1-1}_{\beta A^*,A}(I) X \triangle^{m_2-1}_{\frac{1}{\beta}B^*,B}(I) \neq 0$.*

In the absence of the property $\mathcal{E}_{A,B}(I)^n = E^n_{A,B}(I)$ for all $n \in \mathbb{N}$, the strict (m, X)-isometric property of the pair $(E_{A^*,A}(I), E_{B^*,B}(I))$ for a quasi-affinty X implies

$$\triangle^n_{E_{A^*,A}(I),E_{B^*,B}(I)}(X) = \sum_{j=0}^{n} \binom{n}{j} |A|^{2j} X |B|^{2j};$$

there exist positive integers $m_i \leq m$, $m = m_1 + m_2 - 1$, and a (non-trivial) positive scalar β such that $(\beta|A|, |A|)$ is strict (m_1, I)-isometric, $(\frac{1}{\beta}|B|, |B|)$ is strict (m_2, I)-isometric and $\triangle^{m_1-1}_{\beta|A|,|A|}(I) X \triangle^{m_2-1}_{\frac{1}{\beta}|B|,|B|}(I) \neq 0$.

3. Pairs $(E_{A_1,A_2}, E_{B_1,B_2})$

Proposition 1 fails in the absence of the (fairly restrictive) hypothesis $\mathcal{E}_{A,B}(S)^n = E^n_{A,B}(S)$. This follows from the following elementary example.

Example 1. *Trivially, the pair (I, I) satisfies $\triangle_{I,I}(S) = 0$ for all $S \in B(\mathcal{X})$. Considering the pair $(\mathcal{E}_{I,I}(S_1), \mathcal{E}_{I,I}(S_2))$, the validity of $(ii) + (iii)$ implies (i) in the proof of the proposition implies $\triangle_{\mathcal{E}_{I,I}(S_1),\mathcal{E}_{I,I}(S_2)}(X) = 0$ for all $X \in B(\mathcal{X})$, i.e., $X = S_1 X S_2$ for all S_1, S_2 and $X \in B(\mathcal{X})$. This is absurd.*

Observe that $E^n_{I,I}(S) = S \neq S^n = (\mathcal{E}_{I,I}(S))^n$ and $E^n_{A,B}(I) = A^n B^n \neq (AB)^n = \mathcal{E}_{A,B}(I)^n$. An immediate consequence of examples of the above type is that the proposition cannot be used, contrary to the claim made in [2] (Corollary 1), to deduce results of the the type "(A_1, A_2) is (m_1, I)-isometric and (B_1, B_2) is (m_2, I)-isometric, then $(E_{A_1,A_2}, E_{B_1,B_2})$ is $(m_1 + m_2 - 1, X)$-isometric for all $X \in B(\mathcal{X})$". Indeed, if we let the pair $(E_{A_1,A_2}, E_{B_1,B_2})$ be such that $(A_1, A_2) = (I, I)$ and choose the pair (B_1, B_2) to be (m, I)-isometric for some $m \in \mathbb{N}_+$, then for all $X \in B(\mathcal{X})$,

$$\begin{aligned}
\triangle^m_{E_{A_1,A_2},E_{B_1,B_2}}(X) &= \left(\sum_{j=0}^{m}(-1)^j \binom{m}{j} L^j_{E_{A_1,A_2}} R^j_{E_{B_1,B_2}}\right)(X) \\
&= \sum_{j=0}^{m}(-1)^j \binom{m}{j} L^j_{E_{A_1,A_2}}\left(L^j_{B_1} X R^j_{B_2}\right) \\
&= \sum_{j=0}^{m}(-1)^j \binom{m}{j} L^j_{E_{A_1,A_2}}\left(B^j_1 X B^j_2\right) \\
&= \sum_{j=0}^{m}(-1)^j \binom{m}{j} L^j_{A_1}\left(B^j_1 X B^j_2\right) R^j_{A_2} \\
&= \sum_{j=0}^{m}(-1)^j \binom{m}{j} A^j_1 B^j_1 X B^j_2 A^j_2 \\
&= \sum_{j=0}^{m}(-1)^j \binom{m}{j} B^j_1 X B^j_2 = \triangle^m_{B_1,B_2}(X).
\end{aligned}$$

Evidently, $\triangle^m_{E_{A_1,A_2},E_{B_1,B_2}}(X)$ cannot be 0 for all X (i.e., (ii) and (iii) imply (i) of Proposition 1 fails for pairs $(E_{A_1,A_2}, E_{B_1,B_2})$). We remark here that even though [2] (Theorem 1) makes no explicit mention of the hypothesis $\mathcal{E}_{A,B}(X)^n = E^n_{A,B}(X)$, its use is implicit in the proof of the theorem.

A pair $(\mathcal{X}, \tilde{\mathcal{X}})$ of Banach spaces is a dual pairing if either $\mathcal{X} = \mathcal{X}^*$ or $\mathcal{X} = \tilde{\mathcal{X}}^*$. If we let $x \otimes y'$, $x \in \mathcal{X}$ and $y' \in \mathcal{Y}^*$, $\mathcal{Y}$ a Banach space, denote the rank one operator $\mathcal{Y} \to \mathcal{X}$, $y \to \langle y, y' \rangle x$, then the operator ideal $\mathcal{J}$ between $\mathcal{Y}$ and $\mathcal{X}$ is a linear subspace $B(\mathcal{Y}, \mathcal{X})$ equipped with a Banach norm ν such that (i) $x \otimes y' \in \mathcal{J}$; $\nu(x \otimes y') = \|x\|\|y'\|$ and (ii) $\mathcal{E}_{A,B}(X) = L_A R_B(X) = AXB$, $\nu(AXB) \leq \|A\|\nu(\|X\|)\|B\|$ for all $x \in \mathcal{X}$, $y' \in \mathcal{Y}^*$, $X \in \mathcal{J}$, and $A \in B(\mathcal{X})$ and $B \in B(\mathcal{Y})$. Thus defined, each $\mathcal{J}$ is a tensor product relative to the dual pairings $(\mathcal{X}, \mathcal{X}^*)$ and $(\mathcal{Y}, \mathcal{Y}^*)$ and the bilinear mapping

$$\begin{aligned}
&\mathcal{X} \times \mathcal{Y}^* \to \mathcal{J},\ \langle x, y' \rangle \to x \otimes y', \\
&B(\mathcal{X}) \times B(\mathcal{Y}^*) \to B(\mathcal{J}),\ (A, B^*) \to A \otimes B^*,
\end{aligned}$$

where $A \otimes B^*(X) = AXB = E_{A,B}(X)$ [11] (page 51). It is known, see [9] (Corollary 2) (see also [1,7]), that for $A_i, B_i \in B(\mathcal{X})$, $1 \leq i \leq 2$, $(E_{A_1,A_2}, E_{B_1,B_2})$ is strict (m, X)-isometric if and only if there exist positive integers $m_i \leq m$ and a non-zero scalar β such that

$m = m_1 + m_2 - 1$, $(\beta A_1, A_2)$ is strict (m_1, I)-isometric, $(\frac{1}{\beta}B_2, A_2)$ is strict (m_2, I)-isometric, and $\triangle^{m_1-1}_{\beta A_1,B_1}\left(\triangle^{m_2-1}_{\frac{1}{\beta}B_2,A_2}(X)\right) \neq 0$ for $X \in \mathcal{J}$. This result does not follow from Proposition 2, even for the case in which $\mathcal{X}$ is a Hilbert space and the pair $(E_{A_1,A_2}, E_{B_1,B_2})$ is the pair $(E_{A^*,A}, E_{B^*,B})$. The following theorem, our main result, uses an algebraic argument to prove this result for the case in which the operator pair $(E_{A_1,A_2}, E_{B_1,B_2})$ is strict (m, X)-isometric for a quasi-affinity $X \in B(\mathcal{X})$.

Theorem 1. *Given operators $A_i, B_i \in B(\mathcal{X})$, $1 \leq i \leq 2$, the pair $(E_{A_1,A_2}, E_{B_1,B_2})$ is strict (m, X)-isometric for a quasi-affinity $X \in B(\mathcal{X})$ if and only if there exist positive integers $m_i \leq m$ and a non-trivial scalar β such that $m = m_1 + m_2 - 1$, $(\beta A_1, B_1)$ is strict (m_1, I)-isometric, $(\frac{1}{\beta}B_2, A_2)$ is strict (m_2, I)-isometric, and $\triangle^{m_1-1}_{\beta A_1,B_1}(I)X(\triangle^{m_2-1}_{\frac{1}{\beta}B_2,A_2}(I)) \neq 0$.*

Proof. We start by proving the "only if" part: the proof depends upon a judicious use of the properties of the operator $L^j_{E_{A_1,A_2}}R^j_{E_{B_1,B_2}}$. If the pair $(E_{A_1,A_2}, E_{B_1,B_2})$ is (m, X)-isometric, then

$$\triangle^m_{E_{A_1,A_2},E_{B_1,B_2}}(X) = \left(\sum_{j=0}^{m}(-1)^j\binom{m}{j}L^j_{E_{A_1,A_2}}R^j_{E_{B_1,B_2}}\right)(X) = 0.$$

By definition

$$\begin{aligned}
& L^j_{E_{A_1,A_2}}R^j_{E_{B_1,B_2}}(X) = L^j_{L_{A_1}R_{A_2}}R^j_{L_{B_1}R_{B_2}}(X) \\
= & \left(L^j_{L_{A_1}}L^j_{R_{A_2}}R^j_{L_{B_1}}R^j_{R_{B_2}}\right)(X) \\
= & \left(L^j_{L_{A_1}}R^j_{L_{B_1}}L^j_{R_{A_2}}R^j_{R_{B_2}}\right)(X) \qquad ([L_C, R_D] = 0 \text{ for all operators } C, D) \\
= & \left(L_{L_{A_1}}R_{L_{B_1}}\right)^j X\left(L_{R_{A_2}}R_{R_{B_2}}\right)^j \\
- & L^j_{L_{A_1}}R^j_{L_{B_1}}\left(L^j_{R_{A_2}}XR^j_{R_{B_2}}\right) \\
= & L^j_{L_{A_1}}R^j_{L_{B_1}}\left(R^j_{A_2}XR^j_{B_2}\right) = L^j_{L_{A_1}}R^j_{L_{B_1}}\left(XB^j_2A^j_2\right) \\
= & L^j_{A_1}\left(XB^j_2A^j_2\right)L^j_{B_1} = L^j_{A_1}B^j_1\left(XB^j_2A^j_2\right) = A^j_1B^j_1XB^j_2A^j_2.
\end{aligned} \quad \begin{array}{r}(1)\\ \\ (2)\end{array}$$

For convenience, set $L_{L_{A_1}}R_{L_{B_1}} = C$ and $L_{R_{A_2}}R_{R_{B_2}} = D$. We claim that $\sigma(D) \neq \{0\}$. Let us suppose to the contrary that $\sigma(D) = \{0\}$. Then there exist sequences $\{Z_n\}$ and $\{Z'_n\}$ of unit vectors (in $B(B(\mathcal{X}))$ and its dual space, respectively) such that

$$Z'_n(Z_n) = \langle Z_n, Z'_n\rangle = 1 \text{ for all } n \in \mathbb{N}_+ \text{ and } \lim_{n\to\infty} DZ_n = 0.$$

We have

$$\triangle^m_{E_{A_1,A_2},E_{B_1,B_2}}(X) = \sum_{j=0}^{m}(-1)^j\binom{m}{j}C^jX\lim_{n\to\infty}\langle D^jZ_n, Z'_n\rangle = 0$$

for all j except $j = 0$ when we obtain $X = 0$. The operator X being a quasi-affinity, we have a contradiction. Hence ($0 \notin \sigma_a(D)$ and) there exists a non-trivial scalar $\beta \in \sigma_a(D)$. Assuming $\{Z_n\}$ and $\{Z'_n\}$ to be sequences of unit vectors such that $Z'_n(Z_n) = 1$ for all $n \in \mathbb{N}_+$ and $\lim_{n\to\infty}\langle DZ_n, Z'_n\rangle = \beta$, we have

$$\begin{aligned}
0 &= \triangle^m_{E_{A_1,A_2},E_{B_1,B_2}}(X) \\
&= \sum_{j=0}^{m}(-1)^j\binom{m}{j}C^jX\lim_{n\to\infty}\langle D^jZ_n, Z'_n\rangle \\
&= \left(\sum_{j=0}^{m}(-1)^j\binom{m}{j}(\beta C)^j\right)X \\
&= \left(\sum_{j=0}^{m}(-1)^j\binom{m}{j}(\beta A_1)^jB_1^j\right)X \qquad \text{(see (2))} \\
&= \left(\triangle^m_{\beta A_1,B_1}(I)\right)X.
\end{aligned}$$

The operator X being a quasi-affinity, we conclude $(\beta A_1, B_1)$ is (m, I)-isometric. Consequently there exists a positive integer $m_1 \leq m$ such that $(\beta A_1, B_1)$ is strict (m_1, I)-isometric, and hence the set

$$\{\triangle^j_{\beta A_1,B_1}(I)\}_{j=0}^{m_1-1}, \text{ equivalently } \{\triangle^{m-j}_{\beta A_1,B_1}(I)\}_{j=m-m_1+1}^{m}, \text{ is linearly independent.}$$

Once again, for convenience, set $L_{L_{\beta A_1}}R_{L_{B_1}} = C_\beta$ and $L_{R_{A_2}}R_{R_{\frac{1}{\beta}B_2}} = D_\beta$. Then

$$\begin{aligned}
&\triangle^m_{E_{A_1,A_2},E_{B_1,B_2}}(X) = \triangle^m_{E_{\beta A_1,A_2},E_{B_1,\frac{1}{\beta}B_2}}(X) \\
&= \left(I - L_{L_{\beta A_1}}R_{L_{B_1}}L_{R_{A_2}}R_{R_{\frac{1}{\beta}B_2}}\right)^m(X) \\
&= (I - C_\beta D_\beta)^m(X) \\
&= ((I - C_\beta)D_\beta + (I - D_\beta))^m(X) \\
&= \left(\sum_{j=0}^{m}\binom{m}{j}(I - C_\beta)^{m-j}D_\beta^{m-j}(I - D_\beta)^j\right)(X) \\
&= \left(\sum_{j=0}^{m}\binom{m}{j}\left(\sum_{p=0}^{m-j}(-1)^p\binom{m-j}{p}C_\beta^p\right)D_\beta^{m-j}\left(\sum_{k=0}^{j}(-1)^k\binom{j}{k}D_\beta^k\right)\right)(X).
\end{aligned}$$

Since

$$\begin{aligned}
&D_\beta^{m-j}\left(\sum_{k=0}^{j}(-1)^k\binom{j}{k}D_\beta^k\right)(X) \\
&= X(\frac{1}{\beta}B_2)^{m-j}A_2^{m-j}\left(\sum_{k=0}^{j}(-1)^k\binom{j}{k}(\frac{1}{\beta}B_2)^kA_2^k\right) \\
&= X(\frac{1}{\beta}B_2)^{m-j}A_2^{m-j}\triangle^j_{\frac{1}{\beta}B_2,A_2}(I)
\end{aligned}$$

and

$$\begin{aligned}
&\left(\sum_{p=0}^{m-j}(-1)^p\binom{m-j}{p}C_\beta^p\right)X \\
&= \left(\sum_{p=0}^{m-j}(-1)^p\binom{m-j}{p}(\beta A_1)^pB_1^p\right)X \\
&= \triangle^{m-j}_{\beta A_1,B_1}(I)X,
\end{aligned}$$

we have

$$\triangle^m_{E_{A_1,A_2},E_{B_1,B_2}}(X) = \sum_{j=0}^{m}\binom{m}{j}\triangle^{m-j}_{\beta A_1,B_1}(I)X(\frac{1}{\beta}B_2)^{m-j}A_2^{m-j}\triangle^{j}_{\frac{1}{\beta}B_2,A_2}(I)$$
$$= 0.$$

By the linear independence of the set $\{\triangle^{m-j}_{\beta A_1,B_1}(I)\}$ for all $m-m_1+1 \le j \le m$,

$$X(\frac{1}{\beta}B_2)^{m-j}A_2^{m-j}\triangle^{j}_{\frac{1}{\beta}B_2,A_2}(I) = 0$$

for all $0 \le j \le m_1 - 1$. Since X is a quasi-affinity and $0 \notin \sigma_a(D_\beta)$ (implies $0 \notin \sigma_a(B_2^{m-j}A_2^{m-j})$),

$$\triangle^{j}_{\frac{1}{\beta}B_2,A_2}(I) = 0 \text{ for all } 0 \le j \le m_1 - 1.$$

In particular, upon letting $m - m_1 + 1 = m_2$,

$$\triangle^{m_2}_{\frac{1}{\beta}B_2,A_2}(I) = 0.$$

The strict (m, X)-isometric property of the pair $(E_{A_1,A_2}, E_{B_1,B_2})$ implies also that

$$\begin{aligned}
0 &\neq \triangle^{m-1}_{E_{A_1,A_2},E_{B_1,B_2}}(X)\\
&= \Sigma_{j=0}^{m-1}\binom{m-1}{j}\triangle^{m-1-j}_{\beta A_1,B_1}(I)X(\tfrac{1}{\beta}B_2)^{m-1-j}A_2^{m-1-j}\triangle^{j}_{\frac{1}{\beta}B_2,A_2}(I)\\
&= \Sigma_{j=0}^{m_2-1}\binom{m-1}{j}\triangle^{m-1-j}_{\beta A_1,B_1}(I)X(\tfrac{1}{\beta}B_2)^{m-1-j}A_2^{m-1-j}\triangle^{j}_{\frac{1}{\beta}B_2,A_2}(I)\\
&\quad (\triangle^{j}_{\frac{1}{\beta}B_2,A_2}(I) = 0 \text{ for all } j > m_2)\\
&= \binom{m-1}{m_2-1}\triangle^{m_1-1}_{\beta A_1,B_1}(I)X(\tfrac{1}{\beta}B_2)^{m-1-j}A_2^{m-1-j}\triangle^{m_2-1}_{\frac{1}{\beta}B_2,A_2}(I)\\
&\quad (\triangle^{m-1-j}_{\beta A_1,B_1}(I) = 0 \text{ for all } m-1-j \ge m_1, \text{equivalently, } j \le m_2 - 2)\\
&= \binom{m-1}{m_2-1}\triangle^{m_1-1}_{\beta A_1,B_1}(I)X\triangle^{m_2-1}_{\frac{1}{\beta}B_2,A_2}(I) \qquad (3)\\
&\quad \left(\text{recall}: \triangle^{m_2}_{\frac{1}{\beta}B_2,A_2}(I) = 0 \Longrightarrow (\tfrac{1}{\beta}B_2)^t A_2^t \triangle^{m_2-1}_{\frac{1}{\beta}B_2,A_2}(I) = \triangle^{m_2-1}_{\frac{1}{\beta}B_2,A_2}(I) \text{ for all } t \in \mathbb{N}\right).
\end{aligned}$$

Since $\triangle^{m_2-1}_{\frac{1}{\beta}B_2,A_2}(I) = 0$ would contradict this condition, the pair$(\frac{1}{\beta}B_2, A_2)$ is strict (m_2, I)-isometric.

The proof of the reverse implication is straightforward. Thus, if $(\beta A_1, B_1)$ is strict (m_1, I)-isometric, $(\frac{1}{\beta}B_2, A_2)$ is strict (m_2, I)-isometric, and $m = m_1 + m_2 - 1$, then for every quasi-affinity $X \in B(\mathcal{X})$,

$$\triangle^m_{E_{A_1,A_2},E_{B_1,B_2}}(X) = \sum_{j=0}^{m}\binom{m}{j}\triangle^{m-j}_{\beta A_1,B_1}(I)X(\frac{1}{\beta}B_2)^{m-j}A_2^{m-j}\triangle^{j}_{\frac{1}{\beta}B_2,A_2}(I)$$
$$= 0,$$

since $\triangle^{m-j}_{\beta A_1,B_1}(I) = 0$ for all $m-j \geq m_1$, equivalently, $j \leq m - m_1 = m_2 - 1$, and $\triangle^{j}_{\frac{1}{\beta}B_2,A_2}(I) = 0$ for all $j \geq m_2$. The strictness implies

$$\triangle^{m_1-1}_{\beta A_1,B_1}(I) \neq 0 \neq \triangle^{m_2-1}_{\frac{1}{\beta}B_2,A_2}(I)$$

and this in turn implies $\triangle^{m_1-1}_{\beta A_1,B_1}(I)X(\triangle^{m_2-1}_{\frac{1}{\beta}B_2,A_2}(I)) \neq 0$. □

The proof of Theorem 1 in the case in which $A_1^* = B_1 = A$ and $A_2^* = B_2 = B$, A and B Hilbert space operators, is more straightforward. Thus, if the pair $(E_{A^*,B^*}, E_{A,B})$ is (m, X)-isometric for some quasi-affinity $X \in B(\mathcal{H})$, then

$$\triangle^{m}_{E_{A^*,B^*},E_{A,B}}(X) = \sum_{j=0}^{m}(-1)^j \begin{pmatrix} m \\ j \end{pmatrix} A^{*j}A^jXB^jB^{*j},$$

$0 \notin \sigma_a(B^*)$, and $(0 \neq)\beta_0 \in \sigma_a(B^*)$ implies

$$\left(\sum_{j=0}^{m}(-1)^j \begin{pmatrix} m \\ j \end{pmatrix} \beta^j A^{*j}A^j\right)X = 0 \qquad (\beta = |\beta_0|^2)$$
$$\iff \triangle^{m}_{\beta A^*,A}(I) = 0.$$

Corollary 2. *Given operators $A, B \in B(\mathcal{H})$, the pair $(E_{A^*,B^*}, E_{A,B}))$ is strict (m, X)-isometric for a quasi-affinity $X \in B(\mathcal{H})$ if and only if there exist positive integers $m_i \leq m$ and a non-trivial scalar β such that $m = m_1 + m_2 - 1$, $(\beta A^*, A)$ is strict (m_1, I)-isometric, $(\frac{1}{\beta}B, B^*)$ is strict (m_2, I)-isometric, and $\triangle^{m_1-1}_{\beta A^*,A}(I)X(\triangle^{m_2-1}_{\frac{1}{\beta}B,B^*}(I)) \neq 0$.*

Since $\triangle^{m}_{\beta A^*,A}(I) = 0$ if and only if $\triangle^{m}_{\overline{\beta_0}A^*,\beta_0 A}(I) = 0$, $\overline{\beta_0}\beta_0 = \beta$, the pair of operators $(\overline{\beta_0}A^*, \beta_0 A)$ is (m, I)-isometric; hence, $\sigma_a(\beta_0 A)$ lies in the boundary $\partial\mathbb{D}$ of the unit disc $\mathbb{D}$ in $\mathbb{C}$ and $1 - (\overline{\beta_0}\sigma_a(A^*)(\beta_0\sigma_a(A)) = 0$. There exists a non-trivial scalar λ, $|\lambda| = 1$, such that $\beta_0\alpha = \lambda$ and $\overline{\beta_0\alpha} = \frac{1}{\lambda} = \overline{\lambda}$ for all $\alpha \in \sigma_a(A)$. We assert that $\sigma_a(B^*)$ consists, at most, of two points. For if there exist non-trivial $\overline{\mu}, \overline{\nu} \in \sigma_a(B^*)$, $\mu \neq \beta_0 \neq \nu$, then $\sigma_a(\mu A) = \sigma_a(\beta_0 A) + \sigma_a((\mu - \beta_0)A)$ and $\sigma_a(\nu A) = \sigma_a(\beta_0 A) + \sigma_a((\nu - \beta_0)A)$: since $0 \notin \sigma_a(A)$, not both of these translations of $\sigma_a(\beta_0 A)$ are in $\partial\mathbb{D}$. This argument applies equally to $\sigma_a(A)$; hence $\sigma(A)$ and $\sigma(B)$ consist at most of two points. A similar statement holds for operators $A, B \in B(\mathcal{H})$ such that the pair $(\mathcal{E}_{A^*,A}(I), \mathcal{E}_{B^*,B}(I))$ is a strict (m, X)- isometry for some quasi-affinity $X \in B(\mathcal{H})$. For in this case for every $\beta \in \sigma_a(B)$, β being necessarily non-trivial, the pair $(\overline{\beta}A^*, \beta A)$ is (m_1, I)-isometric for some positive integer $m_1 \leq m$ (see Corollary 1). Thus $\sigma_a(\beta A) \subset \partial\mathbb{D}$. Let $\lambda \in \sigma_a(A)$, and suppose that there exist distinct scalars $\mu, \nu \in \sigma_a(B)$; $\mu, \nu \neq \beta$. Then $\sigma_a(\mu A) = \sigma_a(\beta A) + \sigma_a((\mu - \beta)A)$, $\sigma_a(\nu A) = \sigma_a(\beta A) + \sigma_a((\nu - \beta)A)$, and not both these translations of $\sigma_a(\beta A)$ can be in $\partial(\mathbb{D})$. We remark that both of these classes of operators belong to the class of (m, I)-isometric operators with a finite spectrum [1,9,10,12,13].

4. A Concluding Remark

Let $\mathcal{C}_2(\mathcal{H}) \subseteq B(\mathcal{H})$ denote the operator ideal of Hilbert–Schmidt operators (equipped with the Hilbert–Schmidt operator norm). Given $A, B \in B(\mathcal{H})$, Gu [1] (Theorem 7) proves that $E_{A,B} \in \mathcal{C}_2(\mathcal{H})$ is a strict m-isometry, i.e., the pair $(E^*_{A,B}, E_{A,B})$ is strict (m, T)-isometric for all $T \in \mathcal{C}_2(H)$, if and only if there exists a non-trivial scalar β and integers $m_1, m_2 \in \mathbb{N}$ such that $m = m_1 + m_2 - 1$, βA is strict (m_1, I)-isometric and $\frac{1}{\beta}B$ is strict (m_2, I)-isometric. Observe that if $A, B \in B(\mathcal{H})$ and (A, B) is (m, X)-isometric for a quasi-affinity $X \in B(\mathcal{H})$, then (our purely algebraic argument from Section 2 shows that) there exist $\mu \in \sigma_a(B)$ and $\overline{\nu} \in \sigma_a(A^*)$ such that $(I-\mu A)^m = 0 = (I - \overline{\nu} B^*)^m$. Since $\sigma(\triangle_{A,B}) = 1 - \sigma(A)\sigma(B)$, $\mu\nu = 1$, $(I-\mu A)^m = 0 = (I - \frac{1}{\mu}B)^m$. The operators $\mathcal{E}_{A_1,A_2}(S_1)$ and $\mathcal{E}_{B_1,B_2}(S_2)$ are operators in $B(\mathcal{H})$; if $(\mathcal{E}_{A_1,A_2}(S_1), \mathcal{E}_{B_1,B_2}(S_2))$ is (m,X)-isometric, $X \in B(\mathcal{H})$ a quasi-affinity, then there exists a non-zero scalar β such that $I - \beta\mathcal{E}_{A_1,A_2}(S_1)$ and $I - \frac{1}{\beta}\mathcal{E}_{B_1,B_2}(S_2)$ are m-nilpotent. Thus, if $\mathcal{E}^n_{A_1,A_2}(X) = E^n_{A_1,A_2}(X)$ for all $n \in \mathbb{N}$, then there exists a non-zero scalar β such that $(\beta A_1, A_2)$ is (m, S_1)-isometric and $(\frac{1}{\beta}B_1, B_2)$ is (m, S_2)-isometric. Proposition 2 is a Banach space generalisation of this result. The extension of this algebraic argument to the pair $(E_{A_1,A_2}, E_{B_1,B_2}) \in B(B(\mathcal{X}))^2$ requires a judicious use of the algebraic, especially the commutative, properties of the left/right regularisation operators (in the terminology of Taylor and Lay [14] (Page 392)) L_A and R_B of the algebra $B(\mathcal{X})$. We remark in closing that a proof of the Hilbert space version of this result for the m-null symbols pair $(\mathcal{E}_{A_1,A_2}(S_1), \mathcal{E}_{B_1,B_2}(S_2))$ using arithmetic progressions and a combinatorial argument, thus avoiding analytic arguments, has been given by Marrero [15].

Funding: This research received no external funding.

Data Availability Statement: No data generation or analysis involved.

Conflicts of Interest: The author declares no conflicts of interest.

References

1. Gu, C. Elementary operators which are m-isometric. *Linear Algebra Its Appl.* **2014**, *451*, 49–64. [CrossRef]
2. Marrero, I. Elementary operators with m-null symbols. *Mathematics* **2025**, *73*, 741. [CrossRef]
3. Agler, J. Sub-Jordan operators, Bishop's theorem, spectral inclusions and spectral sets. *J. Oper. Theory* **1982**, *7*, 373–395.
4. Agler, J.; Stankus, M.m-Isometric transformations of Hilbert space I. *Integr. Equ. Oper. Theory* **1995**, *21*, 383–420. [CrossRef]
5. Bayart, F. m-Isometries on Banach Spaces. *Math. Nachr.* **2011**, *284*, 2141–2147. [CrossRef]
6. Bermúdez, T.; Martinón, A.; Noda, J.N. Products of m-isometries. *Linear Algebra Its Appl.* **2013**, *408*, 80–86. [CrossRef]
7. Botelho, F.; Jamison, J. Isometric properties of elementary operators. *Linear Algebra Its Appl.* **2010**, *432*, 357–365. [CrossRef]
8. Duggal, B.P.; Kim, I.H. Structure of elementary operators defining m-left invertible, m-selfadjoint and related classes of operators. *J. Math. Anal. Appl.* **2021**, *495*, 124718. [CrossRef]
9. Duggal, B.P.; Kim, I.H. m-isometric generalised derivations. *Concr. Oper.* **2022**, *9*, 139–150. [CrossRef]
10. Duggal, B.P.; Kim, I.H. m-symmetric operators with elementary operator entries. *Results Math.* **2024**, *79*, 240. [CrossRef]
11. Eschmeier, J. Tensor products and elementary operators. *J. Reine Agnew. Math.* **1988**, *390*, 42–66.
12. Helton, J.W. Infinite dimensional Jordan algebras and Sturm-Liouville conjugation point theory. *Trans. Amer. Math. Soc.* **1970**, *170*, 305–331. [CrossRef]
13. Stankus, M. m-isometries and other linear transformations which are hereditary roots. *Integral Equ. Oper. Theory* **2013**, *75*, 301–321. [CrossRef]
14. Taylor, A.E.; Lay, D.C. *Introduction to Functional Analysis*; John Wiley and Sons: New York, NY, USA, 1980.
15. Marrero, I. On the Symbols of Strictly m-null Elementary Operators. *Mathematics* **2025**, *13*, 2026. [CrossRef]

axioms

MDPI

Article

Relational Almost (ϕ, ψ)-Contractions and Applications to Nonlinear Fredholm Integral Equations

Fahad M. Alamrani, Ebrahem A. Algehyne *, Esmail Alshaban, Adel Alatawi, Hamid I. A. Mohammed and Faizan Ahmad Khan *

Department of Mathematics, Science Faculty, University of Tabuk, P.O. Box 741, Tabuk 71491, Saudi Arabia; fm.alomrani@ut.edu.sa (F.M.A.); ealshaban@ut.edu.sa (E.A.); amalatawi@ut.edu.sa (A.A.); hmohammed@ut.edu.sa (H.I.A.M.)

* Correspondence: e.algehyne@ut.edu.sa (E.A.A.); fkhan@ut.edu.sa (F.A.K.)

Abstract: This paper deals with the fixed-point findings under relational strict almost (ϕ, ψ)-contraction. Our findings complement and strengthen prevailing results. In the course of the procedure, we also derive a related fixed point theorem for strict almost (ϕ, ψ)-contraction. We provide several illustrative examples to support the validity of our outcomes. We also argue about the possibility of a unique solution of a nonlinear Fredholm integral equation via our outcomes.

Keywords: fixed points; binary relation; nonlinear Fredholm integral equations

MSC: 54H25; 47H10; 45B05; 06A75

1. Introduction

The foremost and traditional method in nonlinear functional analysis is the classical Banach contraction principle (abbreviated as BCP). There are numerous generalizations of BCP accessible in the literature. Berinde [1] presented a new generalization of BCP in 2004, which is known as almost contraction.

Definition 1 ([1,2])**.** *A self-map* $\mathbf{f}$ *on a metric space* $(\mathbb{V}, \omega)$ *is known as almost contraction if there exist* $0 < \alpha < 1$ *and* $\ell \geq 0$*, enjoying*

$$\omega(\mathbf{f}v, \mathbf{f}u) \leq \alpha \cdot \omega(v, u) + \ell \cdot \omega(v, \mathbf{f}u), \quad \forall\, v, u \in \mathbb{V}.$$

Making use of symmetry of ω, the aforementioned condition is identical to the following one:

$$\omega(\mathbf{f}v, \mathbf{f}u) \leq \alpha \cdot \omega(v, u) + \ell \cdot \omega(u, \mathbf{f}v), \quad \forall\, v, u \in \mathbb{V}.$$

Theorem 1 ([1])**.** *Every almost contraction map on a complete metric space possesses a fixed point.*

The almost contraction is a weak Picard operator, which means that it does not need to have a unique fixed point but Picard's iterative sequence remains convergent to a fixed point of the map. An almost contraction map is not necessarily continuous but it remains continuous at each of fixed points (c.f. [2]). In addition to the usual contraction, almost contraction extends not only the usual contraction but also several well-known generalized contractions, which include Kannan contraction [3], Chatterjea contraction [4], Zamfirescu contraction, and [5] and a special class of Ćirić's quasi-contraction [6]. In recent years, many fixed point results involving almost contraction conditions have been established, e.g., [7–14].

Babu et al. [15] established a notably restricted category of almost contraction in order to derive a uniqueness theorem.

Definition 2 ([15]). *A self-map* $\mathbf{f}$ *on a metric space* $(\mathbb{V}, \omega)$ *is known as strict almost contraction if there exist* $0 < \alpha < 1$ *and* $\ell \geq 0$*, enjoying*

$$\omega(\mathbf{f}v, \mathbf{f}u) \leq \alpha \cdot \omega(v, u) + \ell \cdot \min\{\omega(v, \mathbf{f}v), \omega(u, \mathbf{f}u), \omega(v, \mathbf{f}u), \omega(u, \mathbf{f}v)\}, \quad \forall\, v, u \in \mathbb{V}.$$

Theorem 2 ([15]). *Every strict almost contraction map on a complete metric space possesses a unique fixed point.*

Metric fixed-point theory continues to be an exquisite field of study for constructing fixed-point outcomes in relational metric space. The contraction condition that leads to such results needs to be satisfied for only comparative elements with regard to the relation. As of right now, relational contractions continue to be weaker than usual contractions.

In 2015, Alam and Imdad [16] launched this progression by establishing an analog of BCP in relational metric space. Numerous outcomes have been proven in this strategy since then. Alam and Imdad [17] investigated certain coincidence and common fixed-point theorems in relational metric space. Alam et al. [18] defined relational analogs of completeness and continuity and utilized the same to improve the relation-theoretic contraction principle. Almarri et al. [19] proved fixed-point theorems for relational Geraghty contractions and provided an application to boundary value problems. Hossain et al. [20] presented relation-theoretic variants of weak contractions and provided applications to nonlinear matrix equations. Hasanuzzaman and Imdad [21] proved Feng–Liu type results in relational metric spaces and gave an application to nonlinear Bernstein operators. Choudhury and Chakraborty [22] established some fixed-point results under multi-valued relational Kannan—Geraghty type contractions employing the concept of w-distance. On the other hand, Antal et al. [23] utilized the idea of w-distance to prove fixed-point results under (φ, ψ, p)-weakly contractive mappings in relational metric space. Relation-theoretic aspects of almost contractions are studied in [24–27]. One of the principal features of relational contractions is that the contraction inequality constitutes acceptable just for comparable elements. As of right now, relational contractions continue to be weaker than corresponding usual contractions; consequently, they have the potential to resolve boundary value problems, nonlinear matrix equations, and integral equations, whereas outcomes about the fixed point in ordinary metric space are not implemented.

Dutta and Choudhury [28] introduced yet another type of contractivity condition depending on a pair ϕ and ψ of auxiliary functions, a so-called (ϕ, ψ)-contraction, which is defined as follows:

$$\phi(\omega(\mathbf{f}v, \mathbf{f}u)) \leq \phi(\omega(v, u)) - \psi(\omega(v, u)).$$

By implementing a new pairing of test functions, Alam et al. [29] enhanced the concept of (ϕ, ψ)-contraction and utilized it to expand the BCP. The relational analog of results due to Alam et al. [29] was subsequently achieved by Sk et al. [30].

In this article, we subsume the concepts of relational contraction, strict almost contraction, and (ϕ, ψ)-contraction as follows:

$$\phi(\omega(\mathbf{f}v, \mathbf{f}u)) \leq \phi(\omega(v, u)) - \psi(\omega(v, u)) + \ell \cdot \min\{\omega(v, \mathbf{f}v), \omega(u, \mathbf{f}u), \omega(v, \mathbf{f}u), \omega(u, \mathbf{f}v)\},$$

where the elements v and u are connected via relation on metric space.

Similar to the relation-theoretic contraction principle [16], in order to prove their relation-theoretic formulations, a few generalized contractions require an arbitrary binary relation for the existence of fixed points of such map. Apart from this, in the context of earlier contraction-condition, transitivity of underlying relation is also required. However, the transitivity requirement is very restrictive. With a view to employing an optimal condition of transitivity, we adopt 'locally finitely $\mathbf{f}$-transitivity', which is relatively weaker than usual transitivity, local transitivity, $\mathbf{f}$-transitivity, and finitely transitivity (c.f. [30–36]). Employing the above contraction-condition and locally finitely $\mathbf{f}$-transitive relation, we prove metrical fixed-point results and present several examples that verify the validity of our findings. Through our results, we characterize the possibility of a unique solution of certain nonlinear Fredholm integral equations when a lower or an upper solution exists.

2. Preliminaries

The sets of natural numbers, whole numbers, real numbers, and nonnegative real numbers will be symbolized by $\mathbb{N}$, $\mathbb{N}_0$, $\mathbb{R}$ and $\mathbb{R}_+$, respectively. Note that a subset of $\mathbb{V}^2$ is designated as a relation on the set $\mathbb{V}$ (Ref. [37]).

Definition 3. *Assuming that $\mathbb{V}$ remains a set, and $\wp$ is a relation on $\mathbb{V}$.*

- *Ref. [16] The elements $v, u \in \mathbb{V}$ are named as $\wp$-comparative if $(v, u) \in \wp$ or $(u, v) \in \wp$. Such a pair is symbolized by $[v, u] \in \wp$.*
- *Ref. [16] A sequence $\{v_\imath\} \subset \mathbb{V}$, satisfying $(v_\imath, v_{\imath+1}) \in \wp$, for all $\imath \in \mathbb{N}$, is named as $\wp$-preserving.*
- *Ref. [38] $\mathbb{U} \subseteq \mathbb{V}$ is named as $\wp$-directed if for any $v, u \in \mathbb{U}$, $\exists\, w \in \mathbb{V}$ enjoying $(v, w) \in \wp$ and $(u, w) \in \wp$.*
- *Ref. [39] For $\mathbb{U} \subseteq \mathbb{V}$, the relation $\wp|_{\mathbb{U}} := \wp \cap \mathbb{U}^2$ on $\mathbb{U}$ is named as restriction of $\wp$ on $\mathbb{U}$.*
- *Ref. [35] For $l \in \mathbb{N} - \{1\}$, $\wp$ is named as l-transitive if for any $v_0, v_1, \ldots, v_l \in \mathbb{V}$,*

$$(v_{i-1}, v_i) \in \wp \text{ for each } i\ (1 \leq i \leq l) \Rightarrow (v_0, v_l) \in \wp.$$

  Thus, the ideas of usual transitivity and 2-transitivity are equivalent.
- *Ref. [36] $\wp$ is named as finitely transitive if for some $l \in \mathbb{N} - \{1\}$, $\wp$ remains l-transitive.*

Definition 4. *Assuming that $\mathbb{V}$ remains a set, $\wp$ is a relation on $\mathbb{V}$, and $\mathbf{f} : \mathbb{V} \to \mathbb{V}$ constitutes a mapping.*

- *Ref. [16] $\wp$ is named as $\mathbf{f}$-closed if for every $v, u \in \mathbb{V}$ enjoying $(v, u) \in \wp$, one has*

$$(\mathbf{f}v, \mathbf{f}u) \in \wp.$$

- *Ref. [31] $\wp$ is named as locally f-transitive if for every $\wp$-preserving sequence $\{u_\imath\} \subset f(\mathbb{V})$ with range $\mathbb{U} = \{u_\imath : \imath \in \mathbb{N}\}$, $\wp|_{\mathbb{U}}$ is transitive.*
- *Ref. [32] $\wp$ is named as locally finitely f-transitive if for every $\wp$-preserving sequence $\{u_\imath\} \subset f(\mathbb{V})$ with range $\mathbb{U} = \{u_\imath : \imath \in \mathbb{N}\}$, $\wp|_{\mathbb{U}}$ is finitely transitive.*

Proposition 1 ([31]). *If $\wp$ is $\mathbf{f}$-closed then for every $\imath \in \mathbb{N}_0$, $\wp$ is $\mathbf{f}^\imath$-closed.*

Remark 1. *The class of finitely transitive relation and the class of locally f-transitive relation both are contained in the class of locally finitely f-transitive relation.*

Definition 5. *Assuming that $(\mathbb{V}, \omega)$ remains metric space, and $\wp$ is a relation on $\mathbb{V}$.*

- *Ref. [16] $\wp$ is named as ω-self-closed if every $\wp$-preserving convergent sequence in $\mathbb{V}$ has a subsequence, each of its terms is $\wp$-comparative to the limit of convergence.*
- *Ref. [17] $(\mathbb{V}, \omega)$ is named as $\wp$-complete metric space if each $\wp$-preserving Cauchy sequence in $\mathbb{V}$ converges.*
- *Ref. [17] A map $\mathbf{f} : \mathbb{V} \to \mathbb{V}$ is named as $\wp$-continuous at $v \in \mathbb{V}$ if for each $\wp$-preserving sequence $\{v_\imath\} \subset \mathbb{V}$ with $v_\imath \xrightarrow{\omega} v$,*

$$\mathbf{f}(v_\imath) \xrightarrow{\omega} \mathbf{f}(v).$$

  A map, which is $\wp$-continuous at each point, is named as $\wp$-continuous.

Lemma 1 ([35]). *In a metric space $(\mathbb{V}, \omega)$, let a sequence $\{v_\imath\}$ be not Cauchy. Then, we can find subsequences $\{v_{\imath_\kappa}\}$ and $\{v_{\jmath_\kappa}\}$ of $\{v_\imath\}$ and a constant $\varepsilon_0 > 0$ such that*

(i) $i \leq \imath_\kappa < \jmath_\kappa,\ \forall\, i \in \mathbb{N}$,

(ii) $\omega(v_{\imath_\kappa}, v_{\jmath_\kappa}) \geq \varepsilon_0, \ \forall \imath \in \mathbb{N}$,
(iii) $\omega(v_{\imath_\kappa}, v_{\rho_\kappa}) < \varepsilon_0, \ \forall \rho_\kappa \in \{\imath_\kappa + 1, \imath_\kappa + 2, \ldots, \jmath_\kappa - 2, \jmath_\kappa - 1\}$.

Moreover, if $\lim_{\imath\to\infty} \omega(v_\imath, v_{\imath+1}) = 0$, *then*

$$\lim_{\imath\to\infty} \omega(v_{\imath_\kappa}, v_{\jmath_\kappa+\lambda}) = \varepsilon_0, \ \forall \lambda \in \mathbb{N}_0.$$

Lemma 2 ([36]). *Let* $\mathbb{V}$ *be a set that is associated with a relation* $\wp$. *If* $\{v_\imath\} \subset \mathbb{V}$ *remains* $\wp$*-preserving sequence and the relation* $\wp$ *is l-transitive on* $\mathbb{U} = \{v_\imath : \imath \in \mathbb{N}_0\}$, *then*

$$(v_\imath, v_{\imath+1+\lambda(l-1)}) \in \wp, \ \forall \imath, \lambda \in \mathbb{N}_0.$$

Let Φ be the collection of auxiliary functions $\phi : \mathbb{R}_+ \to \mathbb{R}_+$ meeting the requirements listed below:

Φ_1: ϕ is right continuous;
Φ_2: ϕ is increasing.

Also, let Ψ be the collection of auxiliary functions $\psi : \mathbb{R}_+ \to \mathbb{R}_+$ meeting the requirements listed below:

Ψ_1: $\psi(t) > 0, \quad \forall t > 0$;
Ψ_2: $\liminf_{t\to r} \psi(t) > 0, \quad \forall r > 0$.

The aforementioned families Φ and Ψ have been described by Alam et al. [29].

Proposition 2 ([29]). *Let* $\phi, \psi : \mathbb{R}_+ \to \mathbb{R}_+$ *be a pair of auxiliary functions such that* ϕ *satisfies axiom* Φ_2 *and* ψ *satisfy axiom* Ψ_1, *verifying*

$$\phi(s) \leq \phi(t) - \psi(t), \quad \forall s \in \mathbb{R}_+ \text{ and } t > 0.$$

Then

$$s < t.$$

By symmetry of metric ω, the following conclusion holds.

Proposition 3. *Given* $\phi \in \Phi$, $\psi \in \Psi$ *and* $\ell \geq 0$, *the following axioms are identical:*

(A) $\phi(\omega(\mathbf{f}v, \mathbf{f}u)) \leq \phi(\omega(v,u)) - \psi(\omega(v,u)) + \ell \cdot \min\{\omega(v,\mathbf{f}v), \omega(u,\mathbf{f}u), \omega(v,\mathbf{f}u), \omega(u,\mathbf{f}v)\}$, *for all* $v, u \in \mathbb{V}$ *with* $(v,u) \in \wp$.
(B) $\phi(\omega(\mathbf{f}v, \mathbf{f}u)) \leq \phi(\omega(v,u)) - \psi(\omega(v,u)) + \ell \cdot \min\{\omega(v,\mathbf{f}v), \omega(u,\mathbf{f}u), \omega(v,\mathbf{f}u), \omega(u,\mathbf{f}v)\}$, *for all* $v, u \in \mathbb{V}$ *with* $[v,u] \in \wp$.

3. Main Results

We look into the fixed point results for relational strict almost (ϕ, ψ)-contractions.

Theorem 3. *Assuming that* $(\mathbb{V}, \omega)$ *is a metric space,* $\mathbf{f} : \mathbb{V} \to \mathbb{V}$ *is a map and* $\wp$ *continues to be a relation on* $\mathbb{V}$. *Furthermore,*

(i) $(v_0, \mathbf{f}v_0) \in \wp$ *for some* $v_0 \in \mathbb{V}$,
(ii) $(\mathbb{V}, \omega)$ *is* $\wp$*-complete,*
(iii) $\wp$ *remains locally finitely* $\mathbf{f}$*-transitive and* $\mathbf{f}$*-closed,*
(iv) $\mathbb{V}$ *is* $\wp$*-continuous, or* $\wp$ *is* ω*-self-closed,*
(v) $\exists\, \phi \in \Phi$, $\psi \in \Psi$ *and* $\ell \geq 0$ *enjoying*

$$\phi(\omega(\mathbf{f}v, \mathbf{f}u)) \leq \phi(\omega(v,u)) - \psi(\omega(v,u)) + \ell \cdot \min\{\omega(v,\mathbf{f}v), \omega(u,\mathbf{f}u), \omega(v,\mathbf{f}u), \omega(u,\mathbf{f}v)\},$$
$$\forall\, v, u \in \mathbb{V} \text{ with } (v,u) \in \wp.$$

Then, $\mathbf{f}$ *admits a fixed point.*

Proof. Given $v_0 \in \mathbb{V}$. Construct a sequence $\{v_\imath\} \subset \mathbb{V}$, enjoying

$$v_\imath := \mathbf{f}^\imath(v_0) = \mathbf{f}(v_{\imath-1}), \quad \forall\, \imath \in \mathbb{N}. \tag{1}$$

By assumption (i), $\mathbf{f}$-closedness of $\wp$ and Proposition 1, we obtain

$$(\mathbf{f}^\imath v_0, \mathbf{f}^{\imath+1} v_0) \in \wp,$$

which owing to (1) reduces to

$$(v_\imath, v_{\imath+1}) \in \wp, \quad \forall\, \imath \in \mathbb{N}_0. \tag{2}$$

Hence, $\{v_\imath\}$ is a $\wp$-preserving sequence.

Let us denote $\omega_\imath := \omega(v_\imath, v_{\imath+1})$. If $\omega_{\imath_0} = \omega(v_{\imath_0}, v_{\imath_0+1}) = 0$ for some $\imath_0 \in \mathbb{N}_0$, then in lieu of (1), one has $\mathbf{f}(v_{\imath_0}) = v_{\imath_0}$. Hence, $v_{\imath_0}$ serves as a fixed point of $\mathbf{f}$ and thus our task is over.

In case $\omega_\imath > 0$, for every $\imath \in \mathbb{N}_0$, using item (v), (1) and (2), we obtain

$$\begin{aligned} \phi(\omega_\imath) &= \phi(\omega(v_\imath, v_{\imath+1})) = \phi(\omega(\mathbf{f}v_{\imath-1}, \mathbf{f}v_\imath)) \\ &\leq \phi(\omega(v_{\imath-1}, v_\imath)) - \psi(\omega(v_{\imath-1}, v_\imath)) + \ell \cdot \min\{\omega(v_{\imath-1}, v_\imath), \omega(v_\imath, v_{\imath+1}), \omega(v_{\imath-1}, v_{\imath+1}), 0\}, \end{aligned}$$

so that

$$\phi(\omega_\imath) \leq \phi(\omega_{\imath-1}) - \psi(\omega_{\imath-1}) \quad \forall\, \imath \in \mathbb{N}_0. \tag{3}$$

Using Proposition 2 in (3), we obtain

$$\omega_\imath < \omega_{\imath-1}, \quad \forall\, \imath \in \mathbb{N}.$$

It follows that $\{\omega_\imath\} \subset (0, \infty)$ is a decreasing sequence. Further, as $\{\omega_\imath\}$ is bounded below by '0', $\exists\, \bar{\omega} \geq 0$, verifying

$$\lim_{\imath \to \infty} \omega_\imath = \bar{\omega}. \tag{4}$$

We shall verify that $\bar{\omega} = 0$. Assuming on the contrary that $\bar{\omega} > 0$. Making use of limit superior in (3), we conclude

$$\begin{aligned} \limsup_{\imath \to \infty} \phi(\omega_{\imath+1}) &\leq \limsup_{\imath \to \infty} \phi(\omega_\imath) + \limsup_{\imath \to \infty}[-\psi(\omega_\imath)] \\ &\leq \limsup_{\imath \to \infty} \phi(\omega_\imath) - \liminf_{\imath \to \infty} \psi(\omega_\imath). \end{aligned}$$

Employing right continuity of ϕ, we obtain

$$\phi(\bar{\omega}) \leq \phi(\bar{\omega}) - \liminf_{\imath \to \infty} \psi(\omega_\imath)$$

implying thereby

$$\liminf_{\omega_\imath \to \bar{\omega} > 0} \psi(\omega_\imath) = \liminf_{\imath \to \infty} \psi(\omega_\imath) \leq 0$$

which contradicts axiom Ψ_2 so that $\bar{\omega} = 0$. Thus, we have

$$\lim_{\imath \to \infty} \omega_\imath = 0. \tag{5}$$

Now, we shall verify that $\{v_\imath\}$ is Cauchy. Assuming on the contrary that $\{v_\imath\}$ is not Cauchy. In lieu of Lemma 1, we can find subsequences $\{v_{\imath_\kappa}\}$ and $\{v_{\jmath_\kappa}\}$ of $\{v_\imath\}$ and a constant $\varepsilon_0 > 0$, which satisfy

$$\kappa \leq \imath_\kappa < \jmath_\kappa,\ \omega(v_{\imath_\kappa}, v_{\jmath_\kappa}) \geq \varepsilon_0 > \omega(v_{\imath_\kappa}, v_{\rho_\kappa}), \quad \text{for all } \kappa \in \mathbb{N},\ \rho_\kappa \in \{\imath_\kappa + 1, \imath_\kappa + 2, \ldots, \jmath_\kappa - 2, \jmath_\kappa - 1\}.$$

Owing to (5) and Lemma 1, we obtain

$$\lim_{\kappa\to\infty} \omega(v_{\imath_\kappa}, v_{\jmath_\kappa+\lambda}) = \varepsilon_0, \ \forall\, \lambda \in \mathbb{N}_0. \tag{6}$$

By (1), we have $\mathbb{U} := \{v_\imath : \imath \in \mathbb{N}_0\} \subset \mathbf{f}(\mathbb{V})$. By locally finitely f-transitivity of $\wp$, we can find $l \in \{2, 3, \cdots\}$ for which $\wp|_{\mathbb{U}}$ is l-transitive. Employing the fact: $\imath_\kappa < \jmath_\kappa$ and $l - 1 > 0$ and by division algorithm, we obtain

$$\jmath_\kappa - \imath_\kappa = (l-1)(p_\kappa - 1) + (l - q_\kappa)$$

$$p_\kappa - 1 \geq 0,\ 0 \leq l - q_\kappa < l - 1$$

$$\Longleftrightarrow \begin{cases} \jmath_\kappa + q_\kappa = \imath_\kappa + 1 + p_\kappa(l-1) \\ \quad p_\kappa \geq 1,\ 1 < q_\kappa \leq l. \end{cases}$$

Clearly, $q_\kappa \in (1, l]$. Thus, we can determine the subsequences $\{v_{\jmath_\kappa}\}$ and $\{v_{\imath_\kappa}\}$ of $\{v_\imath\}$ (verifying (6)) for which $q_\kappa = q$ (a constant). Thus, we have

$$\imath'_\kappa = \jmath_\kappa + q = \imath_\kappa + 1 + p_\kappa(l-1). \tag{7}$$

By (6) and (7), we obtain

$$\lim_{\kappa\to\infty} \omega(v_{\imath_\kappa}, v_{\imath'_\kappa}) = \lim_{\kappa\to\infty} \omega(v_{\imath_\kappa}, v_{\jmath_\kappa+q}) = \varepsilon_0. \tag{8}$$

Use of triangular inequality yields that

$$\omega(v_{\imath_\kappa+1}, v_{\imath'_\kappa+1}) \leq \omega(v_{\imath_\kappa+1}, v_{\imath_\kappa}) + \omega(v_{\imath_\kappa}, v_{\imath'_\kappa}) + \omega(v_{\imath'_\kappa}, v_{\imath'_\kappa+1})$$

and

$$\omega(v_{\imath_\kappa}, v_{\imath'_\kappa}) \leq \omega(v_{\imath_\kappa}, v_{\imath_\kappa+1}) + \omega(v_{\imath_{\kappa+1}}, v_{\imath'_\kappa+1}) + \omega(v_{\imath'_\kappa+1}, v_{\imath'_\kappa}).$$

Therefore, we have

$$\begin{aligned} \omega(v_{\imath_\kappa}, v_{\imath'_\kappa}) - \omega(v_{\imath_\kappa}, v_{\imath_\kappa+1}) - \omega(v_{\imath'_\kappa+1}, v_{\imath'_\kappa}) &\leq \omega(v_{\imath_{\kappa+1}}, v_{\imath'_\kappa+1}) \\ &\leq \omega(v_{\imath_\kappa+1}, v_{\imath_\kappa}) + \omega(v_{\imath_\kappa}, v_{\imath'_\kappa}) + \omega(v_{\imath'_\kappa}, v_{\imath'_\kappa+1}). \end{aligned}$$

Employing $\kappa \to \infty$ and by (5) and (8), above inequality becomes

$$\lim_{\kappa\to\infty} \omega(v_{\imath_\kappa+1}, v_{\imath'_\kappa+1}) = \varepsilon_0. \tag{9}$$

Owing to (7) and Lemma 2, we conclude $(v_{\imath_\kappa}, v_{\imath'_\kappa}) \in \wp$. Denote $\delta_\kappa := \omega(v_{\imath_\kappa}, v_{\imath'_\kappa})$. Employing the assumption (v), we obtain

$$\begin{aligned} \phi(\omega(v_{\imath_\kappa+1}, v_{\imath'_\kappa+1})) &= \phi(\omega(\mathbf{f}v_{\imath_\kappa}, \mathbf{f}v_{\imath'_\kappa})) \leq \phi(\omega(v_{\imath_\kappa}, v_{\imath'_\kappa})) - \psi(\omega(v_{\imath_\kappa}, v_{\imath'_\kappa})) \\ &\quad + \ell \cdot \min\{\omega(v_{\imath_\kappa}, \mathbf{f}v_{\imath_\kappa}), \omega(v_{\imath'_\kappa}, \mathbf{f}v_{\imath'_\kappa}), \omega(v_{\imath_\kappa}, \mathbf{f}v_{\imath'_\kappa}), \omega(v_{\imath'_\kappa}, \mathbf{f}v_{\imath_\kappa})\} \end{aligned}$$

so that

$$\phi(\omega(v_{\imath_\kappa+1}, v_{\imath'_\kappa+1})) \leq \phi(\delta_\kappa) - \psi(\delta_\kappa) + \ell \cdot \min\{\omega_{\imath_\kappa}, \omega_{\imath'_\kappa}, \omega(v_{\imath_\kappa}, v_{\imath'_\kappa+1}), \omega(v_{\imath'_\kappa}, v_{\imath_\kappa+1})\}. \tag{10}$$

Using upper limit in (10), we obtain

$$\limsup_{\kappa\to\infty} \phi(\omega(v_{\imath_\kappa+1}, v_{\imath'_\kappa+1})) \leq \limsup_{\kappa\to\infty} \phi(\delta_\kappa) + \limsup_{\kappa\to\infty}[-\psi(\delta_\kappa)] + \ell \cdot \min\{0, 0, \varepsilon_0, \varepsilon_0\}.$$

Due to right continuity of ϕ and (8), we conclude

$$\phi(\varepsilon_0) \leq \phi(\varepsilon_0) - \liminf_{\kappa\to\infty} \psi(\delta_\kappa)$$

yielding thereby

$$\liminf_{\kappa\to\infty} \psi(\delta_\kappa) \leq 0,$$

which arises a contradiction. Thus, $\{v_\imath\}$ is $\wp$-preserving Cauchy. Using $\wp$-completeness of $\mathbb{V}$, $\exists\, \bar{v} \in \mathbb{V}$ verifying $v_\imath \xrightarrow{\omega} \bar{v}$.

Ultimately, we utilize assumption (iv) to enclose the evidence. Assume that $\mathbf{f}$ is a $\wp$-continuous map. As $\{v_\imath\}$ remains $\wp$-preserving verifying $v_\imath \xrightarrow{\omega} \bar{v}$, $\wp$-continuity of $\mathbf{f}$ yields that $v_{\imath+1} = \mathbf{f}(v_\imath) \xrightarrow{\omega} \mathbf{f}(\bar{v})$ so that $\mathbf{f}(\bar{v}) = \bar{v}$.

Otherwise, assuming that $\wp$ is ω-self-closed. Consequently, we can find a subsequence $\{v_{\imath_\kappa}\}$ of $\{v_\imath\}$ satisfying $[v_{\imath_\kappa}, \bar{v}] \in \wp$, $\forall\, \imath \in \mathbb{N}$. Now, we claim that

$$\lim_{\kappa\to\infty} \omega(v_{\imath_\kappa+1}, \mathbf{f}\bar{v}) = 0. \tag{11}$$

Whenever $v_{\imath_\kappa} = \bar{v}$ for some $\kappa \in \mathbb{N}$. Then, we have $v_{\imath_\kappa+1} = \mathbf{f}(v_{\imath_\kappa}) = \mathbf{f}(\bar{v})$ yielding thereby

$$\lim_{\kappa\to\infty} \omega(v_{\imath_\kappa+1}, \mathbf{f}\bar{v}) = 0.$$

i.e., (11) holds. Now, we consider $v_{\imath_\kappa} \neq \bar{v}$ so that $\omega(v_{\imath_\kappa}, \bar{v}) > 0$ for all $\kappa \in \mathbb{N}$. On the contrary, assume that

$$\lim_{\kappa\to\infty} \omega(v_{\imath_\kappa+1}, \mathbf{f}\bar{v}) = \epsilon > 0.$$

Using assumption (v), we obtain

$$\begin{aligned}\phi(\omega(v_{\imath_\kappa+1}, \mathbf{f}\bar{v})) &= \phi(\omega(\mathbf{f}v_{\imath_\kappa}, \mathbf{f}\bar{v})) \leq \phi(\omega(v_{\imath_\kappa}, \bar{v})) - \psi(\omega(v_{\imath_\kappa}, \bar{v})) \\ &\quad + \ell \cdot \min\{\omega_{\imath_\kappa}, \omega(\bar{v}, \mathbf{f}\bar{v}), \omega(v_{\imath_\kappa}, \mathbf{f}\bar{v}), \omega(\bar{v}, v_{\imath_\kappa+1})\}.\end{aligned}$$

Using upper limit in above and right continuity of ϕ, we obtain

$$\phi(\epsilon) \leq \phi(0) - \liminf_{\kappa\to\infty} \psi(\omega(v_{\imath_\kappa}, \bar{v})) + \ell \cdot \min\{0, \omega(\bar{v}, \mathbf{f}\bar{v}), \epsilon, 0\}$$

so that

$$\liminf_{\kappa\to\infty} \psi(\omega(v_{\imath_\kappa}, \bar{v})) \leq \phi(0) - \phi(\epsilon).$$

Using the fact $\epsilon > 0$ and monotone property of ϕ, above inequality implies that

$$\liminf_{\kappa\to\infty} \psi(\omega(v_{\imath_\kappa}, \bar{v})) \leq 0,$$

which is a contradiction. Therefore, (11) holds and hence, we have

$$v_{\imath_\kappa+1} \xrightarrow{\omega} \mathbf{f}(\bar{v}).$$

This concludes that $\mathbf{f}(\bar{v}) = \bar{v}$. Thus, $\bar{v}$ is a fixed point of $\mathbf{f}$. □

Theorem 4. *In keeping with the predictions of Theorem 3,* $\mathbf{f}$ *exhibits a unique fixed point if* $\mathbf{f}(\mathbb{V})$ *is* $\wp$*-directed.*

Proof. By Theorem 3, $\exists\, \bar{v}, \bar{u} \in \mathbb{V}$ which enjoys

$$\mathbf{f}(\bar{v}) = \bar{v} \text{ and } \mathbf{f}(\bar{u}) = \bar{u}. \tag{12}$$

As $\bar{v}, \bar{u} \in \mathbf{f}(\mathbb{V})$, by our assumption, $\exists\, w \in \mathbb{V}$ verifying

$$(\bar{v}, w) \in \wp \quad \text{and} \quad (\bar{u}, w) \in \wp. \tag{13}$$

Denote $\varrho_\imath := \omega(\bar{v}, \mathbf{f}^\imath w)$. Using (12), (13) and assumption (v), one obtains

$$\begin{aligned} \phi(\varrho_\imath) &= \phi(\omega(\mathbf{f}\bar{v}, \mathbf{f}(\mathbf{f}^{\imath-1}w))) \\ &\leq \phi(\omega(\bar{v}, \mathbf{f}^{\imath-1}w)) - \psi(\omega(\bar{v}, \mathbf{f}^{\imath-1}w)) + \ell \cdot \min\{0, \omega(\mathbf{f}^{\imath-1}w, \mathbf{f}^\imath w), \omega(\bar{v}, \mathbf{f}^\imath w), \omega(\mathbf{f}^{\imath-1}w, \bar{v})\} \\ &= \phi(\varrho_{\imath-1}) - \psi(\varrho_{\imath-1}) \end{aligned}$$

so that

$$\phi(\varrho_\imath) \leq \phi(\varrho_{\imath-1}) - \psi(\varrho_{\imath-1}). \tag{14}$$

If $\exists\, \imath_0 \in \mathbb{N}$ for which $\varrho_{\imath_0} = 0$, then we have $\varrho_{\imath_0} \leq \varrho_{\imath_0-1}$. Otherwise $\varrho_\imath > 0$, $\forall\, \imath \in \mathbb{N}$. By Proposition 2, (14) reduces to $\varrho_\imath < \varrho_{\imath-1}$. Hence, in both cases, we have

$$\varrho_\imath \leq \varrho_{\imath-1}.$$

By applying reasoning similar to Theorem 3, above inequality becomes

$$\lim_{\imath\to\infty} \varrho_\imath = \lim_{\imath\to\infty} \omega(\bar{v}, \mathbf{f}^\imath w) = 0. \tag{15}$$

Similarly, one can find

$$\lim_{\imath\to\infty} \omega(\bar{u}, \mathbf{f}^\imath w) = 0. \tag{16}$$

By using (15), (16) and triangular inequality, we conclude

$$\omega(\bar{v}, \bar{u}) = \omega(\bar{v}, \mathbf{f}^\imath w) + \omega(\mathbf{f}^\imath w, \bar{u}) \to 0 \quad \text{as} \quad \imath \to \infty$$

implying thereby $\bar{v} = \bar{u}$. Therefore, $\mathbf{f}$ possesses a unique fixed point. □

Under full relation $\wp = \mathbb{V}^2$, Theorem 4 reduces to the following result in abstract metric space.

Corollary 1. *Assuming that $(\mathbb{V}, \omega)$ remains a complete metric space and $\mathbf{f} : \mathbb{V} \to \mathbb{V}$ is a map. If there exist $\phi \in \Phi$, $\psi \in \Psi$ and $\ell \geq 0$, enjoying*

$$\phi(\omega(\mathbf{f}v, \mathbf{f}u)) \leq \phi(\omega(v, u)) - \psi(\omega(v, u)) + \ell \cdot \min\{\omega(v, \mathbf{f}v), \omega(u, \mathbf{f}u), \omega(v, \mathbf{f}u), \omega(u, \mathbf{f}v)\}, \quad \textit{for all } v, u \in \mathbb{V},$$

then $\mathbf{f}$ possesses a unique fixed point.

In particular, for $\phi(t) = t$ and $\psi(t) = (1-\alpha)t$ where $0 < \alpha < 1$, Corollary 1 reduces to Theorem 2.

Setting $\ell = 0$ in Theorem 3, we deduce the following outcome of Sk et al. [30].

Corollary 2 ([30])**.** *Assuming that $(\mathbb{V}, \omega)$ is a metric space, $\mathbf{f} : \mathbb{V} \to \mathbb{V}$ is a map and $\wp$ continues to be a relation on $\mathbb{V}$. Furthermore,*

(i) *$(v_0, \mathbf{f}v_0) \in \wp$ for some $v_0 \in \mathbb{V}$,*
(ii) *$(\mathbb{V}, \omega)$ is $\wp$-complete,*
(iii) *$\wp$ remains locally finitely $\mathbf{f}$-transitive and $\mathbf{f}$-closed,*
(iv) *$\mathbb{V}$ is $\wp$-continuous, or $\wp$ is ω-self-closed,*
(v) *$\exists\, \phi \in \Phi$ and $\psi \in \Psi$ enjoying*

$$\phi(\omega(\mathbf{f}v, \mathbf{f}u)) \leq \phi(\omega(v, u)) - \psi(\omega(v, u)), \qquad \forall\, v, u \in \mathbb{V} \textit{ with } (v, u) \in \wp.$$

Then, $\mathbf{f}$ admits a fixed point.

Let $\varphi : \mathbb{R}_+ \to \mathbb{R}_+$ be a function verifying $\varphi(t) < t$, for all $t > 0$ and $\limsup_{s \to t^+} \varphi(s) < t$, for all $t > 0$. Taking $\phi(t) = t$ and $\psi(t) = t - \varphi(t)$ in Theorem 3, we deduce the following outcome of Alharbi and Khan [26].

Corollary 3 ([26]). *Assuming that $(\mathbb{V}, \omega)$ is a metric space, $\mathbf{f} : \mathbb{V} \to \mathbb{V}$ is a map and $\wp$ continues to be a relation on $\mathbb{V}$. Furthermore,*

(i) $(\mathrm{v}_0, \mathbf{f}\mathrm{v}_0) \in \wp$ *for some* $\mathrm{v}_0 \in \mathbb{V}$,
(ii) $(\mathbb{V}, \omega)$ *is* $\wp$*-complete,*
(iii) $\wp$ *remains locally* $\mathbf{f}$*-transitive and* $\mathbf{f}$*-closed,*
(iv) $\mathbb{V}$ *is* $\wp$*-continuous, or* $\wp$ *is* ω*-self-closed,*
(v) $\exists$ *a function* $\varphi : \mathbb{R}_+ \to \mathbb{R}_+$, *verifying* $\varphi(t) < t$, *for all* $t > 0$ *and* $\limsup_{s \to t^+} \varphi(s) < t$, *for all* $t > 0$, *and* $\ell \geq 0$, *enjoying*

$$\omega(\mathbf{f}\mathrm{v}, \mathbf{f}\mathrm{u}) \leq \varphi(\omega(\mathrm{v}, \mathrm{u})) + \ell \cdot \min\{\omega(\mathrm{v}, \mathbf{f}\mathrm{v}), \omega(\mathrm{u}, \mathbf{f}\mathrm{u}), \omega(\mathrm{v}, \mathbf{f}\mathrm{u}), \omega(\mathrm{u}, \mathbf{f}\mathrm{v})\},$$
$$\forall\, \mathrm{v}, \mathrm{u} \in \mathbb{V} \text{ with } (\mathrm{v}, \mathrm{u}) \in \wp.$$

Then, $\mathbf{f}$ *admits a fixed point.*

4. Examples

The following examples are provided for evidence of the results established in the preceding section.

Example 1. *Consider $\mathbb{V} := \mathbb{R}^2$ with the metric ω defined by*

$$\omega((\mathrm{v}, \mathrm{u}), (\mathrm{w}, \mathrm{z})) = \frac{|\mathrm{v} - \mathrm{w}| + |\mathrm{u} - \mathrm{z}|}{2} \quad \forall (\mathrm{v}, \mathrm{u}), (\mathrm{w}, \mathrm{z}) \in \mathbb{V}.$$

On $\mathbb{V}$, take a relation $\wp$ given by

$$\wp = \{((\mathrm{v}, \mathrm{u}), (\mathrm{w}, \mathrm{z})) \in \mathbb{V}^2 : \mathrm{w} - \mathrm{v} \geq 0, \mathrm{u} - \mathrm{z} \geq 0\}.$$

Then $(\mathbb{V}, \omega)$ is $\wp$-complete metric space. Define a map $f : \mathbb{V} \to \mathbb{V}$ as

$$f(\mathrm{v}, \mathrm{u}) = \left(\frac{\mathrm{v} - 2\mathrm{u}}{4}, \frac{\mathrm{u} - 2\mathrm{v}}{4} \right), \quad \forall (\mathrm{v}, \mathrm{u}) \in \mathbb{V}.$$

Then, $\wp$ is f-closed as well as ω-self-closed.

Define

$$\phi(t) = \frac{t}{2}, \; \psi(t) = \frac{t}{16}.$$

Then $\phi \in \Phi$ and $\psi \in \Psi$. Take $(\mathrm{v}, \mathrm{u}), (\mathrm{w}, \mathrm{z}) \in \mathbb{V}$ verifying $((\mathrm{v}, \mathrm{u}), (\mathrm{w}, \mathrm{z})) \in \wp$. One has

$$\begin{aligned} \phi(\omega(f(\mathrm{v}, \mathrm{u}), f(\mathrm{w}, \mathrm{z}))) &= \frac{\omega(f(\mathrm{v}, \mathrm{u}), f(\mathrm{w}, \mathrm{z}))}{2} \\ &= \frac{1}{8}(|(\mathrm{v} - \mathrm{w}) + 2(\mathrm{z} - \mathrm{u})| + |(\mathrm{z} - \mathrm{u}) + 2(\mathrm{v} - \mathrm{w})|) \\ &= \frac{3}{16}(\mathrm{v} - \mathrm{w} + \mathrm{z} - \mathrm{u}), \end{aligned}$$

i.e.,

$$\phi(\omega(f(\mathrm{v}, \mathrm{u}), f(\mathrm{w}, \mathrm{z}))) = \frac{3}{16}(\mathrm{v} - \mathrm{w} + \mathrm{z} - \mathrm{u}). \tag{17}$$

Additionally,

$$\begin{aligned}\phi(\omega((v,u),(w,z))) - \psi(\omega((v,u),(w,z))) &= \frac{\omega((v,u),(w,z))}{2} - \frac{\omega((v,u),(w,z))}{16} \\ &= \frac{7}{16}\omega((v,u),(w,z)) \\ &= \frac{7}{32}(v - w + z - u),\end{aligned}$$

i.e.,

$$\phi(\omega((v,u),(w,z))) - \psi(\omega((v,u),(w,z))) = \frac{7}{32}(v - w + z - u). \tag{18}$$

From (17) *and* (18), *one obtains*

$$\begin{aligned}\phi(\omega(f(v,u),f(w,z))) \leq\ & \phi(\omega((v,u),(w,z))) - \psi(\omega((v,u),(w,z))) + \ell \cdot \min\{\omega((v,u),f(v,u)), \\ & \omega((w,z),f(w,z)), \omega((v,u),f(w,z)), \omega((w,z),f(v,u))\},\end{aligned}$$

where $\ell \geq 0$ is arbitrary. Thus, the contractivity condition (v) holds. Further, here $f(\mathbb{V})$ is also $\wp$-directed and hence by Theorem 4, f enjoys a unique fixed point $v = (0,0)$.

Example 2. *Take $\mathbb{V} := (-1,1]$ with the usual metric ω. On $\mathbb{V}$, define a binary relation $\wp$ by*

$$\wp = \{(v,u) \in \mathbb{V}^2 : v > u \geq 0\}.$$

Then $(\mathbb{V},\omega)$ is a $\wp$-complete metric space.

Define

$$\phi(t) = \begin{cases} t, & \text{if } 0 \leq t \leq 1 \\ t^2, & \text{if } t > 1 \end{cases} \quad \text{and} \quad \psi(t) = \begin{cases} \frac{t^2}{2}, & \text{if } 0 \leq t \leq 1, \\ 1, & \text{if } t > 1. \end{cases}$$

Then, $\phi \in \Phi$ and $\psi \in \Psi$. Define a map $f : \mathbb{V} \to \mathbb{V}$ as

$$f(v) - \begin{cases} v+1, & \text{if } -1 < v < 0, \\ v - \frac{v^2}{2}, & \text{if } 0 \leq v \leq 1. \end{cases}$$

Take $v, u \in \mathbb{V}$ with $(v,u) \in \wp$, then $v > u \geq 0$. Thus, we have

$$\begin{aligned}\phi(\omega(fv,fu)) &= (v - \frac{1}{2}v^2) - (u - \frac{1}{2}u^2) \\ &= (v-u) - \frac{1}{2}(v-u)(v+u) \leq (v-u) - \frac{1}{2}(v-u)^2 \\ &\leq \phi(\omega(v,u)) - \psi(\omega(v,u)) + \min\{\omega(v,fv), \omega(u,fu), \omega(v,fu), \omega(u,fv)\}.\end{aligned}$$

Therefore, f verifies condition (v) of Theorem 3. Here $\wp$ is locally finitely f-transitive and f-closed. Left over the predictions of Theorems 3 and 4 are satisfied and f enjoys a unique fixed point $v = 0$.

Example 3. *Let $\mathbf{V} = [0,1)$ with Euclidean metric ω. Let $f : \mathbf{V} \to \mathbf{V}$ be a map defined by*

$$f(v) = \begin{cases} \frac{v}{2}, & \text{if } v \in \mathbb{Q} \cap \mathbf{V} \\ 0, & \text{if } v \in \mathbb{Q}^c \cap \mathbf{V}. \end{cases}$$

On $\mathbb{V}$, define a binary relation $\wp$ by

$$\wp = \{(v,u) \in \mathbb{V}^2 : vu \in \{v,u\}.$$

Then, $\wp$ is locally finitely f-transitive, f-closed as well as ω-self-closed.

Define

$$\phi(t) = t,\ \psi(t) = \frac{t}{2}.$$

Then, $\phi \in \Phi$ *and* $\psi \in \Psi$. *Here, f verifies condition* (v) *of Theorem 3 for* $\ell = 2$. *Left over, the predictions of Theorems 3 and 4 are satisfied and f enjoys a unique fixed point* $\bar{v} = 0$.

Remark 2. *The involved map in Example 3 is not* φ*-contraction as in particular for the pair* $v = \frac{1}{2}$ *and* $u = \frac{1}{\sqrt{2}}$, *we have*

$$\phi(\omega(fv, fu)) = \frac{1}{4}$$

and

$$\begin{aligned}&\phi(\omega(v,u)) - \psi(\omega(v,u)) + \ell \cdot \min\{\omega(v,fv), \omega(u,fu), \omega(v,fu), \omega(u,fv)\}\\ &= \left(\frac{1}{2} - \frac{1}{\sqrt{2}}\right) - \frac{1}{2}\left(\frac{1}{2} - \frac{1}{\sqrt{2}}\right) + 2 \cdot \frac{1}{4} = \frac{3}{4} - \frac{1}{2\sqrt{2}} = \frac{3-\sqrt{2}}{4} > \frac{1}{4}.\end{aligned}$$

Thus, Example 3 cannot work in the context of ordinary metric space, which substantiates the utility of fixed-point outcomes in relational metric space over the corresponding outcomes in ordinary metric space.

5. An Application

Consider the nonlinear Fredholm integral equation of the form:

$$v(s) = \theta(s) + \int_0^1 M(s,\tau)F(\tau, v(\tau))d\tau, \qquad s \in [0,1]. \tag{19}$$

Here $\theta : I \to \mathbb{R}$, $F : I \times \mathbb{R} \to \mathbb{R}$ and $M : I^2 \to \mathbb{R}$ remain functions, where $I := [0,1]$. As usual, $C(I)$ indicates the family of real continuous maps on I.

Definition 6. $\eta \in \mathcal{C}(I)$ *is known as a lower solution of* (19) *if*

$$\eta(s) \leq \theta(s) + \int_0^1 M(s,\tau)F(\tau, \eta(\tau))d\tau,\ \forall\, s \in I.$$

Definition 7. $\mu \in \mathcal{C}(I)$ *is known as an upper solution of* (19) *if*

$$\mu(s) \geq \theta(s) + \int_0^1 M(s,\tau)F(\tau, \mu(\tau))d\tau,\ \forall\, s \in I.$$

Ω shall stand for the family of functions $\varphi : \mathbb{R}_+ \to \mathbb{R}_+$ such that

(i) φ is increasing;
(ii) $\exists\, \psi \in \Psi$ such that $\varphi(t) = t - \psi(t)$, for all $t \in \mathbb{R}_+$.

Theorem 5. *In conjunction with Problem* (19), *assuming that*

(I) θ, F *and* M *are continuous,*
(II) $M(s,\tau) > 0, \quad \forall\, s,\tau \in I,$
(III) $\exists\, \varphi \in \Omega$, *verifying*

$$0 \leq F(s,a) - F(s,b) \leq \varphi(a-b), \quad \forall\, s \in I \text{ and } \forall\, a,b \in \mathbb{R} \text{ with } a \geq b,$$

(IV) $\sup_{s \in I} \int_0^1 M(s,\tau)d\tau = 1.$

Furthermore, the problem has a unique solution if (19) *has a lower solution.*

Proof. On $\mathbb{V} := \mathcal{C}(I)$, define a metric ω by

$$\omega(v,u) = \sup_{s \in I} |v(s) - u(s)|, \quad \forall\, v,u \in \mathbb{V}. \tag{20}$$

On $\mathbb{V}$, define a relation $\wp$ by

$$\wp = \{(v,u) \in \mathbb{V}^2 : v(s) \leq u(s),\ \forall\, s \in I\}. \tag{21}$$

Take a map $\mathbf{f} : \mathbb{V} \to \mathbb{V}$ defined by

$$(\mathbf{f}v)(s) = \theta(s) + \int_0^1 M(s,\tau)F(\tau, v(\tau))d\tau, \quad \forall\, s \in \mathbb{V}. \tag{22}$$

We are going to ensure all of the assertions of Theorems 3 and 4.
(i) If $\eta \in \mathbb{V}$ is a lower solution of (19), then

$$\eta(s) \leq \theta(s) + \int_0^1 M(s,\tau)F(\tau,\eta(\tau))d\tau = (\mathbf{f}\eta)(s)$$

so that $(\eta, \mathbf{f}\eta) \in \wp$.
(ii) $(\mathbb{V}, \omega)$ being a complete metric space is $\wp$-complete.
(iii) Take $v, u \in \mathbb{V}$ verifying $(v,u) \in \wp$. Using assumption (III), we obtain

$$F(s, v(\tau)) - F(s, u(\tau)) \leq 0, \quad \forall\, s, \tau \in I. \tag{23}$$

Making use of (22), (23) and condition (II), we find

$$(\mathbf{f}v)(s) - (\mathbf{f}u)(s) = \int_0^1 M(s,\tau)[F(\tau, v(\tau)) - F(\tau, u(\tau))]d\tau \leq 0,$$

so that $(\mathbf{f}v)(s) \leq (\mathbf{f}u)(s)$, which, using (21), yields that $(\mathbf{f}v, \mathbf{f}u) \in \wp$ and hence $\wp$ remains $\mathbf{f}$-closed. Also, $\wp$ is locally finitely $\mathbf{f}$-transitive.
(iv) Let $\{v_\imath\} \subset \mathbb{V}$ be a $\wp$-preserving sequence such that $v_\imath \xrightarrow{\omega} \varpi \in \mathbb{V}$. Then for every $s \in I$, $\{v_\imath(s)\}$ is an increasing real sequence such that $v_\imath(s) \xrightarrow{\mathbb{R}} \varpi(s)$. This yields that $v_\imath(s) \leq \varpi(s)$, $\forall\, \imath \in \mathbb{N}$ and $\forall\, s \in I$ so that $(v_\imath, \varpi) \in \wp$, $\forall\, \imath \in \mathbb{N}$. Thus, $\wp$ is ω-self-closed.
(v) Take $v, u \in \mathbb{V}$ with $(v,u) \in \wp$. By (III), (20) and (22), we conclude

$$\begin{aligned} \omega(\mathbf{f}v, \mathbf{f}u) &= \sup_{s\in I} |(\mathbf{f}v)(s) - (\mathbf{f}u)(s)| = \sup_{s\in I}[(\mathbf{f}u)(s) - (\mathbf{f}v)(s)] \\ &= \sup_{s\in I} \int_0^1 M(s,\tau)[F(\tau, u(\tau)) - F(\tau, v(\tau))]d\tau \\ &\leq \sup_{s\in I} \int_0^1 M(s,\tau)\varphi(u(\tau) - v(\tau))d\tau. \end{aligned} \tag{24}$$

As φ is increasing and $0 \leq u(\tau) - v(\tau) \leq \omega(v,u)$, we obtain $\varphi(u(\tau) - v(\tau)) \leq \varphi(\omega(v,u))$ and hence (24) reduces to

$$\omega(\mathbf{f}v, \mathbf{f}u) \leq \varphi(\omega(v,u)) \sup_{s\in I} \int_0^1 M(s,\tau)d\tau = \varphi(\omega(v,u))$$

so that

$$\begin{aligned} \omega(\mathbf{f}v, \mathbf{f}u) &\leq \omega(v,u) - \psi(\omega(v,u)) + \ell \cdot \min\{\omega(v,\mathbf{f}v), \omega(u,\mathbf{f}u), \omega(v,\mathbf{f}u), \omega(u,\mathbf{f}v))\}, \\ \forall &\quad v,u \in \mathbb{V} \text{ such that } (v,u) \in \wp, \end{aligned}$$

where $\ell \geq 0$ is arbitrary. Now take $v, u \in \mathbb{V}$ arbitrary. Set $w := \max\{\mathbf{f}v, \mathbf{f}u\} \in \mathbb{V}$, then we have $(\mathbf{f}v, w) \in \wp$ and $(\mathbf{f}u, w) \in \wp$. Hence, $\mathbf{f}(\mathbb{V})$ is $\wp$-directed. Consequently, by Theorem 4, $\mathbf{f}$ admits a unique fixed point, which in lieu of (22) remains a unique solution of (19). □

Theorem 6. *In conjunction with Problem* (I)–(IV) *of Theorem 5, the problem* (19) *admits a unique solution if the problem has an upper solution.*

Proof. Consider a metric ω on $\mathbb{V} := C(I)$ and a map $\mathbf{f} : \mathbb{V} \to \mathbb{V}$ like as the proof of Theorem 5. Take a relation $\wp'$ on $\mathbb{V}$ as:

$$\wp' = \{(v, u) \in \mathbb{V}^2 : v(s) \geq u(s),\ \forall\, s \in I\}. \tag{25}$$

If $\mu \in \mathbb{V}$ is an upper solution of (19), then we have

$$\mu(s) \geq \theta(s) + \int_0^1 M(s,\tau)\mathcal{F}(\tau, \mu(\tau))d\tau = (\mathbf{f}\mu)(s)$$

implying thereby $(\mu, \mathbf{f}\mu) \in \wp'$.

Take $v, u \in \mathbb{V}$, verifying $(v, u) \in \wp'$. Using assumption (III), we obtain

$$\mathcal{F}(s, v(\tau)) - \mathcal{F}(s, u(\tau)) \geq 0, \quad \forall\, s, \tau \in I. \tag{26}$$

By (22), (26) and assumption (II), we obtain

$$(\mathbf{f}v)(s) - (\mathbf{f}u)(s) = \int_0^1 M(s,\tau)[\mathcal{F}(\tau, v(\tau)) - \mathcal{F}(\tau, u(\tau))]d\tau \geq 0,$$

so that $(\mathbf{f}v)(s) \geq (\mathbf{f}u)(s)$, which, using (25), yields that $(\mathbf{f}v, \mathbf{f}u) \in \wp'$ and hence $\wp'$ is $\mathbf{f}$-closed.

Let $\{v_\imath\} \subset \mathbb{V}$ be a $\wp'$-preserving sequence such that $v_\imath \xrightarrow{\omega} \varpi \in \mathbb{V}$. Then for every $s \in I$, $\{v_\imath(s)\}$ is a decreasing real sequence such that $v_\imath(s) \xrightarrow{\mathbb{R}} \varpi(s)$. This implies that $v_\imath(s) \geq \varpi(s)$, $\forall\, \imath \in \mathbb{N}$ and $\forall\, s \in I$ so that $(v_\imath, \varpi) \in \wp'$, $\forall\, \imath \in \mathbb{N}$. Therefore, $\wp'$ remains ω-self-closed.

Therefore, all the assumptions of Theorems 3 and 4 are verified for the metric space $(\mathbb{V}, \omega)$, the map $\mathbf{f}$ and the relation $\wp'$. This concludes the proof. □

Intending to illustrate Theorem 5, one considers the following example.

Example 4. *Consider the integral equation of the form* (19)*, whereas* $\theta(s) = 2(1 - 2s^2)$, $\mathcal{F}(\tau, \xi) = \frac{1}{3}\xi$, *and* $M(s,\tau) = 2s\tau$. *Define a function* $\varphi : [0,\infty) \to [0,\infty)$ *by* $\varphi(t) = \frac{2}{3}t$. *Obviously, assumptions* (I)–(IV) *of Theorem 5 is satisfied. Moreover,* $\theta = 0$ *forms a lower solution for the present problem. Therefore, Theorem 5 can be applied to the given problem, and hence,* $v(s) = 2(1 - 2s^2)$ *forms the unique solution of the integral equation.*

6. Conclusions

In this work, we investigated fixed-point outcomes for a strict almost (ϕ, ψ)-contraction map in the relational metric space. The underlying relation in our findings being locally finitely $\mathbf{f}$-transitive is restrictive, but the class of functional contraction is weakened. The findings investigated herewith enrich, improve, and unify several known findings, especially due to Babu et al. [15], Alharbi and Khan [26], Sk et al. [30], and similar others. Several examples are also attempted to convey our outcomes. Our outcomes are applied to compute a unique positive solution of a specific nonlinear Fredholm integral equation where the existence of a unique solution is ensured by the presence of an upper or a lower solution. In the foreseeable future, researchers might extend our findings to a pair of maps or more general distance spaces.

Author Contributions: Conceptualization, E.A.A. and F.A.K.; Methodology, E.A. and A.A.; Formal analysis, H.I.A.M.; Investigation, H.I.A.M.; Resources, F.M.A. and F.A.K.; Writing—original draft, E.A. and A.A.; Writing—review & editing, F.M.A. and E.A.A.; Supervision, F.A.K.; Funding acquisition, F.M.A., E.A. and A.A. All authors have read and approved to the final version of the manuscript.

Funding: This study is received no external funding.

Data Availability Statement: Data are contained within the article.

Acknowledgments: All authors are thankful to two academic editors and two anonymous referees for their lucrative remarks and pertinent comments that helped us improve the depth of present manuscript.

Conflicts of Interest: All authors declare no conflicts of interest.

References

1. Berinde, V. Approximating fixed points of weak contractions using the Picard iteration. *Nonlinear Anal. Forum.* **2004**, *9*, 43–53.
2. Berinde, V.; Păcurar, M. Fixed points and continuity of almost contractions. *Fixed Point Theory* **2008**, *9*, 23–34.
3. Kannan, R. Some results on fixed points. *Bull. Calcutta Math. Soc.* **1968**, *60*, 71–76.
4. Chatterjea, S.K. Fixed point theorem. *C. R. Acad Bulgar Sci.* **1972**, *25*, 727–730. [CrossRef]
5. Zamfirescu, T. Fix point theorems in metric spaces. *Arch. Math.* **1972**, *23*, 292–298. [CrossRef]
6. Ćirić, L.B. A generalization of Banach's contraction principle. *Proc. Am. Math. Soc.* **1974**, *45*, 267—273. [CrossRef]
7. Berinde, V.; Takens, F. *Iterative Approximation of Fixed Points*; Springer: Berlin/Heidelberg, Germany, 2007; Volume 1912.
8. Berinde, M.; Berinde, V. On a general class of multi-valued weakly Picard mappings. *J. Math. Anal. Appl.* **2007**, *326*, 772–782. [CrossRef]
9. Păcurar, M. Sequences of almost contractions and fixed points. *Carpathian J. Math.* **2008**, *24*, 101–109.
10. Berinde, V. General constructive fixed point theorems for Ćirić-type almost contractions in metric spaces. *Carpathian J. Math.* **2008**, *24*, 10–19.
11. Alghamdi, M.A.; Berinde, V.; Shahzad, N. Fixed points of non-self almost contractions. *Carpathian J. Math.* **2014**, *30*, 7–14. [CrossRef]
12. Altun, I.; Acar, Ö. Fixed point theorems for weak contractions in the sense of Berinde on partial metric spaces. *Topol. Appl.* **2012**, *159*, 2642–2648. [CrossRef]
13. Berinde, V.; Vetro, F. Common fixed points of mappings satisfying implicit contractive conditions. *Fixed Point Theory Appl.* **2012**, *105*, 8. [CrossRef]
14. Berinde, V. Stability of Picard iteration for contractive mappings satisfying an implicit relation. *Carpathian J. Math.* **2011**, *27*, 13–23. [CrossRef]
15. Babu, G.V.R.; Sandhy, M.L.; Kameshwari, M.V.R. A note on a fixed point theorem of Berinde on weak contractions. *Carpathian J. Math.* **2008**, *24*, 8–12.
16. Alam, A.; Imdad, M. Relation-theoretic contraction principle. *J. Fixed Point Theory Appl.* **2015**, *17*, 693–702. [CrossRef]
17. Alam, A.; Imdad, M. Relation-theoretic metrical coincidence theorems. *Filomat* **2017**, *31* 4421–4439. [CrossRef]
18. Alam, A.; George, R.; Imdad, M. Refinements to relation-theoretic contraction principle. *Axioms* **2022**, *316*, 6. [CrossRef]
19. Almarri, B.; Mujahid, S.; Uddin, I. New fixed point results for Geraghty contractions and their applications. *J. Appl. Anal. Comput.* **2023** *13*, 2788–2798. [CrossRef]
20. Hossain, A.; Alam, A.; Sessa, S.; Khan, Q.H. Relation-theoretic weak contractions and applications. *Mathematics* **2023**, *11*, 15. [CrossRef]
21. Hasanuzzaman, M.; Imdad, M. A unified Feng–Liu type result in relational metric spaces with an application. *J. Fixed Point Theory Appl.* **2023**, *25*, 13. [CrossRef]
22. Choudhury, B.S.; Chakraborty, P. Fixed point problem of a multi-valued Kannan–Geraghty type contraction via w-distance. *J. Anal.* **2023**, *31*, 439–458. [CrossRef]
23. Antal, S.; Khantwal, D.; Negi, S.; Gairola, U.C. Fixed points theorems for (φ, ψ, p)-weakly contractive mappings via w-distance in relational metric spaces with applications. *Filomat* **2023**, *37*, 7319–7328. [CrossRef]
24. Khan, F.A. Almost contractions under binary relations. *Axioms* **2022**, *441*, 7. [CrossRef]
25. Algehyne, E.A.; Altaweel, N.H.; Areshi, M.; Khan, F.A. Relation-theoretic almost ϕ-contractions with an application to elastic beam equations. *AIMS Math.* **2023**, *8*, 18919–18929. [CrossRef]
26. Alharbi, A.F.; Khan, F.A. Almost Boyd-Wong type contractions under binary relations with applications to boundary value problems. *Axioms* **2023**, *896*, 12. [CrossRef]
27. Khan, F.A.; Aldhabani, M.S.; Alamer, A.; Alshaban, E.; Alamrani, F.M.; Mohammed, H.I.A. Almost nonlinear contractions under locally finitely transitive relations with applications to integral equations. *Mathematics* **2023**, *4749*, 11. [CrossRef]
28. Dutta, P.N.; Choudhury, B.S. A generalisation of contraction principle in metric spaces. *Fixed Point Theory Appl.* **2008**, *2008*, 8. [CrossRef]
29. Alam, A.; Sk, F.; Khan, Q.H. Discussion on generalized nonlinear contractions. *Politehn. Univ. Bucharest Sci. Bull. Ser. A Appl. Math. Phys.* **2022**, *84*, 23–34.

30. Sk, F.; Khan, F.A.; Khan, Q.H.; Alam, A. Relation-preserving generalized nonlinear contractions and related fixed point theorems. *AIMS Math.* **2022**, *7*, 6634–6649. [CrossRef]
31. Alam, A.; Imdad, M. Nonlinear contractions in metric spaces under locally T-transitive binary relations. *Fixed Point Theory* **2018**, *19*, 13–24. [CrossRef]
32. Alam, A.; Arif, M.; Imdad, M. Metrical fixed point theorems via locally finitely T-transitive binary relations under certain control functions. *Miskolc Mathematical Notes* **2019**, *20*, 59–73. [CrossRef]
33. Arif, M.; Imdad, M.; Alam, A. Fixed point theorems under locally T-transitive binary relations employing Matkowski contractions. *Miskolc Math. Notes* **2022**, *23*, 71–83. [CrossRef]
34. Filali, D.; Khan, F.A. Relational strict almost contractions employing test functions and an application to nonlinear integral equations. *Mathematics* **2024**, *12*, 10. [CrossRef]
35. Berzig, M.; Karapinar, E. Fixed Point results for $(\alpha\psi, \beta\phi)$-contractive mappings for a generalized altering distance. *Fixed Point Theory Appl.* **2013**, *2013*, 18. [CrossRef]
36. Turinici, M. Contractive maps in locally transitive relational metric spaces. *Sci. World J.* **2014**, *2014*, 10. [CrossRef] [PubMed]
37. Lipschutz, S. *Schaum's Outlines of Theory and Problems of Set Theory and Related Topics*; McGraw-Hill: New York, NY, USA, 1964.
38. Samet, B.; Turinici, M. Fixed point theorems on a metric space endowed with an arbitrary binary relation and applications. *Commun. Math. Anal.* **2012**, *13*, 82–97.
39. Kolman, B.; Busby, R.C.; Ross, S. *Discrete Mathematical Structures*, 6th ed.; Pearson/Prentice Hall: Hoboken, NJ, USA, 2009.

axioms

MDPI

Article

Fixed-Point Results of *F*-Contractions in Bipolar *p*-Metric Spaces

Nabanita Konwar [1] and Pradip Debnath [2,*]

1 Department of Mathematics, Birjhora Mahavidyalaya, Bongaigaon 783380, Assam, India; nabnitakonwar@gmail.com
2 Department of Mathematical Sciences, Tezpur University, Tezpur 784028, Assam, India
* Correspondence: pradip@tezu.ernet.in

Abstract: In this paper, we present new findings on F-contraction in bipolar p-metric spaces. We establish a covariant Banach-type fixed-point theorem and a contravariant Reich-type fixed-point theorem based on F-contraction in these spaces. Additionally, we include an example that demonstrates the applicability of our results. Our results non-trivially extend this covariant Banach-type fixed-point theorem and contravariant Reich type theorem via the concept of F-contraction.

Keywords: covariant Banach-type fixed-point; contravarient Reich-type fixed-point; fixed point; F-contraction; bipolar p-metric spaces

MSC: 47H10; 54H25; 54E50

1. Introduction

The Banach fixed-point theorem, a key result in mathematics, was established in 1922. Following this, significant advancements occurred in fixed-point theory. In 1989, Bakhtin [1] and, in 1993, Czerwik [2] introduced various contraction conditions in b-metric spaces, extending the concept of metric spaces. In 2016, Mutlu and Gurdal [3,4] defined bipolar metric spaces and developed numerous theorems based on different contractive conditions. For a comprehensive study on the comparison of various definitions of contractive mappings, we refer to the famous work of Rhoades [5]. Wardowski [6] introduced the notion of F-contraction in 2012. For some recent works in F-contractions, we refer to [7–10]. In 2020, Roy and Saha [11] presented the concept of bipolar cone b-metric spaces. Paul et al. [12] proved some common fixed points in bipolar metric spaces. The idea of p-metric spaces was proposed by Parvaneh et al. [13] in 2017. Concurrent developments in b-metric spaces and Branciari distance were presented in [14,15]. Some historial notes, surveys and non-trivial generalizations of metric spaces and different versions of the Banach's fixed-point theorem may be found in [16–21] and in the references therein.

In this paper, we introduce the concept of F-contraction in bipolar p-metric spaces and explore covariant and contravariant fixed-point theorems within this new framework. Additionally, we present an example to illustrate and validate one of the results.

For some very recent interesting covariant and contravariant fixed-point theorems on bipolar and bipolar-p-metric spaces, we refer to the works of Mutlu et al. [22,23] and Roy et al. [24], respectively. In this paper, in particular, we non-trivially extend Theorems 3.2 and 3.4 of [24] using Wardowski's F-contraction [6].

2. Preliminaries

Some important results that are related to the present work are listed below:

Definition 1 ([1,2]). *Suppose $\mathfrak{M}$ is a non-empty set and $\mathfrak{d}_{\mathfrak{b}} : \mathfrak{M} \times \mathfrak{M} \to [0, \infty)$ is a mapping. If $\mathfrak{d}_{\mathfrak{b}}$ satisfies the following conditions:*

(1) $\mathfrak{d}_{\mathfrak{b}}(\varsigma_1, \varsigma_2) = 0$ *if and only if* $\varsigma_1 = \varsigma_2$*;*
(2) $\mathfrak{d}_{\mathfrak{b}}(\varsigma_1, \varsigma_2) = \mathfrak{d}_{\mathfrak{b}}(\varsigma_2, \varsigma_1)$ *for all* $\varsigma_1, \varsigma_2 \in \mathfrak{M}$*;*
(3) There exists a real number $s \geq 1$ *such that* $\mathfrak{d}_{\mathfrak{b}}(\varsigma_1, \varsigma_3) \leq s[\mathfrak{d}_{\mathfrak{b}}(\varsigma_1, \varsigma_2) + \mathfrak{d}_{\mathfrak{b}}(\varsigma_2, \varsigma_3)]$ *for all* $\varsigma_1, \varsigma_2, \varsigma_3 \in \mathfrak{M}$*, then* $\mathfrak{d}_{\mathfrak{b}}$ *is known as a b-metric on* $\mathfrak{M}$ *and* $(\mathfrak{M}, \mathfrak{d}_{\mathfrak{b}})$ *is a b-metric space.*

Definition 2 ([25]). *Suppose* $(\mathfrak{M}, \mathfrak{d}_{\mathfrak{b}})$ *is a b-metric space and* $\{u_n\}$ *is a sequence in* $\mathfrak{M}$*. Then,*
(a) $\{u_n\}$ *is called a convergent sequence in* $(\mathfrak{M}, \mathfrak{d}_{\mathfrak{b}})$*, if for every* $\varepsilon > 0$, $\exists\, n_0 \in \mathbb{N}$*, such that* $\mathfrak{d}_{\mathfrak{b}}(u_n, u) < \varepsilon\ \forall\, n > n_0$*. It is denoted by* $\lim_{n\to\infty} u_n = u$ *or* $u_n \to u$ *as* $n \to \infty$*.*
(b) $\{u_n\}$ *is called a Cauchy sequence in* $(\mathfrak{M}, \mathfrak{d}_{\mathfrak{b}})$ *if for every* $\varepsilon > 0\ \exists\, n_0 \in \mathbb{N}$*, such that* $\mathfrak{d}_{\mathfrak{b}}(u_n, u_{n+p}) < \varepsilon\ \forall\, n > n_0, p > 0$*.*
(c) $(\mathfrak{M}, \mathfrak{d}_{\mathfrak{b}})$ *is called a complete b-metric space if every Cauchy sequence in* $\mathfrak{M}$ *converges to some* $u \in \mathfrak{M}$*.*

Definition 3 ([6]). *Suppose the function* $\mathfrak{F} : (0, \infty) \to (-\infty, +\infty)$ *satisfies the following conditions:*
(F1) $\mathfrak{F}$ *is strictly increasing;*
(F2) For every sequence $\{t_n\}_{n\in\mathbb{N}} \subset (0, \infty)$, $\lim_{n\to\infty} t_n = 0$ *iff* $\lim_{n\to\infty} \mathfrak{F}(t_n) = -\infty$*;*
(F3) There exist $s \in (0, 1)$*, such that* $\lim_{t\to 0} t^s \mathfrak{F}(t) = 0$*.*

Let $\mathcal{F}$ *be the collection of all functions* $\mathfrak{F}$ *and let* $(\mathfrak{M}, d)$ *be a metric space. Then, a mapping* $S : \mathfrak{M} \to \mathfrak{M}$ *is known as an* $\mathfrak{F}$*-contraction if* $\exists\, \tau > 0, \mathfrak{F} \in \mathcal{F}$*, such that* $\forall\, \mathfrak{P}, \mathfrak{q} \in \mathfrak{M}$*, and we have*

$$d(S(\mathfrak{P}), S(\mathfrak{q})) > 0 \Rightarrow \tau + \mathfrak{F}(d(S(\mathfrak{P}), S(\mathfrak{q}))) \leq \mathfrak{F}(d(\mathfrak{P}, \mathfrak{q})).$$

Definition 4 ([13]). *Let* $\mathfrak{X} \neq \phi$*. A mapping* $\mathfrak{d}_{\mathfrak{p}} : \mathfrak{X} \times \mathfrak{X} \longrightarrow [0, \infty)$ *is called an extended b-metric or p-metric if* $\exists$ *a strictly increasing continuous mapping* $\Omega : [0, \infty) \longrightarrow [0, \infty)$ *with* $\Omega^{-1}(t) \leq t \leq \Omega(t), \forall\, t \geq 0$ *and* $\Omega^{-1}(0) = 0 = \Omega(0)$*, such that* $\forall\, x, y, z \in \mathfrak{X}$*, and the following conditions hold:*

(i) $\mathfrak{d}_{\mathfrak{p}}(\varsigma_1, \varsigma_2) = 0$ *iff* $\varsigma_1 = \varsigma_2$*;*
(ii) $\mathfrak{d}_{\mathfrak{p}}(\varsigma_1, \varsigma_2) = \mathfrak{d}_{\mathfrak{p}}(\varsigma_2, \varsigma_1)$*, for all* $\varsigma_1, \varsigma_2 \in \mathfrak{X} \bigcap \mathfrak{Y}$*;*
(iii) $\mathfrak{d}_{\mathfrak{p}}(\varsigma_1, \varsigma_3) \leq \Omega(\mathfrak{d}_{\mathfrak{p}}(\varsigma_1, \varsigma_2) + \mathfrak{d}_{\mathfrak{p}}(\varsigma_2, \varsigma_3))$*.*

Then, $(\mathfrak{X}, \mathfrak{d}_{\mathfrak{p}})$ *is known as a p-metric space.*

Definition 5 ([3]). *Consider two non-empty sets* $\mathfrak{X}$ *and* $\mathfrak{Y}$*. A mapping* $\mathfrak{d}_{\mathfrak{bi}} : \mathfrak{X} \times \mathfrak{Y} \longrightarrow [0, \infty)$ *is called bipolar-metric on* $(\mathfrak{X}, \mathfrak{Y})$ *if it satisfies the following conditions:*

(i) $\mathfrak{d}_{\mathfrak{bi}}(\varsigma_1, \varsigma_2) = 0$ *iff* $\varsigma_1 = \varsigma_2$*;*
(ii) $\mathfrak{d}_{\mathfrak{bi}}(\varsigma_1, \varsigma_2) = \mathfrak{d}_{\mathfrak{bi}}(\varsigma_2, \varsigma_1)$*, for all* $\varsigma_1, \varsigma_2 \in \mathfrak{X} \bigcap \mathfrak{Y}$*;*
(iii) $\mathfrak{d}_{\mathfrak{bi}}(\varsigma_1, \varsigma_3) \leq \mathfrak{d}_{\mathfrak{bi}}(\varsigma_1, \varsigma_2) + \mathfrak{d}_{\mathfrak{bi}}(x_1, \varsigma_2) + \mathfrak{d}_{\mathfrak{bi}}(x_1, \varsigma_3)$*, for all* $(\varsigma_1, \varsigma_2), (x_1, \varsigma_3) \in \mathfrak{X} \times \mathfrak{Y}$*.*

Then, $(\mathfrak{X}, \mathfrak{Y}, \mathfrak{d}_{\mathfrak{bi}})$ *is known as a bipolar-metric space.*

Definition 6 ([24]). *Suppose* Ω *is a strictly increasing continuous function. Consider the two non-empty sets of mappings:*

$$\psi = \{\Omega : [0, \infty) \longrightarrow [0, \infty) : \Omega^{-1}(t) \leq t \leq \Omega(t), \forall t \geq 0\} \text{ and}$$
$$\psi^* = \{\Omega \in \psi : \Omega^{-1}(t_1 + t_2) \leq \Omega^{-1}(t_1) + \Omega^{-1}(t_2), \forall t_1, t_2 \geq 0\}.$$

Let $\mathfrak{X}$ *and* $\mathfrak{Y}$ *be two non-empty sets. A mapping* $p : \mathfrak{X} \times \mathfrak{Y} \longrightarrow [0, \infty)$ *is known as a bipolar p-metric on* $(\mathfrak{X}, \mathfrak{Y})$ *if it satisfies the following three conditions for a function* $\Omega \in \psi$*:*

(i) $p(\varsigma_1, \varsigma_2) = 0$ *iff* $\varsigma_1 = \varsigma_2$*;*
(ii) $p(\varsigma_1, \varsigma_2) = p(\varsigma_2, \varsigma_1)$*, for all* $(\varsigma_1, \varsigma_2) \in (\mathfrak{X} \bigcap \mathfrak{Y})^2$*;*
(iii) $p(\varsigma_1, \varsigma_3) \leq \Omega[p(\varsigma_1, \varsigma_2) + p(x_1, \varsigma_2) + p(x_1, \varsigma_3)]$*, for all* $(\varsigma_1, \varsigma_2), (x_1, \varsigma_3) \in \mathfrak{X} \times \mathfrak{Y}$*.*

And $(\mathfrak{X}, \mathfrak{Y}, p)$ *is called a bipolar p-metric space.*

Remark 1. *The definitions of sequence, Cauchy sequence, convergent sequence etc., in a bipolar p-metric space are exactly the same as in the case of a usual metric space or b-metric space. Hence, we omit their exact definitions to avoid repetition.*

Remark 2. *Any metric space, b-metric space, p-metric space, bipolar metric space, and bipolar b-metric space is also a bipolar p-metric space. As such, the results established in the current paper are also true in the aforementioned less general metric spaces.*

Definition 7 **([24]).** *Consider two pairs of sets $(\mathfrak{X}_1, \mathfrak{Y}_1)$ and $(\mathfrak{X}_2, \mathfrak{Y}_2)$. The function $f : \mathfrak{X}_1 \bigcup \mathfrak{Y}_1 \to \mathfrak{X}_2 \bigcup \mathfrak{Y}_2$ is known as covariant mapping if $f(\mathfrak{X}_1) \subset \mathfrak{X}_2$ and $f(\mathfrak{Y}_1) \subset \mathfrak{Y}_2$ and it is denoted by $f : (\mathfrak{X}_1, \mathfrak{Y}_1) \rightrightarrows (\mathfrak{X}_2, \mathfrak{Y}_2)$.*

Definition 8 **([24]).** *Suppose $(\mathfrak{X}_1, \mathfrak{Y}_1)$ and $(\mathfrak{X}_2, \mathfrak{Y}_2)$ are two pairs of sets. The function $f : \mathfrak{X}_1 \bigcup \mathfrak{Y}_1 \to \mathfrak{X}_2 \bigcup \mathfrak{Y}_2$ is known as contravariant mapping if $f(\mathfrak{X}_1) \subset \mathfrak{Y}_2$ and $f(\mathfrak{Y}_1) \subset \mathfrak{X}_2$ and it is denoted by $f : (\mathfrak{X}_1, \mathfrak{Y}_1) \rightleftharpoons (\mathfrak{X}_2, \mathfrak{Y}_2)$.*

3. Extended Interpolative $\mathfrak{F}$-Contraction

In this section, we present covariant-type and contravariant-type fixed-point theorems.

Theorem 1. *Consider a complete bipolar p-MS $(\mathfrak{X}, \mathfrak{Y}, p)$ for some $\Omega \in \psi^*$ and a covariant mapping $f : (\mathfrak{X}, \mathfrak{Y}, p) \rightrightarrows (\mathfrak{X}, \mathfrak{Y}, p)$ such that*

$$\tau + \mathfrak{F}(p(f(\varsigma_1), f(\varsigma_2))) \leq c_1 \mathfrak{F}(p(\varsigma_1, \varsigma_2))$$

holds for $(\varsigma_1, \varsigma_2) \in \mathfrak{X} \times \mathfrak{Y}$, $\tau > 0$, $c_1 \in \Delta_\Omega$ and for any $p(f(\varsigma_1), f(\varsigma_2)) > 0$.

Then, the function $f : \mathfrak{X} \bigcup \mathfrak{Y} \to \mathfrak{X} \bigcup \mathfrak{Y}$ has a unique fixed point.

Proof. Consider $(\varsigma_0, \zeta_0) \in \mathfrak{X} \times \mathfrak{Y}$. Let us consider the iterative sequences $\varsigma_n \subset \mathfrak{X}$ and $\zeta_n \subset \mathfrak{Y}$ such that $\varsigma_n - f(\varsigma_{n-1}) = f^n(\varsigma_0)$ and $\zeta_n = f(\zeta_{n-1}) - f^n(\zeta_0)$, for all $n \in \mathbb{N}$. Then, $(\{\varsigma_n\}, \{\zeta_n\})$ is a bisequence on $(\mathfrak{X}, \mathfrak{Y}, p)$ and $\varsigma_n \neq \zeta_n$.

The term bisequence means that the sequence $(\{\varsigma_n\}, \{\zeta_n\})$ is a subset of the Cartesian product of $\mathfrak{X}$ and $\mathfrak{Y}$. The concept of convergence of a bisequence is a natural extension of the concept of convergence of a sequence.

We then have

$$\begin{aligned}\tau + \mathfrak{F}(p(\varsigma_n, \zeta_n)) &= \tau + \mathfrak{F}(p(f(\varsigma_{n-1}), f(\zeta_{n-1}))) \\ &\leq c_1 \mathfrak{F}(p(\varsigma_{n-1}, \zeta_{n-1})).\end{aligned}$$

Therefore,

$$\begin{aligned}\mathfrak{F}(p(\varsigma_n, \zeta_n)) &\leq c_1 \mathfrak{F}(p(f(\varsigma_{n-1}), f(\zeta_{n-1}))) - \tau \\ &\leq c_1^2 \mathfrak{F}(p(\varsigma_{n-2}, \zeta_{n-2})) - 2\tau.\end{aligned}$$

Proceeding in this way, we have $\forall n \geq 1$,

$$\mathfrak{F}(p(\varsigma_n, \zeta_n)) \leq c_1^n \mathfrak{F}(p(\varsigma_0, \zeta_0)) - n\tau.$$

Taking the limit as $n \to \infty$,

$$\lim_{n \to \infty} \mathfrak{F}(p(\varsigma_n, \zeta_n)) = -\infty.$$

Then, from the second property of $\mathfrak{F}$-contraction, we have

$$\lim_{n \to \infty} p(\varsigma_n, \zeta_n) = 0.$$

Hence, from the third property of the $\mathfrak{F}$-contraction, $\forall n \in \mathbb{N}\ \exists\, t \in (0,1)$, such that

$$\lim_{n\to\infty} p(\varsigma_n,\zeta_n)^t\mathfrak{F}(p(\varsigma_n,\zeta_n)) = 0.$$

For all $n \in \mathbb{N}$, we have

$$\begin{aligned}
p(\varsigma_n,\zeta_n)^t\mathfrak{F}(p(\varsigma_n,\zeta_n)) - p(\varsigma_n,\zeta_n)^t\mathfrak{F}(p(\varsigma_0,\zeta_0)) \\
&\leq p(\varsigma_n,\zeta_n)^t(c_1^n\mathfrak{F}(p(\varsigma_0,\zeta_0)) - n\tau) - p(\varsigma_n,\zeta_n)^t\mathfrak{F}(p(\varsigma_0,\zeta_0)) \\
&= -p(\varsigma_n,\zeta_n)^t n\tau \\
&\leq 0.
\end{aligned}$$

From the third property of the $\mathfrak{F}$-contraction and taking the limit as $n \to \infty$, we have

$$\lim_{n\to\infty} np(\varsigma_n,\zeta_n)^t = 0$$

Hence, there exist $n_1 \in \mathbb{N}$ such that $np(\varsigma_n,\zeta_n)^t \leq 1$ for all $n \geq n_1$.
Therefore, $p(\varsigma_n,\zeta_n) \leq \frac{1}{n^{1/t}}$ for all $n \geq n_1$.
Again,

$$\begin{aligned}
\mathfrak{F}(p(\varsigma_n,\zeta_{n+1})) &= \mathfrak{F}(p(f(\varsigma_{n-1}),f(\zeta_n))) \\
&\leq c_1\mathfrak{F}(p(\varsigma_{n-1},\zeta_n)) - \tau \\
&\vdots \\
&= c_1^n\mathfrak{F}(p(\varsigma_0,\zeta_1)) - n\tau
\end{aligned}$$

Taking the limit as $n \to \infty$,

$$\lim_{n\to\infty} \mathfrak{F}(p(\varsigma_n,\zeta_{n+1})) = -\infty$$

From the second property of the F-contraction, we have

$$\lim_{n\to\infty} p(\varsigma_n,\zeta_{n+1}) = 0$$

Hence, from the third property of the F-contraction for all $n \in \mathbb{N}$, there exist $t \in (0,1)$, such that

$$\lim_{n\to\infty} p(\varsigma_n,\zeta_{n+1})^t\mathfrak{F}(p(\varsigma_n,\zeta_{n+1})) = 0$$

For all $n \in \mathbb{N}$, we have

$$\begin{aligned}
p(\varsigma_n,\zeta_{n+1})^t\mathfrak{F}(p(\varsigma_n,\zeta_{n+1})) - p(\varsigma_n,\zeta_{n+1})^t\mathfrak{F}(p(\varsigma_0,\zeta_1)) \\
&\leq p(\varsigma_n,\zeta_{n+1})^t(c_1^n\mathfrak{F}(p(\varsigma_0,\zeta_1)) - n\tau) - p(\varsigma_n,\zeta_{n+1})^t\mathfrak{F}(p(\varsigma_0,\zeta_1)) \\
&= -p(\varsigma_n,\zeta_{n+1})^t n\tau \\
&\leq 0.
\end{aligned}$$

From the third property of the $\mathfrak{F}$-contraction and taking the limit as $n \to \infty$, we have

$$\lim_{n\to\infty} np(\varsigma_n,\zeta_{n+1})^t = 0$$

Hence, there exist $n_2 \in \mathbb{N}$, such that $np(\varsigma_n,\zeta_{n+1})^t \leq 1$ for all $n \geq n_2$.
Therefore, $p(\varsigma_n,\zeta_{n+1}) \leq \frac{1}{n^{1/t}}$ for all $n \geq n_2$.
Consider $n_0 = \max\{n_1,n_2\}$.
For some $1 \leq n < m$, we have

$$
\begin{aligned}
& p(\varsigma_n,\zeta_m) \le \Omega[p(\varsigma_n,\zeta_n)+p(\varsigma_{n+1},\zeta_n)+p(\varsigma_{n+1},\zeta_m)] \\
\Rightarrow\ & \Omega^{-1}(p(\varsigma_n,\zeta_m)) \le \frac{1}{n^{\frac{1}{t}}}+\frac{1}{n^{\frac{1}{t}}}+p(\varsigma_{n+1},\zeta_m),\ \text{for all } n\ge n_0 \\
& = \frac{1}{n^{\frac{1}{t}}}+\frac{1}{n^{\frac{1}{t}}}+\Omega[p(\varsigma_{n+1},\zeta_{n+1})+p(\varsigma_{n+2},\zeta_{n+1})+p(\varsigma_{n+2},\zeta_m)] \\
\Rightarrow\ & \Omega^{-2}(p(\varsigma_n,\zeta_m)) \le \Omega^{-1}\left[\frac{1}{n^{\frac{1}{t}}}+\frac{1}{n^{\frac{1}{t}}}\right]+\frac{1}{(n+1)^{\frac{1}{t}}}+\frac{1}{(n+1)^{\frac{1}{t}}}+p(\varsigma_{n+2},\zeta_m)
\end{aligned}
$$

Proceeding in a similar way, we have

$$
\begin{aligned}
\Omega^{-(m-n+1)}(p(\varsigma_n,\zeta_m)) &\le \Omega^{-(m-n)}\left[\frac{1}{n^{\frac{1}{t}}}+\frac{1}{n^{\frac{1}{t}}}\right]+\Omega^{-(m-n)}\left[\frac{1}{(n+1)^{\frac{1}{t}}}+\frac{1}{(n+1)^{\frac{1}{t}}}\right] \\
&+\ldots+\Omega^{-1}\left[\frac{1}{(m-1)^{\frac{1}{t}}}+\frac{1}{(m-1)^{\frac{1}{t}}}\right]+p(\varsigma_{m+1},\zeta_m) \\
&\le \sum_{i=n}^{m}\Omega^{-(m-i)}\left[\frac{1}{i^{\frac{1}{t}}}+\frac{1}{i^{\frac{1}{t}}}\right],\ \text{for all } n\ge n_0
\end{aligned}
$$

Hence,

$$
p(\varsigma_n,\zeta_m) \le \Omega^{(m-n+1)}\left(\sum_{i=n}^{m}\Omega^{-(m-i)}\left[\frac{1}{i^{\frac{1}{t}}}+\frac{1}{i^{\frac{1}{t}}}\right]\right) \tag{1}
$$

Similarly, for any $1\le m<n$, we can show that

$$
p(\varsigma_n,\zeta_m) \le \Omega^{(m-n+1)}\left(\sum_{i=m}^{n}\Omega^{-(n-i)}\left[\frac{1}{i^{\frac{1}{t}}}+\frac{1}{i^{\frac{1}{t}}}\right]\right) \tag{2}
$$

Since $t\in(0,1)$, the right hand sides of Equations (1) and (2) trend toward 0 as $m,n\to\infty$.

Hence, the series is bi-convergent and $\{\varsigma_n,\zeta_n\}$ is a Cauchy bisequence in $(\mathfrak{X},\mathfrak{Y})$. Let the $\{\varsigma_n,\zeta_n\}$ biconverge to some $u\in\mathfrak{X}\bigcap\mathfrak{Y}$. Then, $\{\varsigma_n\}\to u$ and $\{\zeta_n\}\to u$, where $u\in\mathfrak{X}\bigcap\mathfrak{Y}$ and $\{f(\varsigma_n)\}=\{\varsigma_{n+1}\}$ where $u\in\mathfrak{X}\bigcap\mathfrak{Y}$. Again, since f is continuous, $f(\varsigma_n)\to f(u)$. Therefore, $f(u)=u$. Hence, u is a fixed point of f. If possible, let v is another fixed point of f.Then, we have $f(v)=v$, for some $v\in\mathfrak{X}\bigcap\mathfrak{Y}$.

Then,

$$
\tau \le \mathfrak{F}(p(f(u),f(v)))-\mathfrak{F}(p(u,v))=0
$$

which is a contradiction. Hence, $u=v$. Therefore, f has a unique fixed point in $(\mathfrak{X},\mathfrak{Y},p)$. □

Theorem 2. *Consider a complete bipolar p-MS* $(\mathfrak{X},\mathfrak{Y},p)$ *for some* $\Omega\in\psi^*$ *and a function* $f:(\mathfrak{X},\mathfrak{Y},p)\rightleftharpoons(\mathfrak{X},\mathfrak{Y},p)$*, which is contravariant such that*

$$
\tau+\mathfrak{F}(p(f(\zeta),f(\varsigma)))\le c_1\mathfrak{F}(p(\varsigma,\zeta))+c_2\mathfrak{F}(p(\varsigma,f(\varsigma)))+c_3\mathfrak{F}(p(f(\zeta),\zeta)),
$$

for $(\varsigma,y)\in X\times Y$ *and* $\tau>0$*, where* $c_1,c_2,c_3\ge 0$*, such that* $c_1+c_2+c_3<1$ *and* $\left(\frac{c_1+c_3}{1-c_2}\right)\left(\frac{c_1+c_2}{1-c_2}\right)\in\Delta_\Omega$.

Then, the function $f:\mathfrak{X}\bigcup\mathfrak{Y}\to\mathfrak{X}\bigcup\mathfrak{Y}\ \forall\, t>0,\ c_3t<\Omega^{-1}(t)$ *has a unique fixed point.*

Proof. Consider $\varsigma_0\in\mathfrak{X}$. Let us construct two iterative sequences $\varsigma_n\subset\mathfrak{X}$ and $\zeta_n\subset\mathfrak{Y}$ such that for some $n\ge 0$, we construct $\zeta_n=f(\varsigma_n)$ and $\varsigma_{n+1}=f(\zeta_n)$, for all $n\in\mathbb{N}$.

Then, we have

$$
\begin{aligned}
\tau+\mathfrak{F}(p(\varsigma_n,\zeta_n)) &= \tau+\mathfrak{F}(p(f(\zeta_{n-1}),f(\varsigma_n))) \\
&\leq c_1\mathfrak{F}(p(\varsigma_n,\zeta_{n-1}))+c_2\mathfrak{F}(p(\varsigma_n,f(\varsigma_n))) \\
&\quad +c_3\mathfrak{F}(p(f(\zeta_{n-1}),\zeta_{n-1})) \\
&= (c_1+c_3)\mathfrak{F}(p(\varsigma_n,\zeta_{n-1}))+c_2\mathfrak{F}(p(\varsigma_n,\zeta_n)),\ \text{for all } n\geq 1 \\
\Rightarrow \mathfrak{F}(p(\varsigma_n,\zeta_n))-c_2\mathfrak{F}(p(\varsigma_n,\zeta_n)) &\leq (c_1+c_3)\mathfrak{F}(p(\varsigma_n,\zeta_{n-1}))-\tau \\
\Rightarrow \mathfrak{F}(p(\varsigma_n,\zeta_n)) &\leq \left(\frac{c_1+c_3}{1-c_2}\right)\mathfrak{F}(p(\varsigma_n,\zeta_{n-1}))-\frac{1}{1-c_2}\tau.
\end{aligned}
$$

Again,

$$
\begin{aligned}
\tau+\mathfrak{F}(p(\varsigma_n,\zeta_{n-1})) &= \tau+\mathfrak{F}(p(f(\zeta_{n-1}),f(\varsigma_{n-1}))) \\
&\leq c_1\mathfrak{F}(p(\varsigma_{n-1},\zeta_{n-1}))+c_2\mathfrak{F}(p(\varsigma_{n-1},f(\varsigma_{n-1}))) \\
&\quad +c_3\mathfrak{F}(p(f(\zeta_{n-1}),\zeta_{n-1})) \\
&= (c_1+c_2)\mathfrak{F}(p(\varsigma_{n-1},\zeta_{n-1}))+c_3\mathfrak{F}(p(\varsigma_n,\zeta_{n-1})) \\
\Rightarrow (1-c_3)\mathfrak{F}(p(\varsigma_n,\zeta_{n-1})) &\leq (c_1+c_2)\mathfrak{F}(p(\varsigma_{n-1},\zeta_{n-1}))-\tau \\
\Rightarrow \mathfrak{F}(p(\varsigma_n,\zeta_{n-1})) &\leq \left(\frac{c_1+c_2}{1-c_3}\right)\mathfrak{F}(p(\varsigma_{n-1},\zeta_{n-1}))-\frac{1}{1-c_3}\tau,\ \text{for all } n\geq 1.
\end{aligned}
$$

Therefore we have,

$$
\mathfrak{F}(p(\varsigma_n,\zeta_n)) \leq \left(\frac{c_1+c_3}{1-c_2}\right)\left(\frac{c_1+c_2}{1-c_3}\right)\mathfrak{F}(p(\varsigma_{n-1},\zeta_{n-1}))-\left(\frac{c_1+c_3}{1-c_2}\right)\left(\frac{1}{1-c_3}\right)\tau-\frac{1}{1-c_2}\tau
$$

Let $\lambda=\left(\frac{c_1+c_3}{1-c_2}\right)\left(\frac{c_1+c_2}{1-c_3}\right)$, therefore

$$
\mathfrak{F}(p(\varsigma_n,\zeta_n)) \leq \lambda\mathfrak{F}(p(\varsigma_{n-1},\zeta_{n-1}))-\left(\frac{c_1+c_3}{1-c_3}-1\right)\left(\frac{1}{1-c_2}\right)\tau
$$

Proceeding in this way, we have

$$
\mathfrak{F}(p(\varsigma_n,\zeta_n)) \leq \lambda^n\mathfrak{F}(p(\varsigma_0,\zeta_0))-n\left(\frac{c_1+c_3}{1-c_3}-1\right)\left(\frac{1}{1-c_2}\right)\tau
$$

Taking the limit as $n\to\infty$,

$$
\lim_{n\to\infty}\mathfrak{F}(p(\varsigma_n,\zeta_n))=-\infty
$$

Thus, from the second property of the $\mathfrak{F}$-contraction,

$$
\lim_{n\to\infty}p(\varsigma_n,\zeta_n)=0.
$$

Hence, from the third property of the $\mathfrak{F}$-contraction, $\forall n\in\mathbb{N}$, $\exists\, t\in(0,1)$ such that

$$
\lim_{n\to\infty}p(\varsigma_n,\zeta_n)^t\mathfrak{F}(p(\varsigma_n,\zeta_n))=0.
$$

For all $n\in\mathbb{N}$, we have

$$
\begin{aligned}
&p(\varsigma_n,\zeta_n)^t\mathfrak{F}(p(\varsigma_n,\zeta_n))-p(\varsigma_n,\zeta_n)^t\mathfrak{F}(p(\varsigma_0,\zeta_0)) \\
&\quad\leq p(\varsigma_n,\zeta_n)^t\left(\lambda^n\mathfrak{F}(p(\varsigma_0,\zeta_0))-n\left(\frac{c_1+c_3}{1-c_3}-1\right)\left(\frac{1}{1-c_2}\right)\tau\right) \\
&\quad -p(\varsigma_n,\zeta_n)^t\mathfrak{F}(p(\varsigma_0,\zeta_0)) \\
&\quad = -p(\varsigma_n,\zeta_n)^t n\left(\frac{c_1+c_3}{1-c_3}-1\right)\left(\frac{1}{1-c_2}\right)\tau \\
&\quad\leq 0.
\end{aligned}
$$

From the third property of the $\mathfrak{F}$-contraction and considering the limit as $n \to \infty$, we have

$$\lim_{n\to\infty} n\left(\frac{c_1+c_3}{1-c_3}-1\right)\left(\frac{1}{1-c_2}\right)p(\varsigma_n,\zeta_n)^t = 0$$

Hence, there exist $n_1 \in \mathbb{N}$ such that $np(\varsigma_n,\zeta_n)^t \leq 1$ for all $n \geq n_1$.
Therefore, $p(\varsigma_n,\zeta_n) \leq \frac{1}{n^{1/t}}$ for all $n \geq n_1$.
Again,

$$\begin{aligned}
\mathfrak{F}(p(\varsigma_{n+1},\zeta_n)) &= \mathfrak{F}(p(f(\zeta_n),f(\varsigma_n))) \\
&\leq \left(\frac{c_1+c_2}{1-c_2}\right)\mathfrak{F}(p(\varsigma_{n+1},\zeta_n)) - \left(\frac{c_1+c_3}{1-c_3}-1\right)\left(\frac{1}{1-c_2}\right)\tau \\
&\vdots \\
&\leq \lambda^n\mathfrak{F}(p(\varsigma_1,\zeta_0)) - n\left(\frac{c_1+c_3}{1-c_3}-1\right)\left(\frac{1}{1-c_2}\right)\tau \\
&\leq \lambda^n\left(\frac{c_1+c_2}{1-c_3}\right)\mathfrak{F}(p(\varsigma_0,\zeta_0)) - n\left(\frac{c_1+c_2}{1-c_3}\right)\left(\frac{c_1+c_3}{1-c_3}-1\right)\left(\frac{1}{1-c_2}\right)\tau
\end{aligned}$$

Taking the limit as $n \to \infty$,

$$\lim_{n\to\infty}\mathfrak{F}(p(\varsigma_{n+1},\zeta_n)) = -\infty$$

From the second property of the $\mathfrak{F}$-contraction, we have

$$\lim_{n\to\infty} p(\varsigma_{n+1},\zeta_n) = 0$$

Hence, from the third property of the $\mathfrak{F}$-contraction for all $n \in \mathbb{N}$, there exist $t \in (0,1)$, such that

$$\lim_{n\to\infty} p(\varsigma_{n+1},\zeta_n)^t\mathfrak{F}(p(\varsigma_{n+1},\zeta_n)) = 0$$

For all $n \in \mathbb{N}$, we have

$$\begin{aligned}
p(\varsigma_{n+1},\zeta_n)^t\mathfrak{F}(p(\varsigma_{n+1},\zeta_n)) &- p(\varsigma_{n+1},\zeta_n)^t\mathfrak{F}(p(\varsigma_1,\zeta_0)) \\
&\leq p(\varsigma_{n+1},\zeta_n)^t\left[\lambda^n\mathfrak{F}(p(\varsigma_1,\zeta_0)) - n\left(\frac{c_1+c_3}{1-c_3}-1\right)\left(\frac{1}{1-c_2}\right)\tau\right] \\
&- p(\varsigma_{n+1},\zeta_n)^t\mathfrak{F}(p(\varsigma_1,\zeta_0)) \\
&= -p(\varsigma_{n+1},\zeta_n)^t n\left(\frac{c_1+c_3}{1-c_3}-1\right)\left(\frac{1}{1-c_2}\right)\tau \\
&\leq 0.
\end{aligned}$$

From the third property of the $\mathfrak{F}$-contraction and taking the limit as $n \to \infty$, we have

$$\lim_{n\to\infty} np(\varsigma_{n+1},\zeta_n)^t = 0$$

Hence, there exist $n_2 \in \mathbb{N}$, such that $np(\varsigma_n,\zeta_{n+1})^t \leq 1$ for all $n \geq n_2$.
Therefore, $p(\varsigma_{n+1},\zeta_n) \leq \frac{1}{n^{1/t}}$ for all $n \geq n_2$.
Consider $n_0 = \max\{n_1,n_2\}$.
For any $1 \leq n < m$, we have

$$\begin{aligned}
&p(\varsigma_n,\zeta_m) \leq \Omega[p(\varsigma_n,\zeta_n)+p(\varsigma_{n+1},\zeta_n)+p(\varsigma_{n+1},\zeta_m)] \\
\Rightarrow\ &\Omega^{-1}(p(\varsigma_n,\zeta_m)) \leq \frac{1}{n^{\frac{1}{t}}}+\frac{1}{n^{\frac{1}{t}}}+p(\varsigma_{n+1},\zeta_m),\ \text{for all } n \geq n_0 \\
&= \frac{1}{n^{\frac{1}{t}}}+\frac{1}{n^{\frac{1}{t}}}+\Omega[p(\varsigma_{n+1},\zeta_{n+1})+p(\varsigma_{n+2},\zeta_{n+1})+p(\varsigma_{n+2},\zeta_m)] \\
\Rightarrow\ &\Omega^{-2}(p(\varsigma_n,\zeta_m)) \leq \Omega^{-1}\left[\frac{1}{n^{\frac{1}{t}}}+\frac{1}{n^{\frac{1}{t}}}\right]+\frac{1}{(n+1)^{\frac{1}{t}}}+\frac{1}{(n+1)^{\frac{1}{t}}}+p(\varsigma_{n+2},\zeta_m)
\end{aligned}$$

Proceeding in a similar way, we have

$$\begin{aligned}
\Omega^{-(m-n+1)}(p(\varsigma_n,\zeta_m)) &\leq \Omega^{-(m-n)}\left[\frac{1}{n^{\frac{1}{t}}}+\frac{1}{n^{\frac{1}{t}}}\right]+\Omega^{-(m-n)}\left[\frac{1}{(n+1)^{\frac{1}{t}}}+\frac{1}{(n+1)^{\frac{1}{t}}}\right] \\
&+\ldots+\Omega^{-1}\left[\frac{1}{(m-1)^{\frac{1}{t}}}+\frac{1}{(m-1)^{\frac{1}{t}}}\right]+p(\varsigma_{m+1},\zeta_m) \\
&\leq \sum_{i=n}^{m}\Omega^{-(m-i)}\left[\frac{1}{i^{\frac{1}{t}}}+\frac{1}{i^{\frac{1}{t}}}\right],\ \text{for all } n \geq n_0
\end{aligned}$$

Hence,

$$p(\varsigma_n,\zeta_m) \leq \Omega^{(m-n+1)}\left(\sum_{i=n}^{m}\Omega^{-(m-i)}\left[\frac{1}{i^{\frac{1}{t}}}+\frac{1}{i^{\frac{1}{t}}}\right]\right) \tag{3}$$

Similarly, for any $1 \leq m < n$, we can show that

$$p(\varsigma_n,\zeta_m) \leq \Omega^{(m-n+1)}\left(\sum_{i=m}^{n}\Omega^{-(n-i)}\left[\frac{1}{i^{\frac{1}{t}}}+\frac{1}{i^{\frac{1}{t}}}\right]\right) \tag{4}$$

Since $t \in (0,1)$, the right hand sides of Equations (3) and (4) trend to 0 as $m,n \to \infty$. Hence the series is bi-convergent.

Therefore, $\{\varsigma_n,\zeta_n\}$ is a Cauchy bisequence in $(\mathfrak{X},\mathfrak{Y})$.

Let the $\{\varsigma_n,\zeta_n\}$ biconverge to some $\mathfrak{z} \in \mathfrak{X}\bigcap\mathfrak{Y}$.

Then, we have

$$\tau+\mathfrak{F}(p(f(\mathfrak{z}),f(\varsigma_n))) \leq c_1\mathfrak{F}(p(\mathfrak{z},\zeta_n))+c_2\mathfrak{F}(p(\mathfrak{z},f(\mathfrak{z})))+c_3\mathfrak{F}(p(f(\zeta_n),\zeta_n))$$

Moreover,

$$\begin{aligned}
p(f(\mathfrak{z}),\mathfrak{z}) &\leq \Omega[p(f(\mathfrak{z}),f(\varsigma_n))+p(\zeta_n,f(\zeta_n))+p(\zeta_n,\mathfrak{z})] \\
&\leq \Omega[c_1\mathfrak{F}(p(\mathfrak{z},\zeta_n))+c_2\mathfrak{F}(p(\mathfrak{z},f(\mathfrak{z})))+c_3\mathfrak{F}(p(f(\zeta_n),\zeta_n))+p(\zeta_n,f(\zeta_n))+p(\zeta_n,\mathfrak{z})]
\end{aligned}$$

Taking the limit as $n \to \infty$, we obtain

$$p(f(\mathfrak{z}),\mathfrak{z}) \leq \Omega[c_2\mathfrak{F}(p(\mathfrak{z},f(\mathfrak{z})))]$$

If $f(\mathfrak{z}) \neq \mathfrak{z}$, then

$$p(f(\mathfrak{z}),\mathfrak{z}) \leq \Omega[c_2\mathfrak{F}(p(\mathfrak{z},f(\mathfrak{z})))] < p(f(\mathfrak{z}),\mathfrak{z})$$

which is a contradiction.

Hence, $\mathfrak{z}$ is a fixed point of f.

If possible, let $\mathfrak{z}_2$ is another fixed point of f.

Then, we have for $\mathfrak{z},\mathfrak{z}_2 \in \mathfrak{X}\bigcap\mathfrak{Y}$.

$$\begin{aligned}
\tau+p(\mathfrak{z},\mathfrak{z}_2) &= \tau+p(f(\mathfrak{z}),f(\mathfrak{z}_2)) \\
&\leq c_1\mathfrak{F}(p(\mathfrak{z},\mathfrak{z}_2))+c_2\mathfrak{F}(p(\mathfrak{z},f(\mathfrak{z})))+c_3\mathfrak{F}(p(f(\mathfrak{z}_2),\mathfrak{z}_2)) \\
&< \tau+p(\mathfrak{z},\mathfrak{z}_2)
\end{aligned}$$

Therefore, $p(\mathfrak{z}, \mathfrak{z}_2) = 0 \Rightarrow \mathfrak{z} = \mathfrak{z}_2$.
Therefore f has a unique fixed point in $(\mathfrak{X}, \mathfrak{Y}, p)$.
□

4. Example

This section includes an example to validate Theorem 2.

Example 1. *Consider $\mathfrak{X} = [0,2]$ and $\mathfrak{Y} = [2,5]$ and a mapping $p : \mathfrak{X} \times \mathfrak{Y} \to [0,\infty)$ defined as $p(\mathfrak{A}, \mathfrak{B}) = |\mathfrak{A} - \mathfrak{B}|^2$ for all $(\mathfrak{A}, \mathfrak{B}) \in \mathfrak{X} \times \mathfrak{Y}$. Then for the function $\Omega(t) = 3t$ for all $t \geq 0$, $(\mathfrak{X}, \mathfrak{Y}, p)$ is a complete bipolar p-MS such that $\forall\, \mathfrak{v} \in \mathfrak{X} \bigcup \mathfrak{Y}$:*

$$f : (\mathfrak{X}, \mathfrak{Y}, p) \rightrightarrows (\mathfrak{X}, \mathfrak{Y}, p) \text{ defined as,}$$

$$f(\mathfrak{V}) = \frac{(\sqrt{2}+1) - \mathfrak{V}}{\sqrt{2}}$$

Then, for $c_1 = \frac{1}{2}$, $c_2 = 0$, $c_3 = 0$, the map f is a contravariant map.
Next, consider $\tau = \ln \frac{1}{2}$ and $\mathfrak{F}(\alpha) = \ln(\alpha)$.
Now,

$$\begin{aligned}
\tau + \mathfrak{F}(p(f(\varsigma), f(\zeta))) &= \ln\frac{1}{2} + \mathfrak{F}\left(p\left(\frac{(\sqrt{2}+1) - \varsigma}{\sqrt{2}}, \frac{(\sqrt{2}+1) - \zeta}{\sqrt{2}}\right)\right) \\
&= \ln\frac{1}{2} + \mathfrak{F}\left(\left|\frac{(\sqrt{2}+1)}{\sqrt{2}} - \frac{\varsigma}{\sqrt{2}} - \frac{(\sqrt{2}+1)}{\sqrt{2}} + \frac{\zeta}{\sqrt{2}}\right|^2\right) \\
&= \ln\frac{1}{2} + \mathfrak{F}\left(\left|-\frac{\varsigma}{\sqrt{2}} + \frac{\zeta}{\sqrt{2}}\right|^2\right) \\
&= \ln\frac{1}{2} + \ln\left(\frac{\varsigma - \zeta}{\sqrt{2}}\right)^2 \\
&= \ln\frac{1}{2} + 2\left[\ln(\varsigma - \zeta) - \ln\sqrt{2}\right] \\
&= 2[\ln(\varsigma - \zeta)] + \left(\ln\frac{1}{2} - 2\ln\sqrt{2}\right)
\end{aligned}$$

and

$$\begin{aligned}
c_1\mathfrak{F}(p(\varsigma, \zeta)) &= \frac{1}{2}\mathfrak{F}(|\varsigma - \zeta|^2) \\
&= \frac{1}{2}\ln(|\varsigma - \zeta|^2) \\
&= \ln|\varsigma - \zeta|.
\end{aligned}$$

Therefore,

$$\tau + \mathfrak{F}(p(f(\zeta), f(\varsigma))) \leq c_1\mathfrak{F}(p(\varsigma, \zeta)) + c_2\mathfrak{F}(p(\varsigma, f(\varsigma))) + c_3\mathfrak{F}(p(f(\zeta), \zeta)),$$

for $(\varsigma, \zeta) \in \mathfrak{X} \times \mathfrak{Y}$, where $c_1, c_2, c_3 \geq 0$, such that $c_1 + c_2 + c_3 < 1$ and $\frac{1}{4} \in \Delta_\Omega$.
Thus, we observe that all conditions of Theorem 2 are satisfied by f.
Hence, f has a unique fixed point in $(\mathfrak{X}, \mathfrak{Y}, p)$.

5. Conclusions

In this paper, we established new extended versions of a covariant Banach-type fixed-point theorem and a contravariant Rich-type fixed-point theorem in a complete bipolar p-metric space using the concept of F-contraction. As a results of this work, several existing results in the literature on Banach- and Reich-type fixed-point theorems (such as Theorems 3.2 and 3.4 in [24]) may be thought of as special cases of Theorem 1 and Theorem 2, respectively. This work can be extended in future to investigate some new results of the fixed points under different types of contractions as indicated in [5] in bipolar p-metric space. Further, multivalued versions of our results may be investigated, as achieved in the recent interesting paper [22]. Common fixed-point results of such covariant and contravariant mappings may also be studied following the directions of [23].

Author Contributions: Conceptualization, N.K.; Methodology, N.K.; Software, N.K.; Validation, N.K. and P.D.; Formal analysis, N.K. and P.D.; Investigation, N.K.; Writing—original draft, N.K.; Writing—review and editing, P.D. All authors have read and agreed to the published version of the manuscript.

Funding: This research received no external funding.

Data Availability Statement: No new data were created or analyzed in this study. Data sharing is not applicable to this article.

Acknowledgments: The authors are thankful to the learned reviewers for their careful reading of and constructive comments for the improvement of this manuscript.

Conflicts of Interest: The authors declare that they have no competing interests.

References

1. Bakhtin, I.A. The contraction mapping principle in almost metric spaces. *Funct. Anal.* **1989**, *30*, 26–37.
2. Czerwik, S. Contraction mappings in *b*-metric spaces. *Acta Math. Univ. Ostrav.* **1993**, *1*, 5–11.
3. Mutlu, A.; Gurdal, U. Bipolar metric spaces and some fixed point theorems. *J. Nonlinear Sci. Appl.* **2016**, *9*, 5362–5373. [CrossRef]
4. Mutlu, A.; Ozkan, K.; Gurdal, U. Coupled fixed point theorems on bipolar metric spaces. *Eur. J. Pure Appl. Math.* **2017**, *10*, 655–667.
5. Rhoades, B.E. A comparison of various definitions of contractive mappings. *Trans. Amer. Math. Soc.* **1977**, *226*, 257–290. [CrossRef]
6. Wardowski, D. Fixed points of a new type of contractive mappings in complete metric spaces. *Fixed Point Theory Appl.* **2012**, *2012*, 94. [CrossRef]
7. Debnath, P. Optimization through best proximity points for multivalued *F*-contractions. *Miskolc Math. Notes* **2021**, *22*, 143–151. [CrossRef]
8. Debnath, P. Common fixed-point and fixed-circle results for a class of discontinuous F-contractive mappings. *Mathematics* **2022**, *10*, 1605. [CrossRef]
9. Debnath, P. Results on discontinuity at fixed point for a new class of *F*-contractive mappings. *Sahand Commun. Math. Anal.* **2023**, *20*, 21–32.
10. Konwar, N.; Debnath, P. Fixed Point Results for a Family of Interpolative *F*-Contractions in *b*-Metric Spaces. *Axioms* **2022**, *11*, 621. [CrossRef]
11. Roy, K.; Saha, M. Generalized contractions and fixed point theorems over bipolar $cone_{tvs}$ b-metric spaces with an application to homotopy theory. *Mat. Vesnik* **2020**, *72*, 281–296.
12. Paul, J.; Sajid, M.; Chandra, N.; Gairola, U.C. Some common fixed point theorems in bipolar metric spaces and applications. *AIMS Math.* **2023**, *8*, 19004–19017. [CrossRef]
13. Parvaneh, V.; Dinmohammadi, A.; Kadelburg, Z. Coincidence point results for weakly α-admissible pairs in extended b-metric spaces. *J. Math. Anal.* **2017**, *8*, 74–89.
14. Alharbi, N.; Aydi, H.; Felhi, A.; Ozel, C.; Sahmim, S. α-contractive mappings on rectangular *b*-metric spaces and an application to integral equations. *J. Math. Anal.* **2018**, *9*, 47–60.
15. Aydi, H.; Chen, C.M.; Karapinar, E. Interpolative Ćirić-Reich-Rus type contractions via the Branciari distance. *Mathematics* **2019**, *7*, 84. [CrossRef]
16. Boyd, D.W.; Wong, J.S. On nonlinear contractions. *Proc. Amer. Math. Soc.* **1969**, *20*, 458–464. [CrossRef]
17. Chatterjea, S.K. Fixed point theorems. *C. R. Acad. Bulgare Sci.* **1972**, *25*, 727–730. [CrossRef]
18. Ćirić, L. Fixed point theorems for multivalued contractions in complete metric spaces. *J. Math. Anal. Appl.* **2008**, *348*, 499–507. [CrossRef]
19. Debnath, P.; Konwar, N.; Radenović, S. *Metric Fixed Point Theory*; Springer: Singapore; Berlin/Heidelberg, Germany, 2021.
20. Kannan, R. Some results on fixed points. *Bull. Calc. Math. Soc.* **1968**, *60*, 71–77.
21. Meir, A.; Keeler, E. A theorem on contraction mappings. *J. Math. Anal. Appl.* **1969**, *28*, 326–329. [CrossRef]
22. Mutlu, A.; Ozkan, K.; Gurdal, U. Fixed point theorems for multivalued mappings on bipolar metric spaces. *Fixed Point Theory* **2020**, *21*, 271–280. [CrossRef]

23. Mutlu, A.; Ozkan, K.; Gurdal, U. Some common fixed point theorems in bipolar metric spaces. *Turk. J. Math. Comput. Sci.* **2022**, *14*, 346–354. [CrossRef]
24. Roy, K.; Saha, M.; George, R.; Guran, L.; Mitrović, Z.D. Some covariant and contravariant fixed point theorems over Bipolar p-metric spaces and applications. *Filomat* **2022**, *36*, 1755–1767. [CrossRef]
25. George, R.; Radenović, S.; Reshma, K.P.; Shukla, S. Rectangular b-metric space and contraction principles. *J. Nonlinear Sci. Appl.* **2015**, *8*, 1005–1013. [CrossRef]

axioms

MDPI

Article

Fixed Point Results in Modular b-Metric-like Spaces with an Application

Nizamettin Ufuk Bostan and Banu Pazar Varol *

Department of Mathematics, Kocaeli University, 41001 Kocaeli, Türkiye; ufuk.bostan@kocaeli.edu.tr
* Correspondence: banupazar@kocaeli.edu.tr

Abstract: In this study, we introduce a new space called the modular b-metric-like space. We investigate some properties of this new concept and define notions of ξ-convergence, ξ-Cauchy sequence, ξ-completeness and ξ-contraction. The existence and uniqueness of fixed points in the modular b-metric-like space are handled. Moreover, we give some examples and an application to an integral equation to illustrate the usability of the obtained results.

Keywords: modular b-metric-like space; fixed point; contraction principle; integral equation

MSC: 47H09; 47H10; 54H25

1. Introduction

Metric space theory was established by Fréchet [1] and Hausdorff [2]. Banach's fixed point theorem (also known as Banach Contraction Principle), in which the concept of metric space is used, is the cornerstone of fixed point theory. Banach [3] introduced this theorem in 1922, and it has since become one of the most effective theorems in mathematics due to its wide applicability and simplicity.

Czerwik [4] presented generalization of some fixed point theorems of the Banach type, using the idea that some problems, especially the problem of convergence of measurable functions, lead to a generalization of the concept of the metric. This generalization of the concept of metric is called the b-metric by Czerwik [4]. For some fixed point results for a multivalued generalized contraction on a set with two b-metrics, see [5].

Amini-Harandi [6] first introduced a new space called a metric-like space. In this new concept, X is a nonempty set and $\sigma : X \times X \to IR^+$ satisfies all conditions of a metric except that $\sigma(x,x)$ may be different from zero for $x \in X$. Then, Amini-Harandi [6] established the fixed point theory in metric-like spaces by giving some fixed point results in such spaces. For several concepts related to metric-like spaces, such as equal-like points, cluster points, completely separate points, distance between a point and a subset of a metric-like space and distance between two subsets of a metric-like space, see [7].

The concept of b-metric-like space which is generalization of the concepts of metric-like space and b-metric space was presented by Alghamdi et al. [8]. They also investigated the existence of fixed points in a b-metric-like space and provided examples and applications to integral equations.

Nakano [9] introduced the concept of modular spaces. The concept of modular spaces was also studied by Orlicz [10]. Concepts of metric modular and modular metric spaces were introduced by Chistyakov [11,12] who constructed the theory of this structure. According to Chistyakov [13], while the metric on a set represents the non-negative finite distances between any two points of set, the purpose of a metric modular is to represent non-negative (possibly infinite valued) velocities. Some results achieved by Chistyakov are available in [14]. For fixed point results obtained by Chistyakov and applications of them, see [13,15–17]. Chistyakov compiled many of the works on metric modular spaces in [18].

Mongkolkeha et al. [19] obtained some results on the existence of fixed points by proving the fixed point theorems for contraction mappings in modular metric spaces.

Ege and Alaca [20] defined the notion of modular b-metric, which is the generalization of the metric modular, and introduced definitions to prove the Banach contraction principle in this new structure. Then, they gave an application of this principle to the system of linear equations.

Rasham et al. [21] introduced the concept of modular-like metric space. Then, they achieved some fixed point results for two families of set-valued mappings, satisfying a contraction in modular-like metric spaces. In [21], some results in graph theory were improved by using multigraph-dominated functions in modular-like metric spaces. Moreover, applications of fixed point theorems on the existence and uniqueness of the solution of integral equations have been investigated in [21? –23]. For more fixed point results in modular-like metric spaces, see [25].

The theory of fixed points also has very proper applications in geometry besides integral equations, systems of linear equations and differential equations. For example, fixed points of principal E_6-bundles over a compact algebraic curve and of the automorphisms of the vector bundle moduli space over a compact Riemann surface were introduced by Antón-Sancho [26,27]. Furthermore, Antón-Sancho [28] presented the notion of an α-trialitarian G-bundle to describe the fixed points of the automorphism of moduli space.

Despite the important generality of the theory of modular spaces over linear spaces, due to problems arising from multivalued analysis, such as the definition of metric functional spaces, selection principles, and the existence of regular selections of multifunctions, the concepts of modular and corresponding modular linear space are very restrictive. For this reason, Chistyakov introduced a new concept of modular space on an arbitrary set that is consistent with the classical concept. With this paper, our aim is to modulate the b-metric-like space in order not to face these restrictions, allowing us to present a more general form of a metric modular and a modular extension of the concepts in b-metric-like spaces.

In this study, we present the concept of "modular b-metric-like space" by using the approaches in [8,14] and investigate fixed point theorems for contractive mappings in modular b-metric-like space. We give the concepts of a ξ-open (ξ-closed) set, ξ-convergence, ξ-Cauchy sequence, ξ-completeness and ξ-contraction with the help of intelligible examples. Furthermore, we demonstrate the existence of a solution of integral equations to support our results.

2. Preliminaries

This section presents fundamental definitions and concepts to facilitate the comprehension of the primary results. Throughout this paper, IR and IN will be used to denote the set of all real numbers and the set of all positive integer numbers, respectively.

We see that the structure of space changes with the change of axioms and then the concept of modular is combined to these structures below.

Definition 1 ([4]). *Let $X \neq \emptyset$ and $K \geq 1$ be a real number. A mapping $d : X \times X \to [0, \infty)$ is called b-metric on X if the following hold for each $x, y, z \in X$:*

(bM1) $d(x,y) = 0 \Leftrightarrow x = y$;

(bM2) $d(x,y) = d(y,x)$;

(bM3) $d(x,y) \leq K[d(x,z) + d(z,y)]$.

The pair (X, d) is called a b-metric space.

Definition 2 ([6]). *Let $X \neq \emptyset$. A mapping $\sigma : X \times X \to IR^+$ is called metric-like on X if the following hold for each $x, y, z \in X$:*

(ML1) $\sigma(x,y) = 0 \Rightarrow x = y$;

(ML2) $\sigma(x,y) = \sigma(y,x)$;

(ML3) $\sigma(x,z) \leq \sigma(x,y) + \sigma(y,z)$.

The pair (X, σ) is called a metric-like space.

Definition 3 ([8]). *Let $X \neq \emptyset$ and $K \geq 1$ be a real number. A mapping $\rho : X \times X \to [0, \infty)$ is called b-metric-like on X if the following hold for each $x, y, z \in X$:*
(bML1) $\rho(x, y) = 0 \Rightarrow x = y$;
(bML2) $\rho(x, y) = \rho(y, x)$;
(bML3) $\rho(x, z) \leq K[\rho(x, y) + \rho(y, z)]$.
The pair (X, ρ) is called a b-metric-like space.

Example 1 ([8]). *Let $X = [0, \infty)$. Define the function $\rho : X \times X \to [0, \infty)$ by $\rho(x, y) = (x + y)^2$. Then, (X, ρ) is a b-metric-like space with constant $K = 2$.*

Example 2 ([8]). *Let $X = [0, \infty)$. Define the function $\rho : X \times X \to [0, \infty)$ by $\rho(x, y) = (\max\{x, y\})^2$. Then, (X, ρ) is a b-metric-like space with constant $K = 2$.*

Definition 4 ([10]). *Let X be a real linear space. A functional $\delta : X \to [0, \infty]$ is called classical modular on X if the following hold for each $x, y \in X$:*
(CM1) $\delta(0) = 0$;
(CM2) If $\delta(\alpha x) = 0$ for all $\alpha > 0$, then $x = 0$;
(CM3) $\delta(-x) = \delta(x)$;
(CM4) $\delta(\alpha x + \beta y) \leq \delta(x) + \delta(y)$ for all $\alpha, \beta \geq 0$ with $\alpha + \beta = 1$.

Definition 5 ([14]). *Let $X \neq \emptyset$. A mapping $v : (0, \infty) \times X \times X \to [0, \infty]$ is called metric modular on X if the following hold for each $x, y, z \in X$:*
(MM1) $v_\lambda(x, y) = 0 \Leftrightarrow x = y$, for all $\lambda > 0$;
(MM2) $v_\lambda(x, y) = v_\lambda(y, x)$, for all $\lambda > 0$;
(MM3) $v_{\lambda+\mu}(x, z) \leq v_\lambda(x, y) + v_\mu(y, z)$, for all $\lambda, \mu > 0$.

Definition 6 ([20]). *Let $X \neq \emptyset$ and $K \geq 1$ be a real number. A mapping $u : (0, \infty) \times X \times X \to [0, \infty]$ is called modular b-metric on X if the following hold for each $x, y, z \in X$:*
(MbM1) $u_\lambda(x, y) = 0 \Leftrightarrow x = y$, for all $\lambda > 0$;
(MbM2) $u_\lambda(x, y) = u_\lambda(y, x)$, for all $\lambda > 0$;
(MbM3) $u_{\lambda+\mu}(x, z) \leq K[u_\lambda(x, y) + u_\mu(y, z)]$, for all $\lambda, \mu > 0$.
Then, we say that (X, u) is a modular b-metric space.

Definition 7 ([21]). *Let $X \neq \emptyset$. A mapping $w : (0, \infty) \times X \times X \to [0, \infty)$ is called modular-like metric on X if the following hold for each $x, y, z \in X$:*
(MLM1) $w_\lambda(x, y) = 0 \Rightarrow x = y$, for all $\lambda > 0$;
(MLM2) $w_\lambda(x, y) = w_\lambda(y, x)$, for all $\lambda > 0$;
(MLM3) $w_{\lambda+\mu}(x, z) \leq w_\lambda(x, y) + w_\mu(y, z)$, for all $\lambda, \mu > 0$.
Then, (X, w) is called a modular-like metric space.

3. Modular b-Metric-like Space

In this section, we start with the introduction of a modular b-metric-like space and give some properties of this concept besides useful examples to support the structure.

Definition 8. *Let $X \neq \emptyset$ and $s \geq 1$ be a real number. A function $\xi : (0, \infty) \times X \times X \to [0, \infty]$ is called modular b-metric-like on X if it satisfies the following three conditions for each $x, y, z \in X$:*
(MbML1) $\xi_\lambda(x, y) = 0 \Rightarrow x = y$, for all $\lambda > 0$,
(MbML2) $\xi_\lambda(x, y) = \xi_\lambda(y, x)$, for all $\lambda > 0$,
(MbML3) $\xi_{\lambda+\mu}(x, y) \leq s[\xi_\lambda(x, z) + \xi_\mu(z, y)]$, for all $\lambda, \mu > 0$.
Then, the triplet (X, ξ, s) is called modular b-metric-like space.

If we replace (MbML1) with $\xi_\lambda(x, y) = 0 \Leftrightarrow x = y$, then ξ becomes a modular b-metric on X.

In the rest of this paper, for all $\lambda > 0$ and $x, y \in X$, $\xi_\lambda(x, y) = \xi(\lambda, x, y)$ denotes the map $\xi : (0, \infty) \times X \times X \to [0, \infty]$.

Example 3. *Let $X = [0, \infty)$. Define the function $\xi : (0, \infty) \times X \times X \to [0, \infty]$ by $\xi_\lambda(x, y) = \frac{(x+y)^2}{\lambda}$ for all $\lambda > 0$ and $x, y \in X = [0, \infty)$. Then, $(X, \xi, 2)$ is a modular b-metric-like space.*

It is clear that the conditions (MbML1) and (MbML2) hold. For this reason, only the condition (MbML3) will be shown:

(MbML3) Since $(x + y)^2 \leq 2[(x + z)^2 + (z + y)^2]$ for all $x, y, z \in X$, we have

$$\begin{aligned}\frac{(x+y)^2}{\lambda+\mu} &\leq \frac{2}{\lambda+\mu}[(x+z)^2 + (z+y)^2] \\ &= 2[\frac{(x+z)^2}{\lambda+\mu} + \frac{(z+y)^2}{\lambda+\mu}] \\ &\leq 2[\frac{(x+z)^2}{\lambda} + \frac{(z+y)^2}{\mu}]\end{aligned}$$

for all $x, y, z \in X$ and all $\lambda, \mu > 0$.

That means that $\xi_{\lambda+\mu}(x, y) \leq 2[\xi_\lambda(x, z) + \xi_\mu(z, y)]$. Thus, $(X, \xi, 2)$ is a modular b-metric-like space.

The graphical behavior of the function ξ defined as $\xi_\lambda(x, y) = \frac{(x+y)^2}{\lambda}$ on the set $[1, 10] \times [1, 10]$ for the values $\lambda = 1, 2, 3, 4, 5$ is given in the Figure 1. Thus, we get a visual idea about how the function ξ changes on the set $[1, 10] \times [1, 10]$ with the change of the value of λ from 1 to 5.

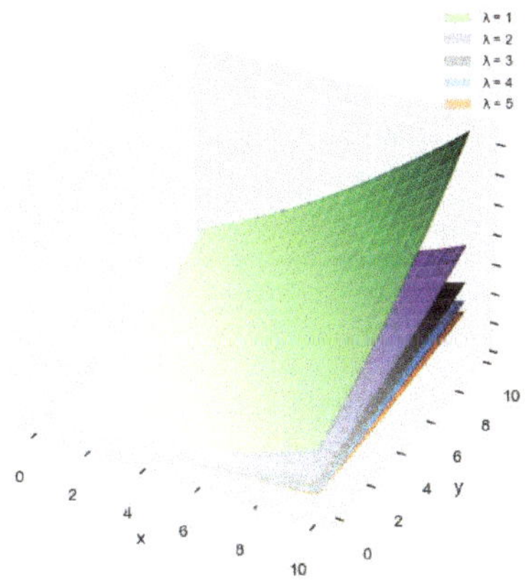

Figure 1. The graphical behavior of the $\xi_\lambda(x, y) = \frac{(x+y)^2}{\lambda}$ with $\lambda = 1, 2, 3, 4, 5$ and $x, y \in [1, 10]$.

Example 4. *Let $X = [0, \infty)$. Define the function $\xi : (0, \infty) \times X \times X \to [0, \infty]$ by $\xi_\lambda(x, y) = \frac{(\max\{x,y\})^2}{\lambda}$ for all $\lambda > 0$ and $x, y \in X = [0, \infty)$. Then, $(X, \xi, 2)$ is a modular b-metric-like space.*

It is clear that the conditions (MbML1) and (MbML2) hold. For this reason, only the condition (MbML3) will be shown:

(MbML3) Since $(\max\{x, y\})^2 \leq 2[(\max\{x, z\})^2 + (\max\{z, y\})^2]$ for all $x, y, z \in X$, we have

$$\begin{aligned}\frac{(\max\{x,y\})^2}{\lambda+\mu} &\leq \frac{2}{\lambda+\mu}[(\max\{x, z\})^2 + (\max\{z, y\})^2] \\ &= 2[\frac{(\max\{x,z\})^2}{\lambda+\mu} + \frac{(\max\{z,y\})^2}{\lambda+\mu}] \\ &\leq 2[\frac{(\max\{x,z\})^2}{\lambda} + \frac{(\max\{z,y\})^2}{\mu}]\end{aligned}$$

for all $x, y, z \in X$ and all $\lambda, \mu > 0$. That means that $\xi_{\lambda+\mu}(x, y) \leq 2[\xi_\lambda(x, z) + \xi_\mu(z, y)]$. Thus, $(X, \xi, 2)$ is a modular b-metric-like space.

Example 5. *Let $\aleph = C[0, L]$ be the set of all continuous real-valued functions defined on $[0, L]$, where $L > 0$. Define the function $\xi : (0, \infty) \times \aleph \times \aleph \to [0, \infty]$ by*

$\xi_\lambda(\varpi(s),\varphi(s)) = \frac{\max_{s\in[0,L]}(|\varpi(s)|+|\varphi(s)|)^2}{\lambda}$ *for all* $\lambda > 0$ *and all* $\varpi,\varphi \in \aleph$. *Then,* $(\aleph,\xi,2)$ *is a modular b-metric-like space.*

It is clear that the conditions (MbML1) and (MbML2) hold. For this reason, only the condition (MbML3) will be shown:

Since $\max_{s\in[0,L]}(|\varpi(s)|+|\varphi(s)|)^2 \le 2[\max_{s\in[0,L]}(|\varpi(s)|+|\kappa(s)|)^2 + \max_{s\in[0,L]}(|\kappa(s)|+|\varphi(s)|)^2]$, *we have*

$$\begin{aligned}
\frac{\max_{s\in[0,L]}(|\varpi(s)|+|\varphi(s)|)^2}{\lambda+\mu} &\le \frac{2}{\lambda+\mu}[\max_{s\in[0,L]}(|\varpi(s)|+|\kappa(s)|)^2 + \max_{s\in[0,L]}(|\kappa(s)|+|\varphi(s)|)^2] \\
&= 2[\frac{\max_{s\in[0,L]}(|\varpi(s)|+|\kappa(s)|)^2}{\lambda+\mu} + \frac{\max_{s\in[0,L]}(|\kappa(s)|+|\varphi(s)|)^2}{\lambda+\mu}] \\
&\le 2[\frac{\max_{s\in[0,L]}(|\varpi(s)|+|\kappa(s)|)^2}{\lambda} + \frac{\max_{s\in[0,L]}(|\kappa(s)|+|\varphi(s)|)^2}{\mu}]
\end{aligned}$$

for all $\varpi,\varphi,\kappa \in \aleph$ *and all* $\lambda,\mu > 0$. *That means that*

$$\xi_{\lambda+\mu}(\varpi,\varphi) \le 2[\xi_\lambda(\varpi,\kappa) + \xi_\mu(\kappa,\varphi)].$$

Thus, $(\aleph,\xi,2)$ *is a modular b-metric-like space.*

Proposition 1. *Let* $X = [0,\infty)$, *and let* (X,d) *be a b-metric-like space with constant* $s \ge 1$. *Define the function* $\xi : (0,\infty) \times X \times X \to [0,\infty]$ *by* $\xi_\lambda(x,y) = \frac{d(x,y)}{\lambda}$ *for all* $\lambda > 0$ *such that* $x,y \in X = [0,\infty)$. *Then,* (X,ξ,s) *is a modular b-metric-like space.*

Proof. (*MbML1*) $\xi_\lambda(x,y) = \frac{d(x,y)}{\lambda} = 0 \Rightarrow d(x,y) = 0$ for all $\lambda > 0$. Hence, we have $x = y$, since d is b-metric-like.

(*MbML2*) $\xi_\lambda(x,y) = \frac{d(x,y)}{\lambda} = \frac{d(y,x)}{\lambda} = \xi_\lambda(y,x)$ for all $\lambda > 0$.

(*MbML3*) Since (X,d) is a b-metric-like space with constant s, we have $d(x,y) \le s[d(x,z) + d(z,y)]$ for all $x,y,z \in X$. It follows that $\frac{d(x,y)}{\lambda+\mu} \le \frac{s}{\lambda+\mu}[d(x,z) + d(z,y)] = s[\frac{d(x,z)}{\lambda+\mu} + \frac{d(z,y)}{\lambda+\mu}] \le s[\frac{d(x,z)}{\lambda} + \frac{d(z,y)}{\mu}]$ for all $x,y,z \in X$ and all $\lambda,\mu > 0$. That means that $\xi_{\lambda+\mu}(x,y) \le s[\xi_\lambda(x,z) + \xi_\mu(z,y)]$. Thus, (X,ξ,s) is a modular b-metric-like space. □

Definition 9. *Let* ξ *be a modular b-metric-like on* X, *and let* x_0 *be an arbitrary element in* X.

Define set X_ξ^{fin} *by* $X_\xi^{fin} \equiv X_\xi^{fin}(x_0) = \{x \in X : \xi_\lambda(x,x_0) < \infty \text{ for all } \lambda > 0\}$.

Definition 10. *Let* (X,ξ,s) *be a modular b-metric-like space. Let* $x \in X$, $r > 0$ *and* $\lambda > 0$. *Then, set* $B_{\xi_\lambda}(x,r) = \{y \in X : |\xi_\lambda(x,y) - \xi_\lambda(x,x)| < r\}$ *is called a* $\xi -$ *open ball relative to* λ *with center* x *and radius* $r > 0$.

Definition 11. *Let* (X,ξ,s) *be a modular b-metric-like space and* U *be a subset of* X. *If there exists* $r_0 > 0$ *such that* $B_{\xi_{\lambda_0}}(x,r_0) \subset U$ *for all* $x \in U$ *and some* $\lambda_0 > 0$, *then* U *is called a* $\xi -$ *open subset of* X.

If $X \backslash U$ *is a* $\xi -$ *open set, then* U *is called a* $\xi -$ *closed set.*

Definition 12. *Let* (X,ξ,s) *be a modular b-metric-like space,* $\{x_n\}_{n\in IN} \subset X_\xi^{fin}$ *and* $x \in X_\xi^{fin}$.

(i) *x is called* $\xi -$ *limit of the sequence* $\{x_n\}_{n\in N}$ *if* $\lim_{n\to\infty} \xi_\lambda(x_n,x) = \xi_\lambda(x,x)$ *for all* $\lambda > 0$; *moreover, we say that the sequence* $\{x_n\}_{n\in N}$ *is* $\xi -$ *convergent to* x *and we denote it by* $x_n \to^\xi x$.

(ii) *Sequence* $\{x_n\}_{n\in N}$ *is called* $\xi -$ *Cauchy if* $\lim_{n,m\to\infty} \xi_\lambda(x_n,x_m)$ *exists and is finite for all* $\lambda > 0$.

(iii) *Modular b-metric-like space* X_ξ^{fin} *is called* $\xi -$ *complete if every* $\xi -$ *Cauchy sequence* $\{x_n\}_{n\in N}$ *is* $\xi -$ *convergent to any* x *such that* $\lim_{n\to\infty} \xi_\lambda(x_n,x) = \xi_\lambda(x,x) = \lim_{n,m\to\infty} \xi_\lambda (x_n,x_m)$ *for all* $\lambda > 0$.

Proposition 2. *Let* (X,ξ,s) *be a modular b-metric-like space, and let* V *be a subset of* X. V *is* ξ*-closed if and only if for any sequence* $\{x_n\} \subset V$, *which is* ξ*-convergent to* $x \in X$, *we have* $x \in V$.

Proof. Suppose that V is a ξ-closed set, $\{x_n\} \subset V$, $x \in X$, $x_n \to^{\xi} x$. Let $x \notin V$. By Definition 11, $X \backslash V$ is a ξ-open set. Since $x \in X \backslash V$, there exists $r_0 > 0$ such that $B_{\xi_{\lambda_0}}(x, r_0) \subset X \backslash V$ for some $\lambda_0 > 0$. Since $x_n \to^{\xi} x$, we have $\lim_{n\to\infty} \xi_\lambda(x_n, x) = \xi_\lambda(x, x)$ for all $\lambda > 0$. In other words, $\lim_{n\to\infty} |\xi_\lambda(x_n, x) - \xi_\lambda(x, x)| = 0$ for all $\lambda > 0$. Hence, for all $\lambda > 0$, there exists $n_0 \in IN$ such that $|\xi_\lambda(x_n, x) - \xi_\lambda(x, x)| < r_0$ for all $n \geq n_0$. Especially for $\lambda = \lambda_0$, we have $|\xi_{\lambda_0}(x_n, x) - \xi_{\lambda_0}(x, x)| < r_0$ for all $n \geq n_0$. Thus, $x_n \subset B_{\xi_{\lambda_0}}(x, r_0) \subset X \backslash V$ for all $n \geq n_0$, which is a contradiction. Hence, $x \in V$.

Conversely, assume that for any sequence $\{x_n\} \subset V$, which is ξ-convergent to $x \in X$, we have $x \in V$. Let $y \in X \backslash V$. We need to show that there exists $r_0 > 0$ such that $B_{\xi_{\lambda_0}}(y, r_0) \cap V = \varnothing$ for some λ_0. Suppose that for all $\lambda > 0$ and $r > 0$, we have

$B_{\xi_\lambda}(y, r_0) \cap V \neq \varnothing$. Then, for all $n \in IN$ and $\lambda > 0$, choose $x_n \in B_{\xi_\lambda}(y, \frac{1}{n}) \cap V \neq \varnothing$. Hence, $|\xi_\lambda(x_n, y) - \xi_\lambda(y, y)| < \frac{1}{n}$ for all $\lambda > 0$ and $n \in IN$. Then, $0 \leq \lim_{n\to\infty} |\xi_\lambda(x_n, y) - \xi_\lambda(y, y)| < \lim_{n\to\infty} \frac{1}{n}$ and we obtain $\lim_{n\to\infty} |\xi_\lambda(x_n, y) - \xi_\lambda(y, y)| = 0$. Therefore, $\lim_{n\to\infty} \xi_\lambda(x_n, y) = \xi_\lambda(y, y)$ for all $\lambda > 0$ and we get $x_n \to^{\xi} x$. Since $\{x_n\} \subset V$, we have $y \in V$ from our assumption, which is a contradiction. Then, for all $y \notin V$, there exists $r_0 > 0$ such that $B_{\xi_{\lambda_0}}(y, r_0) \subset X \backslash V$ for some $\lambda_0 > 0$. Thus, $X \backslash V$ is a ξ-open set. So, V is a ξ-closed set. □

Proposition 3. *Let (X, ξ, s) be a modular b-metric-like space, and let $\{x_n\}$ be a sequence in X such that $\lim_{n\to\infty} \xi_\lambda(x_n, x) = 0$ for all $\lambda > 0$. Then, x is unique.*

Proof. Suppose that there exists $y \in X$ such that $\lim_{n\to\infty} \xi_\lambda(x_n, y) = 0$ for all $\lambda > 0$. Then, for all $\lambda > 0$,

$0 \leq \xi_\lambda(x,y) \leq s[\xi_{\frac{\lambda}{2}}(x, x_n) + \xi_{\frac{\lambda}{2}}(x_n, y)]$.

$\Rightarrow 0 \leq \lim_{n\to\infty} \xi_\lambda(x,y) \leq s[\lim_{n\to\infty} \xi_{\frac{\lambda}{2}}(x, x_n) + \lim_{n\to\infty} \xi_{\frac{\lambda}{2}}(x_n, y)]$

$\Rightarrow 0 \leq \xi_\lambda(x,y) \leq 0$.

Hence, $\xi_\lambda(x,y) = 0$ for all $\lambda > 0$, and $x = y$. □

Remark 1. *In a modular b-metric-like space, the $\xi-$ limit of the $\xi-$ convergent sequence $\{x_n\}$ may not be unique. Let $X = [0, \infty)$. Define the function $d : X \times X \to [0, \infty)$ by $d(x, y) = \max\{x, y\}$. Then, we know that (X, d) is a b-metric-like space with any constant $s \geq 1$. Consider Proposition 1 and define a sequence $\{x_n\} \subset X_\xi^{fin}$ by $\{x_n\} = \{1 + \frac{1}{n}\}$.*

If $x \geq 2$, then $\lim_{n\to\infty} \xi_\lambda(x_n, x) = \lim_{n\to\infty} \frac{d(x_n,x)}{\lambda} = \lim_{n\to\infty} \frac{\max\{x_n,x\}}{\lambda} = \lim_{n\to\infty} \frac{x}{\lambda} = \frac{\max\{x,x\}}{\lambda} = \xi_\lambda(x, x)$ for all $\lambda > 0$. Hence, the sequence $\{x_n\}$ is $\xi-$ convergent to all $x \in X_\xi^{fin}$ with $x \geq 2$.

4. Fixed Point Results

We prove some related fixed point theorems and give examples to support these theorems in this part.

Definition 13. *Let ξ be a modular b-metric-like on X, and let $T : X_\xi^{fin} \to X_\xi^{fin}$ be a mapping. If for every $x, y \in X_\xi^{fin}$ and all $\lambda > 0$ there exists $0 < k < 1$ such that $\xi_\lambda(Tx, Ty) \leq k\xi_\lambda(x, y)$, then the mapping T is called $\xi-$ contraction.*

Theorem 1. *Let (X, ξ, s) be a modular b-metric-like space such that X_ξ^{fin} is ξ-complete. Let $T : X_\xi^{fin} \to X_\xi^{fin}$ be a ξ-contraction with restriction $0 < k < 1$. Then, for the sequence defined as $x_n = Tx_{n-1} = T^n x_0$ where $x_0 \in X_\xi^{fin}$, there exists an element $\bar{x} \in X_\xi^{fin}$ such that $\{x_n\}$ is ξ-convergent to $\bar{x}$ and $\bar{x}$ is a unique fixed point of T.*

Proof. Let $x_0 \in X_\xi^{fin}$ and $\{x_n\} \subset X_\xi^{fin}$ be defined by $x_n = Tx_{n-1} = T^n x_0$. Since T is a ξ-contraction, we obtain

$$\xi_\lambda(T^2x_0, T^2x_1) \leq k\xi_\lambda(Tx_0, Tx_1) \leq k^2\xi_\lambda(x_0, x_1).$$

If this procedure is iterated, we get

$$\xi_\lambda(T^n x_0, T^n x_1) \leq k^n \xi_\lambda(x_0, x_1),$$

for all $\lambda > 0$ and $n \in IN$.

Since $T^n x_1 = T^n(Tx_0) = T^{n+1}x_0 = x_{n+1}$ and $T^n x_0 = x_n$, for all $\lambda > 0$ and $n \in IN$, we have

$$\xi_\lambda(x_n, x_{n+1}) \leq k^n \xi_\lambda(x_0, x_1).$$

Taking the limit as $n \to \infty$ in the above inequality, we get $\lim_{n\to\infty}(k^n \xi_\lambda(x_0, Tx_0)) = \lim_{n\to\infty}(k^n \xi_\lambda(x_0, x_1)) = 0$ because of $k \in (0,1)$ by the definition of the ξ-contraction and $\xi_\lambda(x, Tx) < \infty$ for all $\lambda > 0$ and all $x \in X_\xi^{fin}$.

Then, we have $\lim_{n\to\infty} \xi_\lambda(x_n, x_{n+1}) = 0$ for all $\lambda > 0$. Hence, for all $\lambda > 0$ and $\epsilon > 0$, there exists $n_0 \in IN$ such that $\xi_\lambda(x_n, x_{n+1}) < \epsilon$ for all $n \geq n_0$. Without loss of generality, suppose $m, n \in N$ and $m > n$. Observe that, for $\frac{\lambda}{m-n} > 0$, there exists $n_{\frac{\lambda}{m-n}} \in N$ such that $\xi_{\frac{\lambda}{m-n}}(x_n, x_{n+1}) < \frac{\epsilon}{\sum_{p=1}^{m-n} s^p}$, for all $n \geq n_{\frac{\lambda}{m-n}}$.

Now, we have

$$\begin{aligned}
\xi_\lambda(x_n, x_m) &\leq s\xi_{\frac{\lambda}{m-n}}(x_n, x_{n+1}) + s^2\xi_{\frac{\lambda}{m-n}}(x_{n+1}, x_{n+2}) + ... + s^{m-n}\xi_{\frac{\lambda}{m-n}}(x_{m-1}, x_m) \\
&= s\xi_{\frac{\lambda}{m-n}}(x_n, x_{n+1}) + s^2\xi_{\frac{\lambda}{m-n}}(Tx_n, Tx_{n+1}) + ... + s^{m-n}\xi_{\frac{\lambda}{m-n}}(Tx_{m-2}, Tx_{m-1}) \\
&\leq s\xi_{\frac{\lambda}{m-n}}(x_n, x_{n+1}) + s^2 k\xi_{\frac{\lambda}{m-n}}(x_n, x_{n+1}) + s^3k^2\xi_{\frac{\lambda}{m-n}}(x_n, x_{n+1}) + ... + s^{m-n}k^{m-1-n}\xi_{\frac{\lambda}{m-n}}(x_n, x_{n+1}) \\
&\leq s\xi_{\frac{\lambda}{m-n}}(x_n, x_{n+1}) + s^2\xi_{\frac{\lambda}{m-n}}(x_n, x_{n+1}) + ... + s^{m-n}\xi_{\frac{\lambda}{m-n}}(x_n, x_{n+1}) \\
&= [s + s^2 + s^3 + ... + s^{m-n}]\xi_{\frac{\lambda}{m-n}}(x_n, x_{n+1}) \\
&= \sum_{p=1}^{m-n} s^p \xi_{\frac{\lambda}{m-n}}(x_n, x_{n+1}) \\
&\leq \sum_{p=1}^{m-n} s^p \frac{\epsilon}{\sum_{p=1}^{m-n} s^p} \\
&= \epsilon.
\end{aligned}$$

for all $m > n$ and all $n \geq n_{\frac{\lambda}{m-n}}$.

Therefore, we have $\lim_{n,m\to\infty} \xi_\lambda(x_n, x_m) = 0$; hence, $\{x_n\} \subset X_\xi^{fin}$ is a ξ-Cauchy sequence. Since X_ξ^{fin} is a ξ-complete set, there exists $\overline{x} \in X_\xi^{fin}$ such that $\lim_{n\to\infty} \xi_\lambda(x_n, \overline{x}) = \xi_\lambda(\overline{x}, \overline{x}) = \lim_{n,m\to\infty} \xi_\lambda(x_n, x_m)$ for all $\lambda > 0$. Since $\lim_{n,m\to\infty} \xi_\lambda(x_n, x_m) = 0$ for all $\lambda > 0$, we have $\lim_{n\to\infty} \xi_\lambda(x_n, \overline{x}) = \xi_\lambda(\overline{x}, \overline{x}) = 0$ for all $\lambda > 0$.

It follows that

$$\begin{aligned}
\xi_\lambda(T\overline{x}, \overline{x}) &\leq s[\xi_{\frac{\lambda}{2}}(T\overline{x}, x_n) + \xi_{\frac{\lambda}{2}}(x_n, \overline{x})] \\
&= s[\xi_{\frac{\lambda}{2}}(T\overline{x}, Tx_{n-1}) + \xi_{\frac{\lambda}{2}}(x_n, \overline{x})] \\
&\leq s[k\xi_{\frac{\lambda}{2}}(\overline{x}, x_{n-1}) + \xi_{\frac{\lambda}{2}}(x_n, \overline{x})]
\end{aligned}$$

for all $\lambda > 0$ and all $n \in IN$.

Taking the limit as $n \to \infty$ in the above inequality, we get

$$\begin{aligned}
\lim_{n\to\infty} \xi_\lambda(T\overline{x}, \overline{x}) &\leq \lim_{n\to\infty}(s[k\xi_{\frac{\lambda}{2}}(\overline{x}, x_{n-1}) + \xi_{\frac{\lambda}{2}}(x_n, \overline{x})]) \\
&= s[k \lim_{n\to\infty} \xi_{\frac{\lambda}{2}}(\overline{x}, x_{n-1}) + \lim_{n\to\infty} \xi_{\frac{\lambda}{2}}(x_n, \overline{x})] \\
&= 0
\end{aligned}$$

for all $\lambda > 0$.

It follows that $\xi_\lambda(T\overline{x}, \overline{x}) = 0$ for all $\lambda > 0$. Hence, we have $T\overline{x} = \overline{x}$ from condition $(MbML1)$. Thus, $\overline{x}$ is a fixed point of T. Next, we prove that this fixed point $\overline{x}$ is unique.

Suppose that y is another fixed point of T such that $\overline{x} \neq y$. Therefore, we have $Ty = y$. Since T is a ξ-contraction, we have $\xi_\lambda(\overline{x}, y) = \xi_\lambda(T\overline{x}, Ty) \leq k\xi_\lambda(\overline{x}, y)$ for all $\lambda > 0$.

It follows that $(1-k)\xi_\lambda(\overline{x}, y) \leq 0$. Hence, we have $\xi_\lambda(\overline{x}, y) = 0$ for all $\lambda > 0$. Thus, we get $\overline{x} = y$ from condition $(MbML1)$. □

Example 6. *Let $X = [0,\infty)$. Define the function $\xi : (0,\infty) \times X \times X \to [0,\infty]$ by $\xi_\lambda(x,y) = \frac{d(x,y)}{\lambda}$ for all $\lambda > 0$ such that $d(x,y) = (x+y)^2$ and $x,y \in X = [0,\infty)$. Then, $(X,\xi,2)$ is a modular b-metric-like space such that X_ξ^{fin} is ξ-complete since $X_\xi^{fin} = X$.*

Define the map $T : X_\xi^{fin} \to X_\xi^{fin}$ by $Tx = \alpha x$ such that $\alpha \in (0,1)$. Then, we have $\xi_\lambda(Tx,Ty) = \xi_\lambda(\alpha x,\alpha y) = \frac{(\alpha x+\alpha y)^2}{\lambda} = \frac{\alpha^2(x+y)^2}{\lambda} = \alpha^2\frac{d(x,y)}{\lambda} = \alpha^2\xi_\lambda(x,y)$ for all $\lambda > 0$. Since $\alpha \in (0,1)$, we have $k = \alpha^2 \in (0,1)$. Thus, the mapping T is a ξ-contraction with constant $k = \alpha^2$. Then, by Theorem 1, there exists a unique fixed point $\bar{x} = 0 \in X_\xi^{fin}$ such that $x_n = Tx_{n-1} = T^n x_0$ is ξ-convergent to $\bar{x} = 0$.

Indeed, we have $\lim_{n\to\infty}\xi_\lambda(x_n,0) = \lim_{n\to\infty}\frac{d(x_n,0)}{\lambda} = \lim_{n\to\infty}\frac{(x_n+0)^2}{\lambda} = \lim_{n\to\infty}\frac{(x_n)^2}{\lambda}$ $= \frac{1}{\lambda}(\lim_{n\to\infty}x_n \lim_{n\to\infty}x_n)$. Then, it follows that $x_n = T^n x_0 = T^{n-1}(Tx_0) = T^{n-1}(\alpha x_0) = T^{n-2}(T(\alpha x_0)) = T^{n-2}(\alpha^2 x_0) = \cdots = T^{n-(n-1)}(\alpha^{n-1}x_0) = T(\alpha^{n-1}x_0) = \alpha^n x_0$, and this means that $x_n = \alpha^n x_0$.

Since $x_0 \in X_\xi^{fin}$, we have $x_0 < \infty$. Then, $\lim_{n\to\infty}x_n = \lim_{n\to\infty}\alpha^n x_0 = 0$ since $\alpha \in (0,1)$ and $x_0 < \infty$. Therefore, we have $\lim_{n\to\infty}\xi_\lambda(x_n,0) = \frac{1}{\lambda}(\lim_{n\to\infty}x_n\lim_{n\to\infty}x_n) = 0 = \frac{(0+0)^2}{\lambda} = \xi_\lambda(0,0)$, and this means that $\lim_{n\to\infty}\xi_\lambda(x_n,0) = \xi_\lambda(0,0)$ for all $\lambda > 0$. Also, since $T(0) = \alpha 0 = 0$ holds, 0 is a unique fixed point of T.

Remark 2. *Let (X,ξ,s) be a modular b-metric-like space. Define $\xi_\lambda{}^z : X^2 \to [0,\infty)$ by $\xi_\lambda{}^z(x,y) = |2\xi_\lambda(x,y) - \xi_\lambda(x,x) - \xi_\lambda(y,y)|$. Clearly, $\xi_\lambda{}^z(x,x) = 0$ for all $x \in X$.*

Theorem 2. *Let (X,ξ,s) be a modular b-metric-like space such that X_ξ^{fin} is ξ-complete. Suppose that the mapping $T : X_\xi^{fin} \to X_\xi^{fin}$ is onto and satisfies*

$$\xi_\lambda(Tx,Ty) \geq [r + l\min\{\xi_\lambda{}^z(x,Tx),\xi_\lambda{}^z(y,Ty),\xi_\lambda{}^z(x,Ty),\xi_\lambda{}^z(y,Tx)\}]\xi_\lambda(x,y) \quad (1)$$

for all $x,y \in X_\xi^{fin}$ and all $\lambda > 0$, where $r > s$, $l \geq 0$. Then, T has a unique fixed point.

Proof. Let $x_0 \in X_\xi^{fin}$. Since T is onto mapping, there exists $x_1 \in X_\xi^{fin}$ such that $x_0 = Tx_1$. By continuing this process, we get $x_n = Tx_{n+1}$ for all $n \in IN$. In case $x_{n_0} = x_{n_0+1}$ for some $n_0 \in IN$, we have $Tx_{n_0+1} = x_{n_0+1}$ since $Tx_{n_0+1} = x_{n_0}$. Thus, x_{n_0+1} is a fixed point of T. Now assume that $x_n \neq x_{n+1}$ for all n. From (1) with $x = x_n$ and $y = x_{n+1}$, we get

$$\xi_\lambda(Tx_n,Tx_{n+1}) \geq [r + l\min\{\xi_\lambda{}^z(x_n,Tx_n),\xi_\lambda{}^z(x_{n+1},Tx_{n+1}),\xi_\lambda{}^z(x_n,Tx_{n+1}),\xi_\lambda{}^z(x_{n+1},Tx_n)\}]\xi_\lambda(x_n,x_{n+1})$$

for all $\lambda > 0$.

It follows that

$$\begin{aligned}\xi_\lambda(x_{n-1},x_n) &\geq [r + l\min\{\xi_\lambda{}^z(x_n,x_{n-1}),\xi_\lambda{}^z(x_{n+1},x_n),\xi_\lambda{}^z(x_n,x_n),\xi_\lambda{}^z(x_{n+1},x_{n-1})\}]\xi_\lambda(x_n,x_{n+1}) \\ &= r\xi_\lambda(x_n,x_{n+1})\end{aligned}$$

for all $\lambda > 0$ since $Tx_{n+1} = x_n$ for all $n \in IN$, which implies $\xi_\lambda(x_{n-1},x_n) \geq r\xi_\lambda(x_n,x_{n+1})$. Hence, $\xi_\lambda(x_n,x_{n+1}) \leq \frac{1}{r}\xi_\lambda(x_{n-1},x_n)$, and so we have $\xi_\lambda(x_n,x_{n+1}) \leq h\xi_\lambda(x_{n-1},x_n)$ where $h = \frac{1}{r} < \frac{1}{s}$ since $r > s$. Now, we will show that x_n is a ξ-Cauchy sequence.

Since $\xi_\lambda(x_n,x_{n+1}) \leq h\xi_\lambda(x_{n-1},x_n)$ for all $n \in IN$ and all $\lambda > 0$, we have

$$h\xi_\lambda(x_{n-1},x_n) \leq h(h\xi_\lambda(x_{n-2},x_{n-1})) = h^2\xi_\lambda(x_{n-2},x_{n-1}) \leq h^3\xi_\lambda(x_{n-3},x_{n-2}) \leq \cdots \leq h^n\xi_\lambda(x_0,x_1)$$

which implies $\xi_\lambda(x_n,x_{n+1}) \leq h^n\xi_\lambda(x_0,x_1)$ for all $n \in IN$ and all $\lambda > 0$.

We have

$$\lim_{n\to\infty}(h^n\xi_\lambda(Tx_1,x_1)) = \lim_{n\to\infty}(h^n\xi_\lambda(x_0,x_1)) = 0$$

since $h < \frac{1}{s} \leq 1$ and $\xi_\lambda(Tx,x) < \infty$ for all $\lambda > 0$ and all $x \in X_\xi^{fin}$. It follows that $\lim_{n\to\infty}\xi_\lambda(x_n,x_{n+1}) = 0$ for all $\lambda > 0$. So, for all $\lambda > 0$, we have that for all $\varepsilon > 0$ there exists $n_0 \in IN$ such that $\xi_\lambda(x_n,x_{n+1}) < \varepsilon$ for all $n \in IN$ with $n \geq n_0$. Without loss of generality, suppose $m, n \in IN$ and $m > n$. Observe that, for $\frac{\lambda}{m-n} > 0$, there exists $n_{\frac{\lambda}{m-n}} \in IN$ such that

$$\xi_{\frac{\lambda}{m-n}}(x_n, x_{n+1}) < \frac{\epsilon}{\sum_{p=1}^{m-n} s^p}$$

for all $n \geq n_{\frac{\lambda}{m-n}}$.

Now, we have

$$\begin{aligned}
\xi_\lambda(x_n, x_m) &\leq s\xi_{\frac{\lambda}{m-n}}(x_n, x_{n+1}) + s^2\xi_{\frac{\lambda}{m-n}}(x_{n+1}, x_{n+2}) + \cdots + s^{m-n}\xi_{\frac{\lambda}{m-n}}(x_{m-1}, x_m) \\
&\leq s\xi_{\frac{\lambda}{m-n}}(x_n, x_{n+1}) + s^2 h\xi_{\frac{\lambda}{m-n}}(x_n, x_{n+1}) + s^3h^2\xi_{\frac{\lambda}{m-n}}(x_n, x_{n+1}) + \cdots + s^{m-n}h^{m-1-n}\xi_{\frac{\lambda}{m-n}}(x_n, x_{n+1}) \\
&< s\xi_{\frac{\lambda}{m-n}}(x_n, x_{n+1}) + s^2\xi_{\frac{\lambda}{m-n}}(x_n, x_{n+1}) + \cdots + s^{m-n}\xi_{\frac{\lambda}{m-n}}(x_n, x_{n+1}) \\
&= [s + s^2 + s^3 + \cdots + s^{m-n}]\xi_{\frac{\lambda}{m-n}}(x_n, x_{n+1}) \\
&= \textstyle\sum_{p=1}^{m-n} s^p \xi_{\frac{\lambda}{m-n}}(x_n, x_{n+1}) \\
&\leq \textstyle\sum_{p=1}^{m-n} s^p \frac{\epsilon}{\sum_{p=1}^{m-n} s^p} \\
&= \epsilon
\end{aligned}$$

for all $m > n$ and all $n \geq n_{\frac{\lambda}{m-n}}$.

Thus, we have $\lim_{n\to\infty} \xi_\lambda(x_n, x_m) = 0$. Since $\lim_{n\to\infty} \xi_\lambda(x_n, x_m) = 0$ exists and is finite, $\{x_n\}$ is a ξ-Cauchy sequence. Since $(X_\xi{}^{fin}, \xi, s)$ is ξ-complete, the sequence $\{x_n\}$ in $X_\xi{}^{fin}$ is ξ-convergent to $z_0 \in X_\xi{}^{fin}$ such that

$$\lim_{n\to\infty} \xi_\lambda(x_n, z_0) = \xi_\lambda(z_0, z_0) = \lim_{n,m\to\infty} \xi_\lambda(x_n, x_m)$$

for all $\lambda > 0$.

Since T is onto mapping, there exists $v \in X_\xi{}^{fin}$ such that $Tv = z_0$. From (1) and since $Tx_{n+1} = x_n$, we have

$$\xi_\lambda(x_n, z_0) = \xi_\lambda(Tx_{n+1}, Tv) \geq [r + l\min\{\xi_\lambda{}^z(x_{n+1}, Tx_{n+1}), \xi_\lambda{}^z(v, Tv), \xi_\lambda{}^z(x_{n+1}, Tv), \xi_\lambda{}^z(v, Tx_{n+1})\}]\xi_\lambda(x_{n+1}, v)$$

for all $\lambda > 0$ and all $n \in IN$.

By taking the limit as $n \to \infty$ in the above inequality, we get

$$\lim_{n\to\infty}([r + l\min\{\xi_\lambda{}^z(x_{n+1}, Tx_{n+1}), \xi_\lambda{}^z(v, Tv), \xi_\lambda{}^z(x_{n+1}, Tv), \xi_\lambda{}^z(v, Tx_{n+1})\}]\xi_\lambda(x_{n+1}, v)) \leq \lim_{n\to\infty} \xi_\lambda(x_n, z_0)$$

for all $\lambda > 0$.

It follows that

$$\begin{aligned}
&\lim_{n\to\infty}[r + l\min\{\xi_\lambda{}^z(x_{n+1}, Tx_{n+1}), \xi_\lambda{}^z(v, Tv), \xi_\lambda{}^z(x_{n+1}, Tv), \xi_\lambda{}^z\,(v, Tx_{n+1})\}] \lim_{n\to\infty} \xi_\lambda(x_{n+1}, v) \\
&\leq \lim_{n\to\infty} \xi_\lambda(x_n, z_0)
\end{aligned}$$

for all $\lambda > 0$.

Thus, we have $0 \leq r \lim_{n\to\infty} \xi_\lambda(x_{n+1}, v) \leq \lim_{n\to\infty} \xi_\lambda(x_n, z_0) = 0$ for all $\lambda > 0$ since $\lim_{n\to\infty} \xi_\lambda(x_n, z_0) = \xi_\lambda(z_0, z_0) = \lim_{n,m\to\infty} \xi_\lambda(x_n, x_m) = 0$ for all $\lambda > 0$, which implies $r \lim_{n\to\infty} \xi_\lambda(x_{n+1}, v) = 0$ for all $\lambda > 0$. It follows that $\lim_{n\to\infty} \xi_\lambda(x_{n+1}, v) = 0$ for all $\lambda > 0$ since $r > s \geq 1$. By Proposition 3, v is unique. Also, since $\lim_{n\to\infty} \xi_\lambda(x_n, z_0) = 0$, z_0 is unique again from Proposition 3, that is why we have $v = z_0$. It follows that $Tz_0 = z_0$ since $Tv = z_0$. Thus, z_0 is a fixed point of T. Next, we prove that this fixed point z_0 is unique.

Suppose that y_0 is another fixed point of T such that $z_0 \neq y_0$. Therefore, we have $Ty_0 = y_0$. Thus, from (1), we have

$$\xi_\lambda(Tz_0, Ty_0) \geq r\xi_\lambda(z_0, y_0)$$

for all $\lambda > 0$, which implies $\xi_\lambda(z_0, y_0) \geq r\xi_\lambda(z_0, y_0)$ for all $\lambda > 0$.

It follows that $0 \geq (r-1)\xi_\lambda(z_0, y_0)$ for all $\lambda > 0$.

Since $r > s \geq 1$, which implies $r > 1$, we have $r - 1 > 0$. That is why we have $\xi_\lambda(z_0, y_0) = 0$ for all $\lambda > 0$. Thus, we get $z_0 = y_0$ from condition $(MbML1)$.

If we take $l = 0$ in Theorem 2, then we deduce the following corollary. □

Corollary 1. *Let (X, ξ, s) be a modular b-metric-like space such that $X_\xi{}^{fin}$ is ξ-complete. Suppose that the mapping $T : X_\xi{}^{fin} \to X_\xi{}^{fin}$ is onto and satisfies $\xi_\lambda(Tx, Ty) \geq r\xi_\lambda(x, y)$ for all $x, y \in X_\xi{}^{fin}$ and all $\lambda > 0$, where $r > s$. Then, T has a unique fixed point.*

Example 7. *Let $X = [0, \infty)$. Define the function $\xi : (0, \infty) \times X \times X \to [0, \infty]$ by $\xi_\lambda(x, y) = \frac{d(x,y)}{\lambda}$ for all $\lambda > 0$ such that $d(x, y) = (x + y)^2$ and $x, y \in X = [0, \infty)$. Then, $(X, \xi, 2)$ is a modular b-metric-like space such that $X_\xi{}^{fin}$ is ξ-complete since $X_\xi{}^{fin} = X$. Let $T : X_\xi{}^{fin} \to X_\xi{}^{fin}$ be defined by*

$$Tx = \begin{cases} 4x, & x \in [0,1), \\ 3x + 2, & x \in [1,2), \\ 6x + 1, & x \in [2, \infty). \end{cases}$$

Clearly, T is an onto mapping. Now, we consider the following cases:

$*$ *Let $x, y \in [0, 1)$. Then, $\xi_\lambda(Tx, Ty) = \frac{d(4x,4y)}{\lambda} = \frac{(4x+4y)^2}{\lambda} = \frac{16(x+y)^2}{\lambda} \geq \frac{3(x+y)^2}{\lambda} = 3\xi_\lambda(x, y)$ for all $\lambda > 0$.*

$*$ *Let $x, y \in [1, 2)$. Then, $\xi_\lambda(Tx, Ty) = \frac{d(3x+2,3y+2)}{\lambda} = \frac{(3x+2+3y+2)^2}{\lambda} = \frac{(3x+3y+4)^2}{\lambda} \geq \frac{(3x+3y)^2}{\lambda} = \frac{9(x+y)^2}{\lambda} \geq \frac{3(x+y)^2}{\lambda} = 3\xi_\lambda(x, y)$ for all $\lambda > 0$.*

$*$ *Let $x, y \in [2, \infty)$. Then, $\xi_\lambda(Tx, Ty) = \frac{d(6x+1,6y+1)}{\lambda} = \frac{(6x+1+6y+1)^2}{\lambda} = \frac{(6x+6y+2)^2}{\lambda} \geq \frac{(6x+6y)^2}{\lambda} = \frac{36(x+y)^2}{\lambda} \geq \frac{3(x+y)^2}{\lambda} = 3\xi_\lambda(x, y)$ for all $\lambda > 0$.*

$*$ *Let $x \in [0, 1)$ and $y \in [1, 2)$. Then, $\xi_\lambda(Tx, Ty) = \frac{d(4x,3y+2)}{\lambda} = \frac{(4x+3y+2)^2}{\lambda} \geq \frac{(3x+3y)^2}{\lambda} = \frac{9(x+y)^2}{\lambda} \geq \frac{3(x+y)^2}{\lambda} = 3\xi_\lambda(x, y)$ for all $\lambda > 0$.*

$*$ *Let $x \in [0, 1)$ and $y \in [2, \infty)$. Then, $\xi_\lambda(Tx, Ty) = \frac{d(4x,6y+1)}{\lambda} = \frac{(4x+6y+1)^2}{\lambda} \geq \frac{(4x+4y)^2}{\lambda} = \frac{16(x+y)^2}{\lambda} \geq \frac{3(x+y)^2}{\lambda} = 3\xi_\lambda(x, y)$ for all $\lambda > 0$.*

$*$ *Let $x \in [1, 2)$ and $y \in [2, \infty)$. Then, $\xi_\lambda(Tx, Ty) = \frac{d(3x+2,6y+1)}{\lambda} = \frac{(3x+2+6y+1)^2}{\lambda} = \frac{(3x+6y+3)^2}{\lambda} \geq \frac{(3x+3y)^2}{\lambda} = \frac{9(x+y)^2}{\lambda} \geq \frac{3(x+y)^2}{\lambda} = 3\xi_\lambda(x, y)$ for all $\lambda > 0$.*

That is, $\xi_\lambda(Tx, Ty) \geq r\xi_\lambda(x, y)$ for all $x, y \in X_\xi{}^{fin}$ and all $\lambda > 0$, where $r = 3 > 2 = s$. The conditions of Corollary 1 are satisfied, and T has a unique fixed point $x_0 = 0$.

5. An Application to an Integral Equation

In this section, we investigate the existence of a solution for an integral equation by using Theorem 1.

Consider the following integral equation:

$$\varpi(s) = \int_0^L \varsigma(s, q, \varpi(q))dq, \tag{2}$$

where $L > 0$ and $\varsigma : [0, L] \times [0, L] \times IR \to IR$.

Let $\aleph = C[0, L]$ be the set of all continuous real-valued functions defined on $[0, L]$. Consider the modular b-metric-like given as $\xi_\lambda(\varpi(s), \varphi(s)) = \frac{\max_{s\in[0,L]}(|\varpi(s)|+|\varphi(s)|)^2}{\lambda}$ for all $\lambda > 0$ and all $\varpi, \varphi \in \aleph$. Clearly, $(\aleph, \xi, 2)$ is modular b-metric-like space such that $\aleph_\xi{}^{fin}$ is ξ-complete since $\aleph = \aleph_\xi{}^{fin}$.

Let $\Psi\varpi(s) = \int_0^L \varsigma(s, q, \varpi(q))dq$ for all $\varpi \in \aleph$ and $s \in [0, L]$. Observe that the existence of a solution of (2) is equivalent to the existence of a fixed point of Ψ.

Theorem 3. *Suppose that the following conditions hold. Then, considering the above, the Integral Equation (2) has a unique solution:*

(1) $\varsigma : [0, L] \times [0, L] \times IR \to IR$ is continuous.

(2) There is a continuous function $\delta : [0, L] \times [0, L] \to IR^+$ for all $s, q \in [0, L]$ such that $|\varsigma(s, q, \varpi(q))| + |\varsigma(s, q, \varphi(q))| \leq \vartheta^{\frac{1}{2}}\delta(s, q)(|\varpi(s)| + |\varphi(s)|)$ where $\vartheta \in (0, 1)$.

(3) $\sup_{s\in[0,L]} \int_0^L \delta(s, q)dq \leq 1$.

Proof. For all $s \in [0, L]$, we have

$$\begin{aligned}
\frac{(|\Psi\varpi(s)|+|\Psi\varphi(s)|)^2}{\lambda} &= \frac{(|\int_0^L \varsigma(s,q,\varpi(q))dq|+|\int_0^L \varsigma(s,q,\varphi(q))dq|)^2}{\lambda} \\
&\leq \frac{(\int_0^L |\varsigma(s,q,\varpi(q))|dq+\int_0^L |\varsigma(s,q,\varphi(q))|dq)^2}{\lambda} \\
&= \frac{(\int_0^L |\varsigma(s,q,\varpi(q))|+|\varsigma(s,q,\varphi(q))|dq)^2}{\lambda} \\
&\leq \frac{(\int_0^L \vartheta^{\frac{1}{2}}\delta(s,q)(|\varpi(s)|+|\varphi(s)|)dq)^2}{\lambda} \\
&= \frac{(\int_0^L \vartheta^{\frac{1}{2}}\delta(s,q)((|\varpi(s)|+|\varphi(s)|)^2)^{\frac{1}{2}}dq)^2}{\lambda} \\
&= \frac{\vartheta(|\varpi(s)|+|\varphi(s)|)^2(\int_0^L \delta(s,q)dq)^2}{\lambda} \\
&\leq \frac{\vartheta(|\varpi(s)|+|\varphi(s)|)^2(\sup_{s\in[0,L]}\int_0^L \delta(s,q)dq)^2}{\lambda} \\
&\leq \vartheta\frac{(|\varpi(s)|+|\varphi(s)|)^2}{\lambda}.
\end{aligned}$$

Then, for all $s \in [0, L]$, we have

$$\frac{(|\Psi\varpi(s)| + |\Psi\varphi(s)|)^2}{\lambda} \leq \max_{s\in[0,L]} \vartheta\frac{(|\varpi(s)| + |\varphi(s)|)^2}{\lambda}.$$

It follows that

$$\max_{s\in[0,L]} \frac{(|\Psi\varpi(s)| + |\Psi\varphi(s)|)^2}{\lambda} \leq \max_{s\in[0,L]} \vartheta\frac{(|\varpi(s)| + |\varphi(s)|)^2}{\lambda}.$$

Hence,

$$\frac{\max_{s\in[0,L]}(|\Psi\varpi(s)| + |\Psi\varphi(s)|)^2}{\lambda} \leq \vartheta\frac{\max_{s\in[0,L]}(|\varpi(s)| + |\varphi(s)|)^2}{\lambda}.$$

Thus, we have

$$\xi_\lambda(\Psi\varpi(s), \Psi\varphi(s)) \leq \vartheta\xi_\lambda(\varpi(s), \varphi(s)).$$

Also, observe that all conditions of Theorem 1 are satisfied. Therefore, the operator Ψ has a unique fixed point. This means that the Integral Equation (2) has a unique solution. □

Example 8. *Consider the integral equation below.*

$$\varpi(s) = \frac{1}{3}\int_0^1 q\varpi(q)dq \tag{3}$$

Then, it has a solution in $\aleph$.

Let $\Psi : \aleph \to \aleph$ be defined by $\Psi\varpi(s) = \frac{1}{3}\int_0^1 q\varpi(q)dq$. By setting $\varsigma(s, q, \varpi(q)) = \frac{1}{3}q\varpi(q)$ in Theorem 3, we get

(1) $\varsigma : [0, 1] \times [0, 1] \times IR \to IR$ is continuous.

(2) There is a continuous function $\delta(s, q) = q$ for all $s, q \in [0, 1]$ such that

$$\begin{aligned} |\varsigma(s,q,\varpi(q))| + |\varsigma(s,q,\varphi(q))| &= |\tfrac{1}{3}q\varpi(q)| + |\tfrac{1}{3}q\varphi(q)| \\ &= \tfrac{1}{3}q(|\varpi(q)| + |\varphi(q)|) \\ &\leq \tfrac{1}{2}q(|\varpi(q)| + |\varphi(q)|) \\ &= (\tfrac{1}{4})^{\frac{1}{2}}q(|\varpi(q)| + |\varphi(q)|) \\ &= \vartheta^{\frac{1}{2}}\delta(s,q)(|\varpi(q)| + |\varphi(q)|) \end{aligned}$$

where $\vartheta = \frac{1}{4} \in (0,1)$.

(3) $\sup_{s\in[0,1]} \int_0^1 \delta(s,q)dq = \sup_{s\in[0,1]} \int_0^1 qdq \leq 1$.

Hence, all conditions of Theorem 3 are satisfied. Therefore, the problem (3) *has a solution in* $\aleph$.

6. Conclusions

Fixed point results are important to solve many mathematical problems, such as differential equations, integral equations, and systems of linear equations. That is why we provided some fixed point results on a new space called a modular b-metric-like space and an application of these results to an integral equation. Our work is useful from a theoretical and applied perspective, as the result of this paper enables the further development of fixed point theory and its application. Also, our results may provide motivation for researchers to improve fixed point theory by working in this new space. New contraction mappings can be defined on this new space; thus, different application areas can be found.

Author Contributions: Conceptualization, B.P.V. and N.U.B.; Software, B.P.V.; Formal analysis, N.U.B.; Investigation, N.U.B; Resources, B.P.V.; Data curation, N.U.B; Writing—original draft, B.P.V. and N.U.B.; Supervision, B.P.V.; Project administration, B.P.V. All authors contributed equally in writing this article. All authors have read and agreed to the published version of the manuscript.

Funding: This research received no external funding.

Data Availability Statement: Data are contained within the article.

Conflicts of Interest: The authors declare no conflict of interest.

References

1. Fréchet, M.M. Sur quelques points du calcul fonctionnel. *Rend. Circ. Mat. Palermo* **1906**, *22*, 1–72. [CrossRef]
2. Hausdorff, F. *Grundzüge der Mengenlehre*, Veit and Company: Leipzig, Germany, 1914.
3. Banach, S. Sur les opérations dans les ensembles abstraits et leur application aux équations intégrales. *Fundam. Math.* **1922**, *3*, 133–181. [CrossRef]
4. Czerwik, S. Contraction mappings in b-metric spaces. *Acta Math. Inform. Univ. Ostrav.* **1993**, *1*, 5–11.
5. Boriceanu, M. *Fixed Point Theory for Multivalued Generalized Contraction on a Set with Two b-Metrics*; Studia Universitatis Babeş-Bolyai Mathematica: Cluj-Napoca, Romania, 2009; Volume LIV.
6. Amini-Harandi, A. Metric-like spaces, partial metric spaces and fixed points. *Fixed Point Theory Appl.* **2012**, *2012*, 204. [CrossRef]
7. Hosseini, A.; Fošner, A. On the Structure of Metric-like Spaces. *Sahand Commun. Math. Anal.* **2019**, *14*, 159–171.
8. Alghamdi, M.A.; Hussain, N.; Salimi, P. Fixed point and coupled fixed point theorems on b-metric-like spaces. *J. Inequalities Appl.* **2013**, *2013*, 402. [CrossRef]
9. Nakano, H. *Modulared Semi-Ordered Linear Spaces*; Tokyo Mathematical Book Series; Maruzen Company Limited: Tokyo, Japan, 1950.
10. Orlicz, W. A note on modular spaces. *I Bull. De L'académie Pol. Des Sci. Série Des Sci. Mathématiques Astron. Et Phys.* **1961**, *9*, 157–162.
11. Chistyakov, V.V. Metric modulars and their application. *Dokl. Math.* **2006**, *73*, 32–35. [CrossRef]
12. Chistyakov, V.V. Modular metric spaces generated by F-modulars. *Folia Math.* **2008**, *15*, 3–24.
13. Chistyakov, V.V. A fixed point theorem for contractions in modular metric spaces. *arXiv* **2011**, arXiv:1112.5561.
14. Chistyakov, V.V. Modular metric spaces, I: Basic concepts. *Nonlinear Anal.* **2010**, *72*, 1–14. [CrossRef]
15. Chistyakov, V.V. Fixed points of modular contractive maps. *Dokl. Math.* **2012**, *86*, 515–518. [CrossRef]
16. Chistyakov, V.V. Modular contractions and their application. In *Models, Algorithms, and Technologies for Network Analysis, Springer Proceedings in Mathematics and Statistics*; Springer: New York, NY, USA, 2013; Volume 32, pp. 65–92.
17. Chistyakov, V.V. Modular Lipschitzian and contractive maps. In *Optimization, Control, and Applications in the Information Age, Springer Proceedings in Mathematics and Statistics*; Migdalas, A., Karakitsiou, A., Eds.; Springer International Publishing: Cham , Switzerland, 2015; Volume 130, pp. 1–15.

18. Chistyakov, V.V. *Metric Modular Spaces, Theory and Applications*; Springer International Publishing: Cham, Switzerland, 2015.
19. Mongkolkeha, C.; Sintunavarat, W.; Kumam, P. Fixed point theorems for contraction mappings in modular metric spaces. *Fixed Point Theory Appl.* **2011**, *2011*, 93. [CrossRef]
20. Ege, M.E.; Alaca, C. Some results for modular b-metric spaces and an application to system of linear equations. *Azerbaijan J. Math.* **2018**, *8*, 3–14.
21. Rasham, T.; Shoaib, A.; Park, C.; De La Sen, M.; Aydi, H.; Lee, J.R. Multivalued fixed point results for two families of mappings in modular-like metric spaces with applications. *Complexity* **2020**, *2020*, 1–10. [CrossRef]
22. Ali, F.; Ali, J.; Rodríguez-López, R. Approximation of fixed points and the solution of a nonlinear integral equation. *Nonlinear Funct. Anal. Appl.* **2021**, *26*, 869–885.
23. Ali, J.; Jubair, M. Estimation of common fixed points of SKC mappings and an application to fractional differential equations. *J. Anal.* **2023**, *32*, 889–913. [CrossRef]
24. Özger, F.; Temizer Ersoy, M.; Ödemiş Özger, Z. Existence of Solutions: Investigating Fredholm Integral Equations via a Fixed-Point Theorem. *Axioms* **2024**, *13*, 261. [CrossRef]
25. Das, D.; Narzary, S.; Bora, N. Some Fixed Point Results in Modular-like Metric Spaces and Partial Modular-like Metric Spaces with Its Non-Archimedean Version. *Adv. Appl. Math. Sci.* **2022**, *21*, 5997–6016.
26. Antón-Sancho, Á. Fixed points of principal E_6-bundles over a compact algebraic curve. *Quaest. Math.* **2023**, *47*, 501–513. [CrossRef]
27. Antón-Sancho, Á. Fixed Points of Automorphisms of the Vector Bundle Moduli Space Over a Compact Riemann Surface. *Mediterr. J. Math.* **2023**, *21*, 20. [CrossRef]
28. Antón-Sancho, Á. Triality and automorphisms of principal bundles moduli spaces. *Adv. Geom.* **2024**, *24*, 421–435.

axioms

MDPI

Article

Enriched $\mathcal{Z}$-Contractions and Fixed-Point Results with Applications to IFS

Ibrahim Alraddadi [1], Muhammad Din [2], Umar Ishtiaq [3], Mohammad Akram [1,*] and Ioannis K. Argyros [4,*]

[1] Department of Mathematics, Faculty of Science, Islamic University of Madinah, Madinah 42351, Saudi Arabia; ialraddadi@iu.edu.sa
[2] Department of Mathematics and Statistics, Faculty of Science and Technology, Thammasat University Rangsit Center, Pathum Thani 12120, Thailand; muhammad.din@dome.tu.ac.th
[3] Department of Mathematics, Quaid-i-Azam University, Islamabad 45320, Pakistan; umarishtiaq000@gmail.com or umar.32411007@math.qau.edu.pk
[4] Department of Computing and Mathematical Sciences, Cameron University, Lawton, OK 73505, USA
* Correspondence: akramkhan_20@rediffmail.com or akram@iu.edu.sa (M.A.); iargyros@cameron.edu (I.K.A.)

Abstract: In this manuscript, we initiate a large class of enriched $(d, \mathfrak{Z})$-$\mathcal{Z}$-contractions defined on Banach spaces and prove the existence and uniqueness of the fixed point of these contractions. We also provide an example to support our results and give an existence condition for the uniqueness of the solution to the integral equation. The results provided in the manuscript extend, generalize, and modify the existence results. Our research introduces novel fixed-point results under various contractive conditions. Furthermore, we discuss the iterated function system associated with enriched $(d, \mathfrak{Z})$-$\mathcal{Z}$-contractions in Banach spaces and define the enriched $\mathcal{Z}$-Hutchinson operator. A result regarding the convergence of Krasnoselskii's iteration method and the uniqueness of the attractor via enriched $(d, \mathfrak{Z})$-$\mathcal{Z}$-contractions is also established. Our discoveries not only confirm but also significantly build upon and broaden several established findings in the current body of literature.

Keywords: Banach space; Hutchinson operator; fixed point; Krasnoselskii's iteration

MSC: 47H10; 54H25

1. Introduction

The theory of the fixed point (FP) is an essential part of fractals and the iterated function system (IFS). Basically, the simplest forms of fractals are the compact subsets in Hausdorff spaces that remain unchanged under Hutchinson–Barnsley operators. The concept of an iterated function system (IFS) was initiated to study fractals by Hutchinson [1] and Barnsley [2]. IFSs are, in fact, the natural extension of the classical contraction principle given by Banach [3] in 1922. Fractals, as an IFS, are very important due to their applications in many fields. For example, IFSs have applications in image compression, quantum physics, graphics, wavelet analysis, and many others areas. That is why many computer experts and mathematicians have shown their interest in this active research area. For example, see the work of Andres and Fišer [4], Duvall et al. [5], Kieninger [6], Barnsley and Demko [7], Zhou et al. [8], and the references therein for deep understanding.

Over time, the concept of an IFS has been generalized in many directions. In the past decades, many tools have been created to analyze the unique attractor (or the unique FP of Hutchinson–Barnsley operators) of the fractals. This theory of IFS has been expanded via generalized contractions, multifunctions, countable IFSs, and more. In particular, Kashyap et al. [9] generalized the fractal given by Mandelbrot [10] by using the Krasnoselskii theorem. Maślanka and Strobin [11] explored the generalized IFSs given by the l_∞-sum of a metric space (MS), and Klimek and Kosek [12] discussed the multifunctions, generalized IFSs, and Cantor sets. Torre and others [13–15] studied the more generalized multifunctions. Khumalo et al. [16] studied generalized IFSs for shared attractors in partial MSs.

Very recently, Rizwan et al. [17] generalized the work of Ahmad et al. [18] on fractals with the generalized Θ-Hutchinson operator by using the enriched contraction given by Berinde and Păcurar [19]. Prithvi and colleagues in [20–22] discussed the IFS over generalized Kannan mappings and also gave remarks on countable IFSs via the partial Hausdorff metric and non-conventional IFSs. Sahu et al. [23], Thangaraj et al. [24], and Chandra and Verma [25] constructed fractals via an IFS on Kannan contractions with different conditions. Amit et al. [26] presented the idea of IFS via non-stationary Φ-contractions, while Verma and Priyadarshi [27] worked on general datasets and generated a new type of fractal function. Khojasteh et al. [28] presented FP results via the notion of a simulation function (SF) and $\mathcal{Z}$-contraction. Rhoades [29] studied the continuity and nondecreasing behavior of Φ-contractions.

Throughout the article, we represent the MS by $(\tilde{\Pi}, \mathfrak{u})$, linear normed space by $(\tilde{\Pi}, ||\cdot||)$, and collection of all non-empty and compact subsets of $\tilde{\Pi}$ by $\Lambda(\tilde{\Pi})$. The distance between an element ι^o of $\tilde{\Pi}$ and a subset Υ^o of $\tilde{\Pi}$ is given by:

$$\mathfrak{u}(\iota^o, \Upsilon^o) = \min_{\varrho^o \in \Upsilon^o} \mathfrak{u}(\iota^o, \varrho^o),$$

while the distance between two subsets Υ^o and $\mho$ of $\tilde{\Pi}$ is given by:

$$\mathfrak{D}(\Upsilon^o, \mho) = \max_{\iota^o \in \Upsilon^o} \mathfrak{u}(\iota^o, \mho).$$

Using the above notions, the Hausdorff metric is given by:

$$\mathring{\eth}(\Upsilon^o, \mho) = \max\{\mathfrak{D}(\Upsilon^o, \mho), \mathfrak{D}(\mho, \Upsilon^o)\}.$$

It is noted that, if $\tilde{\Pi}$ is complete, then the Hausdorff space $\Lambda(\tilde{\Pi})$ is also complete. We used the following technical lemma and notions in our main findings.

Lemma 1 ([2]). *Consider $\tilde{\Pi}$ be a MS and $\Upsilon^o, \mho, \mathfrak{C} \in \Lambda(\tilde{\Pi})$. Then, the following holds:*
(i) $\mathfrak{C} \subseteq \mho \Rightarrow \sup_{\iota^o \in \Upsilon^o} \mathfrak{u}(\iota^o, \mathfrak{C}) \leq \sup_{\iota^o \in \Upsilon^o} \mathfrak{u}(\iota^o, \mho)$;
(ii) $\sup_{\iota^o \in \Upsilon^o \cup \mathfrak{C}} \mathfrak{u}(\iota^o, \mho) = \max\{\sup_{\iota^o \in \Upsilon^o} \mathfrak{u}(\iota^o, \mho), \sup_{\iota^o \in \mathfrak{C}} \mathfrak{u}(\iota^o, \mho)\}$;
(iii) If $\{\Upsilon^o{}_i : i = 1, 2, \cdots, \jmath\}$ *and* $\{\mathfrak{C}_i : i = 1, 2, \cdots, \jmath\}$ *are two finite collections of subsets of* $\tilde{\Pi}$, *then*

$$\mathring{\eth}\Big(\bigcup_{i=1}^{\jmath} \Upsilon^o{}_i, \bigcup_{i=1}^{\jmath} \mathfrak{C}_i\Big) \leq \max_{i=1}^{\jmath}\Big\{\mathring{\eth}(\Upsilon^o{}_i, \mathfrak{C}_i)\Big\}.$$

Definition 1 ([2]). *Consider $(\tilde{\Pi}, \mathfrak{u})$ to be a complete MS and $\{\Theta^{(i)} : \tilde{\Pi} \to \tilde{\Pi}$, for all $i = 1, 2, \cdots, \jmath\}$ to be a family of all continuous contraction mappings with contraction factors $\theta_i, \forall i = 1, 2, \cdots, \jmath$. Then, $(\tilde{\Pi}, \Theta^{(1)}, \Theta^{(2)}, \cdots, \Theta^{(\jmath)})$ is named as IFS.*

Definition 2 ([2]). *Any set Υ^o from $\Lambda(\tilde{\Pi})$ is known as the attractor of the IFS if:*

1: $\Theta(\Upsilon^o) = \Upsilon^o$;
2: *$\exists$ an open set $\mho \subseteq \tilde{\Pi}$ for which $\mho \subseteq \Upsilon^o$ and $\lim_{q \to \infty} \Theta^q(\mathfrak{C}) = \Upsilon^o$, for any $\mathfrak{C} \in \Lambda(\tilde{\Pi})$ with $\mathfrak{C} \subseteq \mho$, where the limit is taken with respect to the Hausdorff metric $\mathring{\eth}$.*

The primary outcome in this area was presented by Barnsley in [2], which is expressed as follows:

Theorem 1 ([2]). *Let $(\tilde{\Pi}, \Theta^{(1)}, \Theta^{(2)}, \cdots, \Theta^{(\jmath)})$ be an IFS with contraction factors θ_i, for all $i = 1, 2, \cdots, \jmath$. Then, the operator $\Theta^* : \Lambda(\tilde{\Pi}) \to \Lambda(\tilde{\Pi})$, defined by*

$$\Theta^*(\mathcal{Z}) = \bigcup_{i=1}^{\jmath} \Theta^{(i)}(\Upsilon^o), \quad \forall \Upsilon^o \in \Lambda(\tilde{\Pi}),$$

is also a contraction on $(\Lambda(\tilde{\Pi}), \mathring{\partial})$, with contraction factor $\theta = \max_{i=1}^{\jmath} \theta_i$. Further, Θ^* has a unique attractor, that is, $\exists \Upsilon^{o*} \in \Lambda(\tilde{\Pi})$, such that

$$\Upsilon^{o*} = \Theta^*(\Upsilon^{o*}) = \bigcup_{i=1}^{\jmath} \Theta^{(i)}(\Upsilon^{o*}),$$

and is obtained by $\Upsilon^{o*} = \lim_{q \to \infty} \Theta^{*q}(\mho)$ for any initial choice $\mho \in \Lambda(\tilde{\Pi})$. Here, $\Theta^{*q}(\mho)$ is given by $\Theta^{*q}(\mho) = \Theta^*(\Theta^{*q-1}(\mho))$.

Remark 1 ([17]). *For a given normed space $(\tilde{\Pi}, ||\cdot||)$, we have*

1. *for all Υ^o and $\mho$ of $\tilde{\Pi}$,*

$$\Upsilon^o + \mho := \{\iota^o + \varrho^o : \iota^o \in \Upsilon^o, \varrho^o \in \mho\};$$

2. *for any $\Upsilon^o \subseteq \tilde{\Pi}$, and a real number ν,*

$$\nu\Upsilon^o := \{\nu\iota^o : \iota^o \in \Upsilon^o\}.$$

Recently, Berinde and Păcurar [19] established a wide and novel class of operators called "enriched contractions". This class comprises Banach contractions as well as various other nonexpansive contractions that have been introduced in the literature. They discovered that each enriched contraction has a distinct FP, which can be determined using a Krasnoselskii iteration sequence in the context of Banach spaces. Enriched contraction operators are important because they can include both Banach contractions and non-expansive mappings. In particular, the non-expansive mappings do not always ensure the FPs, but the enriched contraction mappings consistently demonstrated the unique FP.

Definition 3 ([19]). *Let $(\tilde{\Pi}, ||\cdot||)$ be a linear normed space. An operator $\Theta : \tilde{\Pi} \to \tilde{\Pi}$ is known as an enriched contraction if $\exists \mathrm{d} \geq 0$ and $\delta \in [0, \mathrm{d}+1)$ for which, for all $\iota^o, \varrho^o \in \tilde{\Pi}$:*

$$||\mathrm{d}(\iota^o - \varrho^o) + \Theta\iota^o - \Theta\varrho^o|| \leq \delta||\iota^o - \varrho^o||. \tag{1}$$

Lemma 2. *For any mapping Θ and its average operator $\Theta_\delta(\iota^o) = (1-\delta)\iota^o + \delta\Theta\iota^o$ for some $\delta \in [0, 1)$, the set of FPs for both mappings Θ and Θ_δ is the same.*

Recently, Khojasteh et al. [28] presented the notion of a well-known SF as well as the $\mathcal{Z}$-contraction and its FP results, which generalize the several classical FP theorems in the documented literature. A SF with some important examples is given by:

Definition 4 ([28]). *A function $\mathfrak{Z} : [0, \infty)^2 \to \mathbb{R}$ is said to be a SF if it fulfills the conditions listed below:*

(λ_1): $\mathfrak{Z}(0, 0) = 0$;
(λ_2): $\mathfrak{Z}(\iota^o, \varrho^o) < \varrho^o - \iota^o, \quad \forall \iota^o, \varrho^o > 0$;
(λ_3): *for sequences $\{\iota^o{}_l\}, \{\varrho^o{}_l\} \subseteq (0, \infty)$ satisfying $\lim_{l\to\infty} \iota^o{}_l = \lim_{l\to\infty} \varrho^o{}_l > 0$ implies*

$$\limsup_{l\to\infty} \mathfrak{Z}(\iota^o{}_l, \varrho^o{}_l) < 0.$$

The notation $\mathcal{Z}$ is used for the family of all the simulation functions $\mathfrak{Z}$ contained in $\mathcal{Z}$.

Example 1 ([28]). *Consider the mappings* $\mathfrak{Z}_i : [0,\infty)^2 \to \mathbb{R}$ *for* $i = 1,2,3$ *given by:*

1. $\mathfrak{Z}_1(\iota^o, \varrho^o) = \nu(\varrho^o) - \pi(\iota^o)$ *for all* $\iota^o, \varrho^o \in [0,\infty)$, *where* $\pi, \nu : [0,\infty) \to [0,\infty)$ *are the two continuous functions for which* $\nu(\iota^o) = \pi(\iota^o) = 0$ *if and only if* $\iota^o = 0$ *and* $\nu(\iota^o) < \iota^o \leq \pi(\iota^o)$ *for all* $\iota^o > 0$.
2. $\mathfrak{Z}_2(\iota^o, \varrho^o) = \varrho^o - \frac{\pi(\iota^o,\varrho^o)}{\nu(\iota^o,\varrho^o)}$ *for all* $\iota^o, \varrho^o \in [0,\infty)$, *where* $\pi, \nu : [0,\infty) \to (0,\infty)$ *are the two continuous functions for which* $\pi(\iota^o, \varrho^o) > \nu(\iota^o, \varrho^o)$ *for all* $\iota^o, \varrho^o > 0$.
3. $\mathfrak{Z}_3(\iota^o, \varrho^o) = \varrho^o - \pi(\varrho^o) - \iota^o$ *for all* $\iota^o, \varrho^o \in [0,\infty)$, *where* $\pi : [0,\infty) \to [0,\infty)$ *is the continuous function for which* $\pi(\iota^o) = 0$ *if and only if* $\iota^o = 0$.

Then, $\mathfrak{Z}_i$ *for* $i = 1,2,3$ *satisfies all conditions* $(\lambda_1 - \lambda_3)$, *so these are SFs.*

Khojasteh et al. [28], by using the notion of SFs, established the following definition of $\mathcal{Z}$-contraction as follows.

Definition 5 ([28]). *Let* $(\tilde{\Pi}, \mathrm{u})$ *be a MS,* $\Theta : \tilde{\Pi} \to \tilde{\Pi}$ *a mapping, and* $\mathfrak{Z} \in \mathcal{Z}$. *Then,* Θ *is called a* $\mathcal{Z}$*-contraction via SF* $\mathfrak{Z}$ *if:*

$$\mathfrak{Z}(\mathrm{u}(\Theta\iota^o, \Theta\varrho^o), \mathrm{u}(\iota^o, \varrho^o)) \geq 0 \text{ for all } \iota^o, \varrho^o \in \tilde{\Pi}. \tag{2}$$

By using the notion of enriched contraction given by Berinde and Păcurar [19] and the $\mathcal{Z}$-contraction via SF by Khojasteh et al. [28], we found a large class of enriched $(\mathrm{d}, \mathfrak{Z})$-$\mathcal{Z}$-contractions and proved the existence and uniqueness of the fixed point of these contractions in the setting of Banach spaces. We also present an example to support our results and give an existence condition for the uniqueness of the solution of the integral equation. Our research introduces novel FP results under various contractive conditions. Moreover, we also discuss the IFS associated with enriched $(\mathrm{d}, \mathfrak{Z})$-$\mathcal{Z}$-contractions and define the enriched $\mathcal{Z}$-Hutchinson operator in Banach spaces. The convergence of Krasnoselskii's iteration scheme and uniqueness of the attractor via enriched $(\mathrm{d}, \mathfrak{Z})$-$\mathcal{Z}$-contractions is also established.

2. Main Results

In the following section, we present the concept of $(\mathrm{d}, \mathfrak{Z})$-$\mathcal{Z}$-contraction operators and derive results regarding their existence and approximation of the fixed point.

Definition 6. *Let* $(\tilde{\Pi}, ||\cdot||)$ *be a normed space,* $\Theta : \tilde{\Pi} \to \tilde{\Pi}$ *a mapping, and* $\mathfrak{Z} \in \mathcal{Z}$. *Then,* Θ *is called an enriched* $(\mathrm{d}, \mathfrak{Z})$*-*$\mathcal{Z}$*-contraction via some* $\mathfrak{Z}$ *if* $\exists \mathrm{d} \in [0,\infty)$ *such that*

$$\mathfrak{Z}\Big(\frac{1}{\mathrm{d}+1}||\mathrm{d}(\iota^o - \varrho^o) + \Theta\iota^o - \Theta\varrho^o||, ||\iota^o - \varrho^o||\Big) \geq 0, \quad \forall \iota^o, \varrho^o \in \tilde{\Pi}. \tag{3}$$

To highlight the constant d and SF $\mathfrak{Z}$ involved in Definition (6), we call it an enriched $(\mathrm{d}, \mathfrak{Z})$-$\mathcal{Z}$-contraction on $\tilde{\Pi}$. We will now establish some properties of $\mathcal{Z}$-contractions defined in the setting of normed spaces.

Remark 2. *It is noted that, if we put* $\mathrm{d} = 0$ *in Definition (6), then we obtain Definition (5) given by Khojasteh et al. [28]. Therefore, every* $\mathcal{Z}$*-contraction via any* $\mathfrak{Z} \in \mathcal{Z}$ *is an enriched* $(0, \mathfrak{Z})$*-*$\mathcal{Z}$*-contraction.*

Remark 3. *Note that the definition of a SF implies* $\mathfrak{Z}(\iota^o, \varrho^o) < 0, \forall \iota^o \geq \varrho^o > 0$. *Therefore, if* Θ *is a* $(\mathrm{d}, \mathfrak{Z})$*-*$\mathcal{Z}$*-contraction, then*

$$\frac{1}{\mathrm{d}+1}||\mathrm{d}(\iota^o - \varrho^o) + \Theta\iota^o - \Theta\varrho^o|| < ||\iota^o - \varrho^o||, \quad \forall \iota^o, \varrho^o \in \tilde{\Pi},$$

or equivalently,

$$||\Theta_\delta\iota^o - \Theta_\delta\varrho^o|| < ||\iota^o - \varrho^o||, \quad \forall \iota^o, \varrho^o \in \tilde{\Pi}, \tag{4}$$

where $\delta = \frac{1}{d+1}$. *This shows that the transformation of* Θ_δ *is continuous. Thus,* Θ *being the translation and scaling of a continuous function is also continuous. Therefore, every* $\mathcal{Z}$*-contraction mapping is continuous.*

Initially, we present the following result, where we prove the uniqueness of the FP of an enriched $(d, \mathfrak{Z})$-$\mathcal{Z}$-contraction, provided it possesses a FP.

Lemma 3. *Let* $(\tilde{\Pi}, ||\cdot||)$ *be a normed space and* $\Theta : \tilde{\Pi} \to \tilde{\Pi}$ *be an enriched* $(d, \mathfrak{Z})$-$\mathcal{Z}$*-contraction on* $\tilde{\Pi}$. *The FP of* Θ *is unique in* $\tilde{\Pi}$, *provided it possesses a FP.*

Proof. Consider $\iota^o \in \tilde{\Pi}$ be any FP of Θ. On the contrary, we suppose that $\varrho^o \in \Theta$ is any other FP of Θ, with $\iota^o \neq \varrho^o$. It is to be noted that the collection of FPs of both Θ and Θ_δ is the same. Thus, using (3), we obtain the following:

$$0 \leq \mathfrak{Z}(\frac{1}{d+1}||d(\iota^o - \varrho^o) + \Theta\iota^o - \Theta\varrho^o||, ||\iota^o - \varrho^o||) = \mathfrak{Z}(||\Theta_\delta\iota^o - \Theta_\delta\varrho^o||, ||\iota^o - \varrho^o||) = \mathfrak{Z}(||\iota^o - \varrho^o||, ||\iota^o - \varrho^o). \quad (5)$$

In light of Remark (3), inequality (5) implies a contradiction, and this proves our result. □

Next, we show that, for any enriched $(d, \mathfrak{Z})$-$\mathcal{Z}$-contraction, the corresponding transformation $\Theta_\delta := (1-\delta)I + \delta\Theta$ is always asymptotically regular.

Lemma 4. *Let* $(\tilde{\Pi}, ||\cdot||)$ *be a normed space and* Θ *be any enriched* $(d, \mathfrak{Z})$-$\mathcal{Z}$*-contraction on* $\tilde{\Pi}$. *Then, the averaged operator* Θ_δ *is asymptotically regular.*

Proof. Suppose any arbitrary element $\iota^o \in \tilde{\Pi}$ and $p \in \mathbb{N}$. If $\Theta_\delta^p\iota^o = \Theta^{p-1}\iota^o$, which further becomes $\Theta_\delta\varrho^o = \varrho^o$, then some $\varrho^o = \Theta_\delta^{p-1}\iota^o$. Then, $\Theta_\delta^q\varrho^o = \Theta_\delta^{q-1}\Theta_\delta\varrho^o = \Theta_\delta^{q-1}\varrho^o = \ldots = \Theta_\delta\varrho^o = \varrho^o$, $\forall q \in \mathbb{N}$. So, for a sufficiently large $q \in \mathbb{N}$, we obtain

$$\begin{aligned}||\Theta_\delta^q\iota^o - \Theta_\delta^{q+1}\iota^o|| &= ||\Theta_\delta^{q-p+1}\Theta_\delta^{p-1}\iota^o - \Theta_\delta^{q-p+2}\Theta_\delta^{p-1}\iota^o|| = ||\Theta_\delta^{q-p+1}\varrho^o - \Theta_\delta^{q-p+2}\varrho^o|| \\ &= ||\varrho^o - \varrho^o|| = 0.\end{aligned}$$

Letting $q \to \infty$, we obtain $\lim_{q\to\infty} ||\Theta_\delta^q\iota^o - \Theta_\delta^{q+1}\iota^o|| = 0, \quad \forall \iota^o \in \tilde{\Pi}$. On the other hand, consider $\Theta_\delta^q\iota^o \neq \Theta_\delta^{q-1}\iota^o$, $\forall q \in \mathbb{N}$. So, by using inequality (3), we obtain

$$\begin{aligned}0 &\leq \mathfrak{Z}(||\Theta_\delta^{q+1}\iota^o - \Theta_\delta^q\iota^o||, ||\Theta_\delta^q\iota^o - \Theta_\delta^{q-1}\iota^o||) \\ &= \mathfrak{Z}\Big(||\Theta_\delta\Theta_\delta^q\iota^o - \Theta_\delta\Theta_\delta^{q-1}\iota^o||, ||\Theta_\delta^q\iota^o - \Theta_\delta^{q-1}\iota^o||\Big) \\ &< ||\Theta_\delta^q\iota^o - \Theta_\delta^{q-1}\iota^o|| - ||\Theta_\delta^{q+1}\iota^o - \Theta_\delta^q\iota^o|| \\ \implies &||\Theta_\delta^{q+1}\iota^o - \Theta_\delta^q\iota^o|| < ||\Theta_\delta^q\iota^o - \Theta_\delta^{q-1}\iota^o||.\end{aligned}$$

This shows that $\Big\{||\Theta_\delta^q\iota^o - \Theta_\delta^{q-1}\iota^o||\Big\}$ is a monotonically decreasing sequence of positive real numbers. Therefore, it must be convergent. Let $\lim_{q\to\infty} ||\Theta_\delta^q\iota^o - \Theta_\delta^{q+1}\iota^o|| = s \geq 0$. If $s > 0$, and as Θ is an enriched $(d, \mathfrak{Z})$-$\mathcal{Z}$-contraction, therefore by $(\mathfrak{Z}_3)$, we obtain

$$0 \leq \limsup_{q\to\infty} \mathfrak{Z}\Big(||\Theta_\delta^{q+1}\iota^o - \Theta_\delta^q\iota^o||, ||\Theta_\delta^q\iota^o - \Theta_\delta^{q-1}\iota^o||\Big) < 0,$$

which is a contradiction. This implies that $s = 0$. Equivalently, $\lim_{q\to\infty} ||\Theta_\delta^q\iota^o - \Theta_\delta^{q+1}\iota^o|| = 0$. Thus, Θ_δ is an asymptotically regular mapping on $\tilde{\Pi}$. □

The following result demonstrates that the Krasnoselskii sequence $\{\iota^o{}_q\}$ generated by an enriched $(d, \mathfrak{Z})$-$\mathcal{Z}$-contraction is always bounded.

Lemma 5. *Let* $(\tilde{\Pi}, ||\cdot||)$ *be a normed space and* $\Theta : \tilde{\Pi} \to \tilde{\Pi}$ *be an enriched* $(\mathrm{d}, \mathfrak{Z})$*-*$\mathcal{Z}$*-contraction. Then, the Krasnoselskii sequence* $\{\iota^o{}_q\}$ *generated by* Θ *with initial value* $\iota^o{}_0 \in \iota^o$ *is a bounded sequence, where* $\iota^o{}_q = (1-\delta)\iota^o{}_{q-1} + \delta\Theta\iota^o{}_{q-1}, \forall q \in \mathbb{N}$ *and* $\delta = \frac{1}{\mathrm{d}+1}$*.*

Proof. For any arbitrary point $\iota^o{}_0 \in \tilde{\Pi}$, define the Krasnoselskii sequence $\{\iota^o{}_q\}$ given by $\iota^o{}_q = (1-\delta)\iota^o{}_{q-1} + \delta\Theta\iota^o{}_{q-1} = \Theta_\delta\iota^o{}_{q-1}, \forall q \in \mathbb{N}$. Assume that $\{\iota^o{}_q\}$ is not bounded. Then, without loss of generality, we can suppose that $\iota^o{}_{q+p} \neq \iota^o{}_q, \forall q, p \in \mathbb{N}$. As the sequence $\{\iota^o{}_q\}$ is not bounded, so we must find a sub-sequence $\{\iota^o{}_{q_k}\}$ such that $q_1 = 1$ and, for each $k \in \mathbb{N}, q_{k+1}$ is the minimum integer such that $||\iota^o{}_{q_{k+1}} - \iota^o{}_{q_k}|| > 1$. Also, we obtain

$$||\iota^o{}_m - \iota^o{}_{q_k}|| \leq 1, \qquad q_k \leq m \leq q_{k+1} - 1. \tag{6}$$

Therefore, by utilizing inequality (6) and the triangular inequality, we have

$$\begin{aligned} 1 < ||\iota^o{}_{q_{k+1}} - \iota^o{}_{q_k}|| &\leq ||\iota^o{}_{q_{k+1}} - \iota^o{}_{q_{k+1}-1}|| + ||\iota^o{}_{q_{k+1}-1} - \iota^o{}_{q_k}|| \\ &\leq ||\iota^o{}_{q_{k+1}} - \iota^o{}_{q_{k+1}-1}|| + 1. \end{aligned}$$

Taking $k \to \infty$ and using Lemma (4), we obtain

$$\lim_{k\to\infty} ||\iota^o{}_{q_{k+1}} - \iota^o{}_{q_k}|| = 1.$$

By inequality (3), we conclude that $||\iota^o{}_{q_{k+1}} - \iota^o{}_{q_k}|| \leq ||\iota^o{}_{q_{k+1}-1} - \iota^o{}_{q_k-1}||$. Therefore, we obtain the following by the aid of triangular inequality as follows:

$$\begin{aligned} 1 < ||\iota^o{}_{q_{k+1}} - \iota^o{}_{q_k}|| &\leq ||\iota^o{}_{q_{k+1}-1} - \iota^o{}_{q_k-1}|| \\ &\leq ||\iota^o{}_{q_{k+1}-1} - \iota^o{}_{q_k}|| + ||\iota^o{}_{q_k} - \iota^o{}_{q_k-1}|| \\ &\leq 1 + ||\iota^o{}_{q_k} - \iota^o{}_{q_k-1}||. \end{aligned}$$

Taking $k \to \infty$ and using Lemma (4), we obtain

$$\lim_{k\to\infty} ||\iota^o{}_{q_{k+1}-1} - \iota^o{}_{q_k-1}|| = 1.$$

Now, since Θ is an enriched $(\mathrm{d}, \mathfrak{Z})$-$\mathcal{Z}$-contraction, from condition $\mathfrak{Z}_3$, we have

$$\begin{aligned} 0 &\leq \limsup_{k\to\infty} \mathfrak{Z}(||\Theta_\delta\iota^o{}_{q_{k+1}-1} - \Theta_\delta\iota^o{}_{q_k-1}||, ||\iota^o{}_{q_{k+1}-1} - \iota^o{}_{q_k-1}||) \\ &= \limsup_{k\to\infty} \mathfrak{Z}(||\iota^o{}_{q_{k+1}} - \iota^o{}_{q_k}||, ||\iota^o{}_{q_{k+1}-1} - \iota^o{}_{q_k-1}||) < 0, \end{aligned}$$

which is a contradiction. This complete the proof. □

In the next result, we prove the existence of the FP of an enriched $(\mathrm{d}, \mathfrak{Z})$-$\mathcal{Z}$-contraction.

Theorem 2. *Let* $(\tilde{\Pi}, ||\cdot||)$ *be a Banach space and* $\Theta : \tilde{\Pi} \to \tilde{\Pi}$ *be an enriched* $(\mathrm{d}, \mathfrak{Z})$*-*$\mathcal{Z}$*-contraction. Then,* Θ *has a unique FP in* $\tilde{\Pi}$ *and, for every initial guess* $\iota^o{}_0 \in \tilde{\Pi}$*, the Krasnoselskii sequence* $\{\iota^o{}_q\}$*, defined by* $\iota^o{}_q = \Theta_\delta\iota^o{}_{q-1}, \forall q \in \mathbb{N}$*, converges to the FP of* Θ*, where* $\delta = \frac{1}{\mathrm{d}+1}$*.*

Proof. From the definition of an enriched $(\mathrm{d}, \mathfrak{Z})$-$\mathcal{Z}$-contraction, we can write

$$\mathfrak{Z}(\delta||(\frac{1}{\delta} - 1)(\iota^o - \varrho^o) + \Theta\iota^o - \Theta\varrho^o||, ||\iota^o - \varrho^o||) \geq 0, \quad \forall \iota^o, \varrho^o \in \tilde{\Pi},$$

or equivalently,

$$\mathfrak{Z}(||\Theta_\delta\iota^o - \Theta_\delta\varrho^o||, ||\iota^o - \varrho^o||) \geq 0, \quad \forall \iota^o, \varrho^o \in \tilde{\Pi}. \tag{7}$$

Let $\iota^o{}_0 \in \tilde{\Pi}$ be an arbitrary initial point, and let $\{\iota^o{}_q\}$ be the Krasnoselskii sequence defined by $\iota^o{}_q = \Theta_\delta \iota^o{}_{q-1}$ for all $q \in \mathbb{N}$. First, we will demonstrate that the sequence $\{\iota^o{}_q\}$ is Cauchy. To accomplish this, take

$$\mathfrak{C}_q = \sup\{||\iota^o{}_i - \iota^o{}_j|| : i, j \geq q\}.$$

Observe that the sequence $\{\mathfrak{C}_q\}$ is a monotonically decreasing sequence of positive real numbers. According to Lemma (5), the sequence $\{\iota^o{}_q\}$ is bounded, which implies that $\mathfrak{C}_q < \infty$ for all $q \in \mathbb{N}$. Therefore, the sequence $\{\mathfrak{C}_q\}$ is monotonic and bounded, which implies it is convergent. This means there exists a non-negative real number $\mathfrak{C} \geq 0$ such that $\lim_{q\to\infty} \mathfrak{C}_q = \mathfrak{C}$. We aim to prove that $\mathfrak{C} = 0$. If $\mathfrak{C} > 0$, then according to the definition of $\mathfrak{C}_q$, for every $k \in \mathbb{N}$, there exist indices q_k and m_k such that $m_k > q_k \geq k$ and

$$\mathfrak{C}_k - \frac{1}{k} < ||\iota^o{}_{m_k} - \iota^o{}_{q_k}|| \leq \mathfrak{C}_k.$$

Hence,

$$\lim_{k\to\infty} ||\iota^o{}_{m_k} - \iota^o{}_{q_k}|| = \mathfrak{C}. \tag{8}$$

Using inequality (4) and the triangular inequality we have

$$\begin{aligned}||\iota^o{}_{m_k} - \iota^o{}_{q_k}|| &= ||\Theta_\delta \iota^o{}_{m_k-1} - \Theta_\delta \iota^o{}_{q_k-1}|| \\ &< ||\iota^o{}_{m_k-1} - \iota^o{}_{q_k-1}|| \\ &< ||\iota^o{}_{m_k-1} - \iota^o{}_{m_k}|| + ||\iota^o{}_{m_k} - \iota^o{}_{q_k}|| + ||\iota^o{}_{q_k} - \iota^o{}_{q_k-1}||.\end{aligned}$$

Using Lemma (4), inequality (8) and letting $k \to \infty$ in the above inequality, we obtain

$$\lim_{k\to\infty} ||\iota^o{}_{m_k-1} - \iota^o{}_{q_k-1}|| = \mathfrak{C}. \tag{9}$$

Since Θ is an enriched $(\mathrm{d}, \mathfrak{Z})$-$\mathcal{Z}$-contraction, using inequalities (4), (8), (9), and (λ_3), we have

$$0 \leq \limsup_{k\to\infty} \mathfrak{Z}(||\iota^o{}_{m_k-1} - \iota^o{}_{q_k-1}||, ||\iota^o{}_{m_k} - \iota^o{}_{q_k}||) < 0,$$

which is a contradiction, and it proves that $\mathfrak{C} = 0$. So, $\{\iota^o{}_q\}$ is a Cauchy sequence. Since $\tilde{\Pi}$ is a Banach space, there exists $\iota^{o*} \in \tilde{\Pi}$ such that $\lim_{n\to\infty} \iota^o{}_q = \iota^{o*}$. Next, we prove that the point ι^{o*} will remain fixed under Θ_δ, and therefore it would also be the FP of Θ. Suppose $\Theta_\delta \iota^{o*} \neq \iota^{o*}$; then,

$$\begin{aligned}0 &\leq \limsup_{q\to\infty} \mathfrak{Z}(||\Theta_\delta \iota^o{}_q - \Theta_\delta \iota^{o*}||, ||\iota^o{}_q - \iota^{o*}||) \\ &\leq \limsup_{q\to\infty} [||\iota^o{}_q - \iota^{o*}|| - ||\iota^o{}_{q+1} - \Theta_\delta \iota^{o*}||] \\ &= -||\iota^{o*} - \Theta_\delta \iota^{o*}||.\end{aligned}$$

This leads to a contradiction. Thus, this shows that $||\iota^{o*} - \Theta_\delta \iota^{o*}|| = 0$, that is, $\Theta_\delta \iota^{o*} = \iota^{o*}$. Thus, ι^{o*} is a FP of Θ_δ and so is the FP of Θ as well. Uniqueness of the FP follows from Lemma (3). □

Example 2. *Let $\tilde{\Pi} = [0,1]$ be a real normed space with the norm defined by $||\iota^o - \varrho^o|| = |\iota^o - \varrho^o|, \ \forall \iota^o, \varrho^o \in \tilde{\Pi}$. Then, $(\tilde{\Pi}, ||\cdot||)$ is a Banach space. Define an operator $\Theta : \tilde{\Pi} \to \tilde{\Pi}$ as $\Theta(\iota^o) = \frac{\iota^o(1-\iota^o)}{1+\iota^o}, \ \forall \iota^o \in [0,1]$. If $\mathrm{d} = 1$, then $\delta = \frac{1}{2}$. Thus, the mapping Θ_δ becomes $\Theta_\delta \iota^o = \frac{\iota^o}{\iota^o+1}, \ \forall \iota^o \in \tilde{\Pi}$. Then, Θ is an enriched $(\mathrm{d}, \mathfrak{Z})$-$\mathcal{Z}$-contraction, where $\mathrm{d} = 1$ and $\mathfrak{Z}(\iota^o, \varrho^o) = \frac{\varrho^o}{\varrho^o+1} - \iota^o, \ \forall \iota^o, \varrho^o \in [0, \infty)$. In particular, if $\iota^o, \varrho^o \in \tilde{\Pi}$, then*

$$
\begin{aligned}
\mathfrak{Z}(||\Theta_{\frac{1}{2}}\iota^{o} - \Theta_{\frac{1}{2}}\varrho^{o}||, ||\iota^{o} - \varrho^{o}||) &= \frac{||\iota^{o} - \varrho^{o}||}{1 + ||\iota^{o} - \varrho^{o}||} - ||\Theta_{\frac{1}{2}}\iota^{o} - \Theta_{\frac{1}{2}}\varrho^{o}|| \\
&= \frac{|\iota^{o} - \varrho^{o}|}{1 + |\iota^{o} - \varrho^{o}|} - \left| \frac{\iota^{o}}{\iota^{o} + 1} - \frac{\varrho^{o}}{\varrho^{o} + 1} \right| \\
&= \frac{|\iota^{o} - \varrho^{o}|}{1 + |\iota^{o} - \varrho^{o}|} - \left| \frac{|\iota^{o} - \varrho^{o}|}{(\iota^{o} + 1)(\varrho^{o} + 1)} \right| \geq 0.
\end{aligned}
$$

Note that all the conditions of Theorem (2) are satisfied and hence both $\Theta_{\frac{1}{2}}$ and Θ have a unique FP $\iota^{o*} = 0 \in \tilde{\Pi}$.

If we choose $\mathrm{d} = 0$ in Theorem (2), then we obtain Theorem 2.8 in Khojasteh et al. [28] in the setting of Banach spaces as follows.

Corollary 1. *Consider a Banach space $(\tilde{\Pi}, ||\cdot||)$ and an operator $\Theta : \tilde{\Pi} \to \tilde{\Pi}$, which is an enriched $(0, \mathfrak{Z})$-$\mathcal{Z}$-contraction. That is,*

$$\mathfrak{Z}(||\Theta\iota^{o} - \Theta\varrho^{o}||, ||\mathfrak{x} - \mathfrak{y}||) \geq 0, \quad \forall \mathfrak{x}, \mathfrak{y} \in \tilde{\Pi}.$$

Then, Θ has a unique FP in $\tilde{\Pi}$.

In the following, we obtain some well-known and novel results in the FP theory with an enriched-type contraction and the SFs. For example, the FP result of Berinde and Păcurar [19] is given in terms of the SF as follows.

Corollary 2. *Consider a Banach space $(\tilde{\Pi}, ||\cdot||)$ with an operator $\Theta : \tilde{\Pi} \to \tilde{\Pi}$ satisfying*

$$||\mathrm{d}(\iota^{o} - \varrho^{o}) - \Theta\iota^{o} + \Theta\varrho^{o}|| \leq \theta(\mathrm{d} + 1)||\iota^{o} - \varrho^{o}||, \quad \forall \iota^{o}, \varrho^{o} \in \tilde{\Pi},$$

where $\theta \in [0, 1)$ and $\mathrm{d} \in [0, \infty)$. Then, Θ has a unique FP in $\tilde{\Pi}$.

Proof. Define $\mathfrak{Z}_E : [0, \infty)^2 \to \mathbb{R}$ by

$$\mathfrak{Z}_E(\iota^{o}, \varrho^{o}) = \theta\varrho^{o} - \iota^{o}, \quad \forall \varrho^{o}, \iota^{o} \in [0, \infty).$$

It is clear that the mapping Θ is an enriched $(\mathrm{d}, \mathfrak{Z}_E)$-$\mathcal{Z}$-contraction with respect to $\mathfrak{Z}_E \in \mathcal{Z}$. Therefore, the result follows by taking $\mathfrak{Z} = \mathfrak{Z}_E$ in Theorem (2). □

Next, we have the Rhoades FP theorem [29] in terms of the enriched and SFs in the setting of normed spaces as follows.

Corollary 3. *Consider a Banach space $(\tilde{\Pi}, ||\cdot||)$ with an operator $\Theta : \tilde{\Pi} \to \tilde{\Pi}$ satisfying*

$$\frac{1}{\mathrm{d} + 1}||\mathrm{d}(\iota^{o} - \varrho^{o}) - \Theta\iota^{o} - \Theta\varrho^{o}|| \leq ||\iota^{o} - \varrho^{o}|| - \pi(||\iota^{o} - \varrho^{o}||), \quad \forall \iota^{o}, \varrho^{o} \in \tilde{\Pi},$$

where $\pi : [0, \infty) \to [0, \infty)$ is a lower semi-continuous function, and $\pi^{-1}(0) = \{0\}$. Then, Θ has a unique FP in $\tilde{\Pi}$.

Proof. Define $\mathfrak{Z}_r : [0, \infty)^2 \to \mathbb{R}$ by

$$\mathfrak{Z}_r(\iota^{o}, \varrho^{o}) = \varrho^{o} - \pi(\varrho^{o}) - \iota^{o}, \quad \forall \varrho^{o}, \iota^{o} \in [0, \infty).$$

It is clear that the mapping Θ is an enriched $(\mathrm{d}, \mathfrak{Z}_r)$-$\mathcal{Z}$-contraction with respect to $\mathfrak{Z}_r \in \mathcal{Z}$. Therefore, the result follows by taking $\mathfrak{Z} = \mathfrak{Z}_r$ in Theorem (2). □

Rhoades [29] studied the continuity and nondecreasing behavior of the function Φ with $\lim_{t \to \infty} \psi(\iota^{o}) = \infty$. In Corollary (3), we changed these assumptions by the lower semi-continuity of Φ. Hence, our result is a proper generalization of the results given by Rhoades [29] in the setting of Banach spaces via enriched techniques.

Corollary 4. *Consider a Banach space* $(\tilde{\Pi}, ||\cdot||)$ *with an operator* $\Theta : \tilde{\Pi} \to \tilde{\Pi}$ *satisfying*

$$\frac{1}{\mathrm{d}+1}||\mathrm{d}(\iota^o - \varrho^o) - \Theta\iota^o - \Theta\varrho^o|| \leq \pi(||\iota^o - \varrho^o||)||\iota^o - \varrho^o||, \quad \forall \iota^o, \varrho^o \in \tilde{\Pi},$$

where $\pi : [0, +\infty) \to [0, 1)$ *is a function for which* $\limsup_{\iota^o \to \mathfrak{r}^+} \pi(\iota^o) < 1$, *for all* $\mathfrak{r} > 0$. *Then,* Θ *has a unique FP.*

Proof. Define $\mathfrak{Z}_w : [0, \infty)^2 \to \mathbb{R}$ by

$$\mathfrak{Z}_w(\iota^o, \varrho^o) = \varrho^o \pi(\varrho^o) - \iota^o, \quad \forall \varrho^o, \iota^o \in [0, \infty),$$

and follow Theorem (2) to achieve the result. □

Corollary 5. *Consider a Banach space* $(\tilde{\Pi}, ||\cdot||)$ *with an operator* $\Theta : \tilde{\Pi} \to \tilde{\Pi}$ *satisfying*

$$\frac{1}{\mathrm{d}+1}||\mathrm{d}(\iota^o - \varrho^o) - \Theta\iota^o - \Theta\varrho^o|| \leq \pi(||\iota^o - \varrho^o||), \quad \forall \iota^o, \varrho^o \in \tilde{\Pi},$$

where $\pi : [0, +\infty) \to [0, +\infty)$ *is an upper semi-continuous function for which* $\pi(\iota^o) < \iota^o, \quad \forall \iota^o > 0$ *and* $\pi(0) = 0$. *Then,* Θ *has a unique FP.*

Proof. Define the simulation operator $\mathfrak{Z}_q : [0, \infty)^2 \to \mathbb{R}$ by

$$\mathfrak{Z}_q(\iota^o, \varrho^o) = \pi(\varrho^o) - \iota^o, \quad \forall \varrho^o, \iota^o \in [0, \infty),$$

and apply Theorem (2) to complete the proof □

Corollary 6. *Consider a Banach space* $(\tilde{\Pi}, ||\cdot||)$ *with an operator* $\Theta : \tilde{\Pi} \to \tilde{\Pi}$ *satisfying*

$$\int_0^{\frac{1}{\mathrm{d}+1}||\mathrm{d}(\iota^o - \varrho^o) + \Theta\iota^o - \Theta\varrho^o||} \pi(\theta) d\theta \leq ||\iota^o - \varrho^o||, \quad \forall \iota^o, \varrho^o \in \tilde{\Pi},$$

where $\pi : [0, \infty) \to [0, \infty)$ *is a function such that* $\int_0^\epsilon \pi(\theta) d\theta$ *exists and* $\int_0^\epsilon \pi(\theta) d\theta > \epsilon$ *for each* $\epsilon > 0$. *Then,* Θ *has a unique FP in* $\tilde{\Pi}$.

Proof. Define $\mathfrak{Z}_l : [0, \infty) \to \mathbb{R}$ by

$$\mathfrak{Z}_l(\iota^o, \varrho^o) = \varrho^o - \int_0^{\iota^o} \pi(\theta) d\theta, \quad \forall \varrho^o, \iota^o \in [0, \infty).$$

Then, apply Theorem (2) to obtain the conclusion. □

Enriched $(\mathrm{d}, \mathfrak{Z})$-$\mathcal{Z}$-contractions and their IFSs provide advanced methods for solving complex problems in optimization, image processing, and dynamical systems. They enable more robust algorithms, improved computational efficiency, and enhanced simulation accuracy, offering better modeling and new approaches for iterative processes and fixed points.

3. An Application

We suppose the following integral equation, $\forall \lambda \in \mathcal{I} = [a, b]$,

$$\iota^o(\lambda) = \varrho^o(\lambda) + \int_a^b \mathcal{J}(\lambda, \sigma) z(\sigma, \iota^o(\sigma)) d\sigma - (1 - \delta)\iota^o(\lambda), \tag{10}$$

where $\varrho^o : \mathcal{I} \to \mathbb{R}, \mathcal{J} : \mathcal{I}^2 \to \mathbb{R}, \mathrm{z} : \mathcal{I} \times \mathbb{R} \to \mathbb{R}$ are continuous functions, and $\delta = \frac{1}{\mathrm{d}+1}$ with $\mathrm{d} \in [0,\infty)$. In the following, we prove the existence of a unique solution to the integral Equation (10) in $\tilde{\Pi} = \mathfrak{C}(\mathcal{I}, \mathbb{R})$ as an application of our previous results. For this, define a self-mapping $\Theta : \tilde{\Pi} \to \tilde{\Pi}$ by

$$\Theta\iota^o(\lambda) = \varrho^o(\lambda) + \int_a^b \mathcal{J}(\lambda,\sigma)\mathrm{z}(\sigma,\iota^o(\sigma))d\sigma - (1-\delta)\iota^o(\lambda), \quad \forall\lambda \in \mathcal{I}. \tag{11}$$

For $\delta \in [0,1)$, we obtain

$$\Theta_\delta\iota^o(\lambda) = \delta\varrho^o(\lambda) + \delta\int_a^b \mathcal{J}(\lambda,\sigma)\mathrm{z}(\sigma,\iota^o(\sigma))d\sigma, \quad \forall\lambda \in \mathcal{I}. \tag{12}$$

Then, the existence of the FP of (11) and the existence of the solution to the integral Equation (10) are equivalent to each other. We use the FP technique to show the existence of the solution to (10).

We take the following norm $\tilde{\Pi}$, which makes it the Banach space

$$||\iota^o - \varrho^o|| = \sup_{\lambda\in\mathcal{I}} |\iota^o(\lambda) - \varrho^o(\lambda)|.$$

Further, we assume the following conditions to analyze the existence of the solution of the integral Equation (10):

1. $\sup_{\lambda\in\mathcal{I}} \int_a^b |\mathcal{J}(\lambda,\sigma)|d\sigma \leq \frac{1}{b-a}$;
2. $|\mathrm{z}(\sigma,\iota^o(\sigma)) - \mathrm{z}(\sigma,\varrho^o(\sigma))| \leq \frac{1}{\delta}\theta(||\iota^o - \varrho^o||), \quad \forall\iota^o, \varrho^o \in \tilde{\Pi}$,

where $\theta : [0,\infty) \to [0,\infty)$ is a nondecreasing upper semi-continuous operator with $\theta(\iota^o) < \iota^o, \quad \forall\iota^o > 0$ and $\theta(0) = 0$.

Theorem 3. *The solution to the integral Equation (10) is unique in $\tilde{\Pi}$ if assumptions 1 and 2 are satisfied.*

Proof. Consider the following $\forall\lambda \in \mathcal{I}$ and $\mathrm{d} \in [0,\infty)$,

$$\begin{aligned}
\frac{1}{\mathrm{d}+1}||\mathrm{d}(\iota^o - \varrho^o) + \Theta\iota^o - \Theta\varrho^o|| &= ||\Theta_\delta\iota^o - \Theta_\delta\varrho^o|| \\
&= \sup_{\lambda\in\mathcal{I}} |\Theta_\delta\iota^o - \Theta_\delta\varrho^o| \\
&= \sup_{\lambda\in\mathcal{I}} |\delta\varrho^o(\lambda) + \delta\int_a^b \mathcal{J}(\lambda,\sigma)\mathrm{z}(\sigma,\iota^o(\sigma))d\sigma \\
&- \delta\varrho^o(\lambda) - \delta\int_a^b \mathcal{J}(\lambda,\sigma)\mathrm{z}(\sigma,\varrho^o(\sigma))d\sigma| \\
&= \delta \sup_{\lambda\in\mathcal{I}} |\int_a^b \mathcal{J}(\lambda,\sigma)[\mathrm{z}(\sigma,\iota^o(\sigma)) - \mathrm{z}(\sigma,\varrho^o(\sigma))]d\sigma| \\
&\leq \delta \sup_{\lambda\in\mathcal{I}} \int_a^b |\mathcal{J}(\lambda,\sigma)[\mathrm{z}(\sigma,\iota^o(\sigma)) - \mathrm{z}(\sigma,\varrho^o(\sigma))]|d\sigma \\
&\leq \delta \sup_{\lambda\in\mathcal{I}} \int_a^b |\mathcal{J}(\lambda,\sigma)| \cdot |\mathrm{z}(\sigma,\iota^o(\sigma)) - \mathrm{z}(\sigma,\varrho^o(\sigma))|d\sigma \\
&\leq \theta(||\iota^o - \varrho^o||) \cdot \sup_{\lambda\in\mathcal{I}} \int_a^b |\mathcal{J}(\lambda,\sigma)|d\sigma \\
&\leq \frac{1}{b-a} \cdot \theta(||\iota^o - \varrho^o||) \\
&\leq \theta(||\iota^o - \varrho^o||).
\end{aligned}$$

Hence, all the assumptions of Corollary (5) are satisfied, so Θ has a unique FP. Equivalently, the solution to the integral Equation (10) is unique in $\tilde{\Pi}$. □

4. Application to the Iterated Function System

In this part, we list applications of our results to the iterated functions system via enrichment and SFs $\mathfrak{Z} \in \mathcal{Z}$. The first result in this direction is given below.

Theorem 4. *Let Θ be an enriched $(\mathrm{d}, \mathfrak{Z})$-$\mathcal{Z}$-contraction on linear normed space $\tilde{\Pi}$ and define the operator $\tilde{\Theta} : \Lambda(\tilde{\Pi}) \to \mathcal{P}(\tilde{\Pi})$ by $\tilde{\Theta}(Y^o) = \{\Theta(\iota^o) : \iota^o \in Y^o\}, \quad \forall Y^o \in \Lambda(\tilde{\Pi})$. Then,*

1. *$\tilde{\Theta}$ maps $\Lambda(\tilde{\Pi})$ to $\Lambda(\tilde{\Pi})$;*
2. *$\tilde{\Theta}$ is also an enriched $(\mathrm{d}, \mathfrak{Z})$-$\mathcal{Z}$-contraction on $\Lambda(\tilde{\Pi})$,*

where $\mathcal{P}(\tilde{\Pi})$ is the power set of $\tilde{\Pi}$.

Proof. Initially, we demonstrate that $\tilde{\Theta}$ maps elements from $\Lambda(\tilde{\Pi})$ to $\Lambda(\tilde{\Pi})$. Since Θ is an enriched $(\mathrm{d}, \mathfrak{Z})$-contraction, from λ_2 and inequality (4), we obtain

$$||\frac{\mathrm{d}(\iota^o - \varrho^o) + \Theta\iota^o - \Theta\varrho^o}{\mathrm{d}+1}|| < ||\iota^o - \varrho^o||$$
$$\Longrightarrow ||\Theta_\delta\iota^o - \Theta_\delta\varrho^o|| < ||\iota^o - \varrho^o||.$$

This implies that Θ_δ is a contractive mapping and, is therefore continuous. Thus,

$$Y^o \in \Lambda(\tilde{\Pi}) \Rightarrow \Theta_\delta(Y^o) \in \Lambda(\tilde{\Pi}).$$

This means that Θ_δ sends elements from $\Lambda(\tilde{\Pi})$ to $\Lambda(\tilde{\Pi})$. Subsequently, the sum of any number of compact sets and the scalar multiplication of a compact set by any constant remain compact. Consequently, $\tilde{\Theta}$ also maps elements from $\Lambda(\tilde{\Pi})$ to $\Lambda(\tilde{\Pi})$ as $\Theta_\delta(Y^o) = (1-\delta)Y^o + \delta\tilde{\Theta}(Y^o)$.

Next, take $Y^o, \mho \in \Lambda(\tilde{\Pi})$. Then, from λ_2 and inequality (4), we obtain

$$||\Theta_\delta\iota^o - \Theta_\delta\varrho^o|| < ||\iota^o - \varrho^o||, \quad \forall \iota^o, \varrho^o \in \tilde{\Pi}.$$

Thus,

$$\mathfrak{D}(\Theta_\delta\iota^o, \Theta_\delta\mho) = \inf_{\varrho^o \in \mho} ||\Theta_\delta\iota^o - \Theta_\delta\varrho^o|| < \inf_{\varrho^o \in \mho} ||\iota^o - \varrho^o|| = \mathfrak{D}(\iota^o, \mho). \tag{13}$$

Similarly,

$$\mathfrak{D}(\Theta_\delta\varrho^o, \Theta_\delta Y^o) < \mathfrak{D}(\varrho^o, Y^o). \tag{14}$$

Now, using the definition of Hausdorff metric $\mathring{\partial}$, (13), and (14), we obtain

$$\begin{aligned}\frac{\mathring{\partial}(\mathrm{d}Y^o + \tilde{\Theta}Y^o, \mathrm{d}\mho + \tilde{\Theta}\mho)}{\mathrm{d}+1} &= \mathring{\partial}(\Theta_\delta Y^o, \Theta_\delta\mho) \\ &= \max\{\sup_{\iota^o \in Y^o} D(\Theta_\delta\iota^o, \Theta_\delta\mho), \sup_{\varrho^o \in \mho} \mathfrak{D}(\Theta_\delta\varrho^o, \Theta_\delta Y^o)\} \\ &< \max\{\sup_{\iota^o \in Y^o} \mathfrak{D}(\iota^o, \mho), \sup_{\varrho^o \in \mho} D(\varrho^o, Y^o)\} \\ &= \mathring{\partial}(Y^o, \mho).\end{aligned} \tag{15}$$

Using assumption λ_2, we obtain

$$\mathfrak{Z}(\frac{\mathring{\partial}(\mathrm{d}Y^o + \tilde{\Theta}Y^o, \mathrm{d}\mho + \tilde{\Theta}\mho)}{\mathrm{d}+1}, \mathring{\partial}(Y^o, \mho)) \geq 0.$$

This shows that $\tilde{\Theta}$ is an enriched $(\mathrm{d}, \mathfrak{Z})$-$\mathcal{Z}$-contraction on $(\Lambda(\tilde{\Pi}), \mathring{\partial})$. □

Definition 7. *Suppose a normed space $(\tilde{\Pi}, ||\cdot||)$ together with a finite class $\{\Theta^{(i)}, i = 1, 2, \cdots, \jmath\}$ of enriched $(\mathrm{d}, \mathfrak{Z})$-$\mathcal{Z}$-contractions. Then, the operator $\mathcal{Y} : \Lambda(\tilde{\Pi}) \to \Lambda(\tilde{\Pi})$ defined by*

$$\mathcal{Y}(\mathrm{Y}^o) = \bigcup_{i=1}^{\jmath} \Theta^{(i)}(\mathrm{Y}^o), \quad \forall \mathrm{Y}^o \in \Lambda(\tilde{\Pi}),$$

is called the $\mathcal{Z}$-Hutchinson contraction.

Definition 8. *Consider a normed space $(\tilde{\Pi}, ||\cdot||)$ with a class $\{\Theta^{(i)}, i = 1, 2, \cdots, \jmath\}$ of enriched $(\mathrm{d}, \mathfrak{Z})$-$\mathcal{Z}$-contractions that is said to be a $\mathcal{Z}$-IFS, and it is denoted by $(\tilde{\Pi}; \Theta^{(i)}, i = 1, 2, \cdots, \jmath)$.*

Lemma 6. *Let $(\tilde{\Pi}, ||\cdot||)$ be a normed space together with a finite class $\{\Theta^{(i)}, i = 1, 2, \cdots, \jmath\}$ of enriched $(\mathrm{d}, \mathfrak{Z})$-$\mathcal{Z}$-contractions. Then, the $\mathcal{Z}$-Hutchinson operator is also an enriched $(\mathrm{d}, \mathfrak{Z})$-$\mathcal{Z}$-contraction.*

Proof. For some given $\jmath \in \mathbb{N}$ with $\jmath \geq 2$, let $\{\Theta^{(\mathrm{i})} : \tilde{\Pi} \to \tilde{\Pi} : \mathrm{i} = 1, 2, \ldots \jmath\}$ be a family of enriched $(\mathrm{d}, \mathfrak{Z})$-$\mathcal{Z}$-contractions and $\mathrm{Y}^o, \mho \in \Lambda(\tilde{\Pi})$. Then, from Lemma 1, we obtain

$$\begin{aligned}
\frac{\mathring{\partial}(\mathrm{d}\mathrm{Y}^o + \tilde{\Theta}\mathrm{Y}^o, \mathrm{d}\mho + \tilde{\Theta}\mho)}{\mathrm{d}+1} &= \mathring{\partial}(\Theta_\delta \mathrm{Y}^o, \Theta_\delta \mho) \\
&= \mathring{\partial}(\bigcup_{\mathrm{i}=1}^{\jmath} \Theta^{(\mathrm{i})}{}_\delta \mathrm{Y}^o, \bigcup_{\mathrm{i}=1}^{\jmath} \Theta^{(\mathrm{i})}{}_\delta \mho) \\
&\leq \max_{1 \leq \mathrm{i} \leq \jmath} \{\mathring{\partial}(\Theta^{(\mathrm{i})}{}_\delta \mathrm{Y}^o, \Theta^{(\mathrm{i})}{}_\delta \mho)\} \\
&\leq \mathring{\partial}(\mathrm{Y}^o, \mho).
\end{aligned}$$

Therefore, using (λ_2), we obtain

$$\mathfrak{Z}(\frac{\mathring{\partial}(\mathrm{d}\mathrm{Y}^o + \tilde{\Theta}\mathrm{Y}^o, \mathrm{d}\mho + \tilde{\Theta}\mho)}{\mathrm{d}+1}, \mathring{\partial}(\mathrm{Y}^o, \mho)) \geq 0, \quad \forall \mathrm{Y}^o, \mho \in \Lambda(\tilde{\Pi}).$$

Accordingly, the proof is complete. □

Theorem 5. *Let $(\tilde{\Pi}, ||\cdot||)$ be a linear normed space with a finite class $\{\Theta^{(i)}, i = 1, 2, \cdots, \jmath\}$ of enriched $(\mathrm{d}, \mathfrak{Z})$-$\mathcal{Z}$-contractions. Then,*

1. *$\mathcal{Y}$ also maps $\Lambda(\tilde{\Pi})$ to itself;*
2. *the $\mathcal{Z}$-Hutchinson operator has a unique FP, say $\mathrm{Y}^{o*} \in \Lambda(\tilde{\Pi})$;*
3. *the sequence $(\mathrm{Y}^o{}_q)$, $\forall q \in \mathbb{N}$, and $\delta = \frac{1}{\mathrm{d}+1}$, as defined by $\mathrm{Y}^o{}_{q+1} = (1-\delta)\mathrm{Y}^o{}_q + \delta \mathcal{Y} \mathrm{Y}^o{}_q$, converges to $\mathrm{Y}^{o*} \in \Lambda(\tilde{\Pi})$.*

Proof. Since each $\Theta^{(\mathrm{i})}$ for $\mathrm{i} = 1, 2, \ldots, \jmath$ is an enriched $(\mathrm{d}, \mathfrak{Z})$-$\mathcal{Z}$-contraction, conclusion (1) can be directly deduced from the definition of Θ and Theorem (4). In addition, conclusions (2) and (3) follow from Lemma (3) and Theorem (2). □

Definition 9. *An operator $\Theta : \Lambda(\tilde{\Pi}) \to \Lambda(\tilde{\Pi})$, where $(\tilde{\Pi}, ||\cdot||)$ is a normed space, is said to be a generalized enriched $(\mathrm{d}, \mathfrak{Z})$-$\mathcal{Z}$-Hutchinson operator or simply generalized enriched $\mathcal{Z}$-Hutchinson operator if there exists a constant $\mathrm{d} \in [0, \infty)$ and a SF $\mathfrak{Z} \in \mathcal{Z}$ such that*

$$\mathfrak{Z}(\mathring{\partial}(\frac{\mathrm{d}\mathrm{Y}^o + \Theta\mathrm{Y}^o}{\mathrm{d}+1}, \frac{\mathrm{d}\mho + \Theta\mho}{\mathrm{d}+1}), \mathcal{N}_\Theta(\mathrm{Y}^o, \mho) \geq 0, \quad \mathrm{Y}^o, \mho \in \Lambda(\tilde{\Pi}), \tag{16}$$

where

$$\mathcal{N}_{\Theta}(\Upsilon^{o},\mho)=\max\Big\{\mathring{\eth}(\Upsilon^{o},\mho),\mathring{\eth}\Big(\Upsilon^{o},\frac{d\Upsilon^{o}+\Theta\Upsilon^{o}}{d+1}\Big),\mathring{\eth}\Big(\mho,\frac{d\mho+\Theta\mho}{d+1}\Big),$$
$$\frac{1}{2}\Big[\mathring{\eth}\Big(\Upsilon^{o},\frac{d\mho+\Theta\mho}{d+1}\Big)+\mathring{\eth}\Big(\mho,\frac{d\Upsilon^{o}+\Theta\Upsilon^{o}}{d+1}\Big)\Big],$$
$$\mathring{\eth}\Big(\frac{1}{d+1}\Big[\frac{d(d\Upsilon^{o}+\Theta\Upsilon^{o})}{d+1}+\Theta\Big(\frac{d\Upsilon^{o}+\Theta\Upsilon^{o}}{d+1}\Big)\Big],\frac{d\Upsilon^{o}+\Theta\Upsilon^{o}}{d+1}\Big),$$
$$\mathring{\eth}\Big(\frac{1}{d+1}\Big[\frac{d(d\Upsilon^{o}+\Theta\Upsilon^{o})}{d+1}+\Theta\Big(\frac{d\Upsilon^{o}+\Theta\Upsilon^{o}}{d+1}\Big)\Big],\mho\Big),$$
$$\mathring{\eth}\Big(\frac{1}{d+1}\Big[\frac{d(d\Upsilon^{o}+\Theta\Upsilon^{o})}{d+1}+\Theta\Big(\frac{d\Upsilon^{o}+\Theta\Upsilon^{o}}{d+1}\Big)\Big],\frac{d\mho+\Theta\mho}{d+1}\Big)\Big\}.$$

Lemma 7. *Let* $(\tilde{\Pi},||\cdot||)$ *be a normed space and* $\Theta:\Lambda(\tilde{\Pi})\to\Lambda(\tilde{\Pi})$ *be a generalized enriched* $(d,\mathfrak{Z})$*-*$\mathcal{Z}$*-Hutchinson operator. Then, the Krasnoselskii iteration scheme* $\{\Upsilon^{o}{}_{n}\}$ *obtained by* Θ *with initial guess* $\Upsilon^{o}{}_{0}\in\delta(\iota^{o})$ *is a bounded sequence, where* $\Upsilon^{o}{}_{q}=(1-\delta)\Upsilon^{o}{}_{q-1}+\delta\Theta\Upsilon^{o}{}_{q-1},\forall q\in\mathbb{N}$, *and* $\delta=\frac{1}{d+1}$.

Proof. By the definition of the generalized enriched $(d,\mathfrak{Z})$-$\mathcal{Z}$-Hutchinson operator, we have, for $\forall\Upsilon^{o},\mho\in\Lambda(\tilde{\Pi})$,

$$\mathfrak{Z}(\mathring{\eth}(\Theta_{\delta}\Upsilon^{o},\Theta_{\delta}\mho),\mathcal{N}_{\Theta_{\delta}}(\Upsilon^{o},\mho))\geq 0, \tag{17}$$

where

$$\mathcal{N}_{\Theta_{\delta}}(\Upsilon^{o},\mho)=\max\{\mathring{\eth}(\Upsilon^{o},\mho),\mathring{\eth}(\Upsilon^{o},\Theta_{\delta}\Upsilon^{o}),\mathring{\eth}(\mho,\Theta_{\delta}\mho),\frac{1}{2}\Big[\mathring{\eth}(\Upsilon^{o},\Theta_{\delta}\mho)+\mathring{\eth}(\mho,\Theta_{\delta}\Upsilon^{o})\Big],$$
$$\mathring{\eth}(\Theta_{\delta}^{2}\Upsilon^{o},\Theta_{\delta}\Upsilon^{o}),\mathring{\eth}(\Theta_{\delta}^{2}\Upsilon^{o},\mho),\mathring{\eth}(\Theta_{\delta}^{2}\Upsilon^{o},\Theta_{\delta}\mho)\}.$$

Let $\Upsilon^{o}{}_{0}\in\Lambda(\tilde{\Pi})$ be any arbitrary element and generate the sequence as $\Upsilon^{o}{}_{q+1}=(1-\delta)\Upsilon^{o}{}_{q}+\delta\Theta\Upsilon^{o}{}_{q},\forall q\geq 0$. Assume that $\{\Upsilon^{o}{}_{q}\}$ is not bounded. Then, without loss of generality, we can suppose that $\Upsilon^{o}{}_{q+p}\neq\Upsilon^{o}{}_{q},\forall q,p\in\mathbb{N}$. As the sequence $\{\Upsilon^{o}{}_{q}\}$ is not bounded, we must find a sub-sequence $\{\Upsilon^{o}{}_{q_k}\}$ such that $q_1=1$ and, for each $k\in\mathbb{N},q_{k+1}$ is the minimum integer such that $\mathring{\eth}(\Upsilon^{o}{}_{q_{k+1}},\Upsilon^{o}{}_{q_k})>1$. Also, we obtain

$$\mathring{\eth}(\Upsilon^{o}{}_{m},\Upsilon^{o}{}_{q_k})\leq 1,\qquad q_k\leq m\leq q_{k+1}-1. \tag{18}$$

Therefore, by utilizing inequality (18) and the triangular inequality, we have

$$1<\mathring{\eth}(\Upsilon^{o}{}_{q_{k+1}},\Upsilon^{o}{}_{q_k})\leq\mathring{\eth}(\Upsilon^{o}{}_{q_{k+1}},\Upsilon^{o}{}_{q_{k+1}-1})+\mathring{\eth}(\Upsilon^{o}{}_{q_{k+1},1}-\Upsilon^{o}{}_{q_k})$$
$$\leq\mathring{\eth}(\Upsilon^{o}{}_{q_{k+1}},\Upsilon^{o}{}_{q_{k+1}-1})+1.$$

Taking $k\to\infty$ and using Lemma (4), we obtain

$$\lim_{k\to\infty}\mathring{\eth}(\Upsilon^{o}{}_{q_{k+1}},\Upsilon^{o}{}_{q_k})=1. \tag{19}$$

Substituting $\Upsilon^{o}=\Upsilon^{o}{}_{q}$ and $\mho=\Upsilon^{o}{}_{q+1}$ in the inequality (17), we obtain

$$0\leq\mathfrak{Z}(\mathring{\eth}(\Theta_{\delta}\Upsilon^{o}{}_{k},\Theta_{\delta}\Upsilon^{o}{}_{k+1}),\mathcal{N}_{\Theta_{\delta}}(\Upsilon^{o}{}_{k},\Upsilon^{o}{}_{k+1}))=\mathfrak{Z}(\mathring{\eth}(\Upsilon^{o}{}_{k+1},\Upsilon^{o}{}_{k+2}),\mathcal{N}_{\Theta_{\delta}}(\Upsilon^{o}{}_{k},\Upsilon^{o}{}_{k+1})), \tag{20}$$

where

$$\mathcal{N}_{\Theta_\delta}(Y^o{}_k, Y^o{}_{k+1}) = \max\Big\{\mathring{\partial}(Y^o{}_k, Y^o{}_{k+1}), \mathring{\partial}(Y^o{}_k, \Theta_\delta(Y^o{}_k)), \mathring{\partial}(Y^o{}_{k+1}, \Theta_\delta(Y^o{}_{k+1}))$$
$$\frac{\mathring{\partial}(Y^o{}_k, \Theta_\delta(Y^o{}_{k+1})) + \mathring{\partial}(Y^o{}_{k+1}, \Theta_\delta(Y^o{}_k))}{2}$$
$$\mathring{\partial}\Big(\Theta_\delta^2(Y^o{}_k), \Theta_\delta(Y^o{}_k)\Big), \mathring{\partial}\Big(\Theta_\delta^2(Y^o{}_k), Y^o{}_{k+1}\Big), \mathring{\partial}\Big(\Theta_\delta^2(Y^o{}_k), \Theta_\delta(Y^o{}_{k+1})\Big)\Big\}$$
$$= \max\Big\{\mathring{\partial}(Y^o{}_k, Y^o{}_{k+1}), \mathring{\partial}(Y^o{}_k, Y^o{}_{k+1}), \mathring{\partial}(Y^o{}_{k+1}, Y^o{}_{k+2})$$
$$\frac{\mathring{\partial}(Y^o{}_k, Y^o{}_{k+2}) + \mathring{\partial}(Y^o{}_{k+1}, Y^o{}_{k+1})}{2},$$
$$\mathring{\partial}(Y^o{}_{k+2}, Y^o{}_{k+1}), \mathring{\partial}(Y^o{}_{k+2}, Y^o{}_{k+1}), \mathring{\partial}(Y^o{}_{k+2}, Y^o{}_{k+2})\Big\}$$
$$\leq \max\left\{\mathring{\partial}(Y^o{}_k, Y^o{}_{k+1}), \mathring{\partial}(Y^o{}_{k+1}, Y^o{}_{k+2}), \frac{\mathring{\partial}(Y^o{}_k, Y^o{}_{k+1}) + \mathring{\partial}(Y^o{}_{k+1}, Y^o{}_{k+2})}{2}\right\}$$
$$= \max\Big\{\mathring{\partial}(Y^o{}_k, Y^o{}_{k+1}), \mathring{\partial}(Y^o{}_{k+1}, Y^o{}_{k+2})\Big\}.$$

Therefore, using inequality (20) and λ_2, we obtain

$$\begin{aligned}
0 &\leq \mathfrak{Z}(\mathring{\partial}(Y^o{}_{k+1}, Y^o{}_{k+2})), \mathcal{N}_{\Theta_\delta}(Y^o{}_k, Y^o{}_{k+1})) \\
&\leq \mathfrak{Z}(\mathring{\partial}(Y^o{}_{k+1}, Y^o{}_{k+2})), \max\Big\{\mathring{\partial}(Y^o{}_k, Y^o{}_{k+1}), \mathring{\partial}(Y^o{}_{k+1}, Y^o{}_{k+2})\Big\}) \\
&< \max\Big\{\mathring{\partial}(Y^o{}_k, Y^o{}_{k+1}), \mathring{\partial}(Y^o{}_{k+1}, Y^o{}_{k+2})\Big\} - \mathring{\partial}(Y^o{}_{k+1}, Y^o{}_{k+2})) \\
\Longrightarrow \mathring{\partial}(Y^o{}_{k+1}, Y^o{}_{k+2}) &< \max\Big\{\mathring{\partial}(Y^o{}_k, Y^o{}_{k+1}), \mathring{\partial}(Y^o{}_{k+1}, Y^o{}_{k+2})\Big\}.
\end{aligned}$$

This implies that

$$\mathring{\partial}(Y^o{}_{k+1}, Y^o{}_{k+2}) < \mathring{\partial}(Y^o{}_k, Y^o{}_{k+1}). \tag{21}$$

Thus, by inequality (21), we conclude that $\mathring{\partial}(Y^o{}_{q_{k+1}}, Y^o{}_{q_k}) \leq \mathring{\partial}(Y^o{}_{q_{k+1}-1}, Y^o{}_{q_k-1})$. Further, using (21), (18), (19), and the triangular inequality, we have

$$\begin{aligned}
1 < \mathring{\partial}(Y^o{}_{q_{k+1}}, Y^o{}_{q_k}) &\leq \mathring{\partial}(Y^o{}_{q_{k+1}-1}, Y^o{}_{q_k-1}) \\
&\leq \mathring{\partial}(Y^o{}_{q_{k+1}-1}, u^o{}_{q_k}) + \mathring{\partial}(Y^o{}_{q_k}, Y^o{}_{q_k-1}) \\
&\leq 1 + \mathring{\partial}(Y^o{}_{q_k}, Y^o{}_{q_k-1}).
\end{aligned}$$

Taking $k \to \infty$ and using Lemma (4), we obtain

$$\lim_{k\to\infty} \mathring{\partial}(Y^o{}_{q_{k+1}-1}, Y^o{}_{q_k-1}) = 1.$$

Now, since Θ is a generalized enriched $(\mathrm{d}, \mathfrak{Z})$-$\mathcal{Z}$-Hutchinson operator, from condition $\mathfrak{Z}_3$, we have

$$\begin{aligned}
0 &\leq \limsup_{k\to\infty} \mathfrak{Z}\Big(\mathring{\partial}(\Theta_\delta Y^o{}_{q_{k+1}-1}, \Theta_\delta Y^o{}_{q_k-1}), \mathring{\partial}(Y^o{}_{q_{k+1}-1}, Y^o{}_{q_k-1})\Big) \\
&= \limsup_{k\to\infty} \mathfrak{Z}\Big(\mathring{\partial}(Y^o{}_{q_{k+1}}, Y^o{}_{q_k}), \mathring{\partial}(Y^o{}_{q_{k+1}-1}, Y^o{}_{q_k-1})\Big) < 0,
\end{aligned}$$

which is a contradiction. This completes the proof. □

Theorem 6. *Let $(\tilde{\Pi}, ||\cdot||)$ be Banach space and $\Theta : \Lambda(\tilde{\Pi}) \to \Lambda(\tilde{\Pi})$ be a generalized enriched $\mathcal{Z}$-Hutchinson operator. Then,*

1. *the attractor of Θ is unique, say $Y^{o*} \in \Lambda(\tilde{\Pi})$;*

2. *the sequence* $(\Upsilon^o{}_q)$ *defined by*

$$\Upsilon^o{}_{q+1} = (1-\delta)\Upsilon^o{}_q + \delta\Theta\Upsilon^o{}_q, \quad \forall q \geq 0, \tag{22}$$

converges to Υ^{o*} *for any initial point* $\Upsilon^o{}_0 \in \Lambda(\tilde{\Pi})$,

where $\delta = \frac{1}{\mathrm{d}+1}$.

Proof. By the definition of the generalized enriched $(\mathrm{d}, \mathfrak{Z})$-$\mathcal{Z}$-Hutchinson operator, we have, for $\forall \Upsilon^o, \mho \in \Lambda(\tilde{\Pi})$,

$$\mathfrak{Z}(\mathring{\partial}(\Theta_\delta\Upsilon^o, \Theta_\delta\mho), \mathcal{N}_{\Theta_\delta}(\Upsilon^o, \mho)) \geq 0, \tag{23}$$

where

$$\mathcal{N}_{\Theta_\delta}(\Upsilon^o, \mho) = \max\{\mathring{\partial}(\Upsilon^o, \mho), \mathring{\partial}(\Upsilon^o, \Theta_\delta\Upsilon^o), \mathring{\partial}(\mho, \Theta_\delta\mho), \frac{1}{2}\Big[\mathring{\partial}(\Upsilon^o, \Theta_\delta\mho) + \mathring{\partial}(\mho, \Theta_\delta\Upsilon^o)\Big], \\ \mathring{\partial}(\Theta_\delta^2\Upsilon^o, \Theta_\delta\Upsilon^o), \mathring{\partial}(\Theta_\delta^2\Upsilon^o, \mho), \mathring{\partial}(\Theta_\delta^2\Upsilon^o, \Theta_\delta\mho)\}.$$

Let $\Upsilon^o{}_0 \in \Lambda(\tilde{\Pi})$ be any arbitrary element and define the sequence as given in (22). Our aim is to show that this sequence is Cauchy. To do this, take

$$\mathfrak{C}_q = \sup\Big\{\mathring{\partial}(\Upsilon^o{}_l, \Upsilon^o{}_m) : l, m \geq q\Big\}.$$

Observe that the sequence $\{\mathfrak{C}_q\}$ is a monotonically decreasing sequence of positive real numbers. According to Lemma (7), the sequence $\{\Upsilon^o{}_q\}$ is bounded, which implies that $\mathfrak{C}_q < \infty$ for all $q \in \mathbb{N}$. Therefore, the sequence $\{\mathfrak{C}_q\}$ is monotonic and bounded, which implies it is convergent. This means there exists a non-negative real number $\mathfrak{C} \geq 0$ such that $\lim_{q\to\infty} \mathfrak{C}_q = \mathfrak{C}$. We aim to prove that $\mathfrak{C} = 0$. If $\mathfrak{C} > 0$, then according to the definition of $\mathfrak{C}_q$, for every $k \in \mathbb{N}$, there exist indices q_k and m_k such that $m_k > q_k \geq k$ and

$$\mathfrak{C}_k - \frac{1}{k} < \mathring{\partial}(\Upsilon^o{}_{m_k}, \Upsilon^o{}_{q_k}) \leq \mathfrak{C}_k.$$

Hence,

$$\lim_{k\to\infty} \mathring{\partial}(\Upsilon^o{}_{m_k}, \Upsilon^o{}_{q_k}) = \mathfrak{C}. \tag{24}$$

Using inequality (21) and the triangular inequality, we have

$$\mathring{\partial}(\Upsilon^o{}_{m_k}, \Upsilon^o{}_{q_k}) < \mathring{\partial}(\Upsilon^o{}_{m_k-1}, \Upsilon^o{}_{q_k-1}) \\ < \mathring{\partial}(\Upsilon^o{}_{m_k-1}, \Upsilon^o{}_{m_k}) + \mathring{\partial}(\Upsilon^o{}_{m_k}, \Upsilon^o{}_{q_k}) + \mathring{\partial}(\Upsilon^o{}_{q_k}, \Upsilon^o{}_{q_k-1}).$$

Using Lemma (4) and inequality (24) and letting $k \to \infty$ in the above inequality, we obtain

$$\lim_{k\to\infty} \mathring{\partial}(\Upsilon^o{}_{m_k-1}, \Upsilon^o{}_{q_k-1}) = \mathfrak{C}. \tag{25}$$

Since Θ is an enriched $(\mathrm{d}, \mathfrak{Z})$-$\mathcal{Z}$-Hutchinson operator, using inequalities (21), (24), (25), and (λ_3), we therefore have

$$0 \leq \limsup_{k\to\infty} \mathfrak{Z}\Big(\mathring{\partial}(\Upsilon^o{}_{m_k-1}, \Upsilon^o{}_{q_k-1}), \mathring{\partial}(\Upsilon^o{}_{m_k}, \Upsilon^o{}_{q_k})\Big) < 0,$$

which is a contradiction and proves that $\mathfrak{C} = 0$. So, $\{\Upsilon^o{}_q\}$ is a Cauchy sequence. Since $\tilde{\Pi}$ is a Banach space, there exists $\Upsilon^{o*} \in \tilde{\Pi}$ such that $\lim_{q\to\infty} \Upsilon^o{}_q = \Upsilon^{o*}$. Next, we show that Υ^{o*} is a unique FP of Θ. For this purpose, suppose to the contrary that Υ^{o*} is not the FP of Θ. Thus, Υ^{o*} will not be the FP of Θ_δ. By utilizing inequality (23), we have

$$0 \leq \mathfrak{Z}(\mathring{\partial}(\Theta_\delta\Upsilon^o{}_k, \Theta_\delta\Upsilon^{o*}), \mathcal{N}_{\Theta_\delta}(\Upsilon^o{}_k, \Upsilon^{o*})), \tag{26}$$

where

$$
\begin{aligned}
\mathcal{N}_{\Theta_\delta}({Y^o}_k, Y^{o*}) = \max\Big\{ & \mathring{\partial}({Y^o}_k, Y^{o*}), \mathring{\partial}({Y^o}_k, \Theta_\delta {Y^o}_k), \mathring{\partial}(Y^{o*}, \Theta_\delta Y^{o*}), \\
& \frac{\mathring{\partial}({Y^o}_k, \Theta_\delta Y^{o*}) + \mathring{\partial}(Y^{o*}, \Theta_\delta {Y^o}_k)}{2}, \\
& \mathring{\partial}\left(\Theta_\delta^2 {Y^o}_k, \Theta_\delta {Y^o}_k\right), \mathring{\partial}\left(\Theta_\delta^2 {Y^o}_k, Y^{o*}\right), \mathring{\partial}\left(\Theta_\delta^2 {Y^o}_k, \Theta_\delta Y^{o*}\right)\Big\} \\
= \max\Big\{ & \mathring{\partial}({Y^o}_k, Y^{o*}), \mathring{\partial}({Y^o}_k, {Y^o}_{k+1}), \mathring{\partial}(Y^{o*}, \Theta_\delta Y^{o*}), \\
& \frac{\mathring{\partial}({Y^o}_k, \Theta_\delta Y^{o*}) + \mathring{\partial}(Y^{o*}, {Y^o}_{k+1})}{2}, \\
& \mathring{\partial}({Y^o}_{k+2}, {Y^o}_{k+1}), \mathring{\partial}({Y^o}_{k+2}, Y^{o*}), \mathring{\partial}({Y^o}_{k+2}, \Theta_\delta Y^{o*})\Big\}.
\end{aligned}
$$

We now have the following cases:

1. If $\mathcal{N}_{\Theta_\delta}({Y^o}_k, Y^{o*}) = \mathring{\partial}({Y^o}_k, Y^{o*})$, then using the limit as $k \to \infty$ in (26) and λ_2, we obtain

$$
\begin{aligned}
0 &\leq 3(\mathring{\partial}(Y^{o*}, \Theta_\delta Y^{o*}), \mathring{\partial}(Y^{o*}, Y^{o*})) \\
&< \mathring{\partial}(Y^{o*}, Y^{o*}) - \mathring{\partial}(Y^{o*}, \Theta_\delta Y^{o*}) \\
&= -\mathring{\partial}(Y^{o*}, \Theta_\delta Y^{o*}),
\end{aligned}
$$

which is a contradiction.

2. If $\mathcal{N}_{\Theta_\delta}({Y^o}_k, Y^{o*}) = \mathring{\partial}({Y^o}_k, {Y^o}_{k+1})$, then using the limit as $k \to \infty$ in (26) and λ_2, we obtain

$$
\begin{aligned}
0 &\leq 3(\mathring{\partial}(Y^{o*}, \Theta_\delta Y^{o*}), \mathring{\partial}(Y^{o*}, Y^{o*})) \\
&< \mathring{\partial}(Y^{o*}, Y^{o*}) - \mathring{\partial}(Y^{o*}, \Theta_\delta Y^{o*}) \\
&= -\mathring{\partial}(Y^{o*}, \Theta_\delta Y^{o*}),
\end{aligned}
$$

which is a contradiction.

3. If $\mathcal{N}_{\Theta_\delta}({Y^o}_k, Y^{o*}) = \mathring{\partial}(Y^{o*}, \Theta_\delta Y^{o*})$, then using the limit as $k \to \infty$ in (26) and λ_2, we obtain

$$
\begin{aligned}
0 &\leq 3(\mathring{\partial}(Y^{o*}, \Theta_\delta Y^{o*}), \mathring{\partial}(Y^{o*}, \Theta_\delta Y^{o*})) \\
&< \mathring{\partial}(Y^{o*}, \Theta_\delta Y^{o*}) - \mathring{\partial}(Y^{o*}, \Theta_\delta Y^{o*}) \\
&= 0,
\end{aligned}
$$

which further implies $\mathring{\partial}(Y^{o*}, \Theta_\delta Y^{o*}) = 0$ by the aid of λ_1 and is thus a contradiction.

4. If $\mathcal{N}_{\Theta_\delta}({Y^o}_k, Y^{o*}) = \frac{\mathring{\partial}({Y^o}_k, \Theta_\delta Y^{o*}) + \mathring{\partial}(Y^{o*}, {Y^o}_{k+1})}{2}$, then using the limit as $k \to \infty$ in (26) and λ_2, we obtain

$$
\begin{aligned}
0 &\leq 3\left(\mathring{\partial}(Y^{o*}, \Theta_\delta Y^{o*}), \frac{\mathring{\partial}(Y^{o*}, \Theta_\delta Y^{o*}) + \mathring{\partial}(Y^{o*}, Y^{o*})}{2}\right) \\
&= 3\left(\mathring{\partial}(Y^{o*}, \Theta_\delta Y^{o*}), \frac{\mathring{\partial}(Y^{o*}, \Theta_\delta Y^{o*})}{2}\right) \\
&< \mathring{\partial}(Y^{o*}, \Theta_\delta Y^{o*}) - \frac{\mathring{\partial}(Y^{o*}, \Theta_\delta Y^{o*})}{2} \\
&= -\frac{\mathring{\partial}(Y^{o*}, \Theta_\delta Y^{o*})}{2},
\end{aligned}
$$

which is a contradiction.

5. If $\mathcal{N}_{\Theta_\delta}(Y^o{}_k, Y^{o*}) = \mathring{\eth}(Y^o{}_{k+2}, Y^o{}_{k+1})$, then using the limit as $k \to \infty$ in (26) and λ_2, we get

$$\begin{aligned} 0 &\leq \mathfrak{Z}(\mathring{\eth}(Y^{o*}, \Theta_\delta Y^{o*}), \mathring{\eth}(Y^{o*}, Y^{o*})) \\ &< \mathring{\eth}(Y^{o*}, Y^{o*}) - \mathring{\eth}(Y^{o*}, \Theta_\delta Y^{o*}) \\ &= -\mathring{\eth}(Y^{o*}, \Theta_\delta Y^{o*}), \end{aligned}$$

a contradiction.

6. If $\mathcal{N}_{\Theta_\delta}(Y^o{}_k, Y^{o*}) = \mathring{\eth}(Y^o{}_{k+2}, Y^{o*})$, then using the limit as $k \to \infty$ in (26) and λ_2, we obtain

$$\begin{aligned} 0 &\leq \mathfrak{Z}(\mathring{\eth}(Y^{o*}, \Theta_\delta Y^{o*}), \mathring{\eth}(Y^{o*}, Y^{o*})) \\ &< \mathring{\eth}(Y^{o*}, Y^{o*}) - \mathring{\eth}(Y^{o*}, \Theta_\delta Y^{o*}) \\ &= -\mathring{\eth}(Y^{o*}, \Theta_\delta Y^{o*}), \end{aligned}$$

which is a contradiction.

7. If $\mathcal{N}_{\Theta_\delta}(Y^o{}_k, Y^{o*}) = \mathring{\eth}(Y^o{}_{k+2}, \Theta_\delta Y^{o*})$, then using the limit as $k \to \infty$ in (26) and λ_2, we obtain

$$\begin{aligned} 0 &\leq \mathfrak{Z}(\mathring{\eth}(Y^{o*}, \Theta_\delta Y^{o*}), \mathring{\eth}(Y^{o*}, \Theta_\delta Y^{o*})) \\ &< \mathring{\eth}(Y^{o*}, \Theta_\delta Y^{o*}) - \mathring{\eth}(Y^{o*}, \Theta_\delta Y^{o*}) \\ &= 0, \end{aligned}$$

which further implies $\mathring{\eth}(Y^{o*}, \Theta_\delta Y^{o*}) = 0$ by the aid of λ_1 and thus is a contradiction.

Thus, in all cases, $\mathring{\eth}(\Theta_\delta Y^{o*}, Y^{o*}) = 0$. This is to say, Y^{o*} is the FP of Θ_δ and, as such, the FP of Θ. For the purpose of uniqueness, suppose that $Y^o, \mho \in \Lambda(\tilde{\Pi})$ are two distinct FPs of Θ. Then, from (26), we have

$$\begin{aligned} 0 &\leq \mathfrak{Z}(\mathring{\eth}(Y^o, \mho), \mathring{\eth}(\Theta_\delta Y^o, \Theta_\delta \mho)) \\ &< \mathfrak{Z}(\mathring{\eth}(Y^o, \mho), \max\{\mathring{\eth}(Y^o, \mho), \mathring{\eth}(Y^o, \Theta_\delta Y^o), \mathring{\eth}(\mho, \Theta_\delta \mho), \frac{\mathring{\eth}(Y^o, \Theta_\delta \mho) + \mathring{\eth}(\mho, \Theta_\delta Y^o)}{2}, \\ &\quad \mathring{\eth}(\Theta_\delta^2 Y^o, \Theta_\delta Y^o), \mathring{\eth}(\Theta_\delta^2 Y^o, \mho), \mathring{\eth}(\Theta_\delta^2 Y^o, \Theta_\delta \mho)\} \\ &= \mathfrak{Z}(\mathring{\eth}(Y^o, \mho), \mathring{\eth}(Y^o, \mho)) \\ &< \mathring{\eth}(Y^o, \mho) - \mathring{\eth}(Y^o, \mho) \\ &= 0, \end{aligned}$$

which is a contradiction to the supposition. Accordingly, the FP of Θ is unique. □

Example 3. *Take $\mathbb{R}$ as the usual Banach space $||\cdot||$ and a system of finite mappings $\{\Theta^{(i)} : \mathbb{R} \to \mathbb{R},\ \ i = 3, 4, 5\}$ by*

$$\Theta^{(i)}(\iota^o) = 2 - \iota^o - \frac{2\iota^o}{i}, \quad \forall i = 3, 4, 5.$$

Then, for $\mathrm{d} = 1$, we obtain $\delta = \frac{1}{2}$ and $\forall i = 3, 4, 5$,

$$\Theta_\delta^{(i)}(\iota^o) = 1 - \frac{\iota^o}{i}, \quad \forall \iota^o \in \mathbb{R}. \tag{27}$$

Therefore, $|\Theta_\delta^{(i)}(\iota^o) - \Theta_\delta^{(i)}(\varrho^o)| \leq \pi|\iota^o - \varrho^o|, \quad \forall \iota^o, \varrho^o \in \mathcal{X}$*, where* $\pi = \max\{\frac{1}{i} : i = 3,4,5\} = \frac{1}{3}$*. Considering* $\mathfrak{Z} = \mathfrak{Z}_E$ *as defined in Corollary (2) by* $\mathfrak{Z}_E(\iota^o, \varrho^o) = \frac{1}{2}\varrho^o - \iota^o, \quad \forall \varrho^o, \iota^o \in [0,\infty)$*, then we obtain for* $i = 3,4,5$*,*

$$\begin{aligned}
\mathfrak{Z}(||\Theta_\delta^{(i)}(\iota^o) - \Theta_\delta^{(i)}(\varrho^o)||, ||\iota^o - \varrho^o||) &= \mathfrak{Z}(\frac{1}{i}|\iota^o - \varrho^o|, |\iota^o - \varrho^o|) \\
&= \frac{1}{2}|\iota^o - \varrho^o| - \frac{1}{i}|\iota^o - \varrho^o| \\
&\geq \frac{1}{2}|\iota^o - \varrho^o| - \frac{1}{3}|\iota^o - \varrho^o| \\
&= \frac{1}{6}|\iota^o - \varrho^o| \\
\Rightarrow \zeta(||\Theta_\delta^{(i)}(\iota^o) - \Theta_\delta^{(i)}(\varrho^o)||, ||\iota^o - \varrho^o||) &\geq 0.
\end{aligned}$$

Thus, $(\mathbb{R}, \Theta^{(i)} : i = 3,4,5)$ *is an IFS via the enriched* $(\mathrm{d},\mathfrak{Z})$*-*$\mathcal{Z}$*-contractions. Therefore, the mapping* $\Theta : \Lambda(\mathbb{R}) \to \Lambda(\mathbb{R})$ *given by*

$$\Theta(\Upsilon^o) = \cup_{i=3}^5 \Theta^{(i)}(\Upsilon^o), \quad \forall \Upsilon^o \in \Lambda(\mathbb{R})$$

must satisfy the following by Theorem (4)*:*

$$\mathfrak{Z}(\mathring{\partial}(\Theta_\delta^{(i)}(\Upsilon^o), \Theta_\delta^{(i)}(\mho)), \mathring{\partial}(\Upsilon^o, \mho)) \geq 0, \forall \Upsilon^o, \mho \in \Lambda(\mathcal{X}), \quad \forall i = 3,4,5.$$

Therefore, by Theorem 6, Θ *has a unique FP, as* Θ *meets all of its requirements.*

The intricate construction of enriched $(\mathrm{d},\mathfrak{Z})$-$\mathcal{Z}$-contractions is essential for deriving existence and uniqueness results because it broadens classical methods to address more complex scenarios and offers a more profound theoretical framework. Although classical methods may work for simpler cases, generalized contractions and their associated IFSs provide enhanced insights and solutions for more complex problems. This approach enables a more thorough analysis and application, especially for specialized integral equations and advanced operators such as the enriched $\mathcal{Z}$-Hutchinson operator.

5. Conclusions and Future Directions

In conclusion, we introduced a wide class of enriched $(\mathrm{d},\mathfrak{Z})$-$\mathcal{Z}$-contractions defined on Banach spaces and established the existence and uniqueness of their FPs. To validate our findings, we gave a concrete example. In addition, we demonstrated an existence condition confirming the uniqueness of the solution to an integral equation. Moreover, we defined the IFS associated with enriched $(\mathrm{d},\mathfrak{Z})$-$\mathcal{Z}$-contractions in Banach spaces and defined the enriched $\mathcal{Z}$-Hutchinson operator. We also established a result on the convergence of Krasnoselskii's iteration method and the uniqueness of the attractor via enriched $(\mathrm{d},\mathfrak{Z})$-$\mathcal{Z}$-contractions. As a result, our findings not only confirm but also significantly build upon and broaden several established results.

In future work, it would be interesting to examine whether it is possible to deduce Kannan, Chatterjea, interpolative Kannan, and interpolative Chatterjea-type contractions and their FP results in the context of $\mathcal{Z}$-type contractions via enriched techniques. Additionally, investigating the same task for cyclic contractions via enriched techniques could provide valuable insights and further extend the applicability of enriched contractions in various mathematical contexts.

Author Contributions: Conceptualization, I.A., M.D., U.I., M.A. and I.K.A.; methodology, I.A., M.D., U.I., M.A. and I.K.A.; software, I.A., M.D., U.I., M.A. and I.K.A.; validation, I.A., M.D., U.I., M.A. and I.K.A.; formal analysis, I.A., M.D., U.I., M.A. and I.K.A.; investigation, I.A., M.D., U.I., M.A. and I.K.A.; resources, I.A., M.D., U.I., M.A. and I.K.A.; data curation, I.A., M.D., U.I., M.A. and I.K.A.; writing—original draft preparation, I.A., M.D., U.I., M.A. and I.K.A.; writing—review and editing, I.A., M.D., U.I., M.A. and I.K.A.; visualization, I.A., M.D., U.I., M.A. and I.K.A.; supervision, I.A., M.D., U.I., M.A. and I.K.A.; project administration, I.A., M.D., U.I., M.A. and I.K.A.; funding acquisition, I.A., M.D., U.I., M.A. and I.K.A. All authors have read and agreed to the published version of the manuscript.

Funding: This research received no external funding.

Data Availability Statement: Data will be available on demand from the corresponding author.

Acknowledgments: The authors are thankful to the Deanship of Scientific Research, Islamic University of Madinah for providing the support under the Post Publication Program III.

Conflicts of Interest: The authors declare no conflicts of interest.

References

1. Hutchinson, J.E. Fractals and self similarity. *Indiana Univ. Math. J.* **1981**, *30*, 713–747. [CrossRef]
2. Barnsley, M. *Fractals Everywhere*; Academic Press: Boston, MA, USA, 1988.
3. Banach, S. Sur les opérations dans les ensembles abstraits et leur application aux équations intégrales. *Fundam. Math.* **1922**, *3*, 133–181. [CrossRef]
4. Andres, J.; Fišer, J. Metric and topological multivalued fractals. *Int. J. Bifurc. Chaos* **2004**, *14*, 1277–1289. [CrossRef]
5. Duvall, P.F.; Emert, J.W.; Husch, L.S. Iterated function systems, compact semigroups, and topological contractions. In *Lecture Notes in Pure and Applied Mathematics*; CRC Press: Boca Raton, FL, USA, 1993; p. 113.
6. Kieninger, B. *Iterated Function Systems on Compact Hausdorff Spaces*; Shaker: Herzogenrath, Germany, 2002.
7. Barnsley, M.F.; Demko, S. Iterated function systems and the global construction of fractals. *Proc. R. Soc. Lond. Math. Phys. Sci.* **1985**, *399*, 243–275.
8. Zhou, M.; Saleem, N.; Ali, B.; Mohsin, M.; López, de Hierro, A.F.R. Common Best Proximity Points and Completeness of $\mathcal{F}$- MSs. *Mathematics* **2023**, *11*, 281. [CrossRef]
9. Kashyap, S.K.; Sharma, B.K.; Banerjee, A.; Shrivastava, S.C. On Krasnoselskii fixed point theorem and fractal. *Chaos Solitons Fractals* **2014**, *61*, 44–45. [CrossRef]
10. Mandelbrot, B.B. *The Fractal Geometry of Nature*; WH freeman: New York, NY, USA, 1982; Volume 1, pp. 25–74.
11. Maślanka, Ł; Strobin, F. On generalized iterated function systems defined on l_∞-sum of a metric space. *J. Math. Anal. Appl.* **2018**, *461*, 1795–1832. [CrossRef]
12. Klimek, M.; Kosek, M. Generalized iterated function systems, multifunctions and Cantor sets. *Ann. Pol. Math.* **2009**, *1*, 25–41. [CrossRef]
13. Kunze, H.E.; La Torre, D.; Vrscay, E.R. Contractive multifunctions, fixed point inclusions and iterated multifunction systems. *J. Math. Anal. Appl.* **2007**, *330*, 159–173. [CrossRef]
14. La Torre, D. Approximating by Iterated Function Systems and Iterated Multifunction Systems. Convegozo su Metodi Matematicie Stastici per le Assicuraziono e la Finanza 2006, 12. Available online: https://citeseerx.ist.psu.edu/document?repid=rep1&type=pdf&doi=944015231e35c3388605a60fa2b7c18407247336 (accessed on 13 August 2024).
15. Torre, D.L.; Mendivil, F.; Vrscay, E.R. Iterated function systems on multifunctions. In *Math Everywhere: Deterministic and Stochastic Modelling in Biomedicine, Economics and Industry*; Springer: Berlin/Heidelberg, Germany, 2007; pp. 125–138.
16. Khumalo, M.; Nazir, T.; Makhoshi, V. Generalized iterated function system for common attractors in partial metric spaces. *Aims Math.* **2022**, *7*, 13074–13103. [CrossRef]
17. Anjum, R.; Din, M.; Zhou, M. Fractals of two types of enriched (q,θ)-Hutchinson–Barnsley operators. *Chaos Solitons Fractals* **2024**, *181*, 114589. [CrossRef]
18. Ahmad, J.; Al-Mazrooei, A.E.; Rassias, T.M. Fractals of generalized Θ-Hutchinson operator. *Int. J. Nonlinear Anal. Appl.* **2022**, *13*, 1–12.
19. Berinde, V.; Păcurar, M. Approximating fixed points of enriched contractions in Banach spaces. *J. Fixed Point Theory Appl.* **2020**, *22*, 38. [CrossRef]
20. Prithvi, B.V.; Katiyar, S.K. Comments on "Fractal set of generalized countable partial iterated function system with generalized contractions via partial Hausdorff metric". *Topol. Its Appl.* **2024**, *341*, 108687. [CrossRef]
21. Prithvi, B.V.; Katiyar, S.K. Revisiting fractal through nonconventional iterated function systems. *Chaos Solitons Fractals* **2023**, *170*, 113337. [CrossRef]
22. Prithvi, B.V.; Katiyar, S.K. Generalized Kannan Maps with Application to Iterated Function System. In *Advanced Mathematical Analysis and Its Applications*; Chapman and Hall/CRC: Boca Raton, FL, USA, 2023; pp. 179–194.
23. Sahu, D.R.; Chakraborty, A.; Dubey, R.P. K-iterated function system. *Fractals* **2010**, *18*, 139–144. [CrossRef]
24. Thangaraj, C.; Easwaramoorthy, D.; Selmi, B.; Chamola, B.P. Generation of fractals via iterated function system of Kannan contractions in controlled metric space. *Math. Comput. Simul.* **2024**, *222*, 188–198. [CrossRef]
25. Ch, ra, S.; Verma, S.; Abbas, S. Construction of fractal functions using Kannan mappings and smoothness analysis. *arXiv* **2023**, arXiv:2301.03075.
26. Amit, Basotia, V.; Prajapati, A. Non-stationary Φ-contractions and associated fractals. *J. Anal.* **2023**, *31*, 1375–1391. [CrossRef]

27. Verma, M.; Priyadarshi, A. New Type of Fractal Functions for the General Data Sets. *Acta Appl. Math.* **2023**, *187*, 12. [CrossRef]
28. Khojasteh, F.; Shukla, S.; Radenović, S. A new approach to the study of fixed point theory for simulation functions. *Filomat* **2015**, *29*, 1189–1194. [CrossRef]
29. Rhoades, B. Some theorems on weakly contractive maps. *Nonlinear Anal. Theory Methods Appl.* **2001**, *47*, 2683–2693. [CrossRef]

axioms

MDPI

Article

Nonlinear Contractions Employing Digraphs and Comparison Functions with an Application to Singular Fractional Differential Equations

Doaa Filali [1], Mohammad Dilshad [2] and Mohammad Akram [3,*]

[1] Department of Mathematical Science, College of Sciences, Princess Nourah bint Abdulrahman University, Riyadh 84428, Saudi Arabia
[2] Department of Mathematics, University of Tabuk, Tabuk 71491, Saudi Arabia
[3] Department of Mathematics, Islamic University of Madinah, Madinah 42351, Saudi Arabia
* Correspondence: akramkhan_20@rediffmail.com

Abstract: After the initiation of Jachymski's contraction principle via digraph, the area of metric fixed point theory has attracted much attention. A number of outcomes on fixed points in the context of graph metric space employing various types of contractions have been investigated. The aim of this paper is to investigate some fixed point theorems for a class of nonlinear contractions in a metric space endued with a transitive digraph. The outcomes presented herewith improve, extend and enrich several existing results. Employing our findings, we describe the existence and uniqueness of a singular fractional boundary value problem.

Keywords: fixed points; digraphs; singular fractional differential equations

MSC: 47H10; 34A08; 54E35

1. Introduction

Fractional differential equations (abbreviated as FDEs) are generalisations of the ordinary differential equations to an arbitrary non-integer order. In the recent past, FDEs have been studied on account of their remarkable growth and relevance to the field of fractional calculus. For an extensive collection on the background of FDE, we refer the readers to consult [1–5] and the references therein. Various researchers (e.g., [6–11]) have discussed the existence theory of FDE employing the approaches of fixed point theory. Recall that a typical fractional BVP (abbreviation of 'boundary value problem') in a dependent variable ϑ and independent variable θ can be represented by

$$-D^{\iota}\vartheta(\theta) = \hbar\Big(\theta, \vartheta(\theta), D^{\alpha_1}\vartheta(\theta), D^{\alpha_2}\vartheta(\theta), \ldots, D^{\alpha_{r-1}}\vartheta(\theta)\Big)$$

$$\begin{cases} D^{\alpha_i}\vartheta(0) = 0, \quad 1 \le i \le r-1, \\ D^{\alpha_{r-1}+1}\vartheta(0) = 0, \\ D^{\alpha_{r-1}}\vartheta(1) = \sum\limits_{j=1}^{m-2} q_j D^{\alpha_{r-1}}\vartheta(\varpi_j) \end{cases} \tag{1}$$

where

- $r \in \mathbb{N}$, $r \ge 3$ and $r-1 < \iota \le r$,
- $0 < \alpha_1 < \alpha_2 < \cdots < \alpha_{r-2} < \alpha_{r-1}$ and $r-3 < \alpha_{r-1} < \iota - 2$,
- D^{ι} is standard Riemann–Liouville derivative,
- $\hbar \in C\big([0,1] \times \mathbb{R}^r;\ [0,\infty)\big)$,

- $q_j \in \mathbb{R}$ and $0 < \varpi_1 < \varpi_2 < \cdots < \varpi_{m-1} < 1$ with $0 < \sum_{j=1}^{m-2} q_j \varpi_j^{\iota-\alpha_{r-1}-1} < 1$.

Fixed point theory plays in metric space (in short, MS) a central role in nonlinear functional analysis. Throughout the foregoing century, BCP has been expanded and generalised by numerous authors. A common generalisation of this finding is to expand the standard contraction to φ-contraction by means of a proper auxiliary function $\varphi : [0,\infty) \to [0,\infty)$. A variety of generalisations has been developed through effectively modifying φ, resulting in a huge number of articles on this topic. Matkowski [12] invented a new class of φ-contraction that incorporated the concept of comparison functions, which has been further studied in ([13–17]) besides several others. Quite recently, Pant [17] established an interesting non-unique fixed point theorem enlarging the class of φ-contractions in a complete metric space.

In 2008, Jachymski [18] established a very interesting approach in fixed point theory in the setup of graph metric space. Graphs are algebraic structures that subsume the partial ordering. The chief feature of the graphic approach is that the contraction condition is required to hold for merely certain edges of the underlying graph. This approach gave rise to an emerging discipline of research in metric fixed point theory, which led to the appearance of numerous works, e.g., see [19–25]. In 2010, Bojor [19] extended the results of Jachymski [18] to (G,φ)-contraction in the sense of Matkowski [12].

The intent of this manuscript is to expand the outcomes of Bojor [19] adopting the idea of Pant [17] and to prove the fixed point theorems under the enlarged class of (G,φ)-contraction in the setup of graph metric space. Employing the findings proved herewith, we study the existence and uniqueness of positive solutions of a particular form of BVP (1), such that the FDE remains singular.

2. Graph Metric Space

The set of real numbers (resp. natural numbers) are indicated by $\mathbb{R}$ (resp. $\mathbb{N}$). By a graph G, we mean the pair $(V(G), E(G))$, whereas $V(G)$ (known as set of vertices) and a set $E(G)$ (known as set of edges) have a binary relation on $V(G)$.

Definition 1 ([26]). *A graph is named as a digraph (or, directed graph) if every edge remains an ordered pair of vertices.*

Definition 2 ([26]). *The transpose of a graph G, is a graph denoted by G^{-1}, described as*

$$V(G^{-1}) = V(G) \quad and \quad E(G^{-1}) = \{(v,u) \in V(G)^2 : (u,v) \in E(G)\}.$$

Definition 3 ([26]). *Each digraph $G = (V(G), E(G))$ induces an undirected graph $\tilde{G}$, defined by*

$$V(\tilde{G}) = V(G) \quad and \quad E(\tilde{G}) = E(G) \cup E(G^{-1}).$$

Definition 4 ([26]). *For any two vertices v and u in the graph G, a finite sequence $\{v_0, v_1, v_2, \dots v_p\}$ of vertices is said to form a path in G from v to u of length p if $v_0 = v$, $v_p = u$ and $(v_{r-1}, v_r) \in E(G), \forall\, r \in \{1,2,\dots p\}$.*

Definition 5 ([26]). *A graph G is known as connected if any two vertices of G enjoy a path. If $\tilde{G}$ is connected then G is referred as weakly connected.*

Definition 6 ([18]). *Let (V,ϱ) be a MS and $G := (V(G), E(G))$ a digraph. Then the triplet (V,ϱ,G) called a graph MS if*

- *$V(G) = V$;*
- *$E(G)$ contains all loops;*
- *G admits no parallel edge.*

Definition 7 ([20]). *Given a graph MS (V, ϱ, G), G is referred as a (C)-graph if for every sequence $\{v_n\} \subset V$ having the properties: $v_n \to v$ and $(v_n, v_{n+1}) \in E(G)$, for every $n \in \mathbb{N}$, $\exists$ a subsequence $\{v_{n_r}\}$ with $(v_{n_r}, v) \in E(G)$, $\forall\, r \in \mathbb{N}$.*

Definition 8 ([23]). *Given a graph MS (V, ϱ, G), a map $R : V \to V$ is named as G-edge preserving if*

$$(v, u) \in E(G) \Longrightarrow (Rv, Ru) \in E(G).$$

Definition 9 ([24]). *A digraph G is referred as transitive if for all $v, u, w \in V(G)$ with*

$$(v, u) \in E(G) \quad \text{and} \quad (u, w) \in E(G) \Longrightarrow (v, w) \in E(G).$$

Definition 10 ([27]). *An increasing function $\varphi : [0, \infty) \to [0, \infty)$ is named as comparison function if $\lim_{n\to\infty} \varphi^n(t) = 0, \forall\, t > 0$.*

For further discussions on comparison functions, we refer the monographs of Rus [27] and Berinde [28].

Proposition 1 ([27,28]). *Every comparison function φ verifies that $\varphi(t) < t$, $\forall\, t > 0$ and $\varphi(0) = 0$.*

Definition 11 ([29]). *A self-map R defined on a MS (V, ϱ) is referred as*

- *PM (Picard mapping) if* $\mathrm{Fix}(R) = \{v^*\}$ *(a singleton set) and* $R^n(v) \to v^*, \forall\, v \in V$;
- *WPM (weakly Picard mapping) if* $\mathrm{Fix}(R) \neq \emptyset$ *and the sequence* $\{R^n v\}$ *converges to a fixed point of R,* $\forall\, v \in V$.

3. Main Results

Given a digraph $G := (V(G), E(G))$, a self-map R on V and $v \in V(G)$, we adopt the succeeding notations:

$$[v]_G = \{u \in V(G) : \exists \text{ a path in } G \text{ from } v \text{ to } u\};$$

$$V_R = \{v \in V : (v, Rv) \in E(G)\};$$

and

$$\mathrm{Fix}(R) = \{v \in V : R(v) = v\}.$$

We are now going to demonstrate the following fpt in a graph MS over a class of (G, φ)-contractivity condition.

Theorem 1. *Let (V, ϱ, G) be a graph MS whereas (V, ϱ) is a complete MS and G is a transitive. Let $R : V \to V$ be a G-edge preserving map and $V_R \neq \emptyset$. Also, assume that either, R is orbitally G-continuous, or, G is a (C)-graph. If there exists a comparison function φ such that*

$$\varrho(Rv, Ru) \leq \varphi(\varrho(v, u)) \quad \forall\, (v, u) \in E(G) \text{ with } [v \neq R(v) \text{ or } u \neq R(u)], \tag{2}$$

then R is a WPM.

Proof. Take $v_0 \in V_R$ so that $(v_0, Rv_0) \in E(G)$. Construct a sequence $\{v_n\}$ in the following way:

$$v_{n+1} = R^n(v_0) = R(v_n), \quad \forall\, n \in \mathbb{N}_0. \tag{3}$$

Since $(v_0, Rv_0) \in E(G)$ and R is a G-edge preserving, by easy induction, we have

$$(R^n v_0, R^{n+1} v_0) \in E(G)$$

which through (3) simplifies to

$$(v_n, v_{n+1}) \in E(G) \quad \forall\, n \in \mathbb{N}_0. \tag{4}$$

Define $\varrho_n := \varrho(v_n, v_{n+1})$. If there is some $n_0 \in \mathbb{N}_0$ with $\varrho_{n_0} = 0$, then by (3), we find $v_{n_0} = v_{n_0+1} = R(v_{n_0})$; so $v_{n_0} \in \mathrm{Fix}(R)$, unless, we have $\varrho_n > 0$ for every $n \in \mathbb{N}_0$. Then, we have $v_n \neq v_{n+1} = R(v_n)$. On implementing (4) and the contractivity condition (2), we find

$$\varrho_n = \varrho(v_n, v_{n+1}) = \varrho(Rv_{n-1}, Rv_n) \leq \varphi(\varrho(v_{n-1}, v_n)),$$

or,

$$\varrho_n \leq \varphi(\varrho_{n-1}) \quad \forall\, n \in \mathbb{N}_0. \tag{5}$$

Using monotonicity of φ in (5), we have

$$\varrho_n \leq \varphi(\varrho_{n-1}) \leq \varphi^2(\varrho_{n-2}) \leq \cdots \leq \varphi^n(\varrho_0),$$

or,

$$\varrho_n \leq \varphi^n(\varrho_0), \quad \forall\, n \in \mathbb{N}. \tag{6}$$

With $n \to \infty$ in (6) and employing the definition of φ, we find

$$\lim_{n\to\infty} \varrho_n = 0. \tag{7}$$

Choose $\varepsilon > 0$. Then, owing to (7), we can find $n \in \mathbb{N}_0$ allows for

$$\varrho_n < \varepsilon - \varphi(\varepsilon). \tag{8}$$

Now, we seek to verify that $\{v_n\}$ is Cauchy. Implementing the monotonicity of φ, (5) and (8), we find

$$\begin{aligned} \varrho(v_n, v_{n+2}) &\leq \varrho(v_n, v_{n+1}) + \varrho(v_{n+1}, v_{n+2}) = \varrho_n + \varrho_{n+1} \\ &\leq \varrho_n + \varphi(\varrho_n) \\ &< \varepsilon - \varphi(\varepsilon) + \varphi[\varepsilon - \varphi(\varepsilon)] \leq \varepsilon - \varphi(\varepsilon) + \varphi(\varepsilon) \\ &= \varepsilon. \end{aligned}$$

Implementing the monotonicity of φ, transitivity of G, (4), (8), and the contractivity condition (2), we find

$$\begin{aligned} \varrho(v_n, v_{n+3}) &\leq \varrho(v_n, v_{n+1}) + \varrho(v_{n+1}, v_{n+3}) \\ &= \varrho_n + \varrho(Rv_n, Rv_{n+2}) \\ &< \varepsilon - \varphi(\varepsilon) + \varphi(\varrho(v_n, v_{n+2})) \\ &\leq \varepsilon - \varphi(\varepsilon) + \varphi(\varepsilon) \\ &= \varepsilon. \end{aligned}$$

By easy induction, one finds

$$\varrho(v_n, v_{n+p}) < \varepsilon, \quad \forall\, p \in \mathbb{N}.$$

It turns out that $\{v_n\}$ continues to be Cauchy. Through the completeness of (V, ϱ), there exists $v \in V$ whereby $v_n \stackrel{\varrho}{\to} v$.

Suppose that R is orbitally G-continuous. Then, one finds

$$v_{n+1} = R(v_n) \xrightarrow{\varrho} R(v),$$

leading to, in turn, $R(v) = v$. Therefore, v is a fixed point of R. Otherwise, if G is a (C)-graph, then, a subsequence $\{v_{n_k}\}$ of $\{v_n\}$ can be determined that satisfies $(v_{n_k}, v) \in E(G)$ for every $k \in \mathbb{N}_0$. By contractivity condition (2), we have

$$\varrho(v_{n_k+1}, Rv) = \varrho(Rv_{n_k}, Rv) \leq \varphi(\varrho(v_{n_k}, v)), \quad \forall\, k \in \mathbb{N}_0.$$

Using Proposition 1 (whether $\varrho(v_{n_k}, v)$ is zero or non-zero), the above inequality becomes

$$\varrho(v_{n_k+1}, Rv) \leq \varrho(v_{n_k}, v).$$

Taking $k \to \infty$ in the above inequality and using $v_{n_k} \xrightarrow{\varrho} v$, we get

$$v_{n_k+1} \xrightarrow{\varrho} R(v),$$

leading to, in turn, $R(v) = v$. Hence, v is a fixed point of R. □

Next, we present the uniqueness theorem corresponding to Theorem 1.

Theorem 2. *Let (V, ϱ, G) be a graph MS whereas (V, ϱ) is a complete MS and G is a transitive and weakly connected. Let $R : V \to V$ be a G-edge preserving map and $V_R \neq \emptyset$. Also, assume that either, R is orbitally G-continuous, or, G is a (C)-graph. If there exists a comparison function φ such that*

$$\varrho(Rv, Ru) \leq \varphi(\varrho(v, u)) \quad \forall\, (v, u) \in E(G),$$

then R is a PM.

Proof. In regard to Theorem 1, if $v, u \in \mathrm{Fix}(R)$, then, for every $n \in \mathbb{N}_0$, we find

$$R^n(v) = v, \quad R^n(u) = u.$$

By the weak connectedness of G, there is a path $\{w_0, w_1, w_2, \ldots w_p\}$ between v and u, i.e.,

$$w_0 = v,\ w_p = u \text{ and } (w_{r-1}, w_r) \in E(G), \quad \forall\, r \in \{1, 2, \ldots p\}.$$

As R is G-edge preserving, we find for each $0 \leq r \leq p-1$ that

$$(R^n w_r, R^n w_{r+1}) \in E(\tilde{G}), \quad \forall\, n \in \mathbb{N}_0. \tag{9}$$

The application of the triangle inequality reveals that

$$\varrho(v, u) = \varrho(R^n w_0, R^n w_p) \leq \sum_{r=0}^{p-1} \varrho(R^n w_r, R^n w_{r+1}). \tag{10}$$

For every $r (0 \leq r \leq p-1)$, δ_n^r denotes $\varrho(R^n w_r, R^n w_{r+1})$, where $n \in \mathbb{N}_0$. Now, it is claimed that

$$\lim_{n \to \infty} \delta_n^r = 0.$$

To substantiate this, on fixing r, assuming first that $\delta_{n_0}^r = 0$ for some $n_0 \in \mathbb{N}_0$, then, $R^{n_0+1}(w_r) = R^{n_0+1}(w_{r+1})$. Thus, we find $\delta_{n_0+1}^r = \varrho(R^{n_0+1} w_r, R^{n_0+1} w_{r+1}) = 0$; so inductively, we find $\delta_n^r = 0$ for every $n \geq n_0$, so that $\lim_{n\to\infty} \delta_n^r = 0$. In contrast, if $\delta_n^r > 0$ for every $n \in \mathbb{N}_0$, then, by (9) and the contractivity condition (2), we get

$$\begin{aligned} \delta_{n+1}^r &= \varrho(R^{n+1}w_r, R^{n+1}w_{r+1}) \\ &\leq \varphi(\varrho(R^n w_r, R^n w_{r+1})) \\ &= \varphi(\delta_n^r). \end{aligned}$$

Using the monotonicity of φ in (11), we get

$$\delta_n^r \leq \varphi(\delta_{n-1}^r) \leq \varphi^2(\delta_{n-2}^r) \leq \cdots \leq \varphi^n(\delta_0^r)$$

so that

$$\delta_n^r \leq \varphi^n(\delta_0^r). \tag{11}$$

If $\delta_0 = 0$, then by Proposition 1, one gets $\delta_n^r = 0$ yielding thereby $\lim_{n\to\infty} \delta_n = 0$. Otherwise, in case $\delta_0 > 0$, using the limit in (11) and the property of φ, one gets

$$\lim_{n\to\infty} \delta_n^r \leq \lim_{n\to\infty} \varphi^n(\delta_0) = 0.$$

Thus in each case, one has

$$\lim_{n\to\infty} \delta_n^r = 0. \tag{12}$$

Further, (10) can be written as

$$\begin{aligned} \varrho(v,u) = \varrho(R^n w_0, R^n w_p) &\leq \sum_{r=0}^{p-1} \varrho(R^n w_r, R^n w_{r+1}) \\ &\leq \delta_n^0 + \delta_n^1 + \cdots + \delta_n^{p-1} \\ &\to 0 \text{ as } n \to \infty \end{aligned}$$

which yields that $v = u$, so R has a unique fixed point. □

4. Applications to Fractional BVP

Consider the following fractional BVP:

$$\begin{cases} D_{0^+}^{\iota} \vartheta(\theta) + \hbar(\theta, \vartheta(\theta)) = 0, & \forall\, \theta \in (0,1), \\ \vartheta(0) = \vartheta'(0) = \vartheta''(0) = 0, & \vartheta''(1) = \eta\vartheta''(\ell), \end{cases} \tag{13}$$

along with the following assumptions:

- $3 < \iota \leq 4$,
- $0 < \ell < 1$,
- $0 < \eta\ell^{\iota-3} < 1$,
- $\hbar : [0,1] \times [0,\infty) \to [0,\infty)$ is continuous,
- $\hbar$ remains singular at $\theta = 0$, which means $\lim_{\theta\to 0+} \hbar(\theta,\cdot) = \infty$.

Obviously, the BVP (13) is identical to an integral equation given as under

$$\vartheta(\theta) = \int_0^1 G(\theta,\sigma)\hbar(\sigma,\vartheta(\sigma))d\sigma + \frac{\eta\theta^{\iota-1}}{(\iota-1)(\iota-2)(1-\eta\ell^{\iota-3})} \int_0^1 H(\ell,\sigma)\hbar(\sigma,\vartheta(\sigma))d\sigma \tag{14}$$

where the Green function is

$$G(\theta,\sigma) = \begin{cases} \frac{\theta^{\iota-1}(1-\sigma)^{\iota-3} - (\theta-\sigma)^{\iota-1}}{\Gamma(\iota)}, & 0 \leq \sigma \leq \theta \leq 1, \\ \frac{\theta^{\iota-1}(1-\sigma)^{\iota-3}}{\Gamma(\iota)}, & 0 \leq \theta \leq \sigma \leq 1 \end{cases}$$

and the function $H(\theta,\sigma) := \dfrac{\partial^2 G(\theta,\sigma)}{\partial\theta^2}$ becomes

$$H(\theta,\sigma) = \begin{cases} \frac{(\iota-1)(\iota-2)}{\Gamma(\iota)}\left[\theta^{\iota-3}(1-\sigma)^{\iota-3} - (\theta-\sigma)^{\iota-3}\right], & 0 \le \sigma \le \theta \le 1, \\ \frac{(\iota-1)(\iota-2)}{\Gamma(\iota)}\theta^{\iota-3}(1-\sigma)^{\iota-3}, & 0 \le \theta \le \sigma \le 1. \end{cases}$$

As usual, $\Gamma(\cdot)$ and $\beta(\cdot,\cdot)$ will denote the special functions: gamma function and beta function, respectively. Motivated by [8,9], we will determine the unique positive solution of (13).

Proposition 2 ([9]). *The functions G and H enjoy the following properties:*

- *G and H both are continuous;*
- $G(\theta,\sigma) \ge 0$ *and* $H(\theta,\sigma) \ge 0$;
- $G(\theta,1) = 0$;
- $\sup\limits_{0\le\theta\le 1} \int_0^1 G(\theta,\sigma)d\sigma = \frac{2}{(\iota-2)\Gamma(\iota+1)}$;
- $\int_0^1 H(\ell,\sigma)d\sigma = \frac{\ell^{\iota-3}(\iota-1)(1-\ell)}{\Gamma(\iota)}$.

Lemma 1. *If* $0 < \rho < 1$, *then,*

$$\sup_{0\le\theta\le 1} \int_0^1 G(\theta,\sigma)\sigma^{-\rho}d\sigma = \frac{1}{\Gamma(\iota)}(\beta(1-\rho,\iota-2) - \beta(1-\rho,\iota)).$$

Proof. Making use of definition of G, we get

$$\begin{aligned}
\int_0^1 G(\theta,\sigma)\sigma^{-\rho}d\sigma &= \int_0^\theta G(\theta,\sigma)\sigma^{-\rho}d\sigma + \int_\theta^1 G(\theta,\sigma)\sigma^{-\rho}d\sigma \\
&= \int_0^\theta \frac{\theta^{\iota-1}(1-\sigma)^{\iota-3} - (\theta-\sigma)^{\iota-1}}{\Gamma(\iota)}\sigma^{-\rho}d\sigma + \int_\theta^1 \frac{\theta^{\iota-1}(1-\sigma)^{\iota-3}}{\Gamma(\iota)}\sigma^{-\rho}d\sigma \\
&= \int_0^1 \frac{\theta^{\iota-1}(1-\sigma)^{\iota-3}}{\Gamma(\iota)}\sigma^{-\rho}d\sigma - \int_0^\theta \frac{(\theta-\sigma)^{\iota-1}}{\Gamma(\iota)}\sigma^{-\iota}d\sigma \\
&= \frac{\theta^{\iota-1}}{\Gamma(\iota)}\int_0^1 (1-\sigma)^{\iota-3}\sigma^{-\rho}d\sigma - \frac{1}{\Gamma(\iota)}\int_0^\theta (\theta-\sigma)^{\iota-1}\sigma^{-\rho}d\sigma \\
&= \frac{\theta^{\iota-1}}{\Gamma(\iota)}\beta(1-\rho,\iota-2) - \frac{1}{\Gamma(\iota)}I, \qquad (15)
\end{aligned}$$

where

$$I = \int_0^\theta (\theta-\sigma)^{\iota-1}\sigma^{-\rho}d\sigma = \int_0^\theta \left(1-\frac{\sigma}{\theta}\right)^{\iota-1}\theta^{\iota-1}\sigma^{-\rho}d\sigma = \theta^{\theta-\rho}\int_0^\theta \left(1-\frac{\sigma}{\theta}\right)^{\iota-1}\left(\frac{\sigma}{\theta}\right)^{-\rho}\theta d\sigma.$$

Applying the change of variables $v = \sigma/\theta$ so that $\theta dv = d\sigma$ in the above integral, we find

$$I = \theta^{\theta-\rho}\int_0^\theta (1-v)^{\iota-1}v^{-\rho}dv = \theta^{1-\rho}\beta(1-\rho,\iota). \qquad (16)$$

By (15) and (16), we obtain

$$\int_0^1 G(\theta,\sigma)\sigma^{-\rho}d\sigma = \frac{\theta^{\iota-1}}{\Gamma(\iota)}\beta(1-\rho,\iota-2) - \frac{\theta^{\iota-\rho}}{\Gamma(\iota)}\beta(1-\rho,\iota).$$

Defining

$$\phi(\theta) := \frac{\beta(1-\rho,\iota-2)}{\Gamma(\iota)}\theta^{\iota-1} - \frac{\beta(1-\rho,\iota)}{\Gamma(\iota)}\theta^{\iota-\rho}$$

Naturally, the function $\phi(\theta)$ remains increasing on $[0,1]$. Hence, we conclude

$$\sup_{0\leq\theta\leq 1}\int_0^1 G(\theta,\sigma)\sigma^{-\rho}d\sigma = \sup_{0\leq\theta\leq 1}\phi(\theta) = \phi(1) = \frac{1}{\Gamma(\iota)}[\beta(1-\rho,\iota-2)-\beta(1-\rho,\iota)].$$

□

Lemma 2. *If $0<\rho<1$, then,*

$$\int_0^1 H(\ell,\sigma)\sigma^{-\rho}d\sigma = \frac{(\iota-1(\iota-2)}{\Gamma(\iota)}(\ell^{\iota-3}-\ell^{\iota-\rho-2}\beta(1-\rho,\iota-2)),$$

Proof. We have

$$\begin{aligned}
&\int_0^1 H(\ell,\sigma)\sigma^{-\rho}d\sigma = \int_0^\ell H(\ell,\sigma)\sigma^{-\rho}d\sigma + \int_\ell^1 H(\ell,\sigma)\sigma^{-\rho}d\sigma \\
&= \int_0^\ell \frac{(\iota-1)(\iota-2)}{\Gamma(\iota)}\left[\ell^{\iota-3}(1-\sigma)^{\iota-3}-(\ell-\sigma)^{\iota-3}\right]\sigma^{-\rho}d\sigma + \int_\ell^1 \frac{(\iota-1)(\iota-2)}{\Gamma(\iota)}\ell^{\iota-3}(1-\sigma)^{\iota-3}\sigma^{-\rho}d\sigma \\
&= \int_0^1 \frac{(\iota-1)(\iota-2)}{\Gamma(\iota)}\ell^{\iota-3}(1-\sigma)^{\iota-3}\sigma^{-\rho}d\sigma - \int_0^\ell \frac{(\iota-1)(\iota-2)}{\Gamma(\iota)}(\ell-\sigma)^{\iota-3}\sigma^{-\rho}d\sigma \\
&= \frac{(\iota-1)(\iota-2)}{\Gamma(\iota)}\ell^{\iota-3}\int_0^1 (1-\sigma)^{\iota-1}\sigma^{-\rho}d\sigma \\
&- \frac{(\iota-1)(\iota-2)}{\Gamma(\iota)}\int_0^\ell (\ell-\sigma)^{\iota-3}\sigma^{-\rho}d\sigma \\
&= \frac{(\iota-1)(\iota-2)}{\Gamma(\iota)}\ell^{\iota-3}\beta(1-\rho,\iota-2) - \frac{(\iota-1)(\iota-2)}{\Gamma(\iota)}\int_0^\ell (\ell-\sigma)^{\iota-3}\sigma^{-\rho}d\sigma
\end{aligned}$$

In keeping with the argument of the proof of Lemma 1, we conclude

$$\begin{aligned}
\int_0^1 H(\ell,\sigma)\sigma^{-\rho}d\sigma &= \frac{(\iota-1)(\iota-2)}{\Gamma(\iota)}\ell^{\iota-3}\beta(1-\rho,\iota-2) \\
&- \frac{(\iota-1)(\iota-2)}{\Gamma(\iota)}\ell^{\iota-\rho-2}\beta(1-\rho,\iota-2) \\
&= \frac{(\iota-1)(\iota-2)}{\Gamma(\iota)}(\ell^{\iota-3}-\ell^{\iota-\rho-2})\beta(1-\rho,\iota-2).
\end{aligned}$$

□

Remark 1. *Denote*

$$\lambda := \frac{1}{\Gamma(\iota)}\left[\left(1+\frac{\beta(\ell^{\iota-3}-\ell^{\iota-\rho-2})}{1-\beta\ell^{\iota-3}}\right)\beta(1-\rho,\iota-2)-\beta(1-\rho,\iota)\right].$$

Finally, we present the main results.

Theorem 3. *Let the BVP* (13) *satisfy the above standard assumptions. Also, assume that $0<\rho<1$ and that $\theta^\rho\hbar(\theta,\sigma)$ is continuous. If $\mu\in(0,1/\lambda]$ and φ remains a comparison function with*

$$\sigma_1\geq\sigma_2\geq 0 \text{ and } 0\leq\theta\leq 1 \Longrightarrow 0\leq\theta^\rho[\hbar(\theta,\sigma_1)-\hbar(\theta,\sigma_2)]\leq\mu\varphi(\sigma_1-\sigma_2), \quad (17)$$

then, BVP (13) *possesses a unique solution.*

Proof. Endow the following metric on $C[0,1]$:

$$\varrho(\vartheta,\mu) = \sup_{0\leq\theta\leq 1}|\vartheta(\theta)-\mu(\theta)|.$$

Defining

$$V = \{\vartheta \in C[0,1] : \vartheta(\theta) \geq 0\}.$$

Then, (V, ϱ) forms a complete MS. On V, consider the relation

$$E(G) = \{(\vartheta, \mu) \in V^2 : \vartheta(\theta) \leq \mu(\theta), \text{ for each } \theta \in [0,1]\}.$$

Clearly, G is transitive, and (V, ϱ, G) forms a graph MS. Now, choose $\vartheta, \mu \in V$. Define $\omega := \max\{\vartheta, \mu\} \in V$. Then, $\{\vartheta, \omega, \mu\}$ admits a path in $\tilde{G}$ from ϑ to μ. Thus, G remains weakly connected.

We will verify that G is a (C)-graph. Assuming $\{\vartheta_n\} \subset V$ verifying $\vartheta_{\mathrm{n}} \to \vartheta$ and $(\vartheta_{\mathrm{n}}, \vartheta_{\mathrm{n}+1}) \in E(G)$, $\forall$ n $\in \mathbb{N}$. Then, $\forall\, \theta \in [0,1]$, $\{\vartheta_n(\theta)\}$ is an increasing sequence in $\mathbb{R}$ that converges to $\vartheta(\theta)$. Hence, $\forall\, n \in \mathbb{N}$ and $\forall\, \theta \in [0,1]$, we find $\vartheta_n(\theta) \leq \vartheta(\theta)$ so that $(\vartheta_n, \vartheta) \in E(G)$, $\forall\, n \in \mathbb{N}$.

Now, define the map $R : V \to V$ by

$$(R\vartheta)(\theta) = \int_0^1 G(\theta,\sigma)\hbar(\sigma,\vartheta(\sigma))d\sigma + \frac{\eta\theta^{\iota-1}}{(\iota-1)(\iota-2)(1-\eta\ell^{\iota-3})}\int_0^1 H(\ell,\sigma)\hbar(\sigma,\vartheta(\sigma))d\sigma. \tag{18}$$

Let $\mathbf{0} \in V$ be zero function. Then, for every $\theta \in [0,1]$, we find $\mathbf{0}(\theta) \leq (R\mathbf{0})(\theta)$, thereby yielding $(\mathbf{0}, R\mathbf{0}) \in E(G)$. Thus, $\mathbf{0} \in V_R$ i.e., $V_R \neq \emptyset$.

Take $(\vartheta, \mu) \in E(G)$, thereby implying $\vartheta(\theta) \leq \mu(\theta)$, for each $\theta \in [0,1]$. Consequently, we find

$$\begin{aligned}
(R\vartheta)(\theta) &= \int_0^1 G(\theta,\sigma)\hbar(\sigma,\vartheta(\sigma))d\sigma + \frac{\eta\theta^{\iota-1}}{(\iota-1)(\iota-2)(1-\eta\ell^{\iota-3})}\int_0^1 H(\ell,\sigma)\hbar(\sigma,\vartheta(\sigma))d\sigma. \\
&= \int_0^1 G(\theta,\sigma)\sigma^{-\rho}\sigma^{\rho}\hbar(x,\vartheta(\sigma))d\sigma \\
&+ \frac{\eta\theta^{\iota-1}}{(\iota-1)(\iota-2)(1-\eta\ell^{\iota-3})}\int_0^1 H(\ell,\sigma)\sigma^{\ \rho}\sigma^{\rho}\hbar(\sigma,\vartheta(\sigma))d\sigma \\
&\leq \int_0^1 G(\theta,\sigma)\sigma^{-\rho}\sigma^{\rho}\hbar(\sigma,\mu(\sigma))d\sigma \\
&+ \frac{\eta\theta^{\iota-1}}{(\iota-1)(\iota-2)(1-\eta\ell^{\iota-3})}\int_0^1 H(\ell,\sigma)\sigma^{-\rho}\sigma^{\rho}\hbar(\sigma,\mu(\sigma))d\sigma \\
&= \int_0^1 G(\theta,\sigma)\hbar(\sigma,\mu(\sigma))d\sigma + \frac{\eta^{\iota-1}}{(\iota-1)(\iota-2)(1-\eta\ell^{\iota-3})}\int_0^1 H(\ell,\sigma)\hbar(\sigma,\mu(\sigma))d\sigma \\
&= (R\mu)(\theta)
\end{aligned}$$

yielding $(R\vartheta, R\mu) \in E(G)$. Hence, R is G-edge preserving.

On the other hand, for $(\vartheta, \mu) \in E(G)$, we also have

$$\begin{aligned}
\varrho(R\vartheta, R\mu) &= \sup_{0\leq\theta\leq 1}|(R\vartheta)(\theta) - (R\mu)(\theta)| = \sup_{0\leq\theta\leq 1}[(R\mu)(\theta) - (R\vartheta)(\theta)] \\
&= \sup_{0\leq\theta\leq 1}\left[\int_0^1 G(\theta,\sigma)(\hbar(\sigma,\mu(\sigma)) - \hbar(\sigma,\vartheta(\sigma)))\,d\sigma\right. \\
&\left. + \frac{\eta\theta^{\iota-1}}{(\iota-1)(\iota-2)(1-\eta\ell^{\iota-3})}\int_0^1 H(\ell,\sigma)(\hbar(\sigma,\mu(\sigma)) - \hbar(\sigma,v)(\sigma))d\sigma\right] \\
&\leq \sup_{0\leq\theta\leq 1}\int_0^1 G(\theta,\sigma)\sigma^{-\rho}\sigma^{\rho}[\hbar(\sigma,\mu(\sigma)) - \hbar(\sigma,\vartheta(\sigma))]d\sigma \\
&+ \frac{\eta}{(\iota-1)(\iota-2)(1-\eta\ell^{\iota-3})}\int_0^1 H(\ell,\sigma)\sigma^{-\rho}\sigma^{\rho}[\hbar(\sigma,\mu(\sigma)) - \hbar(\sigma,\vartheta)(\sigma)]d\sigma \\
&\leq \sup\int_0^1 G(\theta,\sigma)\sigma^{-\rho}\mu\varphi(\mu(\sigma) - \vartheta(\sigma))d\sigma \\
&+ \frac{\eta}{(\iota-1)(\iota-2)(1-\eta\ell^{\iota-3})}\int_0^1 H(\ell,\sigma)\sigma^{-\rho}\mu\varphi(\mu(\sigma)) - \vartheta(\sigma)d\sigma.
\end{aligned}$$

Using the monotonicity of φ, the above relation reduces to

$$\begin{aligned}\varrho(R\vartheta,R\mu) &\leq \mu\varphi(\varrho(\vartheta,\mu))\sup_{0\leq\theta\leq 0}\int_0^1 G(\theta,\sigma)\sigma^{-\rho}d\sigma \\ &+\frac{\eta}{(\iota-1)(\iota-2)(1-\eta\ell\iota-3)}\mu\varphi(\varrho(\mu,v))\int_0^1 H(\ell,\sigma)\sigma^{\rho}d\sigma \\ &=\mu\varphi(\varrho(\vartheta,\mu))\left[\sup_{0\leq\theta\leq 0}\int_0^1 G(\theta,\sigma)\sigma^{-\rho}d\sigma\right. \\ &\left.+\frac{\eta}{(\iota-1)(\iota-2)(1-\eta\ell^{\iota-3})}\int_0^1 H(\ell,\sigma)\sigma^{-\rho}d\sigma\right]. \end{aligned} \tag{19}$$

Using Lemmas 1 and 2, (19) reduces to

$$\begin{aligned}\varrho(R\vartheta,R\mu) \leq&\mu\varphi(\varrho(\vartheta,\mu))\left[\frac{1}{\Gamma(\iota)}(\beta(1-\rho,\iota-2)-\beta(1-\rho\iota))+\frac{\eta}{(\iota-1)(\iota-2)(1-\eta\ell^{\iota-3})}\right. \\ &\left.\times\frac{(\iota-1)(\iota-2)}{\Gamma(\iota)}\left(\ell^{\iota-3}-\ell^{\iota-\rho-2}\right)\right] \\ &=\mu\varphi(\varrho(\vartheta,\mu))\left[\frac{1}{\Gamma(\iota)}(\beta(1-\rho,\iota-2)-\beta(1-\rho,\iota))\right. \\ &\left.+\frac{\eta(\ell^{\iota-3}-\ell^{\iota-\rho-2})}{(1-\eta\ell^{\iota-3})\Gamma(\iota)}\beta(1-\rho,\iota-2)\right] \\ &=\mu\varphi(\varrho(\vartheta,\mu))\left[\frac{1}{\Gamma(\iota)}\left[\left(1+\frac{\eta(\ell^{\iota-3}-\ell^{\iota-\rho-2})}{1-\eta-\eta\ell^{\iota-3}}\right)\beta(1-\rho,\iota-2)-\beta(1-\rho,\iota)\right]\right] \\ &=\mu\varphi(\varrho(\vartheta,\mu))\lambda.\end{aligned}$$

As $0<\mu\leq 1/\lambda$, the last inequality becomes

$$\varrho(R\vartheta,R\mu)\leq\mu\varphi(\varrho(\vartheta,\mu))\lambda\leq\varphi(\varrho(\vartheta,\mu)). \tag{20}$$

Thus, R verifies the contraction condition mentioned in Theorem 2. Therefore, by Theorem 2, R is a PM. Thus, in view of (14) and (18), the unique fixed point of R will form the unique solution of BVP (13). □

Theorem 4. *Along with the assertions of Theorem 3, BVP* (13) *owns a unique positive solution.*

Proof. By Theorem 3, let $\bar{\varpi}\in V$ be the unique solution of BVP (13). Owing to the fact $\bar{\varpi}\in V$, we have $\bar{\varpi}(\theta)\geq 0, \forall\,\theta\in[0,1]$. This means that $\bar{\varpi}$ is a unique nonnegative solution of given BVP. By contradiction method, we will verify that $\bar{\varpi}$ remains a unique positive solution of the BVP, i.e., $\bar{p}(x)>0$, for all $x\in(0,1)$. If $\exists\, 0<\theta^*<1$ verifying $\bar{\varpi}(\theta^*)=0$, then by (14), we observe that

$$\bar{\varpi}(\theta^*)=\int_0^1 G(\theta^*,\sigma)\hbar(\sigma,\bar{\varpi}(\sigma))d\sigma+\frac{\eta\theta^{*\iota-1}}{(\iota-1)(\iota-2)(1-\eta\ell^{\iota-3})}\int_0^1 H(\ell,\sigma)\hbar(\sigma,x(\sigma))d\sigma=0.$$

By the definition, $\hbar$ is nonnegative. Thus in view of Proposition 2, both summands in RHS are nonnegative. Consequently, we find

$$\begin{aligned}&\int_0^1 G(\theta^*,\sigma)\hbar(\sigma,\bar{\varpi}(\sigma))d\sigma=0, \\ &\int_0^1 H(\ell,\sigma)\hbar(\sigma,\sigma(\sigma))d\sigma=0\end{aligned}$$

thereby implying

$$\begin{cases} G(\theta^*,\sigma)\hbar(\sigma,\varpi(\sigma)) = 0, & a.e.\ (\sigma), \\ H(\ell,\sigma)\hbar(\sigma,\varpi(\sigma)) = 0, & a.e\ (\sigma). \end{cases} \tag{21}$$

Take an arbitrary $\kappa > 0$. By the singular property of $\hbar$, we can find an $\epsilon > 0$ with $\hbar(\sigma,0) > \kappa$, $\forall\,\sigma \in [0,1] \cap (0,\epsilon)$. Note that

$$[0,1] \cap (0,\epsilon) \subset \{\sigma \in [0,1] : \hbar(\sigma,\varpi(\sigma)) > \kappa\}$$

and

$$\aleph([0,1] \cap (0,\epsilon)) > 0,$$

where $\aleph$ denotes the Lebesque measure. Hence, (21) yields that

$$\begin{cases} G(\theta^*,\sigma) = 0, & a.e.\ (\sigma), \\ H(\ell,\sigma) = 0, & a.e.\ (\sigma) \end{cases}$$

which contradicts the fact that $G(\theta^*,\cdot)$ and $H(\ell,\cdot)$ are rational functions. This completes the proof. □

5. Discussions

This article is devoted to prove some outcomes on fixed points under an expanded class of (G,φ)-contraction in the setup of graph metric space. The results presented in this article give new insights into graph metric spaces. Our findings extend, enrich, unify, sharpen and improve a few fixed point theorems, especially due to Matkowski [12], Pant [17], Jachymski [18] and Bojor [19]. Applying our findings, we describe the existence of the unique positive solution of a BVP involving singular fractional differential equations. We can prove the analogues of our results under Boyd–Wong contractions, weak contractions, (ψ,ϕ) contractions, Γ contractions, $\mathcal{Z}$ contractions, and similar others.

Author Contributions: methodology, M.D.; conceptualisation, M.D. and M.A.; writing—original draft preparation, M.D.; writing—review and editing, M.A. and D.F.; funding acquisition, D.F.; validation, M.A. and D.F. All authors have read and agreed to the published version of the manuscript.

Funding: This work is funded by Princess Nourah bint Abdulrahman University, Riyadh, Saudi Arabia, under the Researchers supporting project number (PNURSP2024R174).

Data Availability Statement: The current study utilises no data.

Acknowledgments: All authors would like to offer thanks to the academic editor and three learned referees for their fruitful suggestions and constructive comments towards the improvement of the manuscript. The first author acknowledges the Princess Nourah bint Abdulrahman University Researchers Supporting Project, project number PNURSP2024R174, Princess Nourah bint Abdulrahman University, Riyadh, Saudi Arabia.

Conflicts of Interest: The authors declare no conflicts of interest.

References

1. Podlubny, I. *Fractional Differential Equations*, 1st ed.; Academic Press: San Diego, CA, USA, 1998; p. 340.
2. Daftardar-Gejji, V. *Fractional Calculus and Fractional Differential Equations*; Trends in Mathematics; Birkhäuser-Springer: Singapore, 2019; p. 180.
3. Kilbas, A.A.; Srivastava, H.M.; Trujillo, J.J. *Theory and Applications of Fractional Differential Equations*; North-Holland Mathematics Studies; Elsevier Science B.V.: Amsterdam, The Netherlands, 2006; Volume 204, pp. 1–523.
4. Cevikel, A.C.; Aksoy, E. Soliton solutions of nonlinear fractional differential equations with their applications in mathematical physics. *Rev. Mex. Fís.* **2021**, *67*, 422–428. [CrossRef]
5. Aljethi, R.A.; Kiliçman, A. Analysis of fractional differential equation and its application to realistic data. *Chaos Solitons Fractals* **2023**, *171*, 113446. [CrossRef]
6. Zhou, X.; Wu, W.; Ma, H. A contraction fixed point theorem in partially ordered metric spaces and application to fractional differential equations. *Abstr. Appl. Anal.* **2012**, *2012*, 856302. [CrossRef]

7. Zhai, C.; Hao, M. Fixed point theorems for mixed monotone operators with perturbation and applications to fractional differential equation boundary value problems. *Nonlinear Anal.* **2012**, *75*, 2542–2551. [CrossRef]
8. Liang, S.; Zhang, J. Existence and uniqueness of strictly nondecreasing and positive solution for a fractional three-point boundary value problem. *Comput. Math. Appl.* **2011**, *62*, 1333–1340. [CrossRef]
9. Cabrera, I.J.; Harjani, J.; Sadarangani, K.B. Existence and uniqueness of positive solutions for a singular fractional three-point boundary value problem. *Abstr. Appl. Anal.* **2012**, *2012*, 803417. [CrossRef]
10. Karapınar, E.; Fulga, A.; Rashid, M.; Shahid, L.; Aydi, H. Large contractions on quasi-metric spaces with an application to nonlinear fractional differential equations. *Mathematics* **2019**, *7*, 444. [CrossRef]
11. Abdou, A.A.N. Solving a nonlinear fractional differential equation using fixed point results in orthogonal metric spaces. *Fractal Fract.* **2023**, *7*, 817. [CrossRef]
12. Matkowski, J. Integrable solutions of functional equations. *Diss. Math.* **1975**, *127*, 68.
13. Berinde, V. Approximating fixed points of weak ϕ-contractions using the Picard iteration. *Fixed Point Theory* **2003**, *4*, 131–142.
14. Agarwal, R.P.; El-Gebeily, M.A.; O'Regan, D. Generalized contractions in partially ordered metric spaces. *Appl. Anal.* **2008**, *87*, 109–116. [CrossRef]
15. O'Regan, D.; Petruşel, A. Fixed point theorems for generalized contractions in ordered metric spaces. *J. Math. Anal. Appl.* **2008**, *341*, 1241–1252. [CrossRef]
16. Aydi, H.; Karapinar, E.; Radenović, S. Tripled coincidence fixed point results for Boyd-Wong and Matkowski type contractions. *Rev. R. Acad. Cienc. Exactas Fís. Nat. Ser. A Mat.* **2013**, *107*, 339–353. [CrossRef]
17. Pant, R.P. Extended Φ-contraction mappings. *J. Anal.* **2024**, *32*, 1661–1670. [CrossRef]
18. Jachymski, J. The contraction principle for mappings on a metric space with a graph. *Proc. Amer. Math. Soc.* **2008**, *136*, 1359–1373. [CrossRef]
19. Bojor, F. Fixed point of ϕ-contraction in metric spaces endowed with a graph. *An. Univ. Craiova Ser. Mat. Inform.* **2010**, *37*, 85–92.
20. Aleomraninejad, S.M.A.; Rezapoura, S.; Shahzad, N. Some fixed point results on a metric space with a graph. *Topol. Appl.* **2012**, *159*, 659–663. [CrossRef]
21. Balog, L.; Berinde, V.; Păcurar, M. Approximating fixed points of nonself contractive type mappings in Banach spaces endowed with a graph. *An. Ştiinţ. Univ. "Ovidius" Constanţa Ser. Mat.* **2016**, *24*, 27–43. [CrossRef]
22. Nicolae, A.; O'Regan, D.; Petruşel, A. Fixed point theorems for singlevalued and multivalued generalized contractions in metric spaces endowed with a graph. *Georgian Math. J.* **2011**, *18*, 307–327. [CrossRef]
23. Alfuraidan, M.R.; Khamsi, M.A. Caristi fixed point theorem in metric spaces with a graph. *Abstr. Appl. Anal.* **2014**, *2014*, 303484. [CrossRef]
24. Alfuraidan, M.R.; Bachar, M.; Khamsi, M.A. Almost monotone contractions on weighted graphs. *J. Nonlinear Sci. Appl.* **2016**, *9*, 5189–5195. [CrossRef]
25. Filali, D.; Akram, M.; Dilshad, M. Nonlinear contractions on directed graphs with applications to boundary value problems. *AIMS Math.* **2024**, *9*, 15263–15275. [CrossRef]
26. Johnsonbaugh, R. *Discrete Mathematics*; Prentice-Hall, Inc.: Hoboken, NJ, USA, 1997.
27. Rus, I.A. *Generalized Contractions and Applications*; Cluj University Press: Cluj-Napoca, Romania, 2001.
28. Berinde, V. *Iterative Approximation of Fixed Points*; Springer: Berlin/Heidelberg, Germany, 2007.
29. Petrusel, A.; Rus, I.A. Fixed point theorems in ordered L-spaces. *Proc. Amer. Math. Soc.* **2006**, *134*, 411–418. [CrossRef]

axioms

MDPI

Article

Stability of Fixed Points of Partial Contractivities and Fractal Surfaces

María A. Navascués

Department of Applied Mathematics, Universidad de Zaragoza, 50018 Zaragoza, Spain; manavas@unizar.es

Abstract: In this paper, a large class of contractions is studied that contains Banach and Matkowski maps as particular cases. Sufficient conditions for the existence of fixed points are proposed in the framework of b-metric spaces. The convergence and stability of the Picard iterations are analyzed, giving error estimates for the fixed-point approximation. Afterwards, the iteration proposed by Kirk in 1971 is considered, studying its convergence, stability, and error estimates in the context of a quasi-normed space. The properties proved can be applied to other types of contractions, since the self-maps defined contain many others as particular cases. For instance, if the underlying set is a metric space, the contractions of type Kannan, Chatterjea, Zamfirescu, Ćirić, and Reich are included in the class of contractivities studied in this paper. These findings are applied to the construction of fractal surfaces on Banach algebras, and the definition of two-variable frames composed of fractal mappings with values in abstract Hilbert spaces.

Keywords: partial contractivity; Kirk iteration; fixed-point theorems; fractal maps; contractions; fractal surfaces; fractal frames

MSC: 26A18; 47H10; 28A80; 54H25; 37C25

1. Introduction

M. Fréchet introduced a mapping to measure what he called "l'écart des deux éléments" (distance between two points) in his doctoral thesis [1], presented at the Faculty of Sciences of Paris and published in Italy in 1906. The conditions of this mapping are the axioms of a metric space. The name of metric space, however, is due to F. Hausdorff, who treated the topic in his book "*Grundzüge der Mergenlehre*" of 1914 [2]. Previously, Hilbert [3] and Riemann [4] had shaken the foundations of classical geometry, proposing new axiomatic systems, with precedents in Gauss, Lobachevsky, and Bolyai.

Nowadays, the conditions of a mapping being a distance have been modified in very different ways, giving rise to a great variety of distance spaces (see, for instance, the books [5,6]).

Particularly interesting are the metrics associated with discrete mathematics, that concerns the knowledge and control of complex systems (see [7]). As an example, one may mention the Hamming distance, that measures the number of different bits of two code words, and it quantifies the error of transmission [8].

In this paper, we work with a generalization of a metric space, called in the literature the b-metric or quasi-metric space, that substitutes the triangular inequality by a more general condition. Closely related to metric theory (that gives rise to a class of topological spaces) is fixed-point theory, that establishes conditions for a self-map $T : X \to X$ in order to have a fixed point. The problem of finding a fixed point is intrinsically linked to the sought for solutions of one or several equations, since the equality $x = Tx$ admits the form $x - Tx = 0$, in the case of an underlying vector space X. Important and recent applications of fixed-point theorems can be found in references [9,10], for instance. But these are not the only implications of the theory, since this area of mathematical knowledge has given rise to modern fields of research like fractal theory and others.

The content of this paper can be summarized as follows. In Section 2, the dynamics of a large class of contractions called $(\varphi - \psi)$-contractivities [11,12] is explored. Some sufficient conditions for the existence of fixed points are proposed, and the convergence of the Picard iterations for their approximation is studied for both cases, single- and multivalued mappings. Some error estimates for the Picard approximation are also given. For a study of multivalued mappings in b-metric spaces the reader may consult the reference [13].

Section 3 studies the stability of the fixed points' $(\varphi - \psi)$-partial contractivities, proving that they are asymptotically stable in the case of their existence.

Section 4 analyzes the iterative algorithm for fixed-point approximation proposed by Kirk in reference [14], when it is applied to a $(\varphi - \psi)$-contractivity defined on a quasi-normed space.

The properties proved can be applied to other types of contractions, since the self-maps considered contain many others as particular cases. For instance, if the underlaying set is a metric space, the contractions of type Kannan, Chatterjea, Zamfirescu, Ćirić, and Reich are included in the class of contractivities studied in this paper (see Corollary 2.2 of reference [11]).

Section 5 considers fractal surfaces whose values lie on Banach algebras. The mappings defining the surfaces are fixed points of an operator on a Bochner functional space. The convergence and stability of Picard and Kirk iterations for their approximation are analyzed, giving in both cases an estimate of the error.

Section 6 studies a particular case, where the vertical contraction is linear and bounded. Fractal convolutions of mappings and operators are defined, and the construction of bivariate fractal frames of the Bochner space of square-integrable mappings on a Hilbert space is undertaken, considering fractal perturbations of standard frames in the same space.

2. Existence of Fixed Points and Convergence of Picard Iterations

In this section, we explore the dynamics of a large class of contractions [11,12]. We provide sufficient conditions for the existence of fixed points, and the convergence of the Picard iterations for their approximation for both single- and multivalued mappings. Some "a priori" error estimates for the Picard approximation are also given.

Let us start with the definition of b-metric space.

Definition 1. *A b-metric space X is a set endowed with a mapping $d : X \times X \to \mathbb{R}^+$ with the following properties:*

1. $d(x,y) \geq 0, d(x,y) = 0$ *if and only if* $x = y$.
2. $d(x,y) = d(y,x)$ *for any* $x, y \in X$.
3. *There exists* $s \geq 1$ *such that* $d(x,y) \leq s(d(x,z) + d(z,y))$ *for any* $x, y, z \in X$.

The constant s is the index of the b-metric space, and d is called a b-metric.

Example 1. *The spaces $l^p(\mathbb{R})$ for $0 < p < 1$ are b-metric spaces of index $s = 2^{1/p}$ with respect to the functional*

$$|x - y|_p = (\sum_{i=1}^{\infty} |x_i - y_i|^p)^{1/p}.$$

Other examples can be found in reference [15], for instance.

Given any $x_0, x_1, \ldots x_n \in X$, where X is a b-metric space with index s, one has the following inequality for $n \geq 2$:

$$d(x_0, x_n) \leq \sum_{k=0}^{n-2} s^{k+1} d(x_k, x_{k+1}) + s^{n-1} d(x_{n-1}, x_n) \leq \sum_{k=0}^{n-1} s^{k+1} d(x_k, x_{k+1}). \tag{1}$$

The next definition can be read in reference [16].

Definition 2. *A map $\varphi : \mathbb{R}^+ \to \mathbb{R}^+$ is called a comparison function if it satisfies the following conditions:*

- *φ is increasing.*
- *$\varphi^n(\delta)$ tends to zero when n tends to infinity for any $\delta > 0$.*

Let X be a b-metric space. A map $T : X \to X$ such that $d(Tx, Ty) \leq \varphi(d(x, y))$ for any $x, y \in X$, where φ is a comparison function, is called a φ-contraction or a Matkowski contraction [17].

Example 2. *The maps $\varphi(\delta) = \delta/(1+\delta)$ and $\varphi(\delta) = r\delta$, where $0 < r < 1$, are comparison functions.*

The first aim of this article is the presentation of a new concept of contractivity, presenting maps that include the usual φ-contractions like a particular case, according to the following definition [11,12].

Definition 3. *Let X be a b-metric space, and $T : X \to X$ be a self-map such that for any $x, y \in X$,*

$$d(Tx, Ty) \leq \varphi(d(x, y)) + \psi(d(x, Tx)). \tag{2}$$

If φ is a comparison function, ψ is positive, and $\psi(0) = 0$, then T is a $(\varphi - \psi)$-partial contractivity. If $\varphi(\delta) = a\delta$, where $0 < a < 1$, and $\psi(\delta) = B\delta$, with $B \geq 0$, T is a partial contractivity.

If ψ is the null function, we have a standard φ-contraction. If further $\varphi(\delta) = a\delta$, where $0 < a < 1$, then T is a Banach contraction.

Example 3. *Let $T(x) = 1/(1+x)$ be defined in $X = [0, +\infty)$. Then, T is a $(\varphi - \psi)$-partial contractivity with $\varphi(\delta) = \delta/(1+\delta)$ and $\psi(\delta) = B\delta$ for $B \geq 0$.*

Example 4. *Let $X = [0, 1]$ and T be defined as $T(x) = x/4$ if $x \in [0, 1/2]$ and $T(x) = x/6$ if $x \in (1/2, 1]$. T is a $(\varphi - \psi)$-partial contractivity with $\varphi(\delta) = \delta/2$ and $\psi(\delta) = \delta$.*

- *If $x, y \in [0, \frac{1}{2}]$, then*

$$|Tx - Ty| = |\frac{x}{4} - \frac{y}{4}| \leq \frac{1}{2}|x - y|,$$

$$|Tx - Ty| = |\frac{x}{4} - \frac{y}{4}| \leq \frac{1}{2}|x - y|.$$

- *If $x, y \in (\frac{1}{2}, 1]$, then*

$$|Tx - Ty| = |\frac{x}{6} - \frac{y}{6}| \leq \frac{1}{2}|x - y|,$$

$$|Tx - Ty| = |\frac{x}{6} - \frac{y}{6}| \leq \frac{1}{2}|x - y|.$$

If $x \in [0, 1/2]$ and $y \in (1/2, 1]$,

$$|Tx - Ty| = |\frac{x}{4} - \frac{y}{6}| \leq |\frac{x}{4}| + |\frac{y}{6}| \leq \frac{1}{3}|y - \frac{y}{6}| + \frac{1}{3}|x - \frac{x}{4}|,$$

$$|Tx - Ty| \leq \frac{1}{3}|x - y| + \frac{1}{3}|x - \frac{y}{6}| + \frac{1}{3}|x - \frac{x}{4}|,$$

$$|Tx - Ty| \leq \frac{1}{3}|x - y| + \frac{2}{3}|x - \frac{x}{4}| + \frac{1}{3}|\frac{x}{4} - \frac{y}{6}|,$$

and finally,

$$|Tx - Ty| \leq \frac{1}{2}|x - y| + |x - \frac{x}{4}|.$$

In the same way,

$$|Tx - Ty| = |\frac{x}{4} - \frac{y}{6}| \leq \frac{1}{3}|x - \frac{x}{4}| + \frac{1}{3}|y - \frac{y}{6}|,$$

$$|Tx - Ty| \leq \frac{1}{3}|x - y| + \frac{1}{3}|y - \frac{x}{4}| + \frac{1}{3}|y - \frac{y}{6}|,$$

$$|Tx - Ty| \leq \frac{1}{3}|x - y| + \frac{1}{3}|y - \frac{y}{6}| + \frac{1}{3}|\frac{y}{6} - \frac{x}{4}| + \frac{1}{3}|y - \frac{y}{6}|,$$

and

$$|Tx - Ty| \leq \frac{1}{2}|x - y| + |y - \frac{y}{6}|.$$

Remark 1. *Let us note that, unlike the φ-contractive case, a partial contractivity need not be continuous.*

In previous articles, we proved that several well known contractivities, like Zamfirescu or quasi-contractions, belong to the class of $(\varphi - \psi)$-partial contractivities, when the constants associated satisfy some restrictions (see, for instance, [12]). The next result can be read in Proposition 15 of the same reference.

Proposition 1. *Let X be a b-metric space and $T : X \to X$ be a $(\varphi - \psi)$-partial contractivity. If T has a fixed point, it is unique.*

We start with a result concerning the orbit separations in the case where $\psi(t) = Bt$, for $B \geq 0$.

Definition 4. *A functional $\varphi : D \subseteq X \to \mathbb{R}$, where X is a real linear space, is sublinear if*

- $\phi(\delta + \delta') \leq \phi(\delta) + \phi(\delta')$ *for any $\delta, \delta' \in D$ such that $\delta + \delta' \in D$.*
- $\phi(\lambda\delta) \leq \lambda\phi(\delta)$ *for any $\lambda > 0$ and $\delta \in D$ such that $\lambda\delta \in D$.*

Example 5. *The absolute value of a real number $\phi(\delta) = |\delta|$ is a sublinear function. In general, a seminorm is sublinear.*

Proposition 2. *Let X be a b-metric space and $T : X \to X$ be a $(\varphi - \psi)$-partial contractivity, where φ is a sublinear comparison function and $\psi(t) = Bt$, for $B \geq 0$. Then, for all $n \geq 1$,*

$$d(T^n x, T^n y) \leq \varphi^n(d(x,y)) + ((\varphi + B.Id)^n - \varphi^n)(d(x,Tx)), \quad (3)$$

where Id denotes the identity map.

If $Fix(T) \neq \emptyset$ and $x^* \in Fix(T)$, then for any $x, y \in X$,

$$d(T^n x, T^n y) \leq s(\varphi^n(d(x,x^*)) + \varphi^n(d(y,x^*))). \quad (4)$$

Consequently, $\lim_{n\to\infty} d(T^n x, T^n y) = 0$.

Proof. For $n = 1$ the result is clear since

$$d(Tx, Ty) \leq \varphi(d(x,y)) + ((\varphi + B.Id) - \varphi)(d(x,Tx)),$$

by definition of $(\varphi - \psi)$-partial contractivity. Let us assume that Formula (3) is valid for $n = k$ and any $x, y \in X$:

$$d(T^k x, T^k y) \leq \varphi^k(d(x,y)) + ((\varphi + B.Id)^k - \varphi^k)(d(x,Tx)).$$

and let us prove it for $n = k+1$. By definition of $(\varphi - \psi)$-partial contractivity for $T^k x, T^k y$,

$$d(T^{k+1}x, T^{k+1}y) \leq \varphi(d(T^k x, T^k y)) + Bd(T^k x, T^{k+1}x).$$

Applying the subadditivity of φ and the inductive hypothesis in the first term of the last sum,

$$\varphi(d(T^k x, T^k y)) \leq \varphi^{k+1}(d(x,y)) + \varphi((\varphi + B.Id)^k - \varphi^k)(d(x,Tx)). \quad (5)$$

For the second summand, applying the inductive hypothesis for x and Tx, we have

$$Bd(T^k x, T^{k+1}x) \leq B\varphi^k(d(x,Tx)) + B((\varphi + B.Id)^k - \varphi^k)(d(x,Tx)) \leq B(\varphi + BId)^k(d(x,Tx)). \quad (6)$$

Let us consider the map $\varphi((\varphi + B.Id)^k - \varphi^k) + B(\varphi + B.Id)^k$. Developing both binomials, and bearing in mind the property of the combinatorial numbers,

$$\binom{k+1}{j} = \binom{k}{j-1} + \binom{k}{j},$$

for $k \in \mathbb{N}$ and $j = 1, \ldots, k$, we obtain that

$$\varphi((\varphi + B.Id)^k - \varphi^k) + B(\varphi + B.Id)^k = (\varphi + B.Id)^{k+1} - \varphi^{k+1}.$$

Thus, adding (5) and (6),

$$d(T^{k+1}x, T^{k+1}y) \leq \varphi^{k+1}(d(x,y)) + ((\varphi + B.Id)^{k+1} - \varphi^{k+1})(d(x,Tx)).$$

and consequently, the result.

If $x^* \in Fix(T)$, then

$$d(T^n x, T^n y) \leq sd(T^n x, x^*) + sd(T^n y, x^*).$$

Applying iteratively the definition of the contractivity,

$$d(T^n x, T^n y) \leq s\varphi^n(d(x,x^*)) + s\varphi^n(d(y,x^*)).$$

The conditions on the comparison function φ imply that

$$d(T^n x, T^n y) \to 0,$$

when n tends to infinity. □

Remark 2. *For the inequality (4), the hypotheses of sublinearity of φ and linearity of ψ are not required.*

Corollary 1. *Let X be a b-metric space and $T : X \to X$ be a partial contractivity, that is to say, $\varphi(\delta) = a\delta$ and $\psi(t) = Bt$, for $B \geq 0$. Then, for all $n \geq 1$,*

$$d(T^n x, T^n y) \leq a^n d(x,y) + ((a+B)^n - a^n)(d(x,Tx)). \quad (7)$$

Consequently, $d(T^n x, T^n y) = O((a+B)^n)$. If $Fix(T) \neq \emptyset$, $d(T^n x, T^n y) = O(a^n)$.

Proof. The rates of orbit separation are straightforward consequences of the expressions (3) and (4). □

Corollary 2. *Let X be a b-metric space and $T : X \to X$ be a partial contractivity, that is to say, $\varphi(\delta) = a\delta$ and $\psi(t) = Bt$, for $B \geq 0$. Then, for all $n \geq 1$,*

$$d(T^n x, T^{n+1}x) \leq (a+B)^n d(x,Tx).$$

If $a + B < 1$, T is asymptotically regular, that it to say,

$$\lim_{n\to\infty} d(T^n x, T^{n+1}x) = 0,$$

and all the orbits are bounded. If $a + B > 1$, the orbit of an element $x \in X$ may be unbounded. For $B = 0$ all the orbits are bounded and they are stable in the sense of Lagrange.

Proof. It suffices to take $y = Tx$ in the inequality (7) to obtain the inequality. The second result comes also from the fact that if $a + B < 1$, T has a fixed point, it is unique (see reference [11]), and all the orbits are convergent to the fixed point, and consequently, they are bounded. □

Remark 3. *In fact, according to (3), T is asymptotically regular if there exists* $r \in \mathbb{R}$ *with* $0 < r < 1$ *such that* $(\varphi + B.Id)(\delta) \leq r\delta < 1$ *for any* $\delta > 0$*, since substituting* $y = Tx$ *into inequality (3),* $d(T^n x, T^{n+1}x) \leq r^n d(x, Tx)$ *and* $d(T^n x, T^{n+1}x)$ *tends to zero when n tends to infinity.*

Example 6. *The* $(\varphi - \psi)$*-partial contractivity satisfying the inequality*

$$d(Tx, Ty) \leq \varphi(d(x,y)) + Bd(x, Tx),$$

for $\varphi(\delta) = \delta/(3+\delta)$ *and* $B = 1/4$ *is asymptotically regular, taking* $r = 7/12$.

Proposition 3. *Let X be a b-metric space and* $T : X \to X$ *be a* $(\varphi - \psi)$*-partial contractivity. Let us assume that there is a fixed point* $x^* \in X$*, then for all* $n \geq 1$

$$d(T^n x, x^*) \leq \varphi^n(d(x, x^*)). \tag{8}$$

Consequently, the Picard iterations of any $x \in X$ *are convergent to the fixed point and the order of convergence is* $\varphi^n(d(x,x^*))$*. If* $\varphi(\delta) = a\delta$ *for* $0 < a < 1$*, the order of convergence is* $O(a^n)$.

Proof. It suffices to apply the definition of $(\varphi - \psi)$-partial contractivity. □

In the following, we give a result of fixed-point existence for $(\varphi - \psi)$-partial contractivities where $\psi(t) = Bt$.

Theorem 1. *If X is a complete b-metric space,* $T : X \to X$ *is a* $(\varphi - \psi)$*-partial contractivity where* $\psi(\delta) = B\delta$*, and there exists a real constant k such that* $0 < k < 1$ *satisfying the inequality*

$$\varphi_B(\delta) := (\varphi + B.Id)(\delta) \leq k\delta, \tag{9}$$

for all $\delta \geq 0$*, then T has a unique fixed point and* $T^n x$ *tends to* x^* *for any* $x \in X$.

Proof. Defining the sequence $x_n := T^n x$, $x_0 := x$, we have

$$d(x_n, x_{n+1}) = d(T(x_{n-1}), T(x_n)) \leq \varphi(d(x_{n-1}, x_n)) + Bd(x_{n-1}, x_n) = \varphi_B(d(x_{n-1}, x_n)),$$

and

$$d(x_n, x_{n+1}) \leq \varphi_B^n(d(x_0, x_1)). \tag{10}$$

If $\varphi_B(\delta) \leq k\delta$, (x_n) is a Cauchy sequence [18], and consequently, it is convergent to $x^* \in X$, let us see that x^* is a fixed point of T.

$$d(x^*, Tx^*) \leq sd(x_{n+1}, x^*) + sd(Tx_n, x^*) \leq sd(x_{n+1}, x^*) + s\varphi(d(x_n, x^*)) + sBd(x_n, Tx_n).$$

For a comparison function $0 \leq \varphi(\delta) < \delta$, and thus, $lim_{\delta \to 0^+} \varphi(\delta) = 0$. Then, all the right-hand terms tend to zero, and consequently, $x^* = Tx^*$. The uniqueness was proved in Proposition 15 of reference [12]. □

Example 7. *A* $(\varphi - \psi)$*-partial contractivity where* $\varphi(\delta) = \delta/(3+\delta)$ *and* $\psi(t) = t/4$ *defined on a complete b-metric space has a unique fixed point.*

Remark 4. *For the case* $\varphi(\delta) = a\delta$*, and* $0 < a < 1$*, we obtain a partial contractivity, and the sufficient conditions for the existence of fixed point are* $a + B < 1$ *and X is complete. This result was proved in reference [11].*

In the next theorem, we give an estimation of the error in the fixed-point approximation. Considering the sequence of Picard iterations (x_n) defined as $x_n = T^n x$, it is clear, by definition of $(\varphi - \psi)$-partial contractivity, that

$$d(x_n, x^*) \leq \varphi^n(d(x_0, x^*)). \tag{11}$$

However, it is difficult to know the distance between an element x_0 and the sought fixed point, thus we will give an error estimation in terms of $d(x_0, x_1)$, a quantity easier to find.

Theorem 2. *Let X be a b-metric space, and T be a $(\varphi - \psi)$-partial contractivity, such that $\psi(\delta) = B\delta$. Let us assume that the maps*

$$\phi_n(\delta) := \sum_{k=0}^{\infty} s^k \varphi_B^{n+k}(\delta) \tag{12}$$

are such that $\phi_n(\delta) < \infty$ for all $n = 1, 2, \ldots$. Then, if $x^* \in Fix(T)$ and $x_n := T^n x$,

$$d(x_n, x^*) \leq s^2 \phi_n(d(x_0, x_1)).$$

Proof. Inequality (1) implies that

$$d(x_n, x_{n+j}) \leq \sum_{k=0}^{j-2} s^{k+1} d(x_{n+k}, x_{n+k+1}) + s^{j-1} d(x_{n+j-1}, x_{n+j})$$

Then, using (10),

$$d(x_n, x_{n+j}) \leq s\Big(\sum_{k=0}^{j-2} s^k \varphi_B^{n+k} d(x_0, x_1)\Big) + s^{j-1} \varphi_B^{n+j-1}(d(x_0, x_1)). \tag{13}$$

If $x^* \in Fix(T)$, then

$$d(x_n, x^*) \leq s d(x_n, x_{n+j}) + s d(x_{n+j}, x^*).$$

Using (13) in the first term of the right-hand side,

$$d(x_n, x^*) \leq s^2\Big(\sum_{k=0}^{j-2} s^k \varphi_B^{n+k} d(x_0, x_1)\Big) + s^j \varphi_B^{n+j-1}(d(x_0, x_1)) + s d(x_{n+j}, x^*).$$

Taking limits when j tends to infinity, the second and third terms of the right-hand side tend to zero, due to the hypothesis of the theorem and inequality (11), respectively. Then,

$$d(x_n, x^*) \leq s^2 \phi_n(d(x_0, x_1)) = s^2 \sum_{k=0}^{\infty} s^k \varphi_B^{n+k}(d(x_0, x_1)).$$

□

Corollary 3. *In the particular case where $\varphi(\delta) = a\delta$ with $0 < a < 1$, we have the following "a priori" error estimation for partial contractivities such that $(a + B)s < 1$:*

$$d(x_n, x^*) \leq s^2 \sum_{k=0}^{\infty} s^k (a + B)^{n+k} d(x_0, x_1) = s^2 (a + B)^n \frac{d(x_0, x_1)}{1 - s(a + B)}.$$

In the case where $B = 0$, T is a Banach contraction, and the former expression generalizes the inequality given by Bakhtin [19,20] for this type of map.

The next result concerns set-valued maps satisfying a condition of partial contractivity type. Let us start with some definitions. Given a metric space X, let us consider the set of all nonempty bounded subsets of X, $\mathcal{B}(X)$. Let us define the functional $D: \mathcal{B}(X) \times \mathcal{B}(X) \to \mathbb{R}^+$,

$$D(A,B) = \sup\{d(a,b) : a \in A, b \in B\}.$$

Let us consider the distance of a point to a set $d(a,B) = \inf\{d(a,b) : b \in B\}$.

Theorem 3. *Let X be a complete b-metric space, and let $\tau : X \to \mathcal{B}(X)$ be a set-valued map. Assume that there exist $a \in \mathbb{R}$, $0 < a < 1$, and $B > 0$ such that $a + B < 1$, satisfying the inequality*

$$D(\tau(x), \tau(y)) \leq ad(x,y) + Bd(x, \tau(x)) \tag{14}$$

for any $x, y \in X$. Then, τ has a fixed point $x^* \in X$, $\tau(x^*) = \{x^*\}$ and there exists a partial contractivity $T : X \to X$ whose unique fixed point is x^*. Additionally,

$$d(T^n x, x^*) \leq (a+B)^n d(x, x^*)$$

and, if $s(a+B) < 1$,

$$d(T^n x, x^*) \leq s^2 (a+B)^n \frac{d(x, Tx)}{1 - s(a+B)}.$$

Proof. Let us define a map $T : X \to X$ such that $Tx \in \tau(x)$ and let us see that T is a partial contractivity:

$$d(Tx, Ty) \leq D(\tau(x), \tau(y)) \leq ad(x,y) + Bd(x, \tau(x)) \leq ad(x,y) + Bd(x, T(x)),$$

for any $x, y \in X$. Consequently, T is a partial contractivity. Since $a + B < 1$, T has a fixed point $x^* \in X$. By definition of T, $x^* \in \tau(x^*)$, and consequently, it is a fixed point of τ as well. Applying the contractivity condition (14),

$$D(\tau(x^*), \tau(x^*)) \leq ad(x^*, x^*) + Bd(x^*, \tau(x^*)).$$

Since $x^* \in \tau(x^*)$ the terms of the right-hand side are null, and $\tau(x^*)$ reduces to the single point x^*.

The error estimate of the statement was proved in Corollary 3. □

Example 8. *Let us consider the closed unit ball in $\mathbb{R}$, $X = \overline{B}(0,1) = [-1,1]$ and $\tau : X \to \mathcal{B}(X)$ defined as $\tau(x) = \overline{B}(\frac{x}{8}, |\frac{x}{8}|)$. Then, $d(x, \tau(x)) = |x - \frac{x}{4}| = |\frac{3x}{4}|$. The map τ fulfills the inequality*

$$D(\tau(x), \tau(y)) \leq \frac{1}{4}|x-y| + \frac{1}{3} d(x, \tau(x))$$

for any $x, y \in X$. The constants a, B satisfy the conditions of Theorem 3 and τ has as a unique fixed point $x = 0$, since $0 \in \tau(0) = \{0\}$ and, if $x \neq 0$, x does not belong to $\tau(x)$.

3. Stability of Fixed Points of a $(\varphi - \psi)$-Partial Contractivity

In this paragraph, we study the fixed-point stability $(\varphi - \psi)$-partial contractivities. We consider $(\varphi - \psi)$-contractivities as described in Definition 3. Let $Fix(T)$ denote the set of fixed points of T. Let us remember that if a $(\varphi - \psi)$-partial contractivity has a fixed point, it is unique. Let $N(x^*)$ denote the set of neighborhoods of $x^* \in X$.

Definition 5. *Le X be a b-metric space, $T : X \to X$ and $G \subseteq X$. Then, G is positively invariant if $T(G) \subseteq G$.*

Proposition 4. *If X is a b-metric space, and T is a $(\varphi - \psi)$-partial contractivity with a fixed point x^*, then any (open or closed) ball centered at the fixed point x^* is a positively invariant set.*

Proof. Let $x \in B(x^*, r)$ for $r > 0$, then applying the definition of $(\varphi - \psi)$-partial contractivity,

$$d(Tx, x^*) \leq \varphi(d(x, x^*)) < d(x, x^*) < r,$$

since a comparison function satisfies the inequality $\varphi(\delta) < \delta$ for all $\delta > 0$ (see, for instance, [16]). Hence, $T(B(x^*, r)) \subseteq B(x^*, r)$. □

Definition 6. *Le X be a b-metric space, $T : X \to X$ and $x^* \in Fix(T)$. Then, x^* is stable if for any $U \in N(x^*)$ if there exists $V \in N(x^*)$ such that $T^n(V) \subseteq U$ for all $n \geq 0$.*

If x^* is stable and there exists $V \in N(x^*)$ such that $\lim_{n\to\infty} T^n x = x^*$ for any $x \in V$, then x^* is asymptotically stable.

Proposition 5. *Le X be a b-metric space, and $T : X \to X$ be a $(\varphi - \psi)$-partial contractivity such that $Fix(T) \neq \emptyset$. Then, the Picard iterations $(T^n x)$ converge for any $x \in X$ to the fixed point with asymptotical stability.*

Proof. Let $U \in N(x^*)$ and $r > 0$ such that $B(x^*, r) \subseteq U$, Then, if $x \in B(x^*, r)$,

$$d(T^n x, x^*) \leq \varphi^n(d(x, x^*)) \leq d(x, x^*) < r.$$

Consequently, $T^n(B(x^*, r)) \subseteq B(x^*, r) \subseteq U$ for all $n \geq 0$, and x^* is stable. Moreover,

$$d(T^n x, x^*) \leq \varphi^n(d(x, x^*)) \to 0,$$

due to the definition of the comparison function. Hence, x^* is asymptotically stable, and it is a global attractor, as proved previously. □

4. Convergence and Stability of the Kirk Iterations

In this section, the iterative algorithm for fixed-point approximation proposed by Kirk in reference [14] is analyzed for when it is applied to a $(\varphi - \psi)$-contractivity defined on a quasi-normed space.

Definition 7. *If E is a real linear space, the mapping $|\cdot|_s : E \times E \to \mathbb{R}^+$ is a quasi-norm of index s if*

1. $|f|_s \geq 0$; $f = 0$ *if and only if* $|f|_s = 0$.
2. $|\lambda f|_s = |\lambda||f|_s$.
3. *There exists* $s \geq 1$ *such that* $|f + g|_s \leq s(|f|_s + |g|_s)$ *for any* $f, g \in E$.

The space $(E, |\cdot|_s)$ is a quasi-normed space. If E is complete with respect to the b-metric induced by the quasi-norm, then E is a quasi-Banach space. Obviously, if $s = 1$ then E is a normed space.

The index of a quasi-norm is called sometimes the modulus of concavity of X.

Example 9. *The spaces $l^p(\mathbb{R})$ for $0 < p < 1$ are quasi-normed spaces of index $s = 2^{1/p}$ with respect to the functional*

$$|x|_p = (\sum_{i=1}^{\infty} |x_i|^p)^{1/p}.$$

Kirk's algorithm [14] is given by the scheme of order k:

$$y_{n+1} = \sum_{i=0}^{k} \alpha_i T^i y_n, \tag{15}$$

where $k \in \mathbb{N}$, $\alpha_k > 0$, $\alpha_i \geq 0$, for $i = 1, 2, \ldots, k-1$, $\sum_{i=0}^{k} \alpha_i = 1$, and $y_0 \in X$. For $k = 1$, the algorithm agrees with the Krasnoselskii method [21]. If additionally the coefficients change at every step, one has the Mann iteration [22].

Let us define the Kirk operator $T_K : X \to X$, where X is a quasi-normed space, as

$$T_K x = \sum_{i=0}^{k} \alpha_i T^i x.$$

Kirk proved that the set of fixed points of a nonexpansive mapping T in a Banach space agrees with the set of fixed points of T_K, that is to say, $Fix(T) = Fix(T_K)$. He proved also that if $Fix(T) \neq \emptyset$ and X is uniformly convex, then T_K is asymptotically regular, that is to say,

$$\lim_{n\to\infty} ||T_K^{n+1}x - T_K^n x|| = 0.$$

Let us study the convergence and stability of this algorithm for the approximation of the fixed point of a $(\varphi - \psi)$-partial contractivity T in a quasi-normed space.

If $y_0 := y \in X$ and $x^* \in Fix(T)$,

$$|y_{n+1} - x^*|_s = |\sum_{i=0}^{k} \alpha_i (T^i y_n - x^*)|_s \leq \sum_{i=0}^{k-1} \alpha_i s^{i+1} |T^i y_n - x^*|_s + \alpha_k s^k |T^k y_n - x^*|_s.$$

Applying the definition of $(\varphi - \psi)$-partial contractivity,

$$|y_{n+1} - x^*|_s \leq \sum_{i=0}^{k-1} \alpha_i s^{i+1} \varphi^i(|y_n - x^*|_s) + \alpha_k s^k \varphi^k(|y_n - x^*|_s), \tag{16}$$

defining $\varphi^0 := Id$ as always. Let us assume that the map $\phi : \mathbb{R}^+ \to \mathbb{R}^+$ defined as

$$\phi = \sum_{i=0}^{k-1} \alpha_i s^{i+1} \varphi^i + \alpha_k s^k \varphi^k. \tag{17}$$

is a comparison function. In this case, we have

$$|y_{n+1} - x^*|_s \leq \phi(|y_n - x^*|_s),$$

and, in general,

$$|y_n - x^*|_s \leq \phi^n(|y_0 - x^*|_s). \tag{18}$$

Consequently, the Kirk iterations are convergent to the fixed point x^* with asymptotic stability as in the previous section. For the particular case where $\varphi(\delta) = a\delta$, assuming that

$$r := \sum_{i=0}^{k-1} \alpha_i s^{i+1} a^i + \alpha_k s^k a^k < 1,$$

the Kirk algorithm is convergent and stable since, from (18), we have

$$|y_n - x^*|_s \leq r^n |y_0 - x^*|_s. \tag{19}$$

The order of convergence of the iteration is $O(r^n)$. In the normed case, where $s = 1$, this is always true since

$$r = \sum_{i=0}^{k} \alpha_i a^i < 1,$$

due to the conditions on α_i, and we have the following theorem:

Theorem 4. *If X is a normed space, $T : X \to X$ is a $(\varphi - \psi)$-partial contractivity where $\phi(\delta) = a\delta$, $0 < a < 1$, and $x^* \in X$ is a fixed point, the Kirk iteration $(T_K^n x)$ is convergent, asymptotically stable and asymptotically regular for any values of α_i and $x \in X$.*

Kirk proved that the iterates of his algorithm converge weakly to a fixed point of a nonexpansive mapping, according to the next theorem [14].

Theorem 5. *Let X be a uniformly convex Banach space, K be a closed, bounded, and convex subset of X, and $T : K \to K$ be a nonexpansive mapping. Then, for $x \in K$ the sequence $(T_K^n x)$ converges weakly to a fixed point of T.*

We give in the following a variant of this theorem.

Theorem 6. *Let X be a quasi-Banach space, K be a closed and convex subset of X, and $T : K \to K$ be a $(\varphi - \psi)$-contraction where ψ is the null function. Then, $Fix(T) \neq \emptyset$, $Fix(T) = \{x^*\}$, and the Kirk iterations converge strongly to the fixed point x^* for any $x \in K$ if the map ϕ defined in (17) is a comparison function.*

Proof. A $(\varphi - \psi)$-contractivity where $\psi = 0$ is a nonexpansive mapping, since

$$||Tx - Ty|| \leq \varphi(||x - y||) \leq ||x - y||,$$

for any $x, y \in K$. But, according to the hypotheses, T is also a φ-contraction on a complete b-metric space, consequently it has a single fixed point [23] and the Picard iterations are strongly convergent to it. Due to (18), the Kirk iterations have the same properties if ϕ is a comparison function. □

5. Banach-Valued Fractal Surfaces

In this section, we define fractal surfaces whose values lie on Banach algebras. The convergence and stability of Picard and Kirk iterations for their approximation are also analyzed, giving in both cases an estimate of the error.

The mappings defining the surfaces are fixed points of an operator on the space of bivariate p-integrable maps on a Banach algebra $\mathbb{A}$, $\mathcal{B}^p(I \times J, \mathbb{A})$, where I and J are real compact intervals. For $1 \leq p < \infty$ this space is Banach with respect to the norm

$$|f|_p = (\int_{I \times J} ||f(x,y)||^p dxdy)^{1/p},$$

where $|| \cdot ||$ is the norm in $\mathbb{A}$. For $0 < p < 1$, the space is quasi-Banach with modulus of concavity $s = 2^{1/p-1}$. Consequently, in all the cases $\mathcal{B}^p(I \times J, \mathbb{A})$ is a complete b-metric space.

Let us consider partitions for the intervals I and J, $x_0 < x_1 < \ldots < x_M$ for $I = [x_0, x_M]$, and $y_0 < y_1 < \ldots < y_N$ for $J = [y_0, y_N]$, $M, N > 1$. Let us consider subintervals $I_i = [x_{i-1}, x_i)$ for $i = 1, 2, \ldots, M-1$, $I_M = [x_{M-1}, x_M]$ and $J_j = [y_{j-1}, y_j)$ for $j = 1, 2, \ldots, N-1$, $J_N = [y_{N-1}, y_N]$. Let us define the affine maps

$$u_i(x) = c_i x + d_i, \qquad v_j(y) = e_j y + f_j,$$

satisfying the conditions

$$u_i(x_0) = x_{i-1}, \qquad u_i(x_M) = x_i, \qquad v_j(y_0) = y_{j-1}, \qquad v_j(y_N) = y_j, \tag{20}$$

for $i = 1, 2, \ldots, M$ and $j = 1, 2, \ldots, N$. Given two maps $f, g \in \mathcal{B}^p(I \times J, \mathbb{A})$, let us define

$$F_{ij}(x, y, A) = f(u_i(x), u_j(y)) + R_{ij}(x, y, A) - R_{ij}(x, y, g(x, y)),$$

for $(x, y) \in I \times J$ and $A \in \mathbb{A}$, with the same ranges of indexes. The case where $\mathbb{A} = \mathbb{R}$ and $R_{ij}(x, y, z) = \alpha_{ij} z$ was treated in reference [24].

Let us assume that the operator $S_{ij} : \mathcal{B}^p(I \times J, \mathbb{A}) \to \mathcal{B}^p(I \times J, \mathbb{A})$ defined for $h \in \mathcal{B}^p(I \times J, \mathbb{A})$ as

$$S_{ij}(h)(x,y) = R_{ij}(x,y,h(x,y)) \tag{21}$$

is a φ_{ij}-contraction with respect to $|\cdot|_p$ for $i = 1,2,\ldots,M$, $j = 1,2,\ldots,N$. It is an easy exercise to prove that $\varphi(t) := \max_{ij}\{\varphi_{ij}(t)\}$ is also a comparison function.

Let us define the operator

$$Th(x,y) = F_{ij}(u_i^{-1}(x), v_j^{-1}(y), h(u_i^{-1}(x), v_j^{-1}(y))),$$

for $x \in I_i$, and $y \in J_j$. In order to simplify the notation, let us define $H_{ij}(x,y) = (u_i^{-1}(x), v_j^{-1}(y))$ for any i,j and write

$$Th(x,y) = F_{ij}(H_{ij}(x,y), h \circ H_{ij}(x,y))) \tag{22}$$

for $(x,y) \in I_i \times J_j$. Let us see that T is a φ-contraction:

$$|Th - Th'|_p^p = \sum_{i=1}^{M}\sum_{j=1}^{N} \int_{I_i \times J_j} ||R_{ij}(H_{ij}(x,y), h \circ H_{ij}(x,y)) - R_{ij}(H_{ij}(x,y), h' \circ H_{ij}(x,y))||^p dxdy.$$

With the change $u_i^{-1}(x) = x'$, and $v_j^{-1}(y) = y'$, and renaming the variables, we have

$$|Th - Th'|_p^p = \sum_{i=1}^{M}\sum_{j=1}^{N} c_i e_j \int_{I \times J} ||R_{ij}(x,y,h(x,y)) - R_{ij}(x,y,h'(x,y))||^p dxdy.$$

By definition of the operator S_{ij} (21),

$$|Th - Th'|_p^p = \sum_{i=1}^{M}\sum_{j=1}^{N} c_i e_j \int_{I \times J} ||S_{ij}(h)(x,y) - S_{ij}(h')(x,y)||^p dxdy.$$

Using the fact that S_{ij} is a φ-contraction,

$$|Th - Th'|_p^p = \sum_{i=1}^{M}\sum_{j=1}^{N} c_i e_j |S_{ij}(h) - S_{ij}(h')|_p^p \leq \sum_{i=1}^{M}\sum_{j=1}^{N} c_i e_j (\varphi(|h - h'|_p)^p. \tag{23}$$

Consequently,

$$|Th - Th'|_p \leq (\sum_{i=1}^{M}\sum_{j=1}^{N} c_i e_j)^{1/p} \varphi(|h - h'|_p).$$

But $\sum_{i=1}^{M}\sum_{j=1}^{N} c_i e_j = 1$ due to conditions (20), and thus,

$$|Th - Th'|_p \leq \varphi(|h - h'|_p),$$

T is a φ-contraction, and consequently, is a $(\varphi - \psi)$-contractivity with $\psi = 0$. Since $\mathcal{B}^p(I \times J, \mathbb{A})$ is quasi-Banach, and thus, a complete b-metric space, T has a single fixed point $f^\varphi \in \mathcal{B}^p(I \times J, \mathbb{A})$, and the Picard iterations of any point are convergent to it. The graph of f^φ has a fractal structure (see Theorem 5 of reference [25]). The order of convergence is

$$|T^n h - f^\varphi|_p \leq \varphi^n(|h - f^\varphi|_p),$$

for any $h \in \mathcal{B}^p(I \times J, \mathbb{A})$. In the particular case where $\varphi(t) = at$ for $0 < a < 1$, according to Corollary 3,

$$|T^n h - f^\varphi|_p \leq \frac{|Th - h|_p}{1 - a} a^n, \tag{24}$$

for $1 \le p < \infty$, and

$$|T^n h - f^\varphi|_p \le \frac{s^2 |Th - h|_p}{1 - as} a^n \tag{25}$$

for $0 < p < 1$, if $as < 1$, with $s = 2^{1/p-1}$.

The fixed point f^φ satisfies the functional equation

$$f^\varphi(x,y) = f(x,y) + R_{ij}(H_{ij}(x,y), f^\varphi \circ H_{ij}(x,y)) - R_{ij}(H_{ij}(x,y), g \circ H_{ij}(x,y)), \tag{26}$$

for $(x,y) \in I_i \times J_j$.

Let us consider now the Kirk iteration, and the case where $\varphi_{ij}(\delta) = a_{ij}\delta$. Let us define $a := \max_{ij} a_{ij}$ and assume that

$$r := \sum_{i=0}^{k-1} \alpha_i s^{i+1} a^i + \alpha_k s^k a^k < 1. \tag{27}$$

Denoting the Kirk iterates as $\hat{h}_n$, bearing in mind the estimation (19),

$$|\hat{h}_n - f^\varphi|_p \le r^n |\hat{h}_0 - f^\varphi|_p,$$

for $n \ge 0$. Thus, the Kirk iterations are convergent with a rate of convergence $O(r^n)$. This is always true in the normed case ($1 \le p < \infty$) since

$$r = \sum_{i=0}^{k} \alpha_i a^i < 1,$$

due to the definition of α_i.

Consequently, the Kirk iteration is convergent in the normed case for any values of the coefficients, with asymptotic stability. Since the Kirk operator T_K is also a Banach contraction if $r < 1$, we obtain error estimates for Kirk iterations as well:

$$|T_K^n h - f^\varphi|_p \le \frac{|T_K h - h|_p}{1 - r} r^n, \tag{28}$$

for $1 \le p < \infty$, and

$$|T_K^n h - f^\varphi|_p \le \frac{s^2 |T_K h - h|_p}{1 - rs} r^n \tag{29}$$

for $0 < p < 1$, if $rs < 1$, where $s = 2^{1/p-1}$, and r is defined as in (27) in this second case.

6. Fractal Surfaces with Linear Vertical Contractions

Let us consider in this section the case where the vertical contraction operator $S_{ij} : \mathcal{B}^p(I \times J, \mathbb{A}) \to \mathcal{B}^p(I \times J, \mathbb{A})$, defined as $S_{ij}(h)(x,y) = R_{ij}(x,y,h(x,y))$ (see (21)), is linear and bounded.

We will define fractal convolutions of mappings and operators, and we will construct bivariate fractal frames of the Hilbert space $\mathcal{B}^2(I \times J, \mathbb{A})$ as fractal perturbations of standard frames in this space.

For the first part of (23), we have

$$|Th - Th'|_p \le \Big(\sum_{i=1}^{M} \sum_{j=1}^{N} c_i e_j |S_{ij}|_p^p\Big)^{1/p} |h - h'|_p. \tag{30}$$

If

$$C := \Big(\sum_{i=1}^{M} \sum_{j=1}^{N} c_i e_j |S_{ij}|_p^p\Big)^{1/p} < 1, \tag{31}$$

then T is a Banach contraction in a quasi-Banach space. Consequently, it has a fixed point f^φ that is a bivariate mapping $f^\varphi(x,y)$ whose values are in the algebra $\mathbb{A}$.

Some choices for a linear operator may be $S_{ij}(g) = \lambda_{ij}(g \circ c)$, where $c : I \times J \to I \times J$ and $\lambda_{ij} : \mathbb{R} \times \mathbb{R} \to \mathbb{R}$ or $S_{ij}(g) = \lambda_{ij}(g \cdot v)$, with $v : I \times J \to \mathbb{A}$, where $\cdot$ represents the product in the algebra $\mathbb{A}$. In the first case, for $c = Id$ we have the classical vertical contraction of the fractal interpolation functions.

Remark 5. *Let us notice that we use the same notation for the norms of maps and linear operators* ($|\cdot|_p$) *in order to simplify the text.*

The estimation of the Picard iterations for the approximation of the fixed point f^φ (24) and (25) holds in this case as well, substituting a by C, and considering the hypothesis $Cs < 1$ in the second error estimation ($s \neq 1$).

We can define the operator $\mathcal{F}^\varphi : \mathcal{B}^p(I \times J, \mathbb{A}) \to \mathcal{B}^p(I \times J, \mathbb{A})$ that applies every map into its fractal perturbation: $\mathcal{F}^\varphi(f) = f^\varphi$, considering the partition, functions u_i, v_j, operators S_{ij}, and mapping $g \in \mathcal{B}^p(I \times J, \mathbb{A})$. It is an easy exercise to check that

$$|\mathcal{F}^\varphi(f) - f|_p \leq \frac{Cs}{1 - Cs}|f - g|_p,$$

whenever $Cs < 1$. If, additionally, f and g are related by a linear and bounded operator $\mathcal{L}$, that is to say, $g = \mathcal{L}f$, then $\mathcal{F}^\varphi$ is linear and bounded and

$$|\mathcal{F}^\varphi|_p \leq (1 + \frac{Cs|Id - \mathcal{L}|_p}{1 - Cs}).$$

This operator was defined by the author and studied for single-variable real maps and several functional spaces in reference [26].

In the case where $R_{ij}(x,y,A) = \alpha_{ij}(x,y).A$ and $\max_{ij} |\alpha_{ij}|_p < 1$, we obtain an α-fractal surface [24].

Modulating the distance between a mapping $f(x,y)$ and its fractal associated $f^\varphi(x,y)$, one can obtain fractal bases of several functional spaces (see, for instance, [25]). Given that f^φ is obtained by the action of two bivariate mappings f and g, it is possible to define a binary internal operation $*_\varphi$ in the space $\mathcal{B}^p(I \times J, \mathbb{A})$ as

$$f *_\varphi g := f^\varphi.$$

This was called in the real case the fractal convolution of f and g. This operation is linear, that is to say,

$$(\lambda f + \mu f') *_\varphi (\lambda g + \mu g') = \lambda(f *_\varphi g) + \mu(f' *_\varphi g'),$$

for any $f, f', g, g' \in \mathcal{B}^p(I \times J, \mathbb{A})$ and $\lambda, \mu \in \mathbb{R}$. It is also idempotent, that is to say,

$$f *_\varphi f = f,$$

for any $f \in \mathcal{B}^p(I \times J, \mathbb{A})$. Additionally, the map $P : \mathcal{B}^p(I \times J, \mathbb{A}) \times \mathcal{B}^p(I \times J, \mathbb{A}) \to \mathcal{B}^p(I \times J, \mathbb{A})$ defined as $P(f,g) = f *_\varphi g$ is bounded. The details are similar to the real univariate case.

Let us denote by $L(\mathcal{B}^p(I \times J, \mathbb{A}))$ the space of linear and bounded operators on $\mathcal{B}^p(I \times J, \mathbb{A})$. Based on the fractal convolution of maps, it is possible to define an internal operation in the set of operators as

$$(U *_\varphi V)f = (Uf) *_\varphi (Vf),$$

for any $f \in \mathcal{B}^p(I \times J, \mathbb{A})$, and $U, V \in L(\mathcal{B}^p(I \times J, \mathbb{A}))$. The linearity and boundedness of U, V, and P imply that the operator is well defined.

In the following, we consider the case $1 \leq p < \infty$.

Theorem 7. *Let $U, V \in L(\mathcal{B}^p(I \times J, \mathbb{A}))$ and let us assume that U is invertible such that $|Vf|_p \leq |Uf|_p$ for any $f \in \mathcal{B}^p(I \times J, \mathbb{A})$. Then, $U *_\varphi V$ is invertible and*

$$|(U *_\varphi V)|_p \leq \frac{1+C}{1-C}|U|_p, \tag{32}$$

$$|(U *_\varphi V)^{-1}|_p \leq \frac{1+C}{1-C}|U^{-1}|_p, \tag{33}$$

Proof. The proof is similar to that given in Theorem 8 of reference [25]. □

In the case where $p = 2$ and $\mathbb{A} = H$ is a Hilbert space, $\mathcal{B}^2(I \times J, H)$ is Hilbert as well, with respect to the inner product:

$$< f, g >= \int_{I \times J} < f(x,y), g(x,y) > dxdy.$$

In the following, we consider $p = 2$ and we prove that given a frame $(f_m)_{m=0}^{\infty}$ of bivariate functions $f_m(x, y) \in H$, we can construct Hilbert-valued fractal frames with two variables of type

$$(U(f_m) *_\varphi V(f_m))_{m=0}^{\infty}.$$

Let us start by defining a frame in a Hilbert space.

Definition 8. *A sequence $(f_m)_{m=0}^{\infty} \subseteq X$, where X is a Hilbert space is a frame if there exist real positive constants A, B such that*

$$A||f||^2 \leq \sum_{m=0}^{\infty} | < f, f_m > |^2 \leq B||f||^2, \tag{34}$$

for any $f \in X$, where $|| \cdot ||$ denotes the norm associated with the inner product in X. A and B are the bounds of the frame.

Theorem 8. *Let $U, V \in L(\mathcal{B}^2(I \times J, H))$ satisfy the hypotheses given in Theorem 7, and $(f_m)_{m=0}^{\infty} \subseteq \mathcal{B}^2(I \times J, H)$ be a frame with bounds A, B. Then, $((U *_\varphi V)f_m)_{m=0}^{\infty}$ is also a frame with bounds A_φ and B_φ, defined as*

$$A_\varphi := A(\frac{1+C}{1-C})^{-2}|U^{-1}|_2^{-2}$$

and

$$B_\varphi := B(\frac{1+C}{1-C})^{2}|U|_2^{2}.$$

Proof. Let $(U *_\varphi V)^+$ be the adjoint operator of $(U *_\varphi V)$, and $g \in \mathcal{B}^2(I \times J, H)$. Applying the frame inequalities of $(f_m)_{m=0}^{\infty}$ for $f = (U *_\varphi V)^+ g$ one obtains

$$A|(U *_\varphi V)^+ g|_2^2 \leq \sum_{m=0}^{\infty} | < (U *_\varphi V)^+ g, f_m > |_2^2 \leq B|(U *_\varphi V)^+ g|_2^2 \leq B|(U *_\varphi V)|_2^2 |g|_2^2. \tag{35}$$

Since

$$\sum_{m=0}^{\infty} | < (U *_\varphi V)^+ g, f_m > |_2^2 = \sum_{m=0}^{\infty} | < g, (U *_\varphi V) f_m > |_2^2, \tag{36}$$

using (35) and (36) one has

$$A|(U *_\varphi V)^+ g|_2^2 \leq \sum_{m=0}^{\infty} | < g, (U *_\varphi V) f_m > |_2^2 \leq B|(U *_\varphi V)|_2^2 |g|_2^2, \tag{37}$$

and we have the right inequality for the sequence $((U *_\varphi V)f_m)_{m=0}^\infty$. For Theorem 7 we know that $(U *_\varphi V)$ is an invertible operator. Then,

$$|g|_2^2 = |((U *_\varphi V)^+)^{-1} \circ (U *_\varphi V)^+ g|_2^2 \leq |((U *_\varphi V)^+)^{-1}|_2^2 |(U *_\varphi V)^+ g|_2^2,$$

and

$$A|((U *_\varphi V)^+)^{-1}|_2^{-2} |g|_2^2 \leq A|(U *_\varphi V)^+ g|_2^2.$$

Since $|((U *_\varphi V)^+)^{-1}|_2 = |(U *_\varphi V)^{-1}|_2$, then, by (37),

$$A|(U *_\varphi V)^{-1}|_2^{-2} |g|_2^2 \leq \sum_{m=0}^\infty | < g, (U *_\varphi V) f_m > |_2^2 \leq B|(U *_\varphi V)|_2^2 |g|_2^2. \quad (38)$$

Hence, by (32) and (33), $(U(f_m) *_\varphi V(f_m))$ is also a frame and its bounds are A_φ and B_φ, defined as

$$A_\varphi = A\left(\frac{1+C}{1-C}\right)^{-2} |U^{-1}|_2^{-2} \leq A|(U *_\varphi V)^{-1}|_2^{-2}$$

and

$$B_\varphi = B\left(\frac{1+C}{1-C}\right)^{2} |U|_2^2 \geq B|(U *_\varphi V)|_2^2.$$

□

7. Conclusions

This article delves into the concept of $(\varphi - \psi)$-partial contractivity, defined by the author in previous references in the framework of b-metric and quasi-normed spaces. In particular, it provides sufficient conditions for the existence of fixed points for these maps. The convergence and stability of the Picard iterations for the approximation of the fixed points are proved, giving "a priori" error estimates as well.

Kirk's algorithm for the same purpose is analyzed, giving conditions for its convergence and stability. In particular, it is proved that the method enjoys these properties if the underlying space is a normed space and the comparison function φ is linear, in the case of the existence of a fixed point. Some error estimates are also given.

The properties proved can be applied to other types of contractions, since the self-maps considered contain many others as particular cases. For instance, if the underlying set is a metric space, the contractions of type Kannan, Chatterjea, Zamfirescu, Ćirić, and Reich are included in the class of contractivities studied in this paper (see Corollary 2.2 of reference [11]).

These facts are applied to the definition of new fractal surfaces, more general than those studied so far. The construction of fractal frames composed of bivariate mappings is performed, belonging to very general Hilbert functional spaces.

Funding: This research received no external funding.

Data Availability Statement: The original contributions presented in the study are included in the article, further inquiries can be directed to the corresponding author.

Conflicts of Interest: The author declares that the publication of this paper has no conflicts of interest.

References

1. Fréchet, M. Sur quelques points du calcul fonctionnel. *Rend. Circ. Matem. Palermo* **1906**, *XXII*, 1–72. [CrossRef]
2. Hausdorff, F. *Grundzüge der Mergenlehre*; Verlag Von Veit Comp.: Leipzig, Germany, 1914.
3. Hilbert, J. *Grundlagen der Geometrie*; B.G. Teubner: Leipzig, Germany, 1899.
4. Riemann, B. *Über die Hypothesen der Geometrie su Grunde Liegen*; Abhandlungen der Königlinchen Gesellschaft der Wissenschaften zu Götingen; Kessinger Publishing: Whitefish, MT, USA, 1867; p. 13.
5. Gopal, D.; Agarwal, P.; Kumam P. *Metric Structures and Fixed Point Theory*; CRC Press, Chapman and Hall: Boca Ratón, FL, USA, 2021.
6. Kirk, W.; Shahzad, N. *Fixed Point Theory in Distance Spaces*; Springer: Cham, Switzerland, 2014.

7. Deza, M.M.; Deza, E. *Encyclopedia of Distances*; Springer: Berlin/Heidelberg, Germany, 2009.
8. Hamming, R.W. Error detecting and error correcting codes. *Bell Syst. Tech. J.* **1950**, *29*, 147–160. [CrossRef]
9. Border, K.C. *Fixed Point Theorems with Applications to Economics and Game Theory;* Cambridge Universtiy Press: Cambridge, UK, 2010.
10. Huang, H.; Deng, G.; Radenović, S. Fixed point theorems in b-metric spaces with applications to differential equations. *J. Fixed Point Theory Appl.* **2018**, *20*, 52. [CrossRef]
11. Navascués, M.A. Approximation of fixed points and fractal functions by means of different iterative algorithms. *Chaos Solitons Fractals* **2024**, *180*, 114535. [CrossRef]
12. Navascués, M.A.; Mohapatra, R.N. Fixed point dynamics in a new type of contraction in b-metric spaces. *Symmetry* **2024**, *16*, 506. [CrossRef]
13. Ali, B.; Abbas, M. Existence and Ulam-Hyers stability of fixed point problem of generalized Suzuki type (α_*, ψ_φ)-contractive multivalued operators. *Rev. Acad. Cienc. Exactas Fís. Nat. Ser. A Mat.* **2017**, *111*, 1129–1146. [CrossRef]
14. Kirk, W.A. On successive approximation for nonexpansive mappings in Banach spaces. *Glasg. Math. J.* **1971**, *12*, 6–9. [CrossRef]
15. Rano, G.; Bag, T. Quasi-metric space and fixed point theorems. *Int. J. Math. Sci. Comp.* **2013**, *3*, 27–31.
16. Berinde, V. *Iterative Approximation of Fixed Points;* Lecture Notes in Mathematics; Springer: Berlin/Heidelberg, Germany, 2007.
17. Matkowski, J. Integrable solutions of functional equations. *Diss. Math.* **1975**, *127*, 68.
18. Miculescu, R.; Mihail, A. New fixed point theorems for set-valued contractions in b-metric spaces. *J. Fixed Point Theory Appl.* **2017**, *19*, 2153–2163. [CrossRef]
19. Bakhtin I.A. The contraction mapping principle in quasimetric spaces. *Funkt. Anal. Ulianowvskii Gos. Ped. Inst.* **1989**, *30*, 26–37. (In Russian)
20. Cobzas, S.; Czerwik, S. The completion of generalized b-metric spaces and fixed points. *Fixed Point Theory* **2020**, *21*, 133–150. [CrossRef]
21. Krasnoselskii, M.A. Two remarks on the method of successive approximations. *Uspehi Mat. Nauk.* **1955**, *10*, 123–127. (In Russian)
22. Mann, W.R. Mean value methods in iteration. *Proc. Am. Math. Soc.* **1953**, *44*, 506–510. [CrossRef]
23. Kajántó, S.; Lukács, A. A note on the paper "Contraction mapping in b-metric spaces" by Czerwik. *Acta Univ. Sapientiae Math.* **2018**, *10*, 8589. [CrossRef]
24. Navascués, M.A.; Mohapatra R.N.; Akhtar, M.N. Construction of fractal surfaces. *Fractals* **2020**, *28*, 2050033. [CrossRef]
25. Navascués, M.A. Fractal curves in Banach algebras. *Fractal Fract.* **2022**, *6*, 722. [CrossRef]
26. Viswanathan, P.E.; Navascués, M.A. A fractal operator on some standard spaces of functions. *Proc. Edinb. Math. Soc.* **2017**, *60*, 771–786. [CrossRef]

axioms

MDPI

Article

Three Existence Results in the Fixed Point Theory

Alexander J. Zaslavski

Department of Mathematics, The Technion—Israel Institute of Technology, Haifa 32000, Israel; ajzasl@technion.ac.il

Abstract: In the present paper, we obtain three results on the existence of a fixed point for nonexpansive mappings. Two of them are generalizations of the result for F-contraction, while third one is a generalization of a recent result for set-valued contractions.

Keywords: complete metric space; contraction; fixed point; graph; set-valued mapping

MSC: 47H09; 47H10; 54E50

1. Introduction

The work referenced here [1] was the starting point of the fixed point theory of nonexpansive maps, which is a growing field of research; see [2–7]. In particular, the convergence of iterated Bregman projections and of the alternating algorithm were studied in [2], fixed point theorems under Mizoguchi–Takahashi-type conditions were obtained in [3], Ciric-type results were proved in [4], fixed point theory in modular function spaces was discussed in [5] and cyclic contractions were analyzed in [6]. Note that the research on nonexpansive maps in spaces with graphs is of great importance; see [8–12] and the references mentioned therein. In particular, fixed point results on metric spaces with a graph are obtained in [9,11], Reich-type contractions were studied in [8], hybrid methods were studied in [10] and the convergence of fixed points in graphical spaces was considered in [12]. In [13], D. Wardowski introduced an interesting class of mappings which contains Banach contractions and showed the existence of fixed points for these mappings. More precisely, we can assume that (X, ρ) is a complete metric space, $\tau > 0$, $F : (0, \infty) \to R^1$ is a strictly increasing function and that $T : X \to X$ is a mapping such that for every pair of points $u, v \in X$ satisfying $u \neq v$,

$$F(\rho(T(u), T(v))) + \tau \leq F(\rho(u, v)).$$

Assuming two additional assumptions on F, D. Wardowski showed that the mapping of T has a unique fixed point. In the subsequent research it was shown that these two additional assumptions are not necessary. One of the examples of F is the function $\ln(\cdot)$, and in this case the Wardowski contraction is a strict contraction. Wardowski-type contractions were studied in [14–16]. In this work, we obtain three results on the existence of a fixed point for nonexpansive mappings in a complete metric space. Two of them are generalizations of the result by D. Wardowski for F-contraction, while the third one is a generalization of a recent result by S.-H. Cho for set-valued contractions [17].

Assume that (X, ρ) is a complete metric space. Let $\mathbf{N}$ be the set of all natural numbers. We assume that the sum over empty set is zero. For every element $x \in X$ and every real number $r > 0$, set

$$B(x, r) = \{y \in X : \ \rho(x, y) \leq r\}.$$

For every element $\xi \in X$ and each nonempty set $A \subset X$ set

$$\rho(\xi, A) = \inf\{\rho(\xi, \eta) : \ \eta \in A\}.$$

2. The First Result

Assume that (X, ρ) is a complete metric space where ρ is a metric, $K \subset X$ is a nonempty closed set, $\tau > 0$, and $F : (0, \infty) \to R^1$ is an increasing function satisfying

$$F(t) \leq F(s)$$

for each $s > t > 0$ and that $T : K \to X$ is an operator such that for every pair of points $x, y \in K$ satisfying $x \neq y$,

$$F(\rho(T(x), T(y))) + \tau \leq F(\rho(x, y)). \tag{1}$$

Set $T^0(x) = x$, $x \in K$.

D. Wardowski in [13] proved the existence of a fixed point of T in the case when $K = X_0$, assuming that F is strictly increasing. Here, we assume that F is merely increasing in general.

Since the function F is increasing, the following proposition holds [18].

Proposition 1. *There is a countable set $E \subset (0, \infty)$ such that the function F is continuous at every element $z \in (0, \infty) \setminus E$.*

Equation (1) implies the following proposition.

Proposition 2. *For every pair of elements $x, y \in K$, the relation $\rho(T(x), T(y)) \leq \rho(x, y)$ is true.*

Theorem 1. *Assume that $K_0 \subset X$ is a nonempty bounded set and for each integer $n \geq 1$ there is an element $x_n \in K_0$ for which $T^n(x_n) \in X$ is defined. Then, $x_* \in K$ can be found, satisfying $T(x_*) = x_*$.*

Proof. Fix $\theta \in K_0$. $M_0 > 0$ is found, for which

$$\rho(z, \theta) \leq M_0, \; z \in K_0. \tag{2}$$

Proposition 2 and (2) imply that for each $n, m \in \mathbf{N}$,

$$\rho(x_n, x_m) \leq 2M_0,$$

$$\rho(T(x_n), T(\theta)) \leq \rho(x_n, \theta) \leq M_0,$$
$$\rho(T(x_n), \theta) \leq M_0 + \rho(\theta, T(\theta)). \tag{3}$$

Let $\epsilon \in (0, 1)$. We show that the following property holds:

(P1) There exists a natural number n_0 such that for each integer $n > n_0$ and each integer $i \in [n_0, n)$, we have

$$\rho(T^i(x_n), T^{i+1}(x_n)) \leq \epsilon.$$

Choose an integer:

$$n_0 > 1 + \tau^{-1}(F(2M_0 + \rho(\theta, T(\theta))) - F(\epsilon)). \tag{4}$$

Let $n > n_0$ be an integer. In order to prove that (P1) holds in view of Proposition 2, it is enough to prove that

$$\rho(T^{n_0}(x_n), T^{n_0+1}(x_n)) \leq \epsilon.$$

Assume the contrary. Then, according to Proposition 2,

$$\rho(T^{n_0}(x_n), T^{n_0+1}(x_n)) \geq \epsilon, \; i = 0, \ldots, n_0. \tag{5}$$

Equations (1) and (5) imply that for every $i \in \{0, \dots, n_0 - 1\} \setminus \{n_0 - 1\}$,

$$F(\rho(T^{i+1}(x_n), T^{i+2}(x_n))) + \tau \leq F(\rho(T^i(x_n), T^{i+1}(x_n))),$$

$$F(\rho(T^{n_0}(x_n), T^{n_0+1}(x_n))) \leq \tau(1 - n_0) + F(\rho(T(x_n), x_n)). \tag{6}$$

It follows from (3), (5) and (6) that

$$F(\epsilon) \leq F(\rho(T^{n_0}(x_n), T^{n_0+1}(x_n))) \leq \tau(1 - n_0) + F(2M_0 + \rho(\theta, T(\theta))),$$

$$\tau(n_0 - 1) \leq F(2M_0 + \rho(\theta, T(\theta))) - F(\epsilon),$$

$$n_0 \leq 1 + \tau^{-1}(F(2M_0 + \rho(\theta, T(\theta))) - F(\epsilon)).$$

This contradicts inequality (4) and proves property (P1).

We show that the following property holds:

(P2) $n_0 \in \mathbf{N}$ is found, such that for each triplet of integers i, n_1, n_2 satisfying $n_1, n_2, i \geq n_0$, $i \leq n_1, n_2$,

$$\rho(T^i(x_{n_1}), T^i(x_{n_2})) \leq \epsilon.$$

Choose an integer:

$$n_0 > 1 + \tau^{-1}(F(2M_0) - F(\epsilon)). \tag{7}$$

Let $n_1, n_2 \geq n_0$ be integers. In view of Proposition 2, in order to show that property (P2) holds, it is enough to show that

$$\rho(T^{n_0}(x_{n_1}), T^{n_0}(x_{n_2})) \leq \epsilon.$$

Assume the contrary. Then,

$$\rho(T^{n_0}(x_{n_1}), T^{n_0}(x_{n_2})) > \epsilon. \tag{8}$$

Proposition 2 and (1), (2) and (8) imply that for each $i \in \{0, \dots, n_0 - 1\}$,

$$\rho(T^i(x_{n_1}), T^i(x_{n_2})) > \epsilon,$$

$$F(\rho(T^{i+1}(x_{n_1}), T^{i+1}(x_{n_2}))) + \tau \leq F(\rho(T^i(x_{n_1}), T^i(x_{n_2}))),$$

$$\begin{aligned} F(\rho(T^{n_0}(x_{n_1}), T^{n_0}(x_{n_2}))) &\leq (1 - n_0)\tau + F(\rho(x_{n_1}, x_{n_2})) \\ &\leq (1 - n_0)\tau + F(2M_0). \end{aligned} \tag{9}$$

According to (8) and (9),

$$F(\epsilon) \leq \tau(1 - n_0) + F(2M_0), \; n_0 \leq 1 + \tau^{-1}(F(2M_0) - F(\epsilon)).$$

This contradicts (7). Therefore, (P2) holds.

We will prove that the following property is fulfilled:

(P3) $n_* \in \mathbf{N}$ is found, such that for each triplet $i_1, i_2, n \in \mathbf{N}$ satisfying $n_* \leq i_1, i_2 \leq n$,

$$\rho(T^{i_1}(x_n), T^{i_2}(x_n)) \leq \epsilon.$$

According to Proposition 1, we may assume that F is continuous at ϵ. Assume that property (P3) does not hold. Then, for any $k \in \mathbf{N}$, there are integers $i_{k,1}, i_{k_2}, n_k$ for which

$$k \leq i_{k,1} < i_{k,2} \leq n_k, \tag{10}$$

$$\rho(T^{i_{k,1}}(x_{n_k}), T^{i_{k,2}}(x_{n_k})) > \epsilon. \tag{11}$$

In view of property (P1), we may assume that for every integer $k \geq 1$,

$$\rho(T^{i_{k,1}}(x_{n_k}), T^{i_{k,1}+1}(x_{n_k})) \leq \epsilon. \tag{12}$$

Let $k \geq 1$. According to (11) and (12),

$$i_{k,1} + 1 < i_{k,2}$$

and we may assume that

$$\rho(T^{i_{k,1}}(x_{n_k}), T^{i_{k,2}-1}(x_{n_k})) \leq \epsilon. \tag{13}$$

Equations (1) and (13) imply that

$$\begin{aligned} \epsilon &< \rho(T^{i_{k,1}}(x_{n_k}), T^{i_{k,2}}(x_{n_k})) \\ &\leq \rho(T^{i_{k,1}}(x_{n_k}), T^{i_{k,2}-1}(x_{n_k})) + \rho(T^{i_{k,2}-1}(x_{n_k}), T^{i_{k,2}}(x_{n_k})) \\ &\leq \epsilon + \rho(T^{i_{k,2}-1}(x_{n_k}), T^{i_{k,2}}(x_{n_k})). \end{aligned} \tag{14}$$

Property (P1) and (10), (14) imply that

$$\lim_{k \to \infty} \rho(T^{i_{k,1}}(x_{n_k}), T^{i_{k,2}}(x_{n_k})) = \epsilon. \tag{15}$$

Clearly, for each $k \in \mathbf{N}$,

$$\begin{aligned} \rho(T^{i_{k,1}}(x_{n_k}), T^{i_{k,2}}(x_{n_k})) &\leq \rho(T^{i_{k,1}}(x_{n_k}), T^{i_{k,1}+1}(x_{n_k})) \\ &+\rho(T^{i_{k,1}+1}(x_{n_k}), T^{i_{k,2}+1}(x_{n_k})) + \rho(T^{i_{k,2}}(x_{n_k}), T^{i_{k,2}+1}(x_{n_k})). \end{aligned} \tag{16}$$

According to (1) and (11), for each integer $k \geq 1$,

$$F(\rho(T^{i_{k,1}+1}(x_{n_k}), T^{i_{k,2}+1}(x_{n_k}))) \leq F(\rho(T^{i_{k,1}}(x_{n_k}), T^{i_{k,2}}(x_{n_k}))) - \tau. \tag{17}$$

In view of Proposition 2 and (15), we may assume that there exists

$$\Delta = \lim_{k \to \infty} \rho(T^{i_{k,1}+1}(x_{n_k}), T^{i_{k,2}+1}(x_{n_k})). \tag{18}$$

It follows from (15), (17) and (18) that

$$0 \leq \Delta \leq \epsilon. \tag{19}$$

Property (P1) and (15), (18) and (19) imply that

$$\Delta = \epsilon \tag{20}$$

and

$$\epsilon = \lim_{k \to \infty} \rho(T^{i_{k,1}+1}(x_{n_k}), T^{i_{k,2}+1}(x_{n_k})). \tag{21}$$

Since the function F is continuous at ϵ, Equations (15) and (21) imply that

$$\begin{aligned} F(\epsilon) &= \lim_{k \to \infty} F(\rho(T^{i_{k,1}+1}(x_{n_k}), T^{i_{k,2}+1}(x_{n_k}))) \\ &= \lim_{k \to \infty} F(\rho(T^{i_{k,1}}(x_{n_k}), T^{i_{k,2}}(x_{n_k}))). \end{aligned}$$

This contradicts (17) and proves property (P3).

Let $\epsilon > 0$. Property (P3) implies that there exists $n_0 \in \mathbf{N}$ such that for any triplet of integers i_1, i_2, n satisfying $n_0 \leq i_1, i_2 \leq n$,

$$\rho(T^{i_1}(x_n), T^{i_2}(x_n)) \leq \epsilon/4. \tag{22}$$

Property (P2) implies that there exists a natural number $m_0 \geq n_0$ such that for any triplet of integers i, n_1, n_2 satisfying $n_1, n_2, i \geq m_0,\ i \leq n_j,\ j = 1,2$ we have

$$\rho(T^i(x_{n_1}), T^i(x_{n_2})) \leq \epsilon/4. \tag{23}$$

Assume that integers n_1, n_2, i_1, i_2 satisfy

$$m_0 \leq i_1 \leq n_1,\ m_0 \leq i_2 \leq n_2. \tag{24}$$

According to (22)–(24),

$$\rho(T^{i_1}(x_{n_1}), T^{i_2}(x_{n_1})) \leq \epsilon/4,$$

$$\rho(T^{i_1}(x_{n_1}), T^{i_2}(x_{n_2})) \leq \epsilon/4,$$

$$\rho(T^{i_1}(x_{n_1}), T^{i_1}(x_{n_2})) \leq \epsilon/4,\ \rho(T^{i_2}(x_{n_1}), T^{i_2}(x_{n_2})) \leq \epsilon/4.$$

These relations imply that

$$\rho(T^{i_1}(x_{n_1}), T^{i_2}(x_{n_2})) \leq \rho(T^{i_1}(x_{n_1}), T^{i_2}(x_{n_1})) + \rho(T^{i_2}(x_{n_1}), T^{i_2}(x_{n_2})) \leq \epsilon/2. \tag{25}$$

Thus, we have shown that the following property holds:

For (P4), if integers i_1, i_2, n_1, n_2 satisfy (24), then (25) holds.

In view of (P4), the sequences $\{T^{n-1}(x_n)\}_{n=1}^{\infty}$ and $\{T^{n-2}(x_n)\}_{n=2}^{\infty}$ converge and there exists

$$x_* = \lim_{n\to\infty} T^{n-1}(x_n) = \lim_{n\to\infty} T^{n-2}(x_n).$$

In view of Proposition 2, $x_* = T(x_*)$. Theorem 1 is proved. □

The following example illustrates Theorem 1. Assume that X is the collection of all continuous functions on $[0,1]$,

$$\rho(f_1, f_2) = \sup\{|f_1(t) - f_2(t)| :\ t \in [0,1]\},\ f_1, f_2 \in X,$$

$$K = \{f \in X :\ f([0,1]) \subset [0,1]\}$$

and

$$T(f) = 2^{-1}f + 2/3,\ f \in K.$$

Clearly, T is a Wardowski contraction with $F(t) = \ln(t),\ t > 0$ and $\tau = \ln(2)$. The formula above defines T for all $x \in X$, but we consider T to be a mapping from K to X. Evidently, T does not have a fixed point in T. In view of Theorem 1, $n \in \mathbf{N}$ can be found, such that $T^n(x) \notin K$ for any $x \in K$. A direct calculation shows that $n = 3$.

Let us consider the same mapping T with the same F and τ and

$$K = \{f \in X :\ f([0,1]) \subset [0,2]\} \cup \{f \in X :\ f([0,1]) \subset [10,11]\}.$$

It is not difficult to see that

$$T(K) \not\subset K$$

but T has a fixed point in K.

3. The Second Result

Assume that (X, ρ) is a complete metric space, $T : X \to 2^X \setminus \{\emptyset\}$; for each $x \in X$, the set $T(x)$ is closed and a function

$$\phi : [0,\infty) \to [0,\infty)$$

satisfies

$$\lim_{t\to 0}\phi(t) = 0. \tag{26}$$

In [17], it was shown that the set-valued T has a fixed point if for each $(x,y) \in X^2$ and each $u \in T(x)$ there is $v \in T(y)$, such that

$$\rho(u,v) + \phi(\rho(u,v)) \le \phi(\rho(x,y)).$$

Examples of such mappings are considered in [17]. Here, we show that T possesses a fixed point under a weaker assumption. Namely, we assume that the following assumption holds:

(A) For each $x, y \in X$ and each $u \in T(x)$,

$$\inf\{\rho(u,v) + \phi(\rho(u,v)) : v \in T(y)\} \le \phi(x,y). \tag{27}$$

Theorem 2. *1. Assume that* $\{\epsilon_i\}_{i=0}^{\infty} \subset (0,\infty)$,

$$\sum_{i=0}^{\infty} \epsilon_i < \infty, \tag{28}$$

$\{x_i\}_{i=0}^{\infty} \subset X$, *for each* $i \in \mathbf{N} \cup \{0\}$,

$$x_{i+1} \in T(x_i), \tag{29}$$

$$\rho(x_{i+1}, x_{i+2}) + \phi(\rho(x_{i+1}, x_{i+2})) \le \phi(\rho(x_i, x_{i+1})) + \epsilon_i. \tag{30}$$

(This sequence exists according to assumption (A)). Then, the sequence $\{x_i\}_{i=0}^{\infty}$ *converges to a fixed point of* T.

2. Let $\epsilon > 0$. *Then,* $\delta \in (0,\epsilon)$ *can be found such that for each* $x_0 \in X$ *satisfying* $\rho(x_0, T(x_0)) < \delta$, *there exists* $x_* \in B(x_0,\epsilon)$ *such that* $x_* \in T(x_*)$.

Proof. Let us prove Assertion 1. According to (30), for each integer $i \ge 0$,

$$\rho(x_{i+1}, x_{i+2}) \le \phi(\rho(x_i, x_{i+1})) - \phi(\rho(x_{i+1}, x_{i+2})) + \epsilon_i, \tag{31}$$

$$\phi(\rho(x_{i+1}, x_{i+2})) \le \phi(\rho(x_i, x_{i+1})) + \epsilon_i, \tag{32}$$

$$\phi(\rho(x_{i+1}, x_{i+2})) \le \phi(\rho(x_0, x_1)) + \sum_{j=0}^{\infty} \epsilon_j. \tag{33}$$

Let $m > n \ge 1$ be integers. In view of (30),

$$\rho(x_n, x_m) \le \sum_{i=n-1}^{m-1} \rho(x_{i+1}, x_{i+2})$$

$$\le \sum_{i=n-1}^{m-1} (\phi(\rho(x_i, x_{i+1})) - \phi(\rho(x_{i+1}, x_{i+2})) + \epsilon_i)$$

$$= \phi(\rho(x_{n-1}, x_n)) - \phi(\rho(x_{m-1}, x_m)) + \sum_{i=n-1}^{m-1} \epsilon_i. \tag{34}$$

We claim that there exists

$$\lim_{n\to\infty} \phi(\rho(x_n, x_{n+1})).$$

According to (33), the sequence $\{\phi(\rho(x_n, x_{n+1}))\}_{n=0}^{\infty}$ is bounded. Let

$$r = \liminf_{n\to\infty} \phi(\rho(x_n, x_{n+1})). \tag{35}$$

We claim that

$$\lim_{n\to\infty} \phi(\rho(x_n, x_{n+1})) = r.$$

Let $\epsilon > 0$. According to (35), there exists a natural number n_0 such that for each integer $n \geq n_0$,

$$\phi(\rho(x_n, x_{n+1})) \geq r - \epsilon/8. \tag{36}$$

Equations (28) and (35) imply that there exists a natural number $n_1 > n_0$ such that

$$\sum_{i=n_1}^{\infty} \epsilon_i < \epsilon/8, \tag{37}$$

$$\phi(\rho(x_{n_1}, x_{n_1+1})) < r + \epsilon/8. \tag{38}$$

According to (32), (37) and (38), for any integer $n > n_1$,

$$\phi(\rho(x_n, x_{n+1})) \leq \phi(\rho(x_{n_1}, x_{n_1+1})) + \sum_{i=n_1}^{\infty} \epsilon_i < r + \epsilon/8 + \epsilon/8.$$

Thus, for any integer $n > n_1$,

$$|\phi(\rho(x_n, x_{n+1})) - r| < \epsilon/4 \tag{39}$$

and

$$\lim_{n\to\infty} \phi(\rho(x_n, x_{n+1})) = r. \tag{40}$$

According to (34), (37) and (39), for any pair of integers $m > n > n_1$,

$$\rho(x_n, x_m) \leq \phi(\rho(x_{n-1}, x_n)) - \phi(\rho(x_{m-1}, x_m)) + \sum_{i=n_1}^{\infty} \epsilon_i < \epsilon.$$

Thus, $\{x_n\}_{n=0}^{\infty}$ is a Cauchy sequence and there exists

$$x_* = \lim_{n\to\infty} x_n.$$

Assumption (A) and (29) imply that for any $n \in \mathbf{N}$, there exists

$$v_n \in T(x_*)$$

such that

$$\rho(x_{n+1}, v_n) + \phi(\rho(x_{n+1}, v_n)) \leq \phi(\rho(x_n, x_*)) + \epsilon_n \to 0 \text{ as } n \to \infty.$$

According to (26), (28) and (40),

$$\lim_{n\to\infty} \rho(x_{n+1}, v_n) = 0, \ \lim_{n\to\infty} v_n = x_*$$

and $x_* \in T(x_*)$. Assertion 1 is proved.

Let us proved Assertion 2. According to (26), there exists $\delta \in (0, \epsilon)$ such that for each $t \in [0, \delta]$,

$$\phi(t) < \epsilon/4. \tag{41}$$

Assume that $x_0 \in X$ satisfies

$$\rho(x_0, T(x_0)) < \delta. \tag{42}$$

Choose $\{\epsilon_i\}_{i=0}^{\infty} \subset (0,1)$ such that

$$\sum_{i=0}^{\infty} \epsilon_i < \epsilon/4. \tag{43}$$

In view of (42), there is

$$x_1 \in T(x_0)$$

for which

$$\rho(x_0, x_1) < \delta.$$

Assume that a sequence $\{x_i\}_{i=2}^{\infty}$ is as in Assertion 1. Then, there exists

$$x_* = \lim_{n\to\infty} x_n$$

such that

$$x_* \in T(x_*)$$

and in view of (34) and (41)–(43),

$$\sum_{i=1}^{\infty} \rho(x_i, x_{i+1}) \le \phi(\rho(x_0, x_1)) + \sum_{i=0}^{\infty} \epsilon_i$$

$$\le \phi(\rho(x_0, x_1)) + \epsilon/4 < \epsilon/2,$$

$$\sum_{i=1}^{\infty} \rho(x_i, x_{i+1}) < \epsilon,\ \rho(x_*, x_0) < \epsilon.$$

Assertion 2 is proved. □

Theorem 3. *Assume that the function ϕ is bounded, $\epsilon \in (0,1)$,*

$$M_1 > \phi(t),\ t \in [0,\infty), \tag{44}$$

$$n_0 > 2 + 2\epsilon^{-1} M_1 \tag{45}$$

is an integer and that $\{x_i\}_{i=0}^{n_0} \subset X$ satisfies for each integer $i \in \{0, \dots, n_0 - 1\}$,

$$x_{i+1} \subset T(x_i) \tag{46}$$

and for any $i \in \{0, \dots, n_0 - 2\}$,

$$\rho(x_{i+1}, x_{i+2}) + \phi(\rho(x_{i+1}, x_{i+2})) \le \phi(\rho(x_i, x_{i+1})) + \epsilon/2. \tag{47}$$

Then, there exists $j \in \{1, \dots, n_0 - 1\}$, for which

$$\rho(x_j, x_{j+1}) \le \epsilon,\ B(x_j, \epsilon) \cap T(x_j) \ne \emptyset.$$

Proof. Assume that the theorem does not hold. Then,

$$\rho(x_j, x_{j+1}) > \epsilon,\ j \in \{1, \dots, n_0 - 1\}. \tag{48}$$

According to (44), (47) and (48), for each $i \in \{0, \dots, n_0 - 2\}$,

$$\epsilon < \rho(x_{i+1}, x_{i+2}) \le \phi(\rho(x_i, x_{i+1})) - \phi(\rho(x_{i+1}, x_{i+2})) + \epsilon/2$$

and

$$(n_0 - 1)\epsilon < \sum_{i=0}^{n_0-2} \rho(x_{i+1}, x_{i+2})$$

$$\leq 2^{-1}\epsilon(n_0 - 1) + \sum_{i=0}^{n_0-2} \phi(\rho(x_i, x_{i+1})) - \phi(\rho(x_{i+1}, x_{i+2}))$$
$$\leq 2^{-1}\epsilon(n_0 - 1) + \phi(\rho(x_0, x_1)),$$
$$2^{-1}\epsilon(n_0 - 1) \leq M_1$$

and
$$n_0 \leq 1 + 2\epsilon^{-1}M_1.$$

This contradicts (45) and proves Theorem 3. □

Applying Theorem 3 by induction, we can obtain the following result.

Corollary 1. *Assume that the function ϕ is bounded, $\epsilon \in (0,1)$,*
$$M_1 > \phi(t),\ t \in [0,\infty),$$
$$n_0 > 2 + 2\epsilon^{-1}M_1$$
is an integer and that a sequence $\{x_i\}_{i=0}^{\infty} \subset X$ satisfies for any $i \in \mathbf{N} \cup \{0\}$,
$$x_{i+1} \in T(x_i)$$
and
$$\rho(x_{i+1}, x_{i+2}) + \phi(\rho(x_{i+1}, x_{i+2})) \leq \phi(\rho(x_i, x_{i+1})) + \epsilon/2.$$
Then, there exists $\{n_k\}_{k=1}^{\infty} \subset \mathbf{N}$ such that $n_1 \leq n_0$ and that for any $k \in \mathbf{N}$,
$$1 \leq n_{k+1} - n_k,\ \rho(x_{n_k}, x_{n_k+1}) \leq \epsilon.$$

Theorem 4. *Assume that the function ϕ is bounded, $\epsilon \in (0,1)$, $\epsilon_0 \in (0,\epsilon)$,*
$$M_1 > \phi(t),\ t \in [0,\infty),$$
$$\phi(t) \leq \epsilon/2,\ t \in [0,\epsilon_0), \tag{49}$$
$$n_0 > 2 + 2\epsilon_0^{-1}M_1 \tag{50}$$
is an integer,
$$\delta = (2n_0)^{-1}\epsilon_0 \tag{51}$$
and that a sequence $\{x_i\}_{i=0}^{\infty} \subset X$ satisfies for any $i \in \mathbf{N} \cup \{0\}$,
$$x_{i+1} \in T(x_i) \tag{52}$$
and
$$\rho(x_{i+1}, x_{i+2}) + \phi(\rho(x_{i+1}, x_{i+2})) \leq \phi(\rho(x_i, x_{i+1})) + \delta. \tag{53}$$
Then, $\rho(x_i, x_{i+1}) \leq \epsilon$ for each integer $i \geq n_0$.

Proof. Corollary 1 implies that there exists $\{n_k\}_{k=1}^{\infty} \subset \mathbf{N}$ such that $n_1 \leq n_0$ and that for any $k \in \mathbf{N}$,
$$1 \leq n_{k+1} - n_k \leq n_0, \tag{54}$$
$$\rho(x_{n_k}, x_{n_k+1}) \leq \epsilon_0. \tag{55}$$

Let $k \geq 1$ be an integer. According to (49), (51), (53) and (55),
$$\sum_{i=n_k}^{n_{k+1}} \rho(x_i, x_{i+1}) \leq \sum_{i=n_k}^{n_{k+1}} (\phi(\rho(x_i, x_{i+1})) - \phi(\rho(x_{i+1}, x_{i+2}))) + n_0\delta$$

and

$$\epsilon > \epsilon/2 + \epsilon_0/2 \geq \phi(\rho(x_{n_k}, x_{n_k+1})) + n_0\delta \geq \sum_{i=n_k+1}^{n_{k+1}} \rho(x_i, x_{i+1}).$$

This completes the proof of Theorem 4. □

Our results from this section can be applied to the following problem, considered in [17]. Assume that $a < b$ are real numbers, X is the space $C([a,b])$ of all real-valued continuous functions and that

$$\rho(f_1, f_2) = \sup\{|f_1(t) - f_2(t)| : t \in [a,b]\}, \ f_1, f_2 \in X.$$

We consider a Fredholm-type integral inclusion:

$$x(\tau) \in \int_a^b K(\tau, t, x(t))dt + f(\tau), \ \tau \in [a,b].$$

It was shown in [17] that the study of this problem is reduced to the analysis of a fixed point problem

$$T(z) = \{y \in X : y(\tau) \in \int_a^b K(\tau, s, z(s))ds + f(\tau), \ \tau \in [a,b]\}, \ z \in X$$

and that for mapping T, all the assumptions made in this section hold. Therefore, all the results can be applied for T.

4. The Third Result

Assume that (X, ρ) is endowed with a graph G. Let $V(G)$ be the set of its vertices, $E(G)$ be the set of its edges and let

$$(x, x) \in E(G), \ x \in X.$$

Assume that $\tau > 0$, $F : (0, \infty) \to R^1$ is an increasing function and that $T : X \to X$ is a mapping such that for any $(x, y) \in E(G)$ for which $x \neq y$,

$$(T(x), T(y)) \in E(G) \ \text{and} \ F(\rho(T(x), T(y))) + \tau \leq F(\rho(x, y)). \tag{56}$$

Equation (56) implies the following proposition.

Proposition 3. *For any $(x, y) \in E(G)$, $\rho(T(x), T(y)) \leq \rho(x, y)$.*

Proposition 4. *Let $(x, y) \in E(G)$. Then*

$$\lim_{n \to \infty} \rho(T^n(x), T^n(y)) = 0.$$

Proof. We may assume that

$$T^n(x) \neq T^n(y)$$

for each integer $n \geq 0$. According to (56), for any integer $n \in \mathbf{N} \cup \{0\}$,

$$(T^n(x), T^n(y)) \in E(G),$$

$$F(\rho(T^{n+1}(x), T^{n+1}(y))) + \tau \leq F(\rho(T^n(x), T^n(y))),$$

$$F(\rho(T^n(x), T^n(y))) \leq F(\rho(x, y)) - n\tau. \tag{57}$$

Proposition 3 implies that for any $n \in \mathbf{N} \cup \{0\}$,

$$\rho(T^{n+1}(x), T^{n+1}(y)) \leq \rho(T^n(x), T^n(y)).$$

Assume that the proposition does not hold. Then, $\epsilon > 0$ can be found such that for any integer $n \geq 0$,

$$\epsilon \leq \rho(T^n(x), T^n(y)). \tag{58}$$

In view of (57) and (58), for each $n \in \mathbf{N} \cup \{0\}$,

$$F(\epsilon) \leq F(\rho(T^n(x), T^n(y))) \leq F(\rho(x,y)) - n\tau \to -\infty \text{ as } n \to \infty.$$

This contradiction proves Proposition 4. □

Proposition 4 implies the following result.

Proposition 5. *Let $x, y \in X$, $q \in \mathbf{N}$, $\{x_i\}_{i=0}^q \subset X$,*

$$x_0 = x,\ x_q = y,$$

$$(x_i, x_{i+1}) \in E(G),\ i = 0, \ldots, q-1.$$

Then,

$$\lim_{n\to\infty} \rho(T^n(x), T^n(y)) = 0.$$

Proposition 5 implies the following result.

Theorem 5. *Assume that $x \in X$ and there are $q \in \mathbf{N}$ and points $\{y_i\}_{i=0}^q \subset X$ such that*

$$y_0 = x,\ y_q = T(x),$$

$$(y_i, y_{i+1}) \in E(G),\ i = 0, \ldots, q-1.$$

Then,

$$\lim_{i\to\infty} \rho(T^i(x), T^{i+1}(x)) = 0.$$

Theorem 6. *Assume that $x \in X$ and there exist $q \in \mathbf{N}$ and $\{y_i\}_{i=0}^q$ such that*

$$y_0 = x,\ y_q = T(x),$$

$$(y_i, y_{i+1}) \in E(G),\ i = 0, \ldots, q-1.$$

Assume that there exists $m_0 \in \mathbf{N}$ such that the following property holds:
(P) for any pair of nonnegative integers $i < j$, there is

$$p \in \{j, \ldots, j + m_0\}$$

for which

$$(T^i(x), T^p(x)) \in E(G).$$

Then, the sequence $\{T^n(x)\}_{n=0}^\infty$ converges and its limit is a fixed point of T if the graph of T is closed.

Proof. According to Theorem 5,

$$\lim_{n\to\infty} \rho(T^n(x), T^{n+1}(x)) = 0. \tag{59}$$

Let $\epsilon \in (0,1)$. We show that for all sufficiently large $i, j \in \mathbf{N}$,

$$\rho(T^i(x), T^j(x)) \leq \epsilon.$$

Since the collection of all points at which F is not continuous is countable, we may assume that the function F is continuous at ϵ. Choose

$$\delta \in (0, \epsilon/4)$$

such that

$$|F(\xi) - F(\epsilon)| \leq \tau/2 \text{ for any } \xi \in [\epsilon - 4\delta, \epsilon + 4\delta] \tag{60}$$

and set

$$\delta_0 = \delta(4m_0)^{-1}. \tag{61}$$

In view of (59), there exists a natural number n_0 for which

$$\rho(T^i(x), T^{i+1}(x)) \leq \delta_0 \text{ for each integer } i \geq n_0. \tag{62}$$

Assume that

$$j > i \geq n_0$$

are integers. We show that

$$\rho(T^i(x), T^j(x)) \leq \epsilon.$$

Assume the contrary. Then,

$$\rho(T^i(x), T^j(x)) > \epsilon. \tag{63}$$

According to (61) and (62), we may assume that for any $s \in \{i, \dots, j-1\}$,

$$\rho(T^i(x), T^s(x)) \leq \epsilon. \tag{64}$$

According to Equation (62), for any $s \in \{i+1, \dots, i+m_0\}$,

$$\rho(T^i(x), T^s(x)) \leq \delta_0 m_0 < \delta < \epsilon. \tag{65}$$

According to (63) and (65),

$$j > i + m_0, \ j - 1 \geq i + m_0. \tag{66}$$

In view of (66),

$$j - m_0 > i$$

and (P) implies that there is

$$p \in \{j - m_0 - 1, \dots, j-1\} \tag{67}$$

for which

$$(T^i(x), T^p(x)) \in E(G). \tag{68}$$

According to (67) and (68),

$$p \geq i.$$

If

$$T^p(x) = T^i(x),$$

then according to (62) and (67),

$$\rho(T^i(x), T^j(x)) \leq \sum\{\rho(T^s(x), T^{s+1}(x)) : \ s \in \{p, \dots, j-1\}\} \leq m_0\delta_0 \leq \epsilon$$

and this contradicts (63). Therefore,

$$T^p(x) \neq T^i(x). \tag{69}$$

According to (56), (64), (67) and (69),

$$F(\rho(T^{i+1}(x), T^{p+1}(x))) + \tau \le F(\rho(T^i(x), T^p(x))) \le F(\epsilon). \tag{70}$$

It follows from (60) and (70) that

$$\rho(T^{i+1}(x), T^{p+1}(x)) \le \epsilon - 4\delta. \tag{71}$$

According to (61), (62), (67) and (71),

$$\rho(T^i(x), T^j(x)) \le \rho(T^i(x), T^{i+1}(x)) + \rho(T^{i+1}(x), T^{p+1}(x))$$
$$+\rho(T^{p+1}(x), T^j(x)) \le \delta_0 + \epsilon - 4\delta$$
$$+\sum\{\rho(T^s(x), T^{s+1}(x)) : s \in \{p, \dots, j-1\} \setminus \{p\}\} \le \delta_0 + \epsilon - 4\delta + m_0\delta_0 < \epsilon.$$

This contradicts (63) and proves Theorem 6. □

Theorem 6 was proved under assumption (P). It holds in the following two cases. In the first case, X is equipped with an order $\le$ and $(x, y) \in E(G)$ if and only if $x \le y$. In the second case, m is a natural number $A_i \subset X$, $i = 1, \dots, m$ are nonempty closed sets, $A_{m+1} = A_1$, $\cup_{i=1}^m A_i = X$,

$$T : \cup_{i=1}^m A_i \to \cup_{i=1}^m A_i$$

and for any $i \in \{1, \dots, m\}$, any $a \in A_i$, any $b \in A_{i+1}$,

$$T(A_i) \subset A_{i+1},$$

$$F(\rho(T(a), T(b))) + \tau \le F(\rho(a, b))$$

and

$$E(G) = \cup_{i=1}^m (A_i \times A_{i+1}).$$

In this case, T is called a cyclical operator [6].

Let us consider the following example [19]. Assume that $X = [0, \infty)$, $\rho(u, v) = |u - v|$, $u, v \in [0, \infty)$ and that $(u, v) \in E(G)$ if and only if $u \le v$ and

$$(u, v) \in [0, 1] \times [0, 1] \cup \cup_{n=1}^{\infty} (n, n+1] \times (n, n+1],$$

$$T(0) = 0,\ T(u) = 2^{-1}u + n/2,\ u \in (n, n+1],\ n = 0, 1, \dots.$$

It was shown in [19] that for each $(u, v) \in E(G)$,

$$\rho(T(u), T(v)) \le 2^{-1}\rho(u, v).$$

It is not difficult to see that T is a Wardowski contraction with $F(t) = \ln(t),\ t > 0$ and $\tau = \ln(2)$.

5. Conclusions

We consider three fixed point problems, and for each of them establish the existence of a fixed point. In the first and the third cases, we consider single-valued Wardowski type contraction, while in the second case we study Cho-type set-valued contractions. In the second case, we also study approximate fixed points.

Funding: This research received no external funding.

Data Availability Statement: Data are contained within the article.

Conflicts of Interest: The authors declare no conflicts of interest.

References

1. Banach, S. Sur les opérations dans les ensembles abstraits et leur application aux équations intégrales. *Fund. Math.* **1922**, *3*, 133–181. [CrossRef]
2. Bargetz, C.; Medjic, E. On the rate of convergence of iterated Bregman projections and of the alternating algorithm. *J. Math. Anal. Appl.* **2020**, *481*, 23. [CrossRef]
3. Du, W.-S. Some generalizations of fixed point theorems of Caristi type and Mizoguchi–Takahashi type under relaxed conditions. *Bull. Braz. Math. Soc.* **2019**, *50*, 603–624. [CrossRef]
4. Karapinar, E.; Mitrovic, Z.; Ozturk, A.; Radenovic, S. On a theorem of Ciric in b-metric spaces. *Rend. Circ. Mat. Palermo* **2021**, *70*, 217–225. [CrossRef]
5. Khamsi, M.A.; Kozlowski, W.M. *Fixed Point Theory in Modular Function Spaces*; Birkhäuser/Springer: Cham, Switzerland, 2015.
6. Radenovic, S.; Dosenovic, T.; Lampert, T.A.; Golubovic, Z.A. A note on some recent fixed point results for cyclic contractions in b-metric spaces and an application to integral equations. *Appl. Math. Comput.* **2015**, *273*, 155–164. [CrossRef]
7. Rakotch, E. A note on contractive mappings. *Proc. Amer. Math. Soc.* **1962**, *13*, 459–465. [CrossRef]
8. Bojor, F. Fixed point theorems for Reich type contractions on metric spaces with a graph. *Nonlinear Anal.* **2012**, *75*, 3895–3901. [CrossRef]
9. Jachymski, J. The contraction principle for mappings on a metric space with a graph. *Proc. Amer. Math. Soc.* **2008**, *136*, 1359–1373. [CrossRef]
10. Suantai, S.; Donganont, M.; Cholamjiak, W. Hybrid methods for a countable family of G-nonexpansive mappings in Hilbert spaces endowed with graphs. *Mathematics* **2019**, *7*, 936. [CrossRef]
11. Suparatulatorn, R.; Cholamjiak, W.; Suanta, S. A modified S-iteration process for G-nonexpansive mappings in Banach spaces with graphs. *Numer. Algorithms* **2018**, *77*, 479–490. [CrossRef]
12. Younis, M.; Ahmad, H.; Chen, L.; Han, M. Computation and convergence of fixed points in graphical spaces with an application to elastic beam deformations. *J. Geom. Phys.* **2023**, *192*, 104955. [CrossRef]
13. Wardowski, D. Fixed points of a new type of contractive mappings in complete metric spaces. *Fixed Point Theory Appl.* **2012**, *94*, 6. [CrossRef]
14. Fabiano, N.; Kadelburg, Z.; Mirkov, N.; Cavic, V.S.; Radenovic, S. On F-contractions: A Survey. *Contemp. Math.* **2022**, *3*, 327–342. [CrossRef]
15. Parvaneh, M.; Farajzadeh, A.P. On weak Wardowski-Presic-type fixed point theorems via noncompactness measure with applications to a system of fractional integral equations. *J. Nonlinear Convex Anal.* **2023**, *24*, 1–15.
16. Rakocevic, V.; Roy, K.; Saha, M. Wardowski and Ciric type fixed point theorems over non-triangular metric spaces. *Quaest. Math.* **2022**, *45*, 1759–1769. [CrossRef]
17. Cho, S.-H. Fixed point theorems for set-valued contractions in metric spaces. *Axioms* **2024**, *13*, 86. [CrossRef]
18. Rudin, W. *Principles of Mathematical Analysis*; McGraw-Hill: New York, NY, USA, 1964.
19. Uddin, I.; Garodia, C.; Nieto, J.J. Mann iteration for monotone nonexpansive mappings in ordered CAT(0) space with an application to integral equations. *J. Inequal. Appl.* **2018**, *2018*, 339. [CrossRef] [PubMed]

axioms

MDPI

Article

Fixed-Point Results of Generalized (ϕ, Ψ)-Contractive Mappings in Partially Ordered Controlled Metric Spaces with an Application to a System of Integral Equations

Mohammad Akram [1], Salha Alshaikey [2], Umar Ishtiaq [3], Muhammad Farhan [4], Ioannis K. Argyros [5,*] and Samundra Regmi [6,*]

1 Department of Mathematics, Faculty of Science, Islamic University of Madinah, Madinah 42351, Saudi Arabia; akramkhan_20@rediffmail.com
2 Mathematics Department, Al-Qunfudah University College, Umm Al-Qura University, Mecca 24382, Saudi Arabia; sashaikey@uqu.edu.sa
3 Department of Mathematics, Quaid-i-Azam University, Islamabad 45320, Pakistan; umarishtiaq000@gmail.com
4 Department of Mathematics, National University of Modern Languages Islamabad, Multan Campus, Multan 59300, Pakistan; muhammadfarhan@numl.edu.pk
5 Department of Computing and Mathematical Sciences, Cameron University, Lawton, OK 73505, USA
6 Department of Mathematics, University of Houston, Houston, TX 77204, USA
* Correspondence: iargyros@cameron.edu (I.K.A.); sregmi5@uh.edu (S.R.)

Abstract: In this manuscript, we prove numerous results concerning fixed points, common fixed points, coincidence points, coupled coincidence points, and coupled common fixed points for (ϕ, Ψ)-contractive mappings in the framework of partially ordered controlled metric spaces. Our findings introduce a novel perspective on this mathematical context, and we illustrate the uniqueness of our findings through various explanatory examples. Also, we apply the main result to find the existence and uniqueness of the solution of the system of integral equations as an application.

Keywords: fixed point; controlled metric space; contraction mappings; system of integral equations

MSC: 47H10, 54H25

1. Introduction

The fixed-point (FP) theory is a pivotal branch in mathematics and has found extensive applications across various disciplines, ranging from functional analysis and topology to physics, economics, and beyond. The essence of FP theory is the investigation of mappings that retain certain points during transformation, which serves as a foundational tool for understanding equilibrium and stability in various systems. In 1993, Czerwik [1] introduced the notion of the b-metric space (BMS) and proved the Banach contraction principle (BCP) in the framework of the complete BMS. This pioneering work established the groundwork for following research on endeavors in BMSs, establishing a diverse field of study. Further, in 2019, Mlaiki et al. [2] extended this preliminary work by including (Ω, ω)-admissible mappings and generalized quasi-contraction in the setting of BMSs, unveiling deeper insights into the FP results. In 2019, Faraji et al. [3] delved into Geraghty-type contractive mappings, utilizing BMSs to not only present the BCP, but also give the solutions for nonlinear integral equations and highlighting the real-life significance of these theoretical developments. In 2020, subsequent advancements by Abbas et al. [4] presented the generalization of the BCP by introducing the Suzuki-type multi-valued mapping and examining coincident and common FPs in the context of the BMS. These findings acted as accelerators for other research efforts, resulting in a series of consequences and insights throughout the area of the BMS, as indicated by the works [5–8].

In 2018, Mlaiki et al. [9] incorporated controlled functions in the triangle inequality. This novel concept paved the way for a more generalized form of the Banach FP theorem (BFPT), offering a broader scope for applications and theoretical investigations in the FP theory. In 2003, Ran and Reurings [10] used the notion of a partially ordered metric space, and their formulation of the BFPT imposed contractivity conditions exclusively on elements comparable within a partial order, as well as imposed the contractivity condition on the nonlinear map exclusively for elements that can be compared within the partial order. Later, in 2010, Amini-Harandi and Emami [11] investigated the existence and uniqueness of solutions for periodic and boundary-value problems using partially ordered complete metric spaces and the Banach contraction principle (BCP), showcasing the applicability of the FP theory in addressing real-world problems in various domains. In 2022, Farhan et al. [12] discussed Reich-type and (α, F)-contractions in partially ordered double controlled metric-type spaces (PODCMSs), illuminating the solution of nonlinear fractional differential equations through a monotonic iterative approach.

The emergence of coupled FPs (CFPs), initially introduced by Bhaskar and Lakshmikantham [13], was utilized to investigate and analyze the presence and exclusivity of solutions for boundary-value problems. Further, in 2009, Lakshmikantham and Ćirić [14] were the pioneers in introducing the concept of the coupled coincidence FP (CCFP) and coupled common FP for nonlinear contractive mappings with a monotone property in partially ordered complete metric spaces (POCMSs). In 2011, Choudhury et al. [15] with their results applied a control function to extend the coupled contraction mapping theorem (CCMT) developed by Gnana Bhaskar and Lakshmikantham in partially ordered metric spaces to a coupled coincidence point conclusion for two compatible mappings. Additionally, it was assumed that the mappings satisfy a weak contractive inequality. In 2020, Mitiku et al. [16] unified fundamental metrical FP theorems, establishing coincidence points, coupled coincidences, and the CCFP for generalized (ϕ, ψ)-contractive mappings in partially ordered b-metric spaces. For more on this, see the related literature [17–20]. Brzdęk et al. [21] proved a fixed point theorem and the Ulam stability in generalized dq-metric spaces. Antón-Sancho [22,23] presented fixed points of principal E six-bundles over a compact algebraic curve and of the automorphisms of the vector bundle moduli space over a compact Riemann surface.

In this study, our aim is to go deeper into the realm of coincidence points, coupled coincidences, and CCFPs within the context of generalized (ϕ, ψ)-contractive mappings. These results are developed within the framework of partially ordered controlled-type metric spaces.

2. Preliminaries

In this section, we explain some core concepts that will be helpful for the proof of our main results.

Definition 1 ([1]). *Assume a non-empty set Ω and the function $s \geq 1$ to be a given real number. A mapping $\Theta : \Omega \times \Omega \longrightarrow [0, \infty)$ is said to be a b-metric space if the following axioms hold:*

(BM1) $\Theta(w_1, w_2) = 0$ if and only if $w_1 = w_2$;
(BM2) $\Theta(w_1, w_2) = \Theta(w_2, w_1)$ for all $w_1, w_2 \in \Omega$;
(BM3) $\Theta(w_1, w_3) \leq s[(\Theta(w_1, w_2) + \Theta((w_2, w_3)]$ for all $w_1, w_2, w_3 \in \Omega$.

Then, the pair (Ω, Θ) is called a b-metric space.

Definition 2 ([20]). *Consider a non-empty set Ω and $\alpha : \Omega \times \Omega \longrightarrow [1, \infty)$ to be a controlled function. Then, a mapping $\Theta : \Omega \times \Omega \longrightarrow [0, \infty)$ is said to be a controlled metric space if the following axioms hold:*

(CM1) $\Theta(w_1, w_2) = 0$ if and only if $w_1 = w_2$;
(CM2) $\Theta(w_1, w_2) = \Theta(w_2, w_1)$ for all $w_1, w_2 \in \Omega$;

(CM3) $\Theta(w_1, w_3) \leq \alpha(w_1, w_2)\Theta(w_1, w_2) + \alpha(w_2, w_3)\Theta(w_2, w_3)$ for all $w_1, w_2, w_3 \in \Omega$.

Then, the pair (Ω, Θ) is called a controlled metric space.

Definition 3 ([14]). *Assume $(\Omega, \preceq)$ to be a POS, and let $g, h : \Omega \longrightarrow \Omega$ be two mappings. Then, we have the following:*

1. *h is called a monotone non-decreasing sequence, if $h(u) \leq h(v)$, $\forall\, u, v \in \Omega$ with $u \preceq v$;*
2. *An element $u \in \Omega$ is a coincidence CFP of g and h, if $g(u) = h(u) = u$;*
3. *g and h are called commuting, if $(gh)(u) = (hg)(u)\ \forall\, u \in \Omega$;*
4. *g and h are compatible if any sequence (u_p) in Ω with*
$$\lim_{p \longrightarrow +\infty} g(u_p) = \lim_{p \longrightarrow +\infty} h(u_p) = \breve{u}$$
for some $\breve{u} \in \Omega$ implies
$$\lim_{p \longrightarrow +\infty} \Theta(hg(u_p), gh(u_p)) = 0;$$
5. *A pair (g, h) of self-mappings is named weakly compatible if*
$$hg(u_p) = gh(u_p)$$
when $h(u) = g(u)$ for some $u \in \Omega$;
6. *h is called monotone g-non-decreasing if $gu \preceq gv \Longrightarrow hu \preceq hv$ for any $u, v \in \Omega$;*
7. *$\Omega \neq \emptyset$ is said to be a well-ordered set if every two points of it are comparable, i.e., $u \preceq v$ and $v \preceq u$ for $u, v \in \Omega$.*

Definition 4 ([14]). *Assume that $(\Omega, \Theta, \preceq)$ is a POS, and consider two mappings $h : \Omega \times \Omega \longrightarrow \Omega$ and $g : \Omega \longrightarrow \Omega$ such that we have the following:*

1. *h has the mixed g-monotone property if h is non-decreasing g-monotone in its first argument and is non-increasing g-monotone in its second argument, that is, for any $u, v \in \Omega$,*
$$u_1, u_2 \in \Omega,\ gu_1 \preceq gu_2 \Longrightarrow h(u_1, v) \preceq h(u_2, v)$$
and
$$v_1, v_2 \in \Omega,\ gv_1 \preceq gv_2 \Longrightarrow h(v_1, u) \preceq h(v_2, u).$$
2. *An ordered pair element $(u, v) \in \Omega \times \Omega$ is said to be a coupled coincidence point (CCP) of h and g if the following relation holds:*
$$h(u, v) = gu \text{ and } h(v, u) = gv.$$
Also, if g is an identity mapping, then (u, v) is a CFP (CFP) of h.
3. *An element $u \in \Omega$ is said to have a common FP of g and h if*
$$h(u, u) = gu = u.$$
4. *g and h are commutative, if*
$$\forall\, u, v \in \Omega,\ h(gu, gv) = g(hu, hv)$$
g and h are compatible if
$$\lim_{p \longrightarrow +\infty} \Theta(g(h(u_n, v_n)), h(gu_n, gv_n)) = 0$$
and
$$\lim_{p \longrightarrow +\infty} \Theta(g(h(v_n, u_n)), h(gv_n, gu_n)) = 0,$$

whenever $\{u_n\}$ *and* $\{v_n\}$ *are two sequences in* Ω *such that, for all* $u, v \in \Omega$,

$$\lim_{p \longrightarrow +\infty} h(v_n, u_n) = \lim_{p \longrightarrow +\infty} g u_n = u$$

and

$$\lim_{p \longrightarrow +\infty} h(v_n, u_n) = \lim_{p \longrightarrow +\infty} g v_n = v.$$

The results presented here can be utilized for the convergence of a sequence in the controlled metric space (CMS).

Definition 5 ([16]). *Assume that a function* $\phi : [0, +\infty[\longrightarrow [0, +\infty[$ *is an altering distance function if it satisfies the following conditions:*

(a) *It is continuous and non-decreasing;*
(b) $\phi(l) = 0$ *if and only if* $l = 0$.

The set of all alternating distance functions is denoted by Φ.

Example 1. *Define*

$$\phi_1, \phi_2, \phi_3 : [0, +\infty[\rightarrow [0, +\infty[$$

by $\phi_1(l) = 2l$, $\phi_2(l) = 4l^2$, $\phi_3(l) = 7l^4$. *Then, they are alternating distance functions.*

Here, $\psi : R^+ \longrightarrow R^+$ is $\psi(l) = 0$ if and only if $l = 0$. The set of all lower semicontinuous functions is denoted by Ψ.

Assume $(\Omega, \Theta, \preceq, \alpha)$ to be a partially ordered controlled metric space (POCMS) with control function α and a mapping $h : \Omega \longrightarrow \Omega$. Set

$$M(u, v) = \max\left\{ \begin{array}{c} \frac{\Theta(v,hv)[1+\Theta(u,hu)]}{1+\Theta(u,v)}, \frac{\Theta(u,hu)\Theta(v,hv)}{1+\Theta(hu,hv)}, \\ \frac{\Theta(u,hu)\Theta(u,hv)}{1+\Theta(u,hv)+\Theta(v,hu)}, \Theta(u,v) \end{array} \right\} \quad (1)$$

and

$$N(u, v) = \max\left\{ \frac{\Theta(v, hv)[1 + \Theta(u, hu)]}{1 + \Theta(u, v)} \right\}. \quad (2)$$

Now, we introduce the following notions.

Definition 6. *If* $(p, \preceq)$ *is a partially ordered set (POS), then* $(\Omega, \Theta, \preceq, \alpha)$ *is said to be a POCMS.*

Definition 7. *Assume* $(\Omega, \Theta, \preceq, \alpha)$ *is a POCMS, then we have the following:*

1. *A sequence* (u_p) *is said to be convergent to a point* $u \in \Omega$ *if, for each* $\varepsilon > 0$,

$$\lim_{p \longrightarrow +\infty} \Theta(u_p, u) = 0$$

and written as

$$\lim_{p \longrightarrow +\infty} u_p = u;$$

2. (u_p) *is said to be a Cauchy sequence if*

$$\lim_{p,q \longrightarrow +\infty} \Theta(u_p, u_q) = 0;$$

3. *The pair* (Ω, Θ, α) *is called Cauchy if each Cauchy sequence in* Ω *is convergent in it.*

Definition 8. *If* Θ *is a complete metric, then* (Ω, Θ, α) *is called a complete POCMS (CPOCMS).*

Definition 9. *Assume $(\Omega, \Theta, \preceq, \alpha)$ to be a partially ordered controlled metric space (POCMS) with control function α and $\phi \in \Phi, \psi \in \Psi$. A self-mapping:*

$$h : \Omega \longrightarrow \Omega$$

is called a generalized (Φ, Ψ)-contractive mapping if it satisfies the inequality given below:

$$\phi(\alpha\Theta(hu, hv)) \leq \phi(M(u,v)) - \psi(N(u,v)) \tag{3}$$

for any $u, v \in \Omega$ with $u \preceq v$.

Lemma 1. *Assume $(\Omega, \Theta, \preceq, \alpha)$ to be a POCMS with control function α and $\{u_n\}$ and $\{v_n\}$ be two sequences that are α-convergent to u and v, respectively. Then,*

$$\frac{1}{\alpha^2}\Theta(u,v) \leq \lim_{p \longrightarrow +\infty} \inf \Theta(u_p, v_p) \leq \lim_{p \longrightarrow +\infty} \sup \Theta(u_p, v_p) \leq \alpha^2\Theta(u,v).$$

In a special case, if $u = v$, then

$$\Theta(u_p, v_p) = 0.$$

Additionally, for each $\tau \in \Omega$, we have

$$\frac{1}{\alpha}\Theta(u,v) \leq \lim_{p \longrightarrow +\infty} \inf \Theta(u_p, \tau) \leq \lim_{p \longrightarrow +\infty} \sup \Theta(u_p, \tau) \leq \alpha\Theta(u,v).$$

3. Main Results

In this section, we formulate the outcomes concerning the existence of coincidence points, coupled coincidences, and CCFPs in the realm of generalized (ϕ, ψ)-contractive mappings. These findings are developed within the specific setting of the POCMS.

Theorem 1. *Assume $(\Omega, \Theta, \preceq, \alpha)$ to be a CPOCMS with metric Θ and $\alpha : \Omega \times \Omega \longrightarrow [1, \infty)$ to be a controlled function. Assume a mapping $h : \Omega \longrightarrow \Omega$, which is an almost generalized (ϕ, ψ)-contractive mapping and a continuous, non-decreasing mapping with partial order $\preceq$. If there exists a $u_0 \in \Omega$ with $u_0 \preceq hu_0$, then h have the FP in Ω.*

Proof. Assume $u_0 \in \Omega$ to be an arbitrary point in Ω such that $u_0 = hu_0$, then we have a result. Assume $u_0 \preceq hu_0$, and define the sequence $\{u_p\}$ by $u_{p+1} = hu_p$, for all $p \geq 0$. As h is non-decreasing, so by induction, we obtain

$$u_0 \preceq hu_0 = u_1 \preceq \ldots \preceq u_n \preceq hu_n = u_{n+1} \preceq \ldots \tag{4}$$

If there exists $p_o \in N$ such that $u_{p_o} = u_{p_o+1}$, then from (4), u_{p_o} is an FP of h, then we have nothing to prove. Next, we assume that $u_p \neq u_{p+1}$ for all $p \geq 1$. Since $u_p > u_{p-1}$ for $n \geq 1$ and then from the contractive condition (3), we have

$$\begin{aligned} \phi(\Theta(u_p, u_{p+1})) &= \phi(\Theta(hu_{p-1}, u_p)) \\ &\leq \phi(\alpha\Theta(hu_{p-1}, u_p)) \end{aligned}$$

$$\leq \phi(M(u_{p-1}, u_p)) - \psi(N(u_{p-1}, u_p)), \tag{5}$$

then, from (5), we obtain

$$\Theta(u_p, u_{p+1}) = \Theta(hu_{p-1}, hu_p) \leq \frac{1}{\alpha}M(u_{p-1}, u_p) \tag{6}$$

where

$$
\begin{aligned}
M(u_{p-1}, u_p) &= \max\left\{\begin{array}{c} \frac{\Theta(u_p, hu_p)[1+\Theta(u_{p-1}, hu_{p-1})]}{1+\Theta(u_{p-1}, u_p)}, \frac{\Theta(u_{p-1}, hu_{p-1})\Theta(u_p, hu_p)}{1+\Theta(hu_{p-1}, hu_p)}, \\ \frac{\Theta(u_{p-1}, hu_{p-1})\Theta(u_{p-1}, hu_p)}{1+\Theta(u_{p-1}, hu_p)+\Theta(u_p, hu_{p-1})}, \Theta(u_{p-1}, u_p) \end{array}\right\} \\
&= \max\left\{\begin{array}{c} \frac{\Theta(u_p, hu_{p+1})[1+\Theta(u_{p-1}, hu_p)]}{1+\Theta(u_{p-1}, u_p)}, \frac{\Theta(u_{p-1}, u_p)\Theta(u_p, u_{p+1})}{1+\Theta(u_p, u_{p+1})}, \\ \frac{\Theta(u_{p-1}, u_p)\Theta(u_{p-1}, u_{p+1})}{1+\Theta(u_{p-1}, u_{p+1})+\Theta(u_p, u_p)}, \Theta(u_{p-1}, u_p) \end{array}\right\} \\
&\leq \max\{\Theta(u_p, u_{p+1}), \Theta(u_{p-1}, u_p)\},
\end{aligned} \tag{7}
$$

if

$$
\max\{\Theta(u_p, u_{p+1}), \Theta(u_{p-1}, u_p)\} = \Theta(u_p, u_{p+1})
$$

for some $p \geq 1$. So, from (6), it follows that

$$
\Theta(u_p, u_{p+1}) \leq \frac{1}{\alpha}\Theta(u_p, u_{p+1}), \tag{8}
$$

a contradiction. This implies that

$$
\max\{\Theta(u_p, u_{p+1}), \Theta(u_{p-1}, u_p)\} = \Theta(u_p, u_{p+1})
$$

for $p \geq 1$. Hence, from (6), we obtain

$$
\Theta(u_p, u_{p+1}) \leq \frac{1}{\alpha}\Theta(u_{p-1}, u_p). \tag{9}
$$

Since, $\frac{1}{\alpha} \in (0,1)$, then the sequence (u_p) is a Cauchy sequence by [6–9]. As Ω is complete, so there exists some element $\ddot{u} \in \Omega$ such that $u_p \longrightarrow \ddot{u}$. Moreover, the continuity of h implies that

$$
h\ddot{u} = h\left(\lim_{p \longrightarrow +\infty} u_p\right) = \lim_{p \longrightarrow +\infty} hu_p = \lim_{p \longrightarrow +\infty} u_{p+1} = \ddot{u}. \tag{10}
$$

Hence, $\ddot{u}$ is an FP of h in Ω. □

Theorem 2. *Assume $(\Omega, \Theta, \preceq, \alpha)$ to be a CPOCMS with metric Θ. Assume that a non-decreasing sequence $\{u_p\} \longrightarrow \ddot{u}$ in Ω, then $u_p \preceq \ddot{u}$ for all $p \in \mathbb{N}$, i.e., sup $u_p = \ddot{u}$. Let $h : \Omega \longrightarrow \Omega$ be a non-decreasing mapping that satisfies the contractive condition (3). If there exists a $u_0 \in \Omega$ with $u_0 \preceq hu_0$, then h has a fixed point in Ω.*

Proof. Using the proof of the above theorem, we construct a non-decreasing Cauchy sequence $\{u_p\}$, which converges to $\ddot{u}$ in Ω. So, we have $u_p \preceq \ddot{u}$ for any $p \in \mathbb{N}$, which implies that sup $u_p = \ddot{u}$.

Now, we have to prove that $\ddot{u}$ is an FP of h, i.e., $hu = u$. Assume that $hu \neq u$. Let

$$
M(u_p, \ddot{u}) = \max\left\{\begin{array}{c} \frac{\Theta(\ddot{u}, h\ddot{u})[1+\Theta(u_p, hu_p)]}{1+\Theta(u_p, \ddot{u})}, \frac{\Theta(u_p, hu_p)\Theta(\ddot{u}, h\ddot{u})}{1+\Theta(hu_p, h\ddot{u})}, \\ \frac{\Theta(u_p, hu_p)\Theta(u_p, h\ddot{u})}{1+\Theta(u_p, h\ddot{u})+\Theta(\ddot{u}, hu_p)}, \Theta(u_p, \ddot{u}) \end{array}\right\} \tag{11}
$$

and

$$
N(u_p, \ddot{u}) = \max\left\{\frac{\Theta(\ddot{u}, h\ddot{u})[1+\Theta(u_p, hu_p)]}{1+\Theta(u_p, \ddot{u})}, \Theta(u_p, \ddot{u})\right\}. \tag{12}
$$

Letting $p \longrightarrow +\infty$ and by utilizing

$$\lim_{p \longrightarrow +\infty} u_p = \ddot{u},$$

we conclude that

$$\lim_{p \longrightarrow +\infty} M(u_p, \ddot{u}) = \max\{\Theta(\ddot{u}, h\ddot{u}), 0, 0, 0\} = \Theta(\ddot{u}, h\ddot{u}), \tag{13}$$

and

$$\lim_{p \longrightarrow +\infty} N(u_p, \ddot{u}) = \max\{\Theta(\ddot{u}, h\ddot{u}), 0\} = \Theta(\ddot{u}, h\ddot{u}). \tag{14}$$

We know that, for all p, $u_p \preceq u$, then from the contractive condition (3), we obtain

$$\begin{aligned} \phi(\Theta(u_{p+1}, h\ddot{u})) &= \phi(\Theta(hu_p, h\ddot{u})) \leq \phi(\alpha\Theta(hu_p, h\ddot{u})) \\ &\leq \phi(M(u_p, \ddot{u})) - \psi(N(u_p, \ddot{u})). \end{aligned} \tag{15}$$

Letting $p \longrightarrow +\infty$ and using (13) and (14), we obtain

$$\phi(\Theta(\ddot{u}, h\ddot{u})) \leq \phi(\Theta(\ddot{u}, h\ddot{u})) - \psi(\Theta(\ddot{u}, h\ddot{u})) < \Theta(\ddot{u}, h\ddot{u}), \tag{16}$$

which is a contradiction, by the above inequality (16). Thus, $h\ddot{u} = \ddot{u}$. That is, $\ddot{u}$ is an FP of Ω. □

Now, we provide the essential condition for the uniqueness of the FP in Theorems 1 and 2.

Condition 1. *Every pair of elements has a lower bound or an upper bound.*

The above condition states that, $\forall\, u, v \in \Omega$, there exist an element $w \in \Omega$ such that w is comparable to u and v.

Theorem 3. *In addition, the hypothesis of Theorem 1 (or Theorem 2) and Condition 1 gives the uniqueness of an FP of h in Ω.*

Proof. By applying Theorems 1 and 2, we deduce that h has a non-empty set of FPs. Assume that u^* and u^{**} are two FPs of h in Ω. We want to prove that $u^* = u^{**}$. Assume, on the contrary, $u^* \neq u^{**}$, then by the hypothesis, we have

$$\phi(\Theta(hu^*, hu^{**})) \leq \phi(\alpha\Theta(hu^*, hu^{**})) \leq \phi(M(u^*, u^{**})) - \psi(N(u^*, u^{**})). \tag{17}$$

As a consequence, we obtain

$$\Theta(u^*, u^{**}) = \Theta(hu^*, hu^{**}) \leq \frac{1}{\alpha} M(u^*, u^{**}) \tag{18}$$

where

$$\begin{aligned} M(u^*, u^{**}) &= \max\left\{ \begin{array}{c} \frac{\Theta(u^{**}, hu^{**})[1+\Theta(u^*, hu^*)]}{1+\Theta(u^*, u^{**})}, \frac{\Theta(u^*, hu^*)\Theta(u^{**}, hu^{**})}{1+\Theta(hu^*, hu^{**})}, \\ \frac{\Theta(u^*, hu^*)\Theta(u^*, hu^{**})}{1+\Theta(u^*, hu^{**})+\Theta(u^{**}, hu^*)}, \Theta(u^*, u^{**}) \end{array} \right\} \\ &= \max\left\{ \begin{array}{c} \frac{\Theta(u^{**}, u^{**})[1+\Theta(u^*, u^*)]}{1+\Theta(u^*, u^{**})}, \frac{\Theta(u^*, u^*)\Theta(u^{**}, u^{**})}{1+\Theta(u^*, u^{**})}, \\ \frac{\Theta(u^*, u^*)\Theta(u^*, u^{**})}{1+\Theta(u^*, u^{**})+\Theta(u^{**}, u^*)}, \Theta(u^*, u^{**}) \end{array} \right\} \\ &= \max\{0, 0, 0, \Theta(u^*, u^{**})\} = \Theta(u^*, u^{**}). \end{aligned} \tag{19}$$

From inequality (18), we conclude that

$$\Theta(u^*, u^{**}) \leq \frac{1}{\alpha}\Theta(u^*, u^{**}) < \Theta(u^*, u^{**}), \tag{20}$$

which is a contradiction. By deduction, we obtain $u^* = u^{**}$. This completes the proof. □

Assume $(\Omega, \Theta, \preceq, \alpha)$ to be a POCMS with metric Θ and controlled function α. Assume that h, $g : \Omega \longrightarrow \Omega$ are two mappings. Set

$$M_f(u,v) = \max\left\{ \begin{array}{c} \frac{\Theta(gv,hv)[1+\Theta(gu,hu)]}{1+\Theta(gu,hv)}, \frac{\Theta(gu,hu)\Theta(gv,hv)}{1+\Theta(hu,hv)}, \\ \frac{\Theta(gu,hu)\Theta(gu,hv)}{1+\Theta(gu,hv)+\Theta(gv,hu)}, \Theta(gu,gv) \end{array} \right\} \tag{21}$$

and

$$N_f(u,v) = \max\left\{ \frac{\Theta(gv,hv)[1+\Theta(gu,hu)]}{1+\Theta(gu,gv)}, \Theta(gu,gv) \right\}. \tag{22}$$

Definition 10. *Assume $(\Omega, \Theta, \preceq, \alpha)$ to be a POCMS with metric Θ and controlled function α. We define a generalized (ϕ, ψ)-contraction mapping $h : \Omega \longrightarrow \Omega$ with respect to $g : \Omega \longrightarrow \Omega$ for some $\phi \in \Phi$ and $\psi \in \Psi$. Then, we say that $h : \Omega \longrightarrow \Omega$ is a generalized (ϕ, ψ)-contraction mapping if the inequality below holds:*

$$\phi(\alpha\Theta(hu,hv)) \leq \phi\Big(M_f(u,v)\Big) - \psi\Big(N_f(u,v)\Big) < \Theta(\ddot{u}, h\ddot{u}) \tag{23}$$

for any $u, v \in \Omega$ with $hu \preceq hv$; also, $M_f(u,v)$ and $N_f(u,v)$ are already defined in (21) and (22), respectively.

Theorem 4. *Assume $(\Omega, \Theta, \preceq, \alpha)$ to be a POCMS with metric Θ and controlled function α. We define a generalized (ϕ, ψ)-contraction mapping $h : \Omega \longrightarrow \Omega$ with respect to $g : \Omega \longrightarrow \Omega$; here, h and g are continuous such that h is a monotone g-non-decreasing mapping, compatible with g and $h\Omega \subseteq g\Omega$. If, for some $u_o \in \Omega$, such that $gu_o \preceq hp$, then h and g have a coincidence point in Ω.*

Proof. Using the proof of Theorem 2.2 presented in [4], consider two sequences $\{u_p\}$ and $\{v_p\}$ in Ω such that

$$v_p = hu_p = gu_{p+1} \tag{24}$$

for all $p \geq 0$, for which

$$gu_o \preceq gu_1 \preceq \dots gu_p \preceq gu_{p+1} \preceq \dots \tag{25}$$

By using [4], we want to prove that

$$\Theta(v_p, v_{p+1}) \leq \lambda\Theta(v_{p-1}, v_p) \tag{26}$$

for all $p \geq 0$; here, $\lambda \in \left[1, \frac{1}{\alpha}\right)$. Now, by (23) and using (24) and (25), we have

$$\begin{aligned} \phi(\alpha\Theta(v_p, v_{p+1})) &= \phi(\alpha\Theta(hv_p, hv_{p+1})) \\ &\leq \phi(M_g(v_p, v_{p+1})) - \psi(N_g(v_p, v_{p+1})) \end{aligned} \tag{27}$$

where

$$M_g(u_p, u_{p+1}) = \max\left\{ \begin{array}{c} \frac{\Theta(gu_{p+1},hu_{p+1})[1+\Theta(gu_p,hu_p)]}{1+\Theta(gu_p,gu_{p+1})}, \frac{\Theta(gu_p,hu_p)\Theta(gu_{p+1},hu_{p+1})}{1+\Theta(hu_p,hu_{p+1})}, \\ \frac{\Theta(gu_p,hu_p)\Theta(gu_p,hu_{p+1})}{1+\Theta(gu_p,hu_{p+1})+\Theta(hu_{p+1},gu_p)}, \Theta(gu_p, gu_{p+1}) \end{array} \right\}$$
$$= \max\left\{ \begin{array}{c} \frac{\Theta(v_p,v_{p+1})[1+\Theta(v_{p-1},v_p)]}{1+\Theta(v_{p-1},v_p)}, \frac{\Theta(v_{p-1},v_p)\Theta(v_p,v_{p+1})}{1+\Theta(v_p,v_{p+1})}, \\ \frac{\Theta(v_{p-1},v_p)\Theta(v_{p-1},v_{p+1})}{1+\Theta(v_{p-1},v_{p+1})+\Theta(v_p,v_p)}, \Theta(v_{p-1}, v_p) \end{array} \right\}$$
$$\leq \max\{\Theta(v_{p-1}, v_p), \Theta(v_p, v_{p+1})\}$$

and

$$N_g(u_p, u_{p+1}) = \max\left\{ \frac{\Theta(gu_{p+1}, hu_{p+1})[1 + \Theta(gu_p, hu_p)]}{1 + \Theta(gu_p, gu_{p+1})}, \Theta(gu_p, gu_{p+1}) \right\}$$
$$= \max\left\{ \frac{\Theta(v_p, v_{p+1})[1 + \Theta(v_{p-1}, v_p)]}{1 + \Theta(v_{p-1}, v_p)}, \Theta(v_{p-1}, v_p) \right\}$$
$$= \max\{\Theta(v_{p-1}, v_p), \Theta(v_p, v_{p+1})\}.$$

Consequently, from (27), we obtain

$$\phi(\alpha\Theta(v_p, v_{p+1})) \leq \phi\max\{\Theta(v_{p-1}, v_p), \Theta(v_p, v_{p+1})\} - \psi(\max\{\Theta(v_{p-1}, v_p), \Theta(v_p, v_{p+1})\}). \tag{28}$$

If $0 < \Theta(v_{p-1}, v_p) \leq \Theta(v_p, v_{p+1})$ for some $p \in \mathbb{N}$, then, from (28), we obtain

$$\phi(\alpha\Theta(v_p, v_{p+1})) \leq \phi(\Theta(v_p, v_{p+1})) - \psi(\Theta(v_p, v_{p+1})) < \phi(\Theta(v_p, v_{p+1})) \tag{29}$$

or, likewise,

$$\alpha\Theta(v_p, v_{p+1}) \leq \Theta(v_p, v_{p+1}), \tag{30}$$

which is a contradiction. So, from (28), we conclude that

$$\alpha\Theta(v_p, v_{p+1}) \leq \Theta(v_{p-1}, v_p) \tag{31}$$

Therefore, Equation (26) holds, and $\lambda \in \left[1, \frac{1}{\alpha}\right)$. Hence, by Equation (26) and Lemma 3.1 of [5], we deduce that

$$\{v_p\} = \{hu_p\} = \{gu_{p+1}\}$$

is a Cauchy sequence in Ω, and it converges to $\ddot{u} \in \Omega$. Also, as Ω is complete, so

$$\lim_{p \longrightarrow +\infty} hu_p = \lim_{p \longrightarrow +\infty} gu_{p+1} = \ddot{u}.$$

Hence, g and h are compatible, and we obtain

$$\lim_{p \longrightarrow +\infty} \Theta(g(hu_p), h(gu_p)) = 0. \tag{32}$$

Also, g and h are continuous mappings, so we have

$$\lim_{p \longrightarrow +\infty} g(hu_p) = g\ddot{u}, \text{ and } \lim_{p \longrightarrow +\infty} h(gu_p) = h\ddot{u}. \tag{33}$$

Furthermore, by using the triangular inequality and Equations (32) and (33), we obtain

$$\frac{1}{\alpha}\Theta(h\ddot{u}, g\ddot{u}) \leq \Theta(h\ddot{u}, h(gu_p)) + \alpha\Theta(h(gu_p), g(hu_p)) + \alpha\Theta(g(hu_p), g\ddot{u}) \tag{34}$$

Therefore, we find that

$$\Theta(hu, gu) = 0$$

as $p \longrightarrow +\infty$ in (34). Hence, u is a coincidence point of g and h in Ω. □

We deduce the result below by relaxing the continuity in Theorem 4 of g and h.

Theorem 5. *Consider that Ω satisfies, for any non-decreasing sequence $(gu_p) \subset \Omega$ in the above Theorem 4,*

$$\lim_{p \longrightarrow +\infty} g(u_p) = gu$$

in $g\Omega$, where $g\Omega$ is a closed subset of Ω, which implies that

$$gu_p \preceq gu, \ gu \preceq g(gu)$$

for $p \in \mathbb{N}$. If there exists $u_o \in \Omega$ such that $gu_o \preceq hu_o$, then the weakly compatible mappings h and g have a coincidence point in Ω. Furthermore, h and g have a common FP, if h and g commute at their coincidence points.

Proof. As we know that the sequence:

$$\{v_p\} = \{hu_p\} = \{gu_{p+1}\},$$

is a Cauchy sequence, as in above Theorem 4, therefore $g\Omega$ is closed; hence, we have some $\ddot{u} \in \Omega$ such that

$$\lim_{p \longrightarrow +\infty} hu_p = \lim_{p \longrightarrow +\infty} gu_{p+1} = g\ddot{u}.$$

Then, by the hypothesis, we have $gu_p \preceq g\ddot{u}$ for all $p \in \mathbb{N}$. Now, we will examine that $\ddot{u}$ is a coincidence point of h and g. By applying (23), we obtain

$$\phi(\alpha\Theta(hv_p, hu)) \leq \phi(M_g(u_p, u)) - \psi(N_g(u_p, u)) \tag{35}$$

where

$$\begin{aligned} M_g(u_p, \ddot{u}) &= \max\left\{ \begin{array}{c} \frac{\Theta(g\ddot{u},h\ddot{u})\left[1+\Theta(gu_p,hu_p)\right]}{1+\Theta(gu_p,g\ddot{u})}, \frac{\Theta(gu_p,hu_p)\Theta(g\ddot{u},h\ddot{u})}{1+\Theta(hu_p,h\ddot{u})} \\ , \frac{\Theta(gu_p,hu_p)\Theta(gu_p,h\ddot{u})}{1+\Theta(gu_p,h\ddot{u})+\Theta(g\ddot{u},hu_p)}, \Theta(gu_p, g\ddot{u}) \end{array} \right\} \\ &= \max\{\Theta(g\ddot{u}, g\ddot{u}), 0, 0, 0\} \\ &= \Theta(g\ddot{u}, g\ddot{u}) \text{ as } p \longrightarrow \infty \end{aligned}$$

and

$$\begin{aligned} N_g(u_p, \ddot{u}) &= \max\left\{ \frac{\Theta(g\ddot{u}, h\ddot{u})\left[1 + \Theta(gu_p, hu_p)\right]}{1 + \Theta(gu_p, g\ddot{u})}, \Theta(gu_p, g\ddot{u}) \right\} \\ &= \max\{\Theta(g\ddot{u}, g\ddot{u}), 0\} \\ &= \Theta(g\ddot{u}, g\ddot{u}) \text{ as } p \longrightarrow \infty. \end{aligned}$$

So, Equation (35) becomes

$$\phi\left(\alpha \lim_{p \longrightarrow +\infty} \Theta(hu_p, hu)\right) \leq \phi\Theta(g\ddot{u}, h\ddot{u}) - \psi(\Theta(g\ddot{u}, h\ddot{u})) < \phi\Theta(g\ddot{u}, h\ddot{u}). \tag{36}$$

Consequently, we obtain

$$\lim_{p \longrightarrow +\infty} \Theta(hu_p, hu) < \frac{1}{\alpha}\Theta(g\ddot{u}, h\ddot{u}). \tag{37}$$

Moreover, by the triangular inequality, we have

$$\frac{1}{\alpha}\Theta(g\ddot{u},h\ddot{u}) \leq \Theta(g\ddot{u},hu_p) + \Theta(hu_p,h\ddot{u}), \tag{38}$$

then by (38) and (39), this leads to a contradiction, if $g\ddot{u} \neq h\ddot{u}$. Hence, $g\ddot{u} = h\ddot{u}$. Assume that $g\ddot{u} = h\ddot{u} = \varrho$; this mean that g and h commute at point ϱ, then

$$g\varrho = h(g\ddot{u}) = g(h\ddot{u}) = g\varrho$$

and

$$g\ddot{u} = g(g\ddot{u}) = g\varrho.$$

Then, by (36) with $g\ddot{u} = h\ddot{u}$ and $g\varrho = h\varrho$, we obtain

$$\phi(\alpha\Theta(h\ddot{u},h\varrho)) \leq \phi(M_g(\ddot{u},\varrho)) - \psi(N_g(\ddot{u},\varrho)) < \phi(\Theta(h\ddot{u},h\varrho)) \tag{39}$$

or, equivalently,

$$\alpha\Theta(h\ddot{u},h\varrho) \leq \Theta(h\ddot{u},h\varrho).$$

This contradicts the inequality, if $h\ddot{u} \neq h\varrho$. Hence,

$$h\ddot{u} = g\varrho = \varrho.$$

The above relation shows that ϱ is a common FP of h and g. □

Definition 11. *Assume $(\Omega,\Theta,\preceq,\alpha)$ to be a POCMS with metric Θ, controlled function α, $\phi \in \Phi$, and $\psi \in \Psi$. A mapping $h : \Omega \times \Omega \longrightarrow \Omega$ is called an almost generalized (ϕ,ψ)-contraction mapping with respect to $g : \Omega \longrightarrow \Omega$ such that*

$$\phi\left(\alpha^{\hbar}\Theta(h(u,v),h(u^*,v^*))\right) \leq \phi(M(u,v,u^*,v^*)) - \psi(N(u,v,u^*,v^*)) \tag{40}$$

$\forall u,v,u^*,v^* \in \Omega$ and $gu \preceq gu^*$,$gv \succeq gv^*$, $\hbar > 2$, where

$$M_g(u,v,u^*,v^*) = \max\left\{\begin{array}{c} \frac{\Theta(gu^*,h(u^*,v^*))[1+\Theta(gu,h(u,v))]}{1+\Theta(gu,gv)}, \frac{\Theta(gu,h(u,v))\Theta(gu^*,h(u^*,v^*))}{1+\Theta(h(u,v),h(u^*,v^*))}, \\ \frac{\Theta(gu,h(u,v))\Theta(gu,h(u^*,v^*))}{1+\Theta(gu,h(u^*,v^*))+\Theta(gu^*,h(u,v))}, \Theta(gu,gu^*) \end{array}\right\} \tag{41}$$

and

$$N_g(u,v,u^*,v^*) = \max\left\{\frac{\Theta(gu^*,h(u^*,v^*))[1+\Theta(gu,h(u,v))]}{1+\Theta(gu,gv)}, \Theta(gu,gu^*)\right\}.$$

Theorem 6. *Assume $(\Omega,\Theta,\preceq,\alpha)$ to be a POCMS with metric Θ and controlled function α. A mapping $h : \Omega \times \Omega \longrightarrow \Omega$ is called an almost generalized (ϕ,ψ)-contraction mapping with respect to $g : \Omega \longrightarrow \Omega$, and h and g are continuous functions such that h has a mixed g-monotone property and commutes with g. Furthermore, assume that $h(\Omega \times \Omega) \subseteq g(\Omega)$. Then, h and g have a coupled coincidence point in Ω, if there exists an ordered pair $(u_o,v_o) \in (\Omega \times \Omega)$ such that $gu_o \preceq h(u_o,v_o)$ and $gv_o \succeq h(v_o,u_o)$.*

Proof. Now, by the proof of Theorem 2.2 in [4], we can construct two sequences $\{v_p\}$ and $\{u_p\}$ in Ω such that $gu_{p+1} = h(u_p,v_p)$, $gv_{p+1} = h(v_p,u_p)$, for all $p \geq 0$.

Here, $\{gu_p\}$ is a non-decreasing sequence and $\{gv_p\}$ is a non-increasing sequence in Ω. Now, we replace $u = u_p$, $v = v_p$, $u^* = u_{p+1}$, $v^* = v_{p+1}$, in (40):

$$\begin{aligned} \phi\left(\alpha^{\hbar}\Theta(gu_{p+1},gu_{p+2},)\right) &= \phi\left(\alpha^{\hbar}\Theta(h(u_p,v_p),h(u_{p+1},u_{p+2}))\right) \\ &\leq \phi(M_g(u_p,v_p,u_{p+1},v_{p+1})) - \psi(N_g(u_p,v_p,u_{p+1},v_{p+1})) \end{aligned} \tag{42}$$

where
$$M_g(u_p, v_p, u_{p+1}, v_{p+1}) \leq \max\{\Theta(gu_p, gu_{p+1},), \Theta(gu_{p+1}, gu_{p+2},)\} \tag{43}$$
and
$$N_g(u_p, v_p, u_{p+1}, v_{p+1}) = \max\{\Theta(gu_p, gu_{p+1},), \Theta(gu_{p+1}, gu_{p+2},)\}. \tag{44}$$

Consequently, from (42), we have
$$\phi\left(\alpha^{\hbar}\Theta(gu_{p+1}, gu_{p+2},)\right)$$
$$\leq \phi(\max\{\Theta(gu_p, gu_{p+1},), \Theta(gu_{p+1}, gu_{p+2},)\}) \tag{45}$$
$$-\psi(\max\{\Theta(gu_p, gu_{p+1},), \Theta(gu_{p+1}, gu_{p+2},)\}).$$

Likewise, we replace $u = v_{p+1}, v = u_{p+1}, u^* = u_p, v^* = v_p$, in (40), and we obtain
$$\phi\left(\alpha^{\hbar}\Theta(gv_{p+1}, gv_{p+2},)\right)$$
$$\leq \phi(\max\{\Theta(gv_p, gv_{p+1},), \Theta(gv_{p+1}, gv_{p+2},)\})$$
$$-\psi(\max\{\Theta(gv_p, gv_{p+1},), \Theta(gv_{p+1}, gv_{p+2},)\}), \tag{46}$$
based on $\max\{\phi(c), \phi(d)\}$ for all $c, d \in [0, +\infty)$. Then, by (45) and (46), we obtain
$$\phi\left(\alpha^{\hbar}\delta_p\right) \leq \phi(\max\{\Theta(gu_p, gu_{p+1},), \Theta(gu_{p+1}, gu_{p+2},), (gv_p, gv_{p+1},), \Theta(gv_{p+1}, gv_{p+2},)\})$$
$$-\psi(\max\{\Theta(gu_p, gu_{p+1},), \Theta(gu_{p+1}, gu_{p+2},), (gv_p, gv_{p+1},), \Theta(gv_{p+1}, gv_{p+2},)\}), \tag{47}$$
where
$$\delta_p = \max\{\Theta(gu_{p+1}, gu_{p+2},), \Theta(gv_{p+1}, gv_{p+2},)\}. \tag{48}$$

Let us define
$$\Gamma_p = \max\{\Theta(gu_p, gu_{p+1},), \Theta(gu_{p+1}, gu_{p+2},), (gv_p, gv_{p+1},), \Theta(gv_{p+1}, gv_{p+2},)\}, \tag{49}$$
so by Equations (45)–(48), we deduce that
$$\alpha^{\hbar}\delta_p \leq \Gamma_p. \tag{50}$$

Now, we prove
$$\delta_p \leq \lambda\delta_{p-1} \ \forall\ p \geq 1 \text{ where } \lambda = \frac{1}{\alpha^{\hbar}} \in [0, 1). \tag{51}$$

Assume that $\delta_p = \Gamma_p$, then by (50), we obtain $\alpha^{\hbar}\delta_p \leq \delta_{p-1}$, resulting in $\delta_p = 0$. As $\alpha > 0$, therefore (52) is true. If
$$\Gamma_p = \max\{\Theta(gu_p, gu_{p+1},), (gv_p, gv_{p+1},)\},$$
i.e., $\Gamma_p = \delta_{p-1}$, then (50) follows from (51).

By (50), we deduce that $\delta_p \leq \lambda^p\delta_o$. As a result,
$$\Theta(gu_{p+1}, gu_{p+2},) \leq \lambda^p\delta_o \text{ and } \Theta(gv_{p+1}, gv_{p+2},) \leq \lambda^p\delta_o. \tag{52}$$

Thus, according to Lemma 3.1 of [5], the sequences $\{gu_p\}$ and $\{gv_p\}$ are Cauchy sequences in Ω. We can demonstrate that h and g have a coincidence point in Ω by applying the proof of Theorem 2.2 of [10]. □

Corollary 1. *Assume $(\Omega, \Theta, \preceq, \alpha)$ to be a POCMS with metric Θ and controlled function α; also, $h : \Omega \times \Omega \longrightarrow \Omega$ is a continuous mapping, where h satisfies the mixed monotone condition. Assume there exist $\phi \in \Phi$ and $\psi \in \Psi$ such that*

$$\phi\left(\alpha^{\hbar}\Theta(h(u,v),h(u^*,v^*))\right) \leq \phi(M_g(u,v,u^*,v^*)) - \psi(N_g(u,v,u^*,v^*)),$$

$\forall u,v,u^*,v^* \in \Omega$ and $u \preceq u^*, v \succeq v^*, \hbar > 2$, where

$$M_g(u,v,u^*,v^*) = \max\left\{\begin{array}{c} \frac{\Theta(u^*,h(u^*,v^*))[1+\Theta(u,h(u,v))]}{1+\Theta(u,v)}, \frac{\Theta(u,h(u,v))\Theta(u^*,h(u^*,v^*))}{1+\Theta(h(u,v),h(u^*,v^*))}, \\ \frac{\Theta(u,h(u,v))\Theta(u,h(u^*,v^*))}{1+\Theta(u,h(u^*,v^*))+\Theta(u^*,h(u,v))}, \Theta(u,u^*) \end{array}\right\}$$

and

$$N_g(u,v,u^*,v^*) = \max\left\{\frac{\Theta(u^*,h(u^*,v^*))[1+\Theta(u,h(u,v))]}{1+\Theta(u,v)}, \Theta(u,u^*)\right\}$$

Then, h has a CFP in Ω, if there exists $(u_o,v_o) \in \Omega \times \Omega$ such that $u_o \preceq h(u_o,v_o)$ and $v_o \succeq h(v_o,u_o)$.

Proof. Choose $g = I_p$ in Theorem 3.7; we obtain the required proof. □

Corollary 2. *Assume $(\Omega, \Theta, \preceq, \alpha)$ to be a POCMS with metric Θ and controlled function α; also, $h : \Omega \times \Omega \longrightarrow \Omega$ is a continuous mapping, where h satisfies the mixed monotone condition. Assume there exists $\psi \in \Psi$ such that*

$$\Theta(h(u,v),h(u^*,v^*)) \leq \frac{1}{\alpha^{\hbar}}M_g(u,v,u^*,v^*) - \frac{1}{\alpha^{\hbar}}\psi(N_g(u,v,u^*,v^*))$$

$\forall u,v,u^*,v^* \in \Omega$ and $u \preceq u^*, v \succeq v^*, \hbar > 2$, where

$$M_g(u,v,u^*,v^*) = \max\left\{\begin{array}{c} \frac{\Theta(u^*,h(u^*,v^*))[1+\Theta(u,h(u,v))]}{1+\Theta(u,v)}, \frac{\Theta(u,h(u,v))\Theta(u^*,h(u^*,v^*))}{1+\Theta(h(u,v),h(u^*,v^*))}, \\ \frac{\Theta(u,h(u,v))\Theta(u,h(u^*,v^*))}{1+\Theta(u,h(u^*,v^*))+\Theta(u^*,h(u,v))}, \Theta(u,u^*) \end{array}\right\}$$

and

$$N_g(u,v,u^*,v^*) = \max\left\{\frac{\Theta(u^*,h(u^*,v^*))[1+\Theta(u,h(u,v))]}{1+\Theta(u,v)}, \Theta(u,u^*)\right\}.$$

Then, h has a CFP in Ω, if there exists $(u_o,v_o) \in \Omega \times \Omega$ such that $u_o \preceq h(u_o,v_o)$ and $v_o \succeq h(v_o,u_o)$.

Theorem 7. *In Theorem 6, if for all $(u,v),(s,t) \in \Omega \times \Omega$, there exists $(a,b) \in \Omega \times \Omega$ such that $(h(a,b),h(b,a))$ are comparable to $(h(u,v),h(v,u))$ and $(h(s,t),h(t,s))$, then h and g have a unique CFP in $\Omega \times \Omega$.*

Proof. From Theorem 5, we have at least one coupled coincidence point in Ω for h and g. Suppose that $(u,v),(s,t)$ are two CFPs of h and g, i.e., $h(u,v) = gu$, $h(v,u) = gv$ and $h(s,t) = gs$, $h(t,s) = gt$.

Next, we have to demonstrate that $gu = gs$ and $gv = gt$. By hypothesis, there exists $(a,b) \in \Omega \times \Omega$ such that $(h(a,b),h(b,a))$ are comparable to $(h(u,v),h(v,u))$ and $(h(s,t),h(t,s))$.

Assume

$$(h(u,v),h(v,u)) \leq (h(a,b),h(b,a))$$

and
$$(h(s,t),h(t,s)) \leq (h(a,b),h(b,a)).$$

Assume that $a_o^* = a$ and $b_o^* = b$, then by choosing $(a_1^*, b_1^*) \in \Omega \times \Omega$, as

$$ga_1^* = h(a_o^*, b_o^*),\ gb_1^* = h(b_o^*, a_o^*) \text{ for } (p \geq 1).$$

By repeating the procedure performed above, we obtain two sequences $\{ga_p^*\}$ and $\{gb_p^*\}$ in Ω such that

$$ga_{p+1}^* = h\left(a_p^*, b_p^*\right),\ gb_{p+1}^* = h\left(b_p^*, a_p^*\right) \text{ for } (p \geq 1).$$

In the same manner, we define a sequence $\{gu_p\}, \{gv_p\}$ and $\{gs_p\}, \{gt_p\}$ as above in Ω by setting $u_o = u, v_o = v$ and $s_o = s, t_o = t$.

Additionally, we have

$$gu_p \longrightarrow h(u,v), gv_p \longrightarrow h(v,u), gs_p \longrightarrow h(s,t), gt_p \longrightarrow h(t,s) \text{ for } (p \geq 1). \tag{53}$$

As $h(u,v), h(v,u) = (gu, gv) = (gu_1, gv_1)$ is comparable to $(h(a^*,b^*), h(b^*,a^*)) = (ga^*, gb^*) = (ga_1^*, gb_1^*)$, so we obtain

$$(gu_1, gv_1) \leq h(a_1^*, b_1^*).$$

Consequently, we determine that, through induction,

$$(gu_p, gv_p) \leq \left(ga_p^*, gb_p^*\right), \text{ for } (p \geq 1). \tag{54}$$

As a result of (40), we have

$$\begin{aligned}\phi\left(\Theta\left(gu, ga_{p+1}^*\right)\right) &\leq \phi\left(\alpha^{\hbar}\Theta\left(gu, ga_{p+1}^*\right)\right) = \phi\left(\alpha^{\hbar}\Theta\left(h(u,v), h\left(a_p^*, b_p^*\right)\right)\right) \\ &\leq \phi\left(M_g\left(u,v,a_p^*,b_p^*\right)\right) - \psi\left(N_g\left(u,v,a_p^*,b_p^*\right)\right)\end{aligned} \tag{55}$$

where

$$\begin{aligned} M_g\left(u,v,a_p^*,b_p^*\right) &= \max\left\{\begin{array}{c} \frac{\Theta\left(ga_p^*, h\left(a_p^*, b_p^*\right)\right)[1+\Theta(gu,h(u,v))]}{1+\Theta\left(gu, ga_p^*\right)}, \frac{\Theta(gu,h(u,v))\Theta\left(ga_p^*, h\left(a_p^*,b_p^*\right)\right)}{1+\Theta\left(h(u,v), h\left(a_p^*,b_p^*\right)\right)}, \\ \frac{\Theta(gu,h(u,v))\Theta\left(gu,h\left(a_p^*,b_p^*\right)\right)}{1+\Theta\left(gu,h\left(a_p^*,b_p^*\right)\right)+\Theta\left(ga_p^*,h(u,v)\right)}, \Theta\left(gu, ga_p^*\right) \end{array}\right\} \\ &= \max\left\{0,0,0,\Theta\left(gu, ga_p^*\right)\right\} \\ &= \Theta\left(gu, ga_p^*\right) \end{aligned}$$

and

$$\begin{aligned} N_g\left(u,v,a_p^*,b_p^*\right) &= \max\left\{\frac{\Theta\left(ga_p^*, h\left(a_p^*,b_p^*\right)\right)[1+\Theta(gu,h(u,v))]}{1+\Theta\left(gu, ga_p^*\right)}, \Theta\left(gu, ga_p^*\right)\right\} \\ &= \Theta\left(gu, ga_p^*\right). \end{aligned}$$

By using (55), we have

$$\phi\left(\Theta\left(gu, ga_{p+1}^*\right)\right) \leq \phi\left(\Theta\left(gu, ga_p^*\right)\right) - \psi\left(\Theta\left(gu, ga_p^*\right)\right). \tag{56}$$

By using a similar technique, we can demonstrate that

$$\phi\Big(\Theta\Big(gv, gb^*_{p+1}\Big)\Big) \leq \phi\Big(\Theta\Big(gv, gb^*_p\Big)\Big) - \psi\Big(\Theta\Big(gv, gb^*_p\Big)\Big). \tag{57}$$

We have from (57) and (58) that

$$\begin{aligned} & \phi\Big(\max\Big\{\Theta\Big(gu, ga^*_{p+1}\Big), \Theta\Big(gv, gb^*_{p+1}\Big)\Big\}\Big) \\ \leq\ & \phi\Big(\max\Big\{\Theta\Big(gu, ga^*_p\Big), \Theta\Big(gv, gb^*_p\Big)\Big\}\Big) - \psi\Big(\max\Big\{\Theta\Big(gu, ga^*_p\Big), \Theta\Big(gv, gb^*_p\Big)\Big\}\Big) \\ & < \phi\Big(\max\Big\{\Theta\Big(gu, ga^*_p\Big), \Theta\Big(gv, gb^*_p\Big)\Big\}\Big). \end{aligned} \tag{58}$$

Consequently, we obtain, by using the property of ϕ,

$$\max\Big\{\Theta\Big(gu, ga^*_{p+1}\Big), \Theta\Big(gv, gb^*_{p+1}\Big)\Big\} \leq \max\Big\{\Theta\Big(gu, ga^*_p\Big), \Theta\Big(gv, gb^*_p\Big)\Big\},$$

This demonstrates that $\max\Big\{\Theta\Big(gu, ga^*_p\Big), \Theta\Big(gv, gb^*_p\Big)\Big\}$ is a decreasing sequence, and as a result, there exists $\aleph \geq 0$ such that

$$\lim_{p \longrightarrow +\infty} \max\Big\{\Theta\Big(gu, ga^*_p\Big), \Theta\Big(gv, gb^*_p\Big)\Big\} = \aleph.$$

By letting the upper limit in (58) be as $p \longrightarrow +\infty$, we have

$$\phi(\aleph) \leq \phi(\aleph) - \psi(\aleph), \tag{59}$$

whereas we obtain $\phi(\aleph) = 0$, which implies that $\aleph = 0$. Thus,

$$\lim_{p \longrightarrow +\infty} \max\Big\{\Theta\Big(gu, ga^*_p\Big), \Theta\Big(gv, gb^*_p\Big)\Big\} = 0.$$

As a result, we obtain

$$\lim_{p \longrightarrow +\infty} \Theta\Big(gu, ga^*_p\Big) = 0 \text{ and } \lim_{p \longrightarrow +\infty} \Theta\Big(gv, gb^*_p\Big) = 0. \tag{60}$$

By using a similar argument, we obtain

$$\lim_{p \longrightarrow +\infty} \Theta\Big(gs, ga^*_p\Big) = 0 \text{ and } \lim_{p \longrightarrow +\infty} \Theta\Big(gt, gb^*_p\Big) = 0. \tag{61}$$

Hence, by (60) and (61), we obtain $gu = gs$ and $gv = gt$. As $gu = h(u,v)$ and $gv = h(v, uwe)$, then we know that g and h are commutative, and we have

$$g(gu) = g(h(u,v)) = h(gu, gv) \text{ and } g(gv) = g(h(v,u)) = h(gv, gu). \tag{62}$$

Assume that $gu = a^{**}$ and $gv = b^{**}$, then (62) becomes

$$g(a^{**}) = h(a^{**}, b^{**}) \text{ and } g(b^{**}) = h(b^{**}, a^{**}). \tag{63}$$

This shows that (a^{**}, b^{**}) is a CFP of h and g. Thus, it follows that $g(a^{**}) = g(s)$ and $g(b^{**}) = g(t)$, that is $g(a^{**}) = a^{**}$ and $g(b^{**}) = b^{**}$. By (63), we have

$$a^{**} = g(a^{**}) = h(a^{**}, b^{**}) \text{ and } b^{**} = g(b^{**}) = h(b^{**}, a^{**}).$$

Hence, (a^{**}, b^{**}) is a coupled common FP of h and g.

Now, for uniqueness, assume (σ^*, σ^{**}) to be another CFP of h and g, then

$$\sigma^* = g\sigma^* = h(\sigma^*, \sigma^{**}) \text{ and } \sigma^{**} = g\sigma^{**} = h(\sigma^{**}, \sigma^*).$$

As (σ^*, σ^{**}) is another coupled FP of h and g, then we obtain $g\sigma^* = gu = a^{**}$ and $ga^{**} = gv = b^{**}$. Hence, $\sigma^* = g\sigma^* = ga^{**} = a^{**}$ and $\sigma^{**} = g\sigma^{**} = gb^{**} = b^{**}$. This completes the proof. □

Theorem 8. *Additionally, in the hypotheses of Theorem 6, if gu_o and gv_o are comparable, then h and g have a unique common fixed point in Ω.*

Proof. By Theorem 6, h and g have a unique common FP $(u,v) \in \Omega$. It is sufficient to demonstrate that $u = v$. Then, by the hypothesis, gu_o and gv_o are comparable. Now, we assume that $gu_o \preceq gv_o$. So, by induction, we deduce that $gu_p \preceq gv_p$ for all $p \geq 0$. We take the sequence $\{gu_p\}$ and $\{gv_p\}$ from Theorem 5.

Now, by Lemma 1, we obtain

$$\begin{aligned}
\phi\Big(\alpha^{\hbar-2}\Theta(u,v)\Big) &= \phi\Big(\alpha^{\hbar}\frac{1}{\alpha^2}\Theta(u,v)\Big) \leq \lim_{p\longrightarrow+\infty} \sup\phi\Big(\alpha^{\hbar}\Theta(u_{p+1},v_{p+1})\Big) \\
&= \lim_{p\longrightarrow+\infty} \sup\phi(\alpha^{h}\Theta(h(u_p,v_p),h(v_p,u_p))) \\
&\leq \lim_{p\longrightarrow+\infty} \sup\phi(M_g(u_p,v_p,v_p,u_p)) - \lim_{p\longrightarrow+\infty} \inf\psi(N_g(u_p,v_p,v_p,u_p)) \\
&\leq \phi(\Theta(u,v)) - \lim_{p\longrightarrow+\infty} \inf\psi(N_g(u_p,v_p,v_p,u_p)) \\
&< \phi(\Theta(u,v)),
\end{aligned}$$

which is a contradiction. Hence, $u = v$, i.e., h and g have a unique common FP in Ω. □

Remark 1. *We know that the controlled metric space becomes a metric space when we take a function in the triangular inequality equal to 1. Then, the condition of Jachymski's [11] result*

$$\phi(\Theta(h(u,v),h(u^*,v^*))) \leq \phi\max\{\Theta(gu,gu^*),\Theta(gv,gv^*)\} - \psi\max\{\Theta(gu,gu^*),\Theta(gv,gv^*)\}$$

is equal to

$$\phi(\Theta(h(u,v),h(u^*,v^*))) \leq \varphi(\max\{\Theta(gu,gu^*),\Theta(gv,gv^*)\}),$$

where $\phi \in \Phi, \phi \in \Psi$, $\varphi : [0,+\infty) \longrightarrow [0,+\infty)$ is continuous, and $\varphi(t) < t \;\forall\; t > 0$ and $\varphi(t) = 0$ iff $t = 0$. As a result, we generalize and expand the findings of the study by [12–16] and several other comparable results.

Corollary 3. *Assume $(\Omega, \Theta, \preceq, \alpha)$ to be a CPOCMS with metric Θ and controlled function α; also, $h : \Omega \longrightarrow \Omega$ is a continuous non-decreasing mapping with partial order $\preceq$ such that there exists $u_o \in \Omega$ with $u_o \preceq hu_o$. Assume that*

$$\phi(\alpha\Theta(hu,hv)) \leq \phi(M(u,v)) - \psi(M(u,v)). \tag{64}$$

Here, the conditions upon $M(u,v)$ and ϕ, ψ are similar to Theorem 1. Then, h has a unique FP in Ω.

Proof. Setting $M(u,v) = N(u,v)$ in a contractive condition (3) and by utilizing Theorem 1, we obtain the proof. □

Corollary 4. *Assume $(\Omega, \Theta, \preceq, \alpha)$ to be a CPOCMS with metric Θ and controlled function α; also, $h : \Omega \longrightarrow \Omega$ is a continuous non-decreasing mapping with partial order $\preceq$. Now, for any $u, v \in \Omega$ with partial order $u \preceq v$, there exists $k \in [0,1)$ such that*

$$\Theta(hu,hv) \leq \frac{k}{\alpha}\max\left\{\begin{array}{c} \frac{\Theta(v,hv)[1+\Theta(u,hu)]}{1+\Theta(u,v)}, \frac{\Theta(u,hu)\Theta(v,hv)}{1+\Theta(hu,hv)}, \\ \frac{\Theta(u,hu)\Theta(u,hv)}{1+\Theta(u,hv)+\Theta(v,hu)}, \Theta(u,v) \end{array}\right\} \tag{65}$$

if there exists $u_o \in \Omega$ with $u_o \preceq hu_o$, then h has a unique FP in Ω.

Proof. Take $\phi(t) = t$ and $\psi(t) = (1-k)t$, for all $t \in (0, +\infty)$ in Corollary 3 □

Assume $\Omega = \{0,1,2,3\}$. Define $\Theta : \Omega \longrightarrow \Omega$ and $\alpha : \Omega \times \Omega \longrightarrow [1,\infty)$ to be a control function with partial order "$\preceq$"on Ω defined by

$$\begin{aligned} \Theta(u,v) &= 0 \text{ if } u,v \in \Omega \,\&\, u = v \\ \Theta(u,v) &= 2 \text{ if } u,v \in \{0,1,2\} \\ \Theta(u,v) &= 6 \text{ if } u \in \{0,1,2\} \,\&\, v = 3 \\ \Theta(u,v) &= 24 \text{ if } u = 2 \,\&\, v = 3. \end{aligned}$$

Define a mapping $h : \Omega \longrightarrow \Omega$ by $h(0) = h(1) = h(2) = 1$ and $h(3) = 2$. Assume $\phi(t) = \frac{t}{3}$ and $\psi(t) = \frac{t}{6}$ for $t \in [0, \infty+)$, then all conditions of Corollary 3 are fulfilled; hence, h has a fixed point in Ω.

4. Application

In this section, we explore the existence of solutions for a set of nonlinear integral equations by manipulating the findings established in the preceding sections.

Consider the following system of integral equations:

$$\begin{aligned} x(t) &= L(t) + \int_0^T K(t,r)[\theta(r,x(r)) + \vartheta(r,y(r))]dr \\ y(t) &= L(t) + \int_0^T K(t,r)[\theta(r,y(r)) + \vartheta(r,x(r))]dr. \end{aligned}$$

Now, the system of integral equations will be examined under the following assumptions:

(i) $\theta, \vartheta : [0.T] \times \mathbb{R} \longrightarrow \mathbb{R}$ are continuous;
(ii) $L : [0,T] \longrightarrow \mathbb{R}$ is continuous;
(iii) $K : [0,T] \times \mathbb{R} \longrightarrow [0,\infty)$ is continuous;
(iv) There exists a $w > 0$ such that, for all $x, y \in \mathbb{R}$,

$$\begin{aligned} 0 &\leq \theta(r,y) - \theta(r,x) \leq w(y-x), \\ 0 &\leq \vartheta(r,x) - \vartheta(r,y) \leq w(y-x); \end{aligned}$$

(v)

$$2^{4q-4} 3 w^q \max_{t\in[0,T]} \left(\int_0^T |K(t,r)| dr \right)^q < 1;$$

(vi) There exist continuous functions $\alpha^*, \beta^* : [0,T] \longrightarrow \mathbb{R}$ such that

$$\begin{aligned} \alpha^*(t) &\leq L(t) + \int_0^T K(t,r)[\theta(r,\alpha^*(r)) + \vartheta(r,\beta^*(r))]dr, \\ \beta^*(t) &\leq L(t) + \int_0^T K(t,r)[\theta(r,\beta^*(r)) + \vartheta(r,\alpha^*(r))]dr. \end{aligned}$$

Assume that $\Im = C([0,T], \Re)$ is a space of all continuous functions defined on $[0,T]$ provided with the controlled metric space given by

$$\Theta(u,v) = \max_{t\in[0,T]} |u(t) - v(t)|^q$$

for all $u, v \in \Im$, where $\alpha = 2^{q-1}$ and $q \geq 1$. Now, we endow $\Im$ with partial order $\preceq$ given by $u \preceq v \Longleftrightarrow u(t) \preceq v(t)$ for all $t \in [0, T]$.

It is recognized that $(\Im, \Theta, \preceq)$ is regular.

Theorem 9. *Considering the above-mentioned conditions* (i)–(vi) *and that the system of equations have a solution* $\Im^2$, *where* $\Im = C([0, T], \Re)$.

Proof. Now, we assume the operators: $\Im^2 \longrightarrow \Im$ and $F : \Im \longrightarrow \Im$ defined by

$$(\xi_1, \xi_2)(t) = L(t) + \int_0^T K(t,r)[\theta(r, \xi_1(r)) + \vartheta(r, \xi_2(r))]dr$$

and $F(\xi^*) = \xi^*$ for all $t \in [0, T]$, and $\xi_1, \xi_2, \xi^* \in \Im$. Assume $\xi_1, \xi_2 u, v \in \Im$ with $\xi_1 \succeq u$ and $\xi_2 \succeq v$. Since they have a mixed monotone property, we have

$$(u, v) \preceq (\xi_1, \xi_2).$$

Alternatively,

$$\Theta((\xi_1, \xi_2), (u, v)) = \max_{t \in [0,T]} |(\xi_1, \xi_2)(t) - (u, v)(t)|^q.$$

Observe that, for all $t \in [0, T]$ and from (iv) and the fact that for all $a, b, c \geq 0$,

$$(a + b + c)^q \leq 2^{2q-2}a^q + 2^{2q-2}b^q + 2^{2q-2}c^q,$$

we have

$$\begin{aligned}
(|(\xi_1, \xi_2)(t) - (u, v)(t)|)^q &= \left| \begin{array}{l} \int_0^T K(t,r)[\theta(r, \xi_1(r)) - \theta(r, u(r))]dr \\ + \int_0^T K(t,r)[\vartheta(r, \xi_2(r)) - \vartheta(r, v(r))]dr \end{array} \right|^q \\
&\leq \left(\left| \begin{array}{l} \int_0^T K(t,r)[\theta(r, \xi_1(r)) - \theta(r, u(r))]dr \\ + \int_0^T K(t,r)[\vartheta(r, \xi_2(r)) - \vartheta(r, v(r))]dr \end{array} \right| \right)^q \\
&\leq \left(\begin{array}{l} 2^{2q-2} \left| \int_0^T K(t,r)[\theta(r, \xi_1(r)) - \theta(r, u(r))]dr \right|^q \\ + 2^{2q-2} \left| \int_0^T K(t,r)[\theta(r, \xi_2(r)) - \theta(r, v(r))]dr \right|^q \end{array} \right) \\
&\leq 2^{2q-2} \left[\begin{array}{l} \left(\int_0^T |K(t,r)[\theta(r, \xi_1(r)) - \theta(r, u(r))]| dr \right)^q \\ + \left(\int_0^T |K(t,r)[\theta(r, \xi_2(r)) - \theta(r, v(r))]| dr \right)^q \end{array} \right] \\
&\leq 2^{2q-2} j^q \left[\begin{array}{l} \left(\max_{r \in [0,T]} |\xi_1(r) - u(r)| \right)^q \\ + \left(\max_{r \in [0,T]} |\xi_2(r) - v(r)| \right)^q \end{array} \right] \left(\int_0^T |K(t,r)| dr \right)^q \\
&= 2^{2q-2} j^q \left[\begin{array}{l} \max_{r \in [0,T]} |\xi_1(r) - u(r)|^q \\ + \max_{r \in [0,T]} |\xi_2(r) - v(r)|^q \end{array} \right] \left(\int_0^T |K(t,r)| dr \right)^q
\end{aligned}$$

thus

$$\begin{aligned}\max_{r\in[0,T]}((\xi_1,\xi_2)(t)-(u,v)(t))^q &\le 2^{2q-2}j^q[\Theta(\xi_1,u)+\Theta(\xi_2,v)]\max_{t\in[0,T]}\left(\int_0^T|K(t,r)|dr\right)^q\\ &\le 2^{2q-2}j^q\max\{\Theta(\xi_1,u)+\Theta(\xi_2,v)\}\\ &\quad \max_{t\in[0,T]}\left(\int_0^T|K(t,r)|dr\right)^q.\end{aligned}$$

Using the notion of the controlled metric space to emphasize this concept, we obtain

$$\begin{aligned}\max_{r\in[0,T]}((\xi_1,\xi_2)(t)-(u,v)(t))^q &\le 2^{2q-2}j^q[\Theta(\xi_2,v)+\Theta(\xi_1,u)+\Theta(\xi_2,v)]\max_{t\in[0,T]}\left(\int_0^T|K(t,r)|dr\right)^q\\ &\le 2^{2q-2}3j^q\max[\Theta(\xi_2,v),\Theta(\xi_1,u)]\max_{t\in[0,T]}\left(\int_0^T|K(t,r)|dr\right)^q\\ &\le 2^{2q-2}3j^q\max[\Theta(\xi_1,u),\Theta(\xi_2,v),\Theta(\xi_1,u)]\\ &\quad \max_{t\in[0,T]}\left(\int_0^T|K(t,r)|dr\right)^q\end{aligned}$$

and

$$\begin{aligned}\max_{r\in[0,T]}((\xi_2,\xi_1)(t)-(v,u)(t))^q &\le 2^{2q-2}j^q[\Theta(\xi_1,u)+\Theta(\xi_2,v)+\Theta(\xi_2,v)]\max_{t\in[0,T]}\left(\int_0^T|K(t,r)|dr\right)^q\\ &\le 2^{2q-2}3j^q\max[\Theta(\xi_1,u),\Theta(\xi_2,v)]\max_{t\in[0,T]}\left(\int_0^T|K(t,r)|dr\right)^q.\end{aligned}$$

Therefore, based on the three inequalities above, we obtain

$$\begin{aligned}&\max\{\Theta((\xi_1,\xi_2),(u,v)),\Theta((\xi_2,\xi_1),(v,u))\}\\ &\le 2^{2q-2}3j^q\max_{t\in[0,T]}\left(\int_0^T|K(t,r)|dr\right)^q\max\{\Theta(\xi_1,u),\Theta(\xi_2,v)\}\\ &\le \frac{2^{4q-4}3j^q\max_{t\in[0,T]}\left(\int_0^T|K(t,r)|dr\right)^q}{2^{2q-2}}\max\{\Theta(\xi_1,u),\Theta(\xi_2,v)\}\end{aligned}$$

but from (v), we have

$$2^{4q-4}3j^q\max_{t\in[0,T]}\left(\int_0^T|K(t,r)|dr\right)^q<1.$$

This demonstrates that the operator satisfies the contractive condition seen in Corollary 2.8 [19] with $(\varepsilon=2)$. Consider the functions that occur in assumption (vi) as α^*,β^*, Next, by (vi), we obtain

$$\alpha^*\preceq(\alpha^*,\beta^*),\ \ \beta^*\succeq(\alpha^*,\beta^*).$$

With the help of corollary 2.8 in [19], we determine the presence of $\xi_1, \xi_2 \in \Omega$ such that

$$\xi_1 = (\xi_1, \xi_2) \text{ and } \xi_2 = (\xi_2, \xi_1).$$

□

5. Conclusions

In this work, we proved several concrete theorems concerning FPs, common FPs, coincidence points, coupled coincidence points, and coupled common fixed points satisfying (ϕ, Ψ)-contractive mappings in the context of the POCMS. Furthermore, we provided several non-trivial examples and an application to the system of nonlinear integral equations. This work is extendable in the framework of partially ordered double controlled metric spaces, partially ordered fuzzy metric spaces, partially ordered intuitionistic fuzzy metric spaces, and many others.

Author Contributions: Conceptualization, M.A., S.A., U.I. and M.F.; methodology, M.A., U.I., I.K.A. and S.R.; software, M.F. and S.R.; validation, S.A., U.I. and I.K.A.; formal analysis, M.A. and U.I.; investigation, I.K.A.; resources, S.A.; data curation, M.F.; writing—original draft preparation, M.A., U.I., M.F. and S.R.; writing—review and editing, U.I. and I.K.A.; visualization, S.A.; supervision, I.K.A.; project administration, U.I., I.K.A. and S.R.; funding acquisition, M.A., I.K.A. and S.R. All authors have read and agreed to the published version of the manuscript.

Funding: This research received no external funding.

Data Availability Statement: The data will be available upon request from the corresponding author.

Acknowledgments: The authors are thankful to the Deanship of Scientific Research, Islamic University of Madinah, for providing the support under the Post Publication Program III.

Conflicts of Interest: The authors declare no conflicts of interest.

References

1. Czerwik, S. Contraction mappings in *b*-metric spaces. *Acta Math. Inform. Univ. Ostrav.* **1993**, *1*, 5–11.
2. Mlaiki, N.; Dedovic, N.; Aydi, H.; Gardašević-Filipovi ć, M.; Bin-Mohsin, B.; Radenović, S. Some new observations on Geraghty and Ćirić type results in *b*-metric spaces. *Mathematics* **2019**, *7*, 643. [CrossRef]
3. Faraji, H.; Savić, D.; Radenović, S. Fixed point theorems for Geraghty contraction type mappings in *b*-metric spaces and applications. *Axioms* **2019**, *8*, 34. [CrossRef]
4. Abas, M.; Ali, B.; Nazir, T.; Dedović, N.; Bin-Mohsin, B.; Radenović, S. Solutions and Ulam-Hyers stability of differential inclusions involving Suzuki type multivalued mappings on *b* -metric spaces. *Vojnotehnički Glasnik/Military Technical Courier* **2020**, *68*, 438–487. [CrossRef]
5. Hussain, N.; Mitrovic, Z.D. On multi-valued weak quasi-contractions in *b*-metric spaces. *J. Nonlinear Sci. Appl.* **2017**, *10*, 3815–3823. [CrossRef]
6. Zoto, K.; Rhoades, B.E.; Radenović, S. Common fixed point theorems for a class of (s, q)-contractive mappings in *b*- metric-like spaces and applications to integral equations. *Math. Slovaca* **2019**, *69*, 233–247. [CrossRef]
7. Suzuki, T. Basic inequality on a *b*-metric space and its applications. *J. Inequalities Appl.* **2017**, *2017*, 256. [CrossRef] [PubMed]
8. Singh, S.L.; Czerwik, S.; Krol, K.; Singh, A. Coincidences and Fixed Points of Hybrid Contractions. *Tamsui Oxf. J. Math. Sci. (TOJMS)* **2008**, *24*, 401–416.
9. Mlaiki, N.; Aydi, H.; Souayah, N.; Abdeljawad, T. Controlled metric type spaces and the related contraction principle. *Mathematics* **2018**, *6*, 194. [CrossRef]
10. Ran, A.; Reurings, M. A fixed point theorem in partially ordered sets and some applications to matrix equations. *Proc. Am. Math. Soc.* **2004**, *132*, 1435–1443. [CrossRef]
11. Amini-Harandi, A.; Emami, H. A fixed point theorem for contraction type maps in partially ordered metric spaces and application to ordinary differential equations. *Nonlinear Anal. Theory Methods Appl.* **2010**, *72*, 2238–2242. [CrossRef]
12. Farhan, M.; Ishtiaq, U.; Saeed, M.; Hussain, A.; Al Sulami, H. Reich-Type and (α, F)-Contractions in Partially Ordered Double-Controlled Metric-Type Spaces with Applications to Non-Linear Fractional Differential Equations and Monotonic Iterative Method. *Axioms* **2022**, *11*, 573. [CrossRef]
13. Bhaskar, T.G.; Lakshmikantham, V. Fixed point theorems in partially ordered metric spaces and applications. *Nonlinear Anal. Theory Methods Appl.* **2006**, *65*, 1379–1393. [CrossRef]
14. Lakshmikantham, V.; Ćirić, L. Coupled fixed point theorems for nonlinear contractions in partially ordered metric spaces. *Nonlinear Anal. Theory Methods Appl.* **2009**, *70*, 4341–4349. [CrossRef]

15. Choudhury, B.S.; Metiya, N.; Kundu, A. Coupled coincidence point theorems in ordered metric spaces. *Annali Dell'Universita'Di Ferrara* **2011**, *57*, 1–16. [CrossRef]
16. Mitiku, B.; Karusala, K.; Namana, S.R. Some fixed point results of generalized (ϕ, ψ)-contractive mappings in ordered b-metric spaces. *BMC Res. Notes* **2020**, *13*, 537. [CrossRef]
17. Nieto, J.J.; Rodríguez-López, R. Existence and uniqueness of fixed point in partially ordered sets and applications to ordinary differential equations. *Acta Math. Sin. Engl. Ser.* **2007**, *23*, 2205–2212. [CrossRef]
18. Aydi, H.; Karapınar, E.; Shatanawi, W. Tripled coincidence point results for generalized contractions in ordered generalized metric spaces. *Fixed Point Theory Appl.* **2012**, *2012*, 101. [CrossRef]
19. Parvaneh, V.; Rezaei Roshan, J.; Radenović, S. Existence of tripled coincidence points in ordered b-metric spaces and an application to a system of integral equations. *Fixed Point Theory Appl.* **2013**, *2013*, 130. [CrossRef]
20. Ishtiaq, U.; Kattan, D.A.; Ahmad, K., Sessa, S.; Ali, F. Fixed point results in controlled fuzzy metric spaces with an application to the transformation of solar energy to electric power. *Mathematics* **2023**, *15*, 3435. [CrossRef]
21. Brzdęk, J.; Karapınar, E.; Petruşel, A. A fixed point theorem and the Ulam stability in generalized dq-metric spaces. *J. Math. Anal. Appl.* **2018**, *467*, 501–520. [CrossRef]
22. Antón-Sancho, Á. Fixed points of principal E 6-bundles over a compact algebraic curve. *Quaest. Math.* **2024**, *47*, 501–513. [CrossRef]
23. Antón-Sancho, Á. Fixed Points of Automorphisms of the Vector Bundle Moduli Space Over a Compact Riemann Surface. *Mediterr. J. Math.* **2024**, *21*, 20. [CrossRef]

MDPI AG
Grosspeteranlage 5
4052 Basel
Switzerland
Tel.: +41 61 683 77 34

Axioms Editorial Office
E-mail: axioms@mdpi.com
www.mdpi.com/journal/axioms

www.ingramcontent.com/pod-product-compliance
Lightning Source LLC
Chambersburg PA
CBHW061617210926
51850CB00009B/2350